EVERYDAY LIFE IN
ANCIENT GREECE
PEOPLE AND PLACES

EVERYDAY LIFE IN
ANCIENT GREECE
PEOPLE AND PLACES
ART • ARCHITECTURE • THEATRE • GODS AND MYTHS • CULTURE

NIGEL RODGERS

HERMES
HOUSE

CONTENTS

INTRODUCTION

The world we live in today was made by the ancient Greeks. This is no overstatement, although the Greeks had no cars, computers or aircraft and lived very simple lives. The way we perceive both our external and internal worlds springs from the way the Greeks began to think, talk and act, with unprecedented energy, 2,500 years ago. Our architecture, astronomy, technology, medicine, athletics, theatre, maths, drama – history itself – began with the Greeks. The Greek roots of these words reveal how Greeks blazed the way that the Western world has followed since. Without the Greeks, the modern world could not exist today. Insofar as the whole world today follows Western precedents, it ultimately is following the Greeks.

The Greeks did not invent everything, of course. Egyptians and Babylonians had earlier made vital discoveries in architecture and astronomy, and Greek thinking had notable gaps – the Greeks had no concept of zero, for example. But the Greeks enjoyed in their *poleis* (their city-states), a freedom to think and speak that was lacking elsewhere at the time and in most other places for long after. In their open societies they thought and talked freely, forging artistic and intellectual prototypes for millennia to come. This happened despite – or perhaps because of – their relative poverty. Even by the standards of their time, the Greeks were far from rich.

A POWER TO SURPRISE

Greek art still has the power to surprise. People who know only white marble statues of obscure gods or heroes in museum corridors understandably feel that nothing could be more dead and cold than these frigid white males.

Above: The Charioteer of Delphi, *one of the few Greek bronze statues to survive, seems almost hieratically solemn in his long robe. Dating to c.473BC, this was an offering from Hieron, ruler of Syracuse. His eyes still have their original inlay.*

This is the wrong reaction, however. What we usually see today are dull Roman copies, in stone or marble, of lost Greek originals. Those statues, often of bronze and always brilliantly painted, with eyes inlaid with bright stones and hair separately coloured, must have once seemed thrillingly, even alarmingly, alive.

The Riace bronzes are twin statues of athletes (or warriors) fished out of the sea off Italy in 1972. Preserved almost miraculously intact, they give an idea of Greek sculpture at the start of the Classical period. The athletes, made by an unknown but brilliant artist in about 470BC, quiver with muscular energy. With traces of paint still adhering to their lips, teeth and eyes, they look as if they have just stopped exercising in the gymnasium (which is another Greek word for a

Left: The Greeks spread from their cramped peninsula across the whole Mediterranean, founding independent poleis *as they went. Some of the cities, such as Marseilles, Naples and Byzantium (today Istanbul), still thrive.*

Greek concept). Striding confidently forward, they appear in their nakedness almost dangerously alive and glamorous, not at all like cold statues in museums.

Even less survives of Greek painting, but sketchy if vivid murals from royal tombs in Macedonia of *c.*330BC hint at what has been lost. Later Greek painting styles, often dazzlingly realistic, survive in copies made in Pompeii, buried intact by Vesuvius' eruption in AD79.

Greek temples, their architects' supreme achievement, looked very different from today's austere ruins, being painted and even gilded in ways that might strike modern eyes as shockingly gaudy. (Such decoration served to emphasize, not disguise, their form, however.) When complete, the buildings and statues on Athens' Acropolis glittered in the sunlight, trumpeting the pride – or arrogance – of the world's first democracy.

DEMOCRATIC EXCELLENCE

The Greeks never thought that popularity and artistic excellence were incompatible – that their direct democracy must involve cultural or intellectual dumbing down. Classical Athens at its zenith in the 5th century BC demonstrated the exact opposite. The whole citizen body (not the whole population, but a large section of it) voted for the building of the temples on the Acropolis, still among the most admired buildings in the world. The same ordinary citizens listened to day-long performances of plays by Athenian playwrights and then chose the prize-winners. Posterity has generally agreed with their judgements, which cannot be said of every critic.

Greek theatre, however, was not like the theatre today, but more like a combination of opera, ballet, musical and concert. An event of high culture, it was also a political rite for the whole people. Up to 17,000 spectators could sit in the theatre in Athens, which, like all Greek theatres, was open to the sky. Theatre had strong religious connotations, being sacred to Dionysus, god also of wine and ecstasy. Gods and myths were never far from Greek life.

MYTHIC RESONANCES

Every culture has its myths, sometimes embodying archetypal human truths, but few legends have proved so enduringly

Below: This entrance corridor, dating from the 4th century BC, leads to the Stadium at Olympia. This was one of the holiest of Greek shrines, where the quadrennial Olympic Games were held for almost 1,200 years from 776BC.

Above: Taken from the sea off Euboea, this majestic bronze of Zeus, king of the gods, dates from c.460BC. It is one of the finest original Greek statues to have survived.

Below: The Temple of Aphaia on the island of Aegina has survived unusually intact. Built c.510–490BC and sited on a rocky hilltop, it is one of the most complete and perfect examples of a Doric temple.

inspirational as the Greeks'. We still talk casually of someone's Achilles heel, of Pandora's box or Herculean labours. Greek myth has also provided universal metaphors or analogies for some of the greatest modern artists and scientists.

Freud, father of psychoanalysis, kept a statue of the Sphinx – Egyptian in origin, but absorbed into Greek legend at an early date – in his study in Vienna, along with statues of Eros, god of sexual desire. Working on his theory of the Oedipus Complex, derived from Sophocles' tragedy *Oedipus the King*, he wrote: "Oedipus' fate moves us because it might have been our own", making the doomed king of myth a modern everyman. Picasso, before painting *Guernica*, the 20th century's most famous painting, had returned to the myth of the Minotaur, which had long fascinated him. The Minotaur is one of Picasso's most compelling images because this half-human, half-taurine monster of ancient Crete expresses perfectly the artist's anguish about war.

Many 20th-century poets and playwrights turned to Greek mythical archetypes. W.B. Yeats often used Greek myths in his poems and majestically translated Sophocles' tragedy, *Oedipus at Colonus*. T.S. Eliot tried to revive Greek poetic drama in *Sweeney Agonistes* and *The Family Reunion*. W.H. Auden reworked Greek legends in poems such as *The Shield of Achilles* and *Atlantis* to illustrate the dilemmas facing modern humanity. The playwright Eugene O'Neill adopted the themes of the *Oresteia*, a trilogy of plays by Aeschylus, to describe the impact of the American Civil War, while Tennessee Williams recast the myth of Orpheus, the archetypal poet, for his confessional play *Orpheus Descending*. The grandest Greek legend of all, the Trojan War, fascinates Hollywood still.

THE BIRTH OF REASON

Out of the mythic background there emerged the first scientific and philosophical attempts to understand and explain the world, human and natural. Early philosophers were also scientists and mathematicians, with Thales reputedly being the first to predict a solar eclipse in 585BC. Pythagoras, a figure about whom myths cluster, was a philosopher, mathematician and mystic. He traditionally discovered the theory of the triangle bearing his name and suggested that the Earth floats freely in space. This proved immensely stimulating, for it was soon realized that the Earth must be round.

Working in the Museum/Library of Alexandria, the era's intellectual powerhouse, Eratosthenes calculated the globe's circumference remarkably closely. Aristarchus even suggested that the Earth spins around the Sun – a suggestion too far for the age, but one that later inspired Copernicus in the 16th century. In the 2nd century BC, Euclid laid down the elements of maths in books that remained authoritative until almost 1900. In medicine, Hippocrates originated the clinical analytical approach that still underlies modern doctoring. (Many Greek intellectual achievements were to be preserved in the Islamic world during western Europe's Dark Ages.)

The Greeks invented history and philosophy also. Other cultures had shown historical and philosophical interests, but only the Greeks, uniquely free from priests and kings, could examine the past with critical freedom – *historia* actually means 'inquiry'. Only in free cities like Athens could philosophers debate the aims of human life or the nature of the cosmos. (Socrates, pushing Athenian tolerance beyond its limits, was executed, but his trial was unique in Greek history.) Little wonder that Herodotus is known as 'the father of history' or that later Western philosophy has been called 'footnotes to Plato', Socrates' greatest disciple.

ATHLETES AS HEROES

The Greeks were not just intellectuals: they also pioneered competitive sports, for 'gymnasium', 'athletics' and 'Olympics' are Greek words. The Olympic Games, the first great sporting contest, started in 776BC. It was held every four years for almost 1,200 years at Olympia in south-western Greece. (The modern games rekindled the Olympic torch 1,500 years later.) Modern concepts of the perfect body derive from Greek ideals. Physical excellence was seen not as a way of keeping fit – although the Greeks were very fit – but as part of a holistic concept of life, uniting body, mind and spirit. Musical and poetry contests were also held at many games.

Victorious athletes, who won only a crown of olive leaves, returned home to be greeted as heroes, touched with divinity. Statue, such as the *Charioteer of Delphi* were raised to their triumphs, and sacrifices were made to them after their deaths. The suppression of the Olympic Games in AD393 symbolized the passing of ancient Greece.

ATHENS, ROME AND JERUSALEM

By the end of the 1st century BC most Greeks were living under Roman control. This loss of liberty, although resented at the time, had its compensations, for the Romans proved willing preservers and

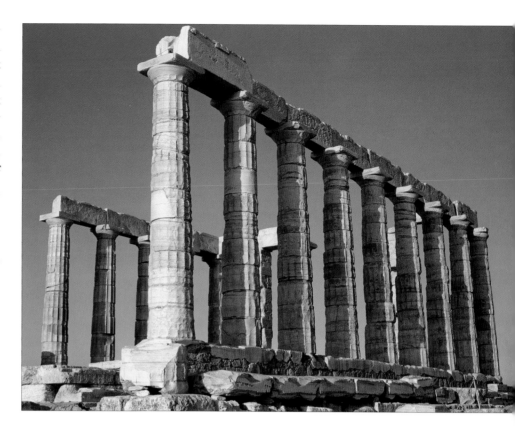

transmitters of Greek culture. Educated Romans such as Cicero studied in Athens, and Cicero later translated much Greek philosophy into Latin.

The same adoption and adaptation shaped Roman literature and religion. Paradoxically, a religion that spoke Greek finally destroyed the world of ancient Greece. Jesus and Pontius Pilate must have talked in Greek, then the common language of every educated man across the Mediterranean world. The New Testament is written in Greek, the word Christ (*Christos*) being Greek for Anointed One.

Without the impact of Hellenism, Christianity might have remained just an obscure heretical Jewish sect – as imperial Rome initially regarded it. As it grew, Christianity was deeply influenced by Plato's philosophy, propagated by two great thinkers: the heretic Origen and the saint Augustine. Rome's political collapse in the west after AD400 hardly interrupted this religious process. Athens, Rome and Jerusalem are still the triple pillars of the Western world. Christian or otherwise, we remain the heirs of Greece.

Above: The Temple of Poseidon at Sunium is superbly sited overlooking the sea. Built around 440BC by an unknown architect, it was a landmark for sailors rounding the cape as they headed for Athens.

Below: The Erechtheum, one of the temples on the Acropolis, was named after the ancestor of Theseus, the legendary king of Athens. It was completed in 405BC.

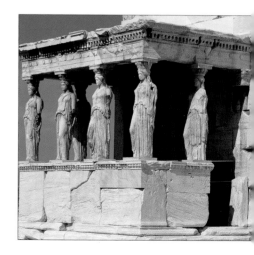

TIMELINE

Ancient Greek history, both cultural and political, stretches back to the early Bronze Age in the Aegean, a time about which very little is definitely known.

The history of ancient Greece, however, does not really end with the end of antiquity, whenever that is defined. (Some time between the 4th and 7th centuries AD is the general consensus). The story of ancient Greece's cultural and intellectual influence continues long after ancient Greece itself had vanished, for the idea or ideal of Greece resurfaced in the 15th century AD in Renaissance Italy and is still powerful today.

Dates and events cluster most thickly around the great central centuries, from 500 to 300BC. This was the Classical Age in Greek culture and politics, to which later generations looked back in awe and often tried to emulate.

All dates mentioned are BC (BCE) unless otherwise stated. Almost all dates before 500BC, and many dates afterwards relating to cultural events, are conjectured or approximate.

Below: The theatre in the Sanctuary of Apollo at Delphi of the 4th century BC.

Above: The Late Minoan palace at Cnossus, Crete, dating to c.1500BC.

2000–600BC

2000BC Building of first palaces in Crete.
1700BC Building of new Cretan palaces after major earthquake.
1600–1550BC Zenith of Minoan art in Crete and Aegean Islands; *Lily Prince* fresco at Cnossus; first royal grave shafts at Mycenae; murals painted in Thira.
***c.*1500BC** Volcanic eruption of Thira ravages central and southern Aegean.
1400BC Destruction of Cnossus palace.
***c.*1300BC** Building of Palace of Nestor at Pylos, of citadel at Tiryns and 'Treasury of Atreus' at Mycenae.
1280BC Building of Lion Gate at Mycenae.
1190BC Traditional date of Trojan War.
1100BC Final collapse of Mycenaean civilization; beginning of Dark Ages.
1050BC Dorian migrations into Greece; Ionian migration to western Asia Minor.
800BC Wooden temple to Hera on Samos; start of Middle Geometric Style.
776BC First Olympic Games (traditional).
***c.*750BC** Foundation of Cumae in Italy, first Greek colony in west; Homer writes *The Iliad.*
730–710BC Homer writes *The Odyssey;* Sparta's first conquest of Messenia; beginning of hoplite fighting.
700BC Hesiod writes *Theogony* and *Works and Days;* Greek colonization of western Mediterranean intensifies.
***c.*650BC** Carving of *Auxere Statuette;* creation of Lion Avenue at Delos.
***c.*630BC** Birth of poet Sappho.
***c.*620BC** Poet Alcaeus born; *Chigi Vase.*
620BC Dracon's Law Code in Athens.

Above: Terrace of the Lions, Delos, a sacral avenue of the 7th century BC.

600–500BC

600BC Aesop traditionally compiles *Fables;* Polymedes of Argos sculpts *Cleobus* and *Biton,* a pair of *kouroi.*
594BC Legislation of Solon in Athens.
590–580s BC Poets Sappho and Alcaeus flourish in Lesbos; Temple of Artemis in Corfu; Temple of Hera at Olympia.
585BC Thales, the 'first philosopher' of Miletus, predicts solar eclipse.
575BC Birth of poet Anacreon.
570BC Births of philosophers Pythagoras and Xenophones of Colophon.
***c.*560BC** *François Vase* made by Cleitias.
550BC Achaemenid Empire of Persia founded by Cyrus the Great; Sparta forms the Peloponnesian League; temples of Zeus and Apollo at Syracuse.
546BC Cyrus conquers Lydia and begins conquest of Ionian Greeks; Pisistratus reaffirms power as *tyrannos* of Athens.
540s BC Temple of Apollo at Corinth begun; temples of Hera at Samos and Artemis at Ephesus built by Theodorus of Samos (died 540BC); Exekias makes *Dionysus in a Ship,* a glazed *kylix* (cup).
525BC Emergence of black figure vases in Athens; birth of playwright Aeschylus; Treasury of Siphnians built at Delphi.
520s BC Pisistratid tyrants start Temple of Olympian Zeus in Athens.
518BC Birth of Theban poet Pindar.
511BC Phrynicus wins prize for his first tragedy.
510BC Temple of Aphaia at Aegina.
508BC Cleisthenes' radical reforms lead to full democracy in Athens.

Above: Athenian Treasury, Delphi, built by the new democracy in 510BC.

Above: The Temple to Poseidon at Sunium built c.440BC.

Above: Caryatids of the Erechtheum on the Acropolis, Athens, 4th century BC.

500–460BC

*c.*500BC Birth of Anaxagoras and Hippodamnus; Heraclitus active.

499BC Outbreak of Ionian Revolt; Athens sends force to help.

496BC Birth of Sophocles.

495BC Birth of Pericles.

494BC Defeat of Ionians by Persia; Phrynicus' play *Fall of Miletus* causes uproar in Athens.

490BC Athenians defeat Persians at Marathon; birth of Pheidias; *Apollo of Piombino* bronze nude cast.

484BC Birth of Euripides.

480BC Battles of Thermopylae and Salamis, Persian fleet destroyed; *Critios Boy* made: first truly classical statue.

479BC Persian army defeated at Battle of Plataea.

477BC Critios and Nesiotes sculpt (2nd) statues of Harmodius and Aristogeiton.

473BC *Charioteer of Delphi* bronze.

472BC Aeschylus's *Persians* staged.

471BC Ostracism of Themistocles.

*c.*470BC Birth of Socrates; death of Phrynicus; Riace bronzes made.

*c.*468BC *Labours of Hercules* frieze carved by 'Master of Olympia'.

467BC Battle of Eurymedon – end of Persian threat to Aegean.

462BC Democratic reforms of Ephialtes and Pericles.

*c.*460BC Outbreak of war between Sparta and Athens; birth of Hippocrates, first great physician; bronze *Zeus* from Sunium cast; *Amazonomachia Vase* made by 'Niobe Master'.

460–430BC

458BC Pericles completes reforms; Aeschylus' *Oresteia*; Long Walls of Athens.

457BC Birth of Thucydides the historian.

456BC Death of Aeschylus; completion of Temple of Zeus at Olympia.

*c.*450BC Birth of Aristophanes; Pheidias completes his first statue of Athena Lemnia; *Apollo* carved for Temple of Zeus at Olympia.

449BC Peace of Callias with Persia; Athens invites Greeks to help her restore her temples.

447BC Parthenon and the Panathenaic frieze (*Elgin Marbles*) begun.

446BC Pindar writes last *Ode;* 30 Years' Peace with Sparta (actually to 431).

443BC Ostracism of Thucydides, son of Melesias, confirms Pericles' supremacy.

440S BC Temples to Hephaestus in Athens and to Poseidon at Sunium.

438BC Gold and ivory giant statue of Athena by Pheidias set up in completed Parthenon; Euripides' *Alcestis* staged; death of Pindar.

437–432BC Propylaea built on Acropolis; Herodotus completes his *History.*

*c.*435BC *Doryphorus* (Spear-carrier) statue by Polyclitus; Anaxagoras and Protagoras teaching in Athens in Pericles' circle.

431BC Outbreak of Peloponnesian War; Pericles' Funeral Oration; Euripides' *Medea*; Pheidias creates gold and ivory statue of Zeus at Olympia.

430BC Plague devastates Athens; Pericles tried and fined; birth of Xenophon; death of Anaxagoras.

429–404BC

*c.*429BC Birth of Plato; Zeuxis, 'master of realism', painting in Athens.

428–425BC Mnesicles builds temple to Athena Nike on Acropolis; Aristophanes' *Acharnanians*; death of Herodotus.

424BC Loss of Amphipolis to Spartans leads to banishment of Thucydides, who starts writing his history of the war.

421BC Peace of Nicias; Paionius sculpts marble *Nike* in Olympia.

415BC Syracusan expedition sails under Nicias and Alcibiades; Alcibiades recalled.

413BC Disastrous loss of Syracusan expedition; Euripides' *Electra*; building of Temple of Apollo at Bassae.

411BC Oligarchic revolution at Athens.

406BC Euripides' *Bacchae* staged in Macedonia; deaths of Euripides and Sophocles.

405BC Athens' defeat at Aegospotamoi.

404BC Surrender of Athens; Long Walls pulled down; dictatorship of The Thirty.

Below: The Parthenon at Athens, the supreme Greek temple, 5th century BC.

Above: Sculpture depicting horse racing, from the Agora, Athens.

Above: Corcyra (Corfu) was one of the most important Corinthian colonies.

Above: Pillars of the Temple of Apollo, Corinth from the 6th century BC.

404–360BC

403BC Restoration of Athenian democracy and general amnesty.

401BC 'March of the 10,000' Greek mercenaries; Xenophon leads them home.

401BC Posthumous production of Sophocles' *Oedipus at Colonnus*.

400BC Death of Thucydides.

399BC Trial and execution of Socrates.

394BC Tombstone of Dexileus at Athens.

393BC Athens completes rebuilding of her Long Walls.

392BC Aristophanes' last play, *Women in Parliament*.

387BC Plato founds his Academy just outside Athens.

386BC The King's Peace: Sparta abandons Ionians in return for Persian support.

384BC Birth of Aristotle; Timotheus builds Temple of Asclepius at Epidaurus.

379BC Anti-Spartan revolution in Thebes led by Epamonindas and Pelopidas.

376BC Athens defeats Spartan fleet at Naxos; Mausolus becomes satrap of Caria; Jason establishes rule in Pherae.

375BC Praxiteles carves *Satyr Pouring Wine* for Athenian Agora.

371BC Peace of Callias between Sparta and Athens; Thebes defeats Spartans at Leuctra, becoming hegemon.

369BC Foundation of Messene and liberation of *helots* by Thebans.

367BC Dionysius I of Syracuse dies, succeeded by Dionysius II; Plato visits Syracuse to teach Dionysius philosophy.

362BC Epamonindas' death at Mantinea ends Thebes' hegemony.

360–330BC

359BC Accession of Philip II of Macedon.

357BC Philip marries Olympias.

356BC Birth of Alexander the Great.

352BC Philip defeats Phocians and becomes *tagus* (ruler) of Thessaly.

350BC Praxiteles sculpts *Aphrodite of Cnidus*; Scopas sculpting Maenads.

354BC Demosthenes' first public speech; murder of Dion in Syracuse.

347BC Death of Plato; Aristotle leaves Athens; building of Mausoleum at Halicarnassus with sculptures by Scopas.

341BC Birth of Epicurus in Samos.

340BC Philip attacks Byzantium; Alexander left as regent of Macedonia; Lysippus sculpts *Apoxymenos*.

338BC Battle of Chaeronaea: Theban and Athenian armies defeated by Philip.

337BC Council of Corinth elects Philip as general to lead anti-Persian crusade.

336BC Philip II murdered; accession of Alexander III.

335BC Alexander destroys Thebes; Aristotle starts teaching at Athens, founds Lyceum; Apelles painting at court of Alexander.

334BC Alexander crosses to Asia; defeats Persians at Granicus; liberates Ionia.

333BC Alexander routs Persians at Issus.

331BC Foundation of Alexandria; trip to consult oracle at Siwah; Alexander routs Persians at Gaugamela; enters Babylon.

330BC Praxiteles carves *Hermes and the Infant Dionysus*; *Abduction of Persephone* murals painted at royal tombs, Vergina; Apelles paints *Battle of Issus* mural.

329–300BC

326BC Alexander reaches northern India, where his troops force him to turn back.

323BC Alexander dies in Babylon; Lamian War, revolt of Greeks against Macedonia.

322BC Ptolemy gains control of Egypt: Greeks defeated by Macedonia; deaths of Demosthenes and Aristotle; Athenian democracy curbed.

c.320BC Ptolemy Leochares sculpts *Apollo Belvedere*; Lysippus sculpts *Hermes*; *Deer Hunt* mosaic from Pella by Gnosis.

317BC Menander's comedy *Dyscolus*.

312BC Seleucus I takes over eastern satrapies; founds Seleucia-on-the-Tigris.

310BC Birth of poet Theocritus and astronomer Aristarchus.

307BC Epicurus settles in Athens and begins teaching philosophy.

c.300BC Zeno of Citium founds Stoic School in Athens.

301BC Battle of Ipsus: division of Hellenistic world into 4 main kingdoms.

Below: The Theseion, Athens, 5th century BC, one of the city's best preserved temples.

Above: Greece's mountainous nature meant the country was relatively poor.

Above: The Cycladic island of Delos was sacred to the god Apollo.

Above: Olympia was the site of Greece's greatest athletic festival.

299–200BC

295BC Ptolemy I founds Library at Alexandria; Euclid starts writing his mathematical *Elements*.
287BC Birth of Archimedes in Syracuse.
281BC Seleucus I defeats and kills Lysimachus, then is murdered himself; Antiochus I succeeds him (to 261).
279BC Building of Pharos at Alexandria.
*c.*275BC Aristarchus of Samos proposes heliocentric theory.
274–232BC Reign of Asoka, first Buddhist emperor in India, of part Greek descent.
270BC Hieron emerges as saviour of Syracuse, assuming crown as Hieron II.
264BC First Punic War between Carthage and Rome starts.
*c.*255BC Bactria breaks away from Seleucid control, its example followed by Parthia.
250BC *Nike* of Samothrace sculpted.
229BC Athens 'buys out' Macedonian garrison, in effect becoming neutral.
*c.*225BC Eratosthenes calculates circumference of the Earth.
221BC Philip V succeeds to Macedonian throne (to 179BC); Ptolemy IV defeats Antiochus III at Raphia (218).
218–201BC Second Punic War.
217BC Peace Conference at Naupactus: warning of the 'shadow of Rome'.
216BC Battle of Cannae.
212BC Fall of Syracuse to Romans: Archimedes killed in the fighting.
202BC Hannibal finally defeated at Zama.
200BC Egypt, defeated by Antiochus III at Ionion, loses southern Syria/Palestine.
200BC *Boy Pulling Thorn from Foot* sculpted.

199–1BC

197BC Rome defeats Macedonia at Cynoscephalae in 2nd Macedonian War.
190BC *The Finding of Telephus* mural painted at Pergamum.
188BC Treaty of Apamea: Seleucids, defeated by Rome, lose Asia Minor.
180–160BC Pergamum Altar erected.
168BC Polybius taken to Rome as hostage.
166BC Romans enslave 150,000 Epirotes, make Delos a free port; slave trade booms.
*c.*150BC Demetrius of Alexandria paints *topographoi* landscapes; First Pompeiian Style of wall painting emerges.
146BC Romans sack Corinth; make Achaea and Macedonia Roman provinces.
120BC Nile Mosaic from Praeneste.
*c.*100BC Hagesandros sculpts *Venus de Milo*; *Alexander Mosaic* made at Pompeii.
86–85BC Sulla sacks Athens.
*c.*80BC Second Pompeiian Style.
78BC Cicero studies at the Academy.
66–63BC Pompey reorganizes the east.
50BC *Laocoön* copy made in Rhodes.
*c.*45BC Cicero writes *Scipio's Dream*.
44BC Caesar assassinated; renewed Roman civil wars.
44–22BC Strabo the geographer active.
42BC Battle of Philippi: Cassius and Brutus defeated by Antony and Octavian; Antony takes eastern empire, winters in Athens.
31BC Battle of Actium: Cleopatra and Antony defeated by Octavian.
30BC Egypt annexed to Roman Empire.
4BC Birth of Seneca, philosopher, and Apollonius of Tyana, mystic; Third Pompeiian Style of wall painting emerges.

AD1–1462

AD14 Augustus, first emperor of Rome, dies.
AD46 Birth of Plutarch, historian.
AD60s Heron active in Alexandria.
AD65 Death of Seneca.
AD87 Birth of Arrian, historian/general.
AD120 Birth of Pausanias, travel writer; building starts on Hadrian's Villa at Tivoli.
AD131 Hadrian completes Temple of Zeus in Athens, becomes *archon* (ruler).
AD140s Ptolemy, astronomer/cartographer, active in Alexandria.
AD160s Galen, physician, active in Rome.
AD169 Emperor Marcus Aurelius starts writing philosophical *Meditations*.
AD204 Birth of Plotinus in Alexandria.
AD250s/60s Plotinus teaching in Rome, Emperor Gallienus among his students.
AD313 Edict of Milan: Emperor Constantine I accepts Christianity.
AD324–30 Constantinople founded as 'New Rome'.
AD361–3 Emperor Julian's *Orations and Letters Against the Christians*.
AD393 Last Olympic Games held.
AD395 Roman Empire finally divided.
AD410 Sack of Rome by Goths.
AD412 St Augustine begins writing *The City of God*.
AD485 Death of Neoplatonist Proclus.
AD529 Justinian I closes Academy and other philosophy schools in Athens.
1438 Gemiston Plethon unveils esoteric Neoplatonism in Italy.
1453 Fall of Constantinople to Turks.
1462 New Platonist Academy founded in Renaissance Florence.

PART ONE

ARCHITECTURE AND ART

Mention 'ancient Greece' and many people will think of temples consisting solely of columns, of blank-eyed white statues of naked men or women without arms. Such 'pure' but boring images are misleading. The temples we see today laid open to the sky are only the sunbleached skeletons of structures once adorned with statues and painted deep crimson, blue and gold. The white marble statues that today seem so chilling are seldom Greek originals (these were usually of bronze and always vividly painted) but dull, semi-competent Roman copies. The art the Greeks themselves created was more intense, astonishing and original than the art now lodged in museums. But it needs a leap of the imagination to realize this, for so much has been lost.

In painting, sculpture and architecture, Greek artists' drive toward ideal form was linked to their increasing skill at realistic depiction. The statues created by Pheidias and Polyclitus in the 5th century BC are both mathematically and anatomically perfect. With them, the human nude became the template for Greek concepts of humanized divinity. Our ideas of the perfect body, along with our ideas of architectural perfection epitomized in the Parthenon, spring from the Greeks. They envisaged the entire world in humanized form, but they also believed that mathematical principles underlie the universe.

The historian Plutarch, describing the temples of the Athenian Acropolis erected 500 years before his lifetime, wrote: "They were created in a short time for all time. Each building in its fitness was even then at once age-old. But in freshness and vigour each seems even now recent and newly made." His words apply equally powerfully to sculpture and to painting.

Left: Part of the Acropolis of Athens in 1857, site of the most famous Greek temples, as seen by the Belgian artist Florent Mols before restoration.

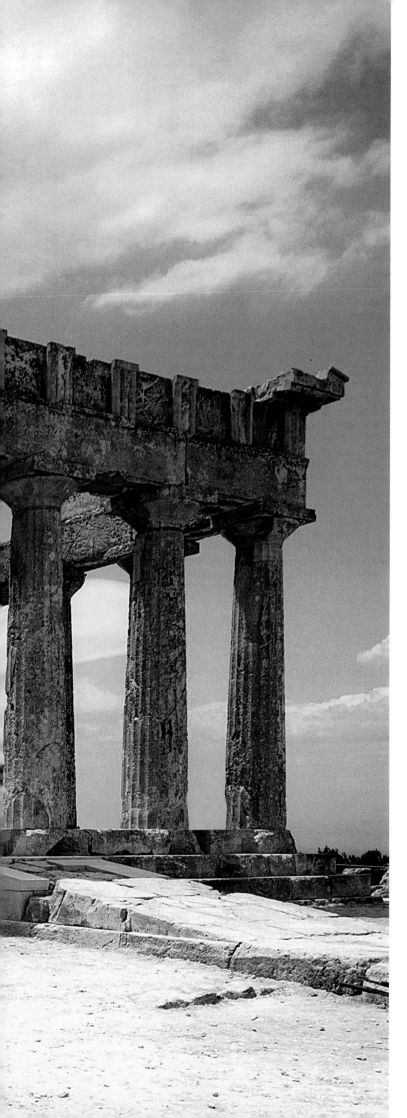

CHAPTER I

THE RISE OF GREEK ARCHITECTURE

Greek architecture, at its zenith in 480–320BC, did not have a long history. The Minoans and Mycenaeans had raised sophisticated buildings, but these were forgotten in the Dark Ages after 1200BC. When the Greeks began building again after 700BC, they started from scratch. Within 300 years they moved from timber and mud-brick huts to the symmetrical all-marble Parthenon in Athens. This meteoric rise owed a little to external influences but it soon became an original, self-sustaining achievement. If, after 400BC, Greek architecture changed only slowly, this did not bother the Greeks. They were less interested in ephemeral fashion than in perfection. This explains why they long stuck to *trabeated* architecture, dependent on column and lintel, although they knew of *arcuated* architecture, which involved the use of arches, vaults and domes.

A Greek temple was intended to be viewed from the outside. Today we see Greek temples almost inside out, with their interiors open to the sky, their exteriors stripped of all colouring and adornment. The Greeks never believed decoration was a crime, although they painted buildings to emphasize the forms, not disguise them. The forms themselves were perfection. Greeks also built *stoas* (porticoes), theatres, council halls and fountains.

Left: All Greek temples were brightly decorated. Only marble skeletons remain, their inner sanctuaries now open to the sky.

MINOAN ARCHITECTURE
2000–1400 BC

The first European architecture emerged in Minoan Crete in c.2000BC. Minoan culture (named after the mythical King Minos) spread across the Aegean, but its centre was Crete. The Minoans' origins remain uncertain, but they were almost certainly not Greeks. Their buildings, while colourful, comfortable and ingenious, lack the Greeks' passion for symmetry. But the Minoans deeply influenced the Mycenaeans, who *were* Greek.

Cretan architecture focused on palaces, not tombs, temples or citadels. The Minoans built palaces not on a superhuman scale to overawe their subjects, as in Egypt or Babylonia, but as cheerfully decorated rambling homes and administrative centres. All had large storerooms with jars containing olive oil and wine. They were also unfortified. This suggests an unusually peaceful culture, possibly relying on a navy for external defence. (Traditionally, Minos was the first ruler of the seas.) Cnossus and Phaestus are the largest, best-excavated palace sites, but there were several other smaller sites, some termed 'royal villas'.

THE FIRST PALACES

The first palaces arose around 2000BC as increased trading links with Asia and Egypt quickened economic life. Asian and Egyptian models may have first inspired Minoan builders but they soon developed distinctive features. These include light-wells, alabaster veneer over walls made of mud-brick, ashlar or gypsum, columns made of inverted tree trunks tapering downwards, and porched courts. Often fine staircases lead to the *piano nobile* (main floor) with the best rooms upstairs, anticipating a later Mediterranean custom.

The most striking feature of the first palaces is the absence of any real plan. Rooms and courtyards seem to have been added piecemeal as need arose. The perhaps deliberate asymmetry has led to Minoan architecture being called 'accumulative'. The overall effect is pleasingly picturesque rather than grandly imposing.

CNOSSUS: HOUSE OF THE DOUBLE AXE

Around 1700BC a devastating earthquake destroyed most major buildings in Crete – the island is notoriously seismic – and all the palaces were rebuilt. This time there are signs of planning at least at Cnossus, the greatest palace, which was colourfully, if controversially, half-restored by the archaeologist Arthur Evans in the early 20th century. He thought that Cnossus now ruled the whole island.

At Cnossus a grand central court 91.5m (nearly 100 yards) long formed the new palace's core. Aligned nearly north–south, the court was flanked by colonnaded terraces rising three, perhaps four floors above. Opening off it to the west lay the Throne Room, the throne flanked by superb griffin frescoes. To the east rose a Grand Staircase, now reconstructed,

Above: The Grand Staircase of the Palace at Cnossus, with its tapering Minoan columns, dates from c.1550BC.

Below: The Palace at Cnossus was laid out around courts, passages and staircases in a seemingly haphazard way – perhaps the origin of the myth of the Labyrinth.

while beneath was the 'Queen's Megaron', decorated with gay frescoes of dolphins. Nearby was a bathroom with running water and flushing toilet, more advanced than anything known much later in classical Greece.

A suite of rooms nearby, the finest on the ground floor, is called the Hall of the Double Axes from the two-bladed axes, religious symbols, carved on its walls. It also served as a throne room. The Hall was open at both ends, with columns separating it from a light well at the west. Beyond a colonnade was another light well. There were no solid internal walls, only wooden partitions fitted with double doors. Open in summer and closed in winter, these kept the apartments comfortable all year. There were similar rooms on the floor above.

West of the courtyard ran a maze of magazines holding vases of oil, connected by dark corridors. These probably inspired the legend of the Labyrinth in which lurked the Minotaur, bull-headed offspring of Queen Pasiphae and a bull, eating Athenian maidens. But the overall

Below: A reconstruction of the Throne Room at Cnossus, where King Minos may once have sat, flanked by painted griffins.

tone of the palace is cheerful. It should really be called the House of the Double Axe, *labrys* meaning 'axe' in Lydian, a language related to old Cretan. Covering 2ha (5 acres), Cnossus was the largest, most sophisticated building in the Mediterranean world. Phaestus and other smaller palaces echoed its splendours, all being brightly painted inside and out, with tapering dark red or blue pillars rising above landscaped gardens. All were destroyed between 1500 and 1400BC.

Above: Phaestus in southern Crete was the site of the second-largest palace, similar in overall design to Cnossus.

Below: Minoan palaces rose to four or even five floors, with light wells flanked by columns.

MYCENAE: A CITADEL-PALACE
1550–1100BC

Above: The Mycenaeans were brilliant engineers, building huge corbelled domes of great sophistication.

Below: The Lion Gate, the monumental entrance to Mycenae, built c.1280BC.

Mycenaean buildings were very different from the Minoans'. The Mycenaeans – whom Homer called Achaeans – had overrun the peninsula by 1900BC. A warlike Greek-speaking people, they came into contact with the Minoans around 1600BC, growing wealthy through trading, raiding or fighting as mercenaries. After 1450BC they dominated Crete itself, trading from Sicily to Egypt. They used their wealth to transform their hill forts into elaborate citadels. Inside them the Achaean warrior-kings built palaces that reveal their debt to Minoan culture.

MYCENAE "RICH IN GOLD"

Greatest of their citadel-palaces was Mycenae, "rich in gold" in Homer's words. Mycenae dominated the fertile Argolid plain, controlling the trade routes to the Corinthian Isthmus. In legend, its rulers, the feuding Atreids, were acknowledged as High Kings by other Greeks. Its lords and those of nearby Tiryns have left the most dramatic fortifications in Bronze Age Europe before the Middle Ages.

At the centre of every Mycenaean palace and large house lay a *megaron* (great hall). Square or rectangular, this room had four pillars around an open circular hearth, often under a lantern roof that let smoke out and light in. The megaron served as the main baronial hall and sometimes as the throne room. (At Mycenae there was another throne room.) A *propylaeum* (ceremonial gateway) was common at the megaron's entrance, often with a porched court in front of that.

All were arranged on a clear axis to create an imposing approach. The axial plan of Mycenaean buildings resurfaced in later Greek architecture. Beyond or above the megaron lay private royal apartments, built of timber and mud-brick like most Mycenaean dwellings. These had murals so Minoan in style that Cretan artists might have been employed, but the themes – horses, chariots, warriors – were very different from Crete. Bathrooms similar to those at Cnossus have been found at Tiryns and elsewhere, but much of Mycenae's royal palace has fallen down a ravine.

THE LION GATE

A visitor to Mycenae at its 13th-century peak would have approached up a steep well-paved chariot road to see the Lion Gate towering above him. Built *c.*1280BC, it was part of massive fortifications enclosing the whole hill. The Lion Gate consists of three giant slabs of cut ashlar, with the lintel surmounted by two great stone-carved lions, whose now-lost heads once turned to snarl downward. The regal menace of this sculpture derives from Hittite models (in Anatolia), but the lions flank a Minoan-style column, revealing a cultural mixture. Entering, the visitor would pass on the right tomb circles from the 16th century BC (where the archaeologist Heinrich Schliemann later found what he thought was the mask of Agamemnon.) A chariot ramp zigzagged up to the palace, but those on foot could use a direct staircase.

While the palace itself was small compared to that at Cnossus, let alone those in Egypt – its court measured only 15 by 9m (50 by 30ft) and the megaron was about the same size – it was flanked by sizeable other houses such as the House of Columns. A smaller version of the palace, its colonnaded court anticipates those of wealthy Greek dwellings 1,000 years later. There were no great temples, the Mycenaeans presumably conducting their worship outside.

'TREASURY OF ATREUS'

The most imposing Mycenaean structure is a tomb, the 'Treasury of Atreus', so-called because of a misconception by its discoverers. Lying outside the citadel and dating from *c.*1280BC, it might have been the tomb of Agamemnon, the Achaean leader in the Trojan Wars, and others of the Atreid dynasty. It is a *tholos*, a circular chamber with a dome made of corbelled stone resembling a beehive. It is entered by a 38m (120ft) long *dromos*, a long narrow passageway burrowing into the earth, with walls of cut stone giving a suitably sepulchral approach. The door to the tomb has tapering sides and an inward slant, a style derived from Egypt. Above it is a triangular opening to relieve pressure on the lintel, once richly decorated with Minoan-style spirals.

The tomb's doors, originally of bronze, were flanked by columns of green limestone crowned with mouldings resembling Egyptian water-lily capitals. The tholos chamber, 13m (43ft) high and 14.5m (47ft 6in) in diameter, had a smooth interior surface once covered with gold, silver and bronze decorations. Although a tholos is not a 'true' dome – a corbelled dome relies on corbelled or projecting stones to close the gap – the 'Treasury of Atreus' remained the world's largest masonry dome until the building of the Pantheon in Rome 1,400 years later.

Below: The so-called 'Treasury of Atreus' at Mycenae, actually a vast royal tholos-type tomb, where the kings of Mycenae were buried in splendour with their treasures.

Above: A reconstruction of the citadel at Mycenae protected by its massive walls, for long the greatest in all Greece.

TIRYNS AND PYLOS
CONTRASTING PALACES 1500–1150 BC

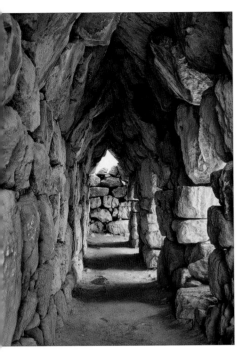

Two very different palaces in the Peloponnese's far corners reveal the variety of Mycenaean palace architecture.

TIRYNS: THE MIGHTY CITADEL

Tiryns, standing on a ridge a few miles to the south-east, is better preserved than Mycenae, though lacking its dramatic legendary associations. Homer called it "mighty-walled". This is, most unusually for Homer, a poetic understatement, for its walls are truly massive, being 6m (20ft) thick and originally even higher.

The upper citadel was fortified in c.1400 BC along the crest of the ridge. Its walls were formed of massive rough-hewn blocks, probably inspired by Hittite examples in Anatolia. (The Mycenaeans and Hittites were in diplomatic and trading contact, so knowledge of the massively fortified Hittite citadel at Hattusa could have reached Greece.) The main Eastern Gate at first opened directly on to the slope but was progressively improved until the gate was approached from the north and then along a passageway between high walls.

Above: A passage within the massive Cyclopean walls of Tiryns, the most complete Mycenaean citadel-palace to have survived.

Below: The megalithic walls at Tiryns, still standing after 3,200 years, which later Greeks thought must be the work of giants.

CYCLOPEAN WALLS

The Greeks who lived after the 12th-century BC collapse of Mycenaean civilization assumed that only the Cyclopes, mythical one-eyed giants of vast strength, if little brain, could have built such massive structures as Mycenae or Tiryns. This was not such an absurd assumption, for the megaliths ('big stones') of the walls of Mycenae, Tiryns and similar palaces are huge stone slabs. On average they weigh 5–7 tons, crudely hammered into place. Some are even larger. The lintel above Mycenae's Lion Gate is estimated to weigh at least 20 tons, being 4.5m (15ft) long by 2m (7ft) wide and 1m (3ft) tall. Mycenae, like most Achaean citadels, stands on top of a steep hill. How builders who had only bronze tools excavated and then transported such huge stones remains unknown. Clearly, the kings of Mycenae could call on massive labour forces, free or servile.

Huge walls, in places 10m (33ft) thick and at least as high, lined this. Galleries in the walls' thickness had embrasures through which defenders could shoot arrows down on to any assailants. A lesser entrance was made on the west side by building out a huge tower with a doorway through it. Along the front of this protruding bastion a pit was dug and a drawbridge installed.

The palace these walls tightly enclosed was, in contrast, very modestly sized. In the 13th century BC it was reconstructed with a Minoan-style outer propylaeum, which measured approximately 13.5 by 13.75m (44 by 46ft) giving on to a smaller propylaeum. Beyond lay the megaron, its plastered floor painted with squares of marine life. Its design perpetuated

Minoan fashions of centuries before. So did the murals of women dressed in fashions seemingly copied from Cnossus. Around the megaron clustered the living apartments, including the bathroom. This had a 20-ton block of limestone as its floor, however, a markedly non-Minoan touch.

THE PALACE OF NESTOR

Safely distant from the Argolid's battle-fields in the south-western Peloponnese are the ruins of the palace called after Nestor, Homer's venerable king. According to legend, Nestor's father came from Thessaly to found a new kingdom in Messenia. Nestor later took 90 ships to fight in the Trojan Wars, forming the second largest Greek contingent. Archaeology seems to confirm legend. An early Mycenaean settlement on a hill overlooking Navarino Bay was replaced about 1300BC by a new palace. This flourished – unwalled, most remarkably for a Mycenaean – for the next 100 years.

The Palace of Nestor is the most complete Mycenaean palace excavated. The new palace was entered from a formal propylaeum through a simple porchway with a single fluted wooden column, with a guard by the door. Across an inner courtyard paved in stucco with great pillars on both sides was a modest megaron and beyond that the Great Megaron, measuring 13 by 11.2m (42 by 37ft). At its centre was a great round hearth with a lantern to let smoke out.

Against the east wall stood the throne, flanked by frescoes of lions, griffins and deer. Here it is easy to imagine that Homeric heroes such as Nestor and Telemachus might have feasted while bards sang of the Trojan War. But Homer is never a wholly reliable guide for archaeologists. Stairs led to domestic rooms above, while to the north-east lay workshops, offices and store-rooms.

The Palace of Nestor at Pylos was, like most Aegean buildings, built of ashlar stone around a timber frame with timber pillars. This made it vulnerable

to fire, and fire destroyed the palace soon after 1200BC. From clay writing tablets baked in that fire we read of preparations to repel the invaders, perhaps northern Dorian tribes. Pylos, last and most graceful of the Mycenaean palaces, was apparently the first to fall. But refugees from Pylos sailed east. Some found shelter in Athens, the 'unsacked city', others sailed on to Ionia in the eastern Aegean.

Above: The magnificently constructed tholos tomb at Pylos, perhaps the royal burial place of the Neleid dynasty mentioned by Homer.

Below: The megaron (reconstructed) of the Palace of Nestor at Pylos, the last-built and most elegant of Mycenaean palaces.

THE DARK AGES
1100–600 BC

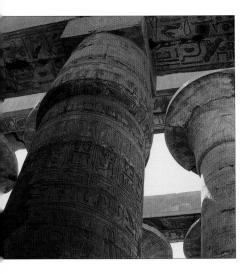

Above: The huge columns of the Temple of Amon at Karnak were a possible influence on early Greek architecture.

Below: The Temple of Hatshepsut, Egypt, was perhaps an influence on early Greek temples.

Some time after 1200BC the Mycenaean world collapsed. In its place emerged a simpler, poorer world with limited horizons and even more limited architecture. Greeks, as we can now call them (*Greek* is a Roman name, they called themselves Hellenes) forgot the reality of Mycenaean life but hazily remembered its legendary heroes. It is uncertain if Dark Age Greeks remembered actual Mycenaean architecture, although they may have been influenced by grand Egyptian temples they saw. But over the next few centuries there was to be no building in stone at all.

THE FIRST BUILDINGS
The oldest structure unearthed is at Lefkandi on Euboea island, dating from *c*.1000BC. Remarkably large – 45 x 9m (150 by *c*.30ft) – it was perhaps a cross

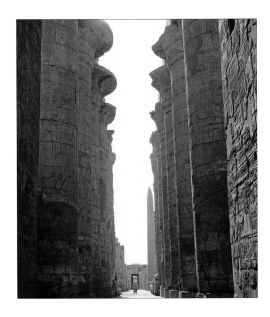

Above: The Hippostyle Hall at Karnak must have awed Greek traders and mercenaries with its imposing stony grandeur.

between a tomb and temple, with a stone base but mud-brick walls and thatch roof, surrounded by a colonnaded court with timber pillars. More typical are two small temples near Corinth to Hera, the wife of Zeus, considered mother of the gods. These were simple wooden thatched huts with timber porches and rounded ends. Around 800BC a temple to Hera was built on Samos. While still built of wood, it anticipates later temples in its strict rectilinear plan. It was large – 30m (100ft) long – and *peripteral*, i.e. its inner *cella* was surrounded by an external colonnade added *c*.750BC. (It was rebuilt several times over the next centuries, each time progressively more grandly.) All these buildings had pitched roofs, unlike most Bronze Age structures.

The whole tradition of Greek architecture probably originated in the carpentry techniques needed to make these timber buildings. So thought Vitruvius, the influential Roman architect writing in the 1st century BC. In the *entablature* of the Doric

While Greece languished in its Dark Age, Egypt recovered from attacks by the 'Peoples of the Sea'. It continued its millennial culture with little perceptible change in its architecture. Greece had strong trading links in the 7th and 6th centuries BC with Egypt, Naucratis being founded as a Greek colony in the Delta. Possibly Greek traders or mercenaries brought home knowledge of the massive, almost Doric-looking columns of the Temple of Amon at Karnak or the Temple of Hatshepshut, Deir El Bahri, the latter dating from *c.*1470BC. Egyptian influence on contemporary Greek sculpture is indisputable, but remains debatable on the development of Greek temples.

order, the first of the three Greek orders of columns (usually demonstrated in the capitals of the columns), *triglyphs* represent the end of the original wooden crossbeams, *guttae* were the pegs used to fasten them and *metopes* were the spaces between the beams. The Greeks stuck faithfully to these forms, often called 'petrified carpentry', long after they began building in stone.

CLAY TILES, STONE COLUMNS

A key development was the invention of terracotta (fired clay) roof tiles after 700BC. Tiles, being much heavier than timber or thatch – some early examples from the mid-7th century weigh 30kg (66lb) each – led to the need for stone columns and masonry walls to support them. They also produced ridge roofs with a shallower pitch. Among the first stone temples, that of Poseidon, on the Corinthian Isthmus of *c.*650BC, had walls wholly of cut stone, but its columns were wooden. At the Temple of Apollo at Thermon in north-western Greece of *c.*630BC, the upper walls were made of mud-brick but its wooden entablature (the superstructure between the capitals

and gutter) had brightly painted terracotta panels showing gorgons and other mythical creatures. Parts of this survive. Its tiled roof was supported by 15 wooden columns on each side and five at each end, a prototypical Doric temple.

By 600BC the Greeks were starting to build temples wholly in stone, with roofs made of terracotta tiles on wooden beams. By then the basic form for later Greek temples was established. Temples, flanked by columns, generally faced east, with their main altars outside. The *procella*, or vestibule, of the east front led directly to the cella, which held the statue of the god or goddess in sacred darkness.

Above: The Temple of Poseidon at Isthmia, dating from c.650BC, *was one of the first Greek temples with stone walls. This picture shows it at a much later date when it was far more ornate.*

Below: The Beach of Aphrodite in Cyprus, the one part of the Greek world where Mycenaean customs long survived almost unchanged.

THE EMERGENCE OF THE GREEK TEMPLE 600–530BC

Above: The Temple of Hera at Samos of c.580BC, whose lower walls still stand, is among the earliest surviving Greek temples. (The columns are of a later date.)

Below: At Selinus (Selinunte) in Sicily, three temples from the 6th century BC remain, with some massive Doric columns intact.

In the 6th century BC the tempo of Greek life began to accelerate. This cultural and social quickening reflected the economic recovery that made even archaic Greece wealthier than the Mycenaean world. Wealth was now more equally spread, also. This affected Greek architecture, for money was spent building temples for all the city, not palaces just for kings. A surge of confidence in building techniques led to the construction of early stone temples.

These temples are large, often with crudely massive Doric columns. The columns' gigantic size may reflect early architects' anxiety about supporting the new tiled roofs and masonry entablatures. Equally possibly, they were built so heavily just to impress.

From the start, all temples were designed to be seen mainly from the outside, as were almost all Greek buildings. At first, columns were overwhelmingly of the Doric order, or type. This consisted of a fluted (grooved) column rising directly from the ground like a tree trunk – early columns were often monoliths –

with a shallow capital supporting an entablature decorated with a triglyph and metope frieze. ('Doric' refers also to one of the two main Greek dialects, the other being Ionian. The Peloponnese, southern Aegean islands and many Sicilian cities were Dorian, but the Doric order was at first the architectural norm even among Ionians. The most perfect Doric temple of all is the Parthenon in Ionian Athens.)

Among the earliest temples with a full Doric order was the Temple of Artemis at Corcyra (Corfu), built *c*.590BC. Long since demolished, its pediment had sculpted figures – a giant gorgon surrounded by panthers at the front to frighten away evil spirits, with a *gigantomachia* (battle of gods and giants) on the sides. Built *c*.580BC, the Temple of Hera at Olympia, site of the Olympic Games, has its base walls still standing, although the present three Doric columns are later. Its cella walls were of limestone masonry at the base but the rest of the structure was still mud-brick.

The Temple of Apollo at Corinth from *c*.540BC has seven giant Doric columns standing. Originally there were six columns at the temple's ends and 15 on each side, each column being a limestone monolith 6.6m (21ft) high covered in stucco. Their bare forms, high above the Gulf Corinth, are still powerfully dramatic. The base under the columns rises in a gentle convex curve, the first example of *entasis*, the device to correct the illusion (if seen from a distance) of drooping in the middle that would arise if the base was really level.

TRIGLYPHS AND METOPES

This temple also shows Greek architects grappling successfully with a fundamental problem of the Doric order: Greek architects insisted on putting a triglyph over each column,

Above: The Temple of Apollo at Corinth dates from c.540BC, *where seven giant Doric columns are still standing. The other 35 have long since fallen.*

symbolizing the weight carried by the column. But they also wanted to end every frieze with a triglyph, not a less-powerful metope. As corner triglyphs could not be placed centrally over corner columns, end columns were placed closer together than the rest, while end metopes are 5cm (2in) wider than the others. Greek architects soon recognized such subtleties.

FIRST TEMPLES IN THE WEST
Founded in 735BC, Syracuse became one of the richest cities in this booming new world. Two Doric temples were built in Syracuse in the mid-6th century BC: the Temple of Olympian Zeus and that of Apollo. Both had 17 columns on each side and six across the end. In the Temple of Apollo, several survive and have been reinstated. They are monoliths, 8m (26ft) high, tapered and irregular in size. Those at the opposite corners of each end differ by as much as 30cm (1ft) in diameter from those at the other. The height of some columns is only four times their diameter. The effect, bulky rather than accomplished, suggests that this was a

pioneer building. At Selinus, in western Sicily, ruins remain of three huge temples, partly restored, dating also from the 6th century BC. All boast massive columns.

On the Italian mainland at Poseidonia (Paestum), the 'Basilica', actually a temple to Hera of the 6th century, has similar monumental columns with vast capitals. The bare virile power of these early temples much impressed visiting Neoclassical architects in the 18th century, who did not realize that originally all temple columns had been stuccoed.

Above: At the Temple of Apollo at Syracuse, built in the 6th century BC, monolithic Doric columns survive, exuding primitive strength.

Below: At Poseidonia (Paestum) in southern Italy, the 'Basilica', actually a temple to Hera of the 6th century BC, has monumental columns with vast overhanging capitals.

THE DEVELOPMENT OF THE GREEK TEMPLE 530–480BC

Above: The upper colonnade of the Temple of Aphaea, c.500BC, which is most unusually part-intact.

Under the Pisistratids, a dynasty of enlightened tyrants who ruled Athens intermittently from 560 to 510BC, the city became increasingly prosperous. It also emerged as one of Greece's leading cultural centres, and now began building proper Doric temples.

The Temple of Athena Polias, the divine guardian of Athens, was probably the very first temple erected on the Acropolis, being built in about 530BC. It had sculptures on its pediments carved in marble and in the round – a double first. Later, a huge temple to Olympian Zeus was started east of the Acropolis but the Pisistratids lost power in 510BC before it had progressed beyond its base plan. (It was finally completed under the Emperor Hadrian in AD130.)

After Athens' triumphant defeat of the Persians at the battle of Marathon in 490BC, a new temple to the city's goddess was started on the Acropolis and a propylaeum built at the Acropolis entrance with fine Doric columns.

However, all the Acropolis' buildings were torched in the two Persian invasions and sacks of 480–479BC, and any reconstructions remain predominately conjectural. While walls and columns were now of stone, roofs still had wooden beams.

THE TEMPLE OF APHAEA

The great Doric Temple of Aphaea, goddess of sailors and hunters on the island of Aegina south of Athens, survives remarkably well. Built *c.*510–490BC, the temple is sited on a rocky hilltop with superb views. Most of its columns survive almost up to roof level, allowing the upper colonnade to be seen half-extant for once. The *pteron* had six monolithic columns on the ends and 12 on the sides, sloping inwards to increase the impression of strength. The columns again have entasis (convex swelling) to make the columns appear regular when seen from afar. The *stylobate* has an upward curve.

Built of local limestone, the Temple of Aphaea now gleams serenely pale gold, but originally it was faced with cream-painted marble stucco and had bright-painted ornamental features such as lions' heads. Its triglyphs and guttae were painted dark blue, while other parts of the entablature were deep red – colours that were later used on the Athenian Parthenon. This again reveals how mistaken earlier ideas about Greek 'pure white marble form' were. Greek temples, like the lives of the Greek themselves, blazed with impassioned colour. The older sculptures from the temple's west pediment depict graceful smiling warriors, while figures on the east front, carved 20 years later, are more heroically muscular, indicating the revolution that was starting to transform Greek sculpture.

Left: The 'Temple of Neptune' at Poseidonia (Paestum) of c.510BC is the best-surviving western temple.

GIANT TEMPLES OF THE WEST

Out in the Greek west, temples were built of remarkable size, splendour and quirkiness. Most notable of these is the Temple of Olympian Zeus at Acragas (Agrigento) in south-western Sicily. Although only founded in 580BC, Acragas was among the wealthiest cities in the Greek world. It built the largest Doric temple ever, measuring 110 by 53m (361 by 173ft), with columns originally 20m (65ft) high.

The temple, started c.505BC, was unfinished when Carthaginians sacked the city in 406BC and almost nothing remains. Raised on a platform 4.5m (15ft) high, its huge outer columns, seven at each end and 14 along the side, were engaged (half-sunk) into the walls. This was a novel idea, perhaps designed to help carry the weight of the large entablature. At the temple's corners, however, the columns were necessarily three-quarters round. Further, the entablature, walls and half-columns were not made of solid masonry blocks but built of relatively small stones. As the diameter of each column exceeded 4m (13ft), this must have made them easier and cheaper to build.

The Acragas temple has another peculiarity, which gives it its nickname 'Temple of the Giants'. From masonry fragments since reassembled and from medieval records, made before the temple was destroyed by quarrying, we know that the temple incorporated huge male figures, about 7.6m (25ft) high, the Atlantes. (They are named after the mythical giant who upheld the heavens on his shoulders.) These titans supported the architrave, standing on a ledge, one between each pillar. Remnants of their vast forms have been tentatively reassembled. It is unlikely that the temple's interior was ever roofed over.

THE 'TEMPLE OF NEPTUNE'

North at Poseidonia (Paestum) on the Italian mainland, the so-called 'Temple of Neptune' (really yet another temple of Hera, that most important of goddesses),

was started c.510BC. It has survived better than any other western temple. Its pediment, outer columns and architraves are still almost intact. It is relatively conventional in plan, with a pteron of six by 14 columns, measuring 24 by 59m (79 by 196ft). Here, too, the external columns, 8.9m (29ft) high, taper sharply, giving this temple also an impression of rugged, almost truculent strength. The western Greeks, rich but remote from the accepted conventions on the mainland, were developing an original, albeit quirky, form of architecture.

Above: A typical Doric temple showing the brightly painted and richly carved frieze and pediment, and the marble pillars, with the slight convex curve known as entasis that made them appear straight.

Below: The Temple of Aphaea on Aegina shows the Doric temple approaching perfection. It was built c.510–490BC.

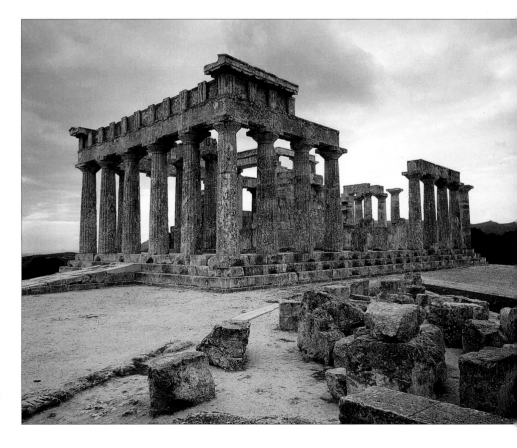

THE IONIC TEMPLE
560–400BC

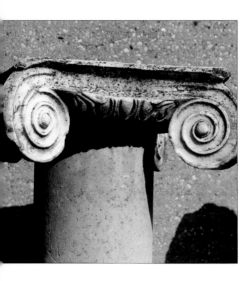

Above: Ionic columns are chiefly identified by their rolled-up forms resembling cushions or rams' horns, which create their distinctive volutes.

While the Doric order at first dominated the Greek world, it was soon rivalled by the Ionic order, a more slender, graceful style of column and capital (head). The Ionic order first appeared in the sophisticated Ionian cities and the Aegean islands in the 6th century BC, spreading to the mainland. It became seen as the feminine order, in contrast to the more 'virile' Doric order.

Preceding the Ionic order was the Aeolian, a capital common in Aeolis in north-western Asia Minor around 600BC. This had *volutes* (spiral scrolls) growing up and out of the column, supporting a rectangular slab. (It is now thought that there was no direct connection between the Aeolian and the Ionian orders, for the oldest Ionic capitals date only from 560BC, while their volutes, in the form of rams' horns or scrolls, turn downward and inward. Also, Aeolic columns had no bases but Ionic columns stood on elaborate bases.)

THE FIRST IONIC TEMPLES

The first true Ionic columns appeared in two vast temples: the Heraion at Samos and the Artemision at Ephesus. Remarkably similar, they were both built in the mid-6th century BC by Theodorus of Samos (died 540BC). An architect of genius, he wrote the first architectural treatise, now lost. King Croesus of Lydia, wealthy overlord of Ephesus, paid for most of its temple. Both buildings were dipteral, i.e. they had a double *pteron* (colonnade), an imposing feature perhaps inspired by Egyptian examples.

Both temples were later destroyed by fire, although that at Ephesus was rebuilt more grandly to become one of the Seven Wonders of the World in the Hellenistic and Roman ages. Both had two rows of eight columns at the entrance, with the columns' spacing and thickness gradually increasing toward the centre to make them look regular seen from afar, as with most Greek temples. At the Heraion on Samos the two central columns were 8.6m (28ft) apart while the outermost pairs were only 5.9m (17ft) apart. It was about 88.4 by 45.7m (290 by 150ft).

The Temple of Artemis at Ephesus was even larger, measuring 109 by 55m (358 by 171ft). Built of limestone covered in marble, the first temple to be so built, its tall, slender columns had richly moulded bases, each with a horizontally fluted *torus*. Sculptural display was ornamental rather than structural in a way that became typically Ionian.

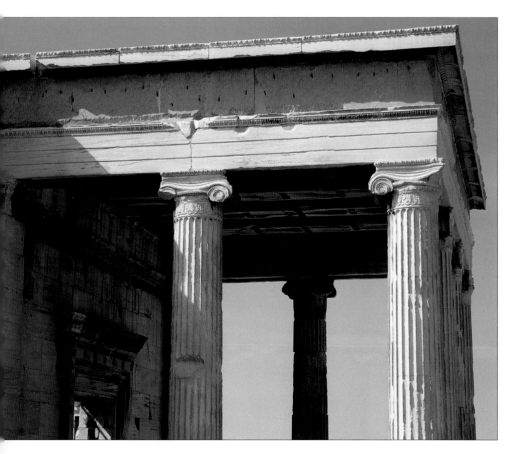

Left: The Ionic columns of the north porch of the Erechtheum, started in 421BC and completed in 405BC, are among the earliest extant uses of the Ionic order in Athens.

Ionic columns had no triglyphs or metopes. Instead, in Asiatic Ionic temples rows of *dentils* ran below the cornice, while in west Aegean Ionic style there was a band of stone, often richly sculpted.

THE TREASURY OF THE SIPHNIANS

One of the first half-extant Ionic temples, built in 525BC, the Treasury of the Siphnians at Delphi, was also the first marble temple on the mainland. Although its base is limestone, its superstructure uses Siphnian marble for the main wall, Naxian for its outer decorations and Parian for its sculptural adornments. Its porch boasts two large free-standing *caryatids* (female statues) similar to those later erected at the Erechtheum on the Athenian Acropolis. The caryatids wear tall hats carved with figures of men and lions. The frieze and even the pediment have sculpted figures carved in high relief, all once brightly painted in red, blue and green. Unpainted, fresh-cut marble must have gleamed blindingly white in strong Greek sunlight.

BUILDING IN MARBLE

Although Greece was blessed with abundant limestone, Greek architects around 500BC began to realize that building completely in marble made it possible to produce far clearer, crisper outlines for both orders of columns. However, marble was very expensive except near quarries. The first major use of marble in temple-building at the Artemision of Ephesus was made possible by King Croesus, a famously rich ruler. Pisistratus reputedly used marble roof tiles for his Temple of Athena Polias in the 530s BC, but he had connections with Paros. Even for the Siphnians, it must have been costly to haul the marble for their small treasury up the mountains to Delphi.

Once they had done so, however, others felt the urge to compete. Cleisthenes, the wealthy Athenian radical aristocrat, probably sponsored the building of the Treasury of the Athenians *c*.500BC. This, also resembling a mini-temple, is the first

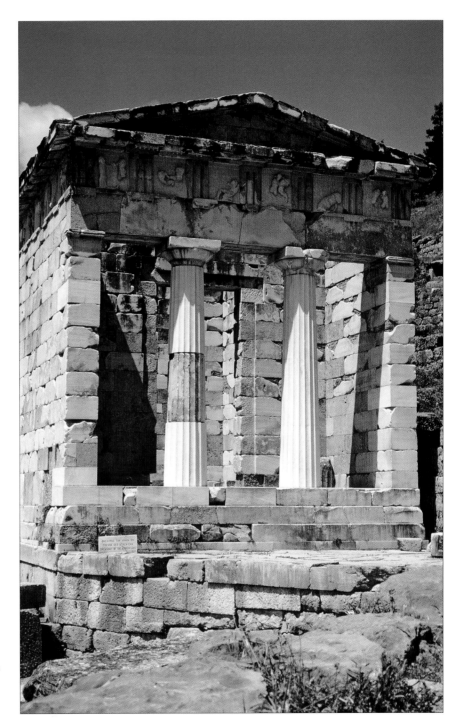

Doric all-marble building. In Athens itself marble remained forbiddingly expensive until a quarry was opened on nearby Mt Pentelicus soon after 500BC. When Athens finally began rebuilding after the end of the Persian wars, it found marble of the highest quality on its doorstep. New claw chisels were needed to work this harder, more brittle material, but the remarkable results on the Acropolis astound us still.

Above: The Treasury of the Athenians at Delphi built soon after 500BC, resembling a mini-temple, is the first Greek all-marble structure, and still Doric in style.

THE PARTHENON
A PERFECT TEMPLE

Above: The Parthenon, perhaps the most famous temple in the world, was built by Ictinus and Callicrates from 447BC. It brought the Doric temple to perfection.

Below: The Parthenon on the Acropolis as it may have looked in its prime, lavishly decorated and colourfully painted. Built as a gleaming statement of Athenian national pride, it housed the great cult statue of Athena, tutelary goddess of the city.

When the Athenians returned to their burnt-out city in 479BC after the Persians had been defeated, they ignored the blackened stumps of their temples on the Acropolis. In the Oath of Plataea that year they had sworn not to rebuild the temples as a reminder of Persian sacrilege in burning them. For decades anyway, they were occupied in fighting Persia. But in 449BC the Persian wars ended with the Peace of Callias. The Athenians then debated what to do with the tribute money still flowing in from their allied (or, increasingly, their subject) states in the Delian League.

Pericles – the radical aristocrat who so dominated the age that he has given his name to it – urged the money be used to rebuild the city's temples. His proposal triggered a violent debate. Some Athenians agreed with Thucydides, son of Melesias, cousin of the historian, that this would be a misuse of the funds. But Pericles won the argument.

Work began in 447BC on what many consider the world's most perfect building: the Parthenon, temple of Athena, virgin (*parthenos*) goddess of the city. Within 15 years the Parthenon had been completed. It has become the archetypal image of ancient Greece.

Above: The frieze running around the Parthenon showing horsemen in the Panathenaic Procession, carved to the general designs of Pheidias.

Pheidias, the great sculptor, had overall charge of the project, but the joint architects were Callicrates and Ictinus. The latter wrote a book about the Parthenon's construction, which, like much Greek literature, has been lost. But the temple itself embodies the key principles of Greek classicism so closely that it has been read almost like a book by successive archaeologists.

> **FOR THE GODS' EYES ONLY?**
> A strange aspect of the Parthenon is the position of the frieze, 161m (534ft) long, running high up around the cella's exterior. Meticulously carved, this must have been almost impossible for contemporary observers to see fully, being overshadowed by the architrave above when the temple was intact. The outer columns would have half-obscured it if seen from far-off. To look at the frieze standing close up on the stylobate must have required painful neck-craning. Possibly it was designed only for the all-seeing eyes of the gods. In this it anticipates Gothic cathedral carvings.

MARBLE COLUMNS AND GILDED STATUES

The building of such a huge marble structure in less than ten years – the sculpting took a further five years to complete – was an unprecedented feat. About 22,000 tons of marble were needed for the Parthenon and the Propylaea, the ceremonial gateway. Fortunately, Mt Pentelicum's quarries were only 13km (8 miles) away. Marble column drums surviving from the burnt earlier temple to Athena were incorporated into the new building, which rested partly on its predecessor's base.

The pteron measured eight by 17 columns, obeying the now canonical rule that the number of columns on the sides should be more than double those on the ends. The columns' height is 5.48 times their diameter, 10.4m (34.3ft) high. The stylobate, as usual, had three steps all round. Sited on the Acropolis' southern edge, the Parthenon remains strikingly visible from miles off. (It also remained essentially intact until its interior was wrecked in an explosion in 1683. That year the Venetians were besieging Athens, held by Turkish troops who were storing gunpowder in the temple. One direct hit gutted the Parthenon.)

In antiquity, worshippers who entered the Acropolis would at first have seen only the temple's carved pediment looming above a flanking wall. As they passed the Propylaea, their eyes would be caught by Pheidias' great outdoor bronze statue of Athena Promachos, 'the warrior', visible far out at sea. Turning a corner, worshippers could finally see the temple's east front ahead and enter the cella. Almost 30m (100ft) long by 10m (34ft) wide and divided in two, this was made of finely cut ashlar blocks. In its inner chamber stood the chryselephantine (gold-ivory over a wooden core) statue of the goddess, Pheidias' masterwork. A two-storeyed Doric colonnade framed the statue, while the outer chamber had internal Ionic columns, a radical innovation inside a Doric temple.

Unusually, all the metopes were sculpted in high relief, the pediments being filled with groups of figures, vividly painted. These include works by Pheidias depicting the city's legends. At each corner a lion's head was carved on the cornice, while above gilded winged victories mounted on *acroteria* seemed poised for flight.

TECHNICAL 'REFINEMENTS'

The Parthenon is renowned for its technical 'refinements', which make it the most accomplished of Doric temples. These include entasis and inward-tilting columns, so that those at the corners do not appear thinner, and the convexity in the stylobate and entablature. All were designed to make the temple look perfectly proportioned when seen from far off. (The columns' tilt means that theoretically they would meet in the sky 2.4km (1½ miles) above.)

Working in marble permitted such sophistication but inevitably required remarkable skills from the workforce. Their efforts produced the archetypal Greek temple.

Above: A view of the Parthenon from the north. It remained astonishingly intact until an explosion during a siege in 1683 blew it apart – it was being used to store gunpowder by the Turks.

Below: The Acropolis of Athens seen from afar, with its unsurpassable group of superb 5th-century BC temples.

ON THE ACROPOLIS
THE OTHER TEMPLES

Above: Jutting out high over the city, the tiny temple to Athena Nike, the first visible to worshippers approaching the Acropolis, was built in 428–425BC, probably by Mnesicles.

Below: The Erechtheum, completed in 405BC, rivals the Parthenon in elegance and surpasses it in ingenuity. It is named after Athens' legendary first king, Erechtheus. The close-spaced supporting caryatids emphasize the building's mass.

Around the Parthenon, smaller temples were subsequently built on the Acropolis, despite the war with the Peloponnesians that started in 431BC. Remarkably, even through the war's increasing disasters, work continued intermittently, bringing Greek classical architecture to its peak.

The Propylaea, the monumental Doric gateway at the west of the Acropolis, was the second building commissioned by Pericles. It was constructed in 437–432BC, work on it stopping before completion as war loomed. Little is known about its architect Mnesicles, but he probably also designed the Athena Nike temple opposite. The Propylaea was approached by a ramp about 25m (65ft) wide, the start of the Panathenaic Way leading down to the Agora (market place). It had two impressive temple-like façades of six Doric columns, one on each side.

IRON BARS AND CUNNING

Mnesicles solved the difficulty of erecting a symmetrical building on a sloping, irregular site by extending the architrave round the flanking buildings on the same level. However, the exterior junction of the Propylaea's separate roofs must have looked awkward. The building is entered through a hexastyle (six-column) Doric porch, the two central columns being wider spaced to let sacrificial animals pass through. Beyond lay an imposing passage with Ionic columns supporting a rich marble ceiling. This, with its coffers (recessed panels) adorned with gold stars on a blue background, was a wonder of its age. It was also very expensive, the building costing 2,000 talents. The architraves over the colonnade were reinforced with iron bars, a remarkable innovation if superfluous structurally. Designing the Propylaea, the first complex building on different levels, required creating harmonious spatial relations between its varied parts. It inspired many later architects.

On the Propylaea's north side lay the *pinakotheke* (the picture gallery), where state banquets were held with platforms for dining couches round the walls. It also housed some of Athens' greatest pictures, depicting victories over the Persians at Marathon and Salamis, all long since lost.

On the other side of the Propylaea the tiny temple to Athena Nike was built, probably by Mnesicles, in *c*.428–425BC. It uses the Ionic order with four monolithic columns only 4m (13ft) high at each end, oddly thick for their size. The aim was probably to avoid too strong a contrast to the solid Propylaea. It had attachments for figures in its pediments and much fine carving, while its little cella is almost square. Jutting out high over the city, this exquisite temple is the first approaching visitors see.

THE ERECHTHEUM

Another Ionic temple on the Acropolis, the Erechtheum rivals the Parthenon in elegance if not size. Started in 421BC after the short-lasting Peace of Nicias and completed in 405BC, the year of Athens'

Above: The Propylaea, the monumental Doric gateway on the west of the Acropolis, was built in 437–432BC, work stopping before its completion as war loomed. Its architect was Mnesicles.

final catastrophic defeat, it was named after the legendary semi-divine first king of Athens. It is in fact a multiple temple, housing shrines to ten different gods and heroes, besides a pit of sacred serpents. Because the site is asymmetrical and on several levels, the Erechtheum is really two semi-detached temples with three porches facing in different directions. The asymmetry is minimized by the noble exterior, united by a harmonious Ionic order and frieze of low-relief figures in white marble on a dark background running around the temple like a belt. The whole Erechtheum, again built of marble, has carvings of an elaboration never repeated elsewhere in Greece.

The central larger temple, dedicated to Athena Polias (guardian), has a huge porch facing north over the city. It housed her ancient wooden statue, dating back to the Bronze Age, besides the supposed tomb of Erechtheus. Its smaller porch, on the south side facing the Parthenon, has famous caryatids (now copies) instead of supporting pillars. These draped female figures are close-spaced to create a massiveness echoing the Parthenon's.

The south porch, lower than the north, is raised on a wall to make it appear level. It was linked internally by a staircase.

The eastern temple was dedicated chiefly to Zeus, whose altar was in the porch. Inside were altars to Hephaestus, the fire god, Erechtheus and Poseidon. At the Erechtheum's west end stood the Pandroseum, an enclosure with the tomb of Cecrops, another Athenian mythical hero, and the sacred olive tree of Athena. Reputedly it sprouted fresh leaves after being burnt by the Persians in 480BC. The Erechtheum's interior suffered from being converted into the Turkish governor's harem under Ottoman rule (1455–1829).

Above: The hill of the Acropolis, towering above Athens, superbly displays the highest achievements of Greek classical architecture.

Below: The Erechtheum was a temple not to one deity but to ten, being in reality two semi-detached buildings with three porches, all on different levels. Its architect may also have been Mnesicles.

OTHER TEMPLES OF THE GOLDEN AGE

Above: The Temple of Poseidon the sea-god at Sunium was built by an unknown architect around 440BC. Superbly sited at Sunium on the point of Attica, it is made of local marble.

Below: The Hephaistion (Theseion) on the west side of the Agora was Athens' first all-marble temple. It was started in 449BC, being designed by the same unknown architect who built that at Sunium. It has survived better than any other Greek temple.

Although the temples on the Acropolis are Athens' most striking, many others were built in the city and across Greece in the 5th century BC. Oldest of the classical temples in central Athens itself was the Hephaistion (once called the Theseion) on the west of the Agora, the city's social and commercial heart.

Started in 449BC, it is the first all-marble Doric temple in Attica but lacks the Parthenon's subtleties. Its use of 'refinements' such as entasis is crudely obvious, so that the building only convinces when seen front-on. Happily, that is how most Athenians would have seen it, as trees or buildings on its sides probably prevented other views. Further, all its sculptured metopes are concentrated on its front or just around its corners. The relatively high entablature of 2m (6ft 6in), coupled with unduly slim columns of 5.7m (18ft 9in), would appear unimpressive if seen otherwise.

In plan the Hephaistion resembles the earlier temple of Zeus at Olympia in the Peloponnese, but is on half its scale,

ATHENS' LARGEST TEMPLE

The Pisistratids had started a gigantic temple to Olympian Zeus east of the Acropolis in c.520BC, its size reflecting both their dynastic pretensions and Zeus' status as supreme deity. They had got no further than its base before their expulsion in 510BC. For the next 350 years the site remained untouched until Antiochus IV, an energetic Seleucid king of Syria, paid for work to restart in 170BC. The architect was Cossutius, a Roman who had worked in the Greek east in opulent Hellenistic style. He continued with the basic plan but gave the temple gigantic columns of the Corinthian order. It was the first time this order had been used so grandly in Athens. But the temple was not completed as Antiochus' death in 164BC cut off funds. Sulla, the Roman general, removed some of the temple's capitals to Rome after sacking Athens in 86–85BC. Only when the philhellenic Emperor Hadrian visited Athens was the great temple finally completed in AD131. Hadrian's plan generally followed Cossutius' designs, but the standard of workmanship was not so fine. The columns are 16.7m (55ft) high and unusually proportioned, their height being equal to 8¾ of their lower diameter. The huge temple finally measured 108 by 41m (354 by 135ft).

measuring 31.7 by 13.7m (104 by 45ft). Possibly its carvings were influenced by those on the Parthenon, where work progressed more rapidly. The Hephaistion became a church in the 6th century AD, which explains why it is so well preserved. (Most temples were not converted to churches, chiefly because they were the wrong shape for Christian worship.)

THE TEMPLE OF POSEIDON

Very similar and probably built by the same unknown architect around 440BC is the Temple of Poseidon the sea-god. It is superbly sited at Sunium on the very tip of Attica. Though built of a less fine local marble, not pentelic, it shows the architect's skills developing. Its dimensions are similar to the Hephaistion's but the columns are 30cm (1ft) higher. Each column has only 16 shallow-carved flutes instead of the usual 20, removing the need for entasis. Whether seen by sailors rounding the cape or by worshippers approaching from land, the temple has always looked marvellous, gleaming hundreds of feet above the sea. It was built on the base of an earlier temple, which is thought to have beeen destroyed by the Persians in the invasion of 480BC.

BASSAE: A RADICAL INTERIOR

Equally impressive but very different is the Temple of Apollo Epikourius, Apollo the Helper, built by the small state of Phigaleia in Arcadia, the most rugged part of the Peloponnese. This was in thanks for divine deliverance from the plague, at least so wrote Pausanias 600 years later, who claimed that its architect was Ictinus who had just designed the Parthenon. But Apollo may have delivered the little state from foreign aggresion, not plague. *Epikouros* in ancient Greek can mean mercenary soldier.

The temple was probably started about 429BC and finished, after interruptions caused by Spartan occupation, in 400BC. Built of grey local limestone – at 1,127m (3,700ft) up amid mountainous ravines, Bassae is too remote to be supplied easily or cheaply with marble – the temple's proportions appear rather old-fashioned, with six by 15 columns. Externally it lacked most of the latest refinements such as entasis, which suggests that the builder was possibly a provincial.

However, its interior was remarkably radical, which suggests that Ictinus was indeed the real architect. Its cella is flanked by impressive Ionic half-columns

(sunk in the wall). Their bases are abnormally flared, echoing the flamboyant capitals. which have three-faced capitals with two volutes (scrolls) and curved tops. Most radical of all was a free-standing column with a Corinthian capital at the south end. (Originally there may have been two others. This column has since perished but is known from drawings.) Bassae is the first known use of the elaborate third order, which became so popular in the Hellenistic and Roman eras.

Above: The Temple of Olympian Zeus is the largest temple in Athens. Started in the 6th century BC, it was only completed in Hadrian's reign (AD117–138).

Below: The Temple of Apollo at Bassae in remote Arcadia was possibly designed by Ictinus, the Parthenon's architect, in 429BC.

THE WORLD'S FIRST THEATRES

Above: The vast theatre at Pergamum, capital of the wealthy Attalid kingdom in north-western Asia Minor, was carved from the steep acropolis side in the 2nd century BC.

Below: The theatre at Priene was small, suiting this tiny polis in Asia Minor. Built c.300BC, it is typical of many Greek theatres.

The Greeks built the world's first permanent theatres to stage their great plays. Athens, which pioneered drama and comedy in the 5th century BC, also pioneered the structural development of the Greek theatre. Its form then spread around the expanding Greek world and was finally taken over and adapted by the Romans. Greek theatres were always open to the sky, although March, the month of the Greater Dionysia and the annual drama contests, can be cold even in Greece.

Theatre in Athens began simply, using a natural hollow on the south slope of the Acropolis in the 6th century BC as its venue. This site was transformed over the next two centuries into the great Theatre of Dionysus, seating up to 17,000 spectators, and was embellished over the succeeding centuries into the Roman era. Classical plays are still performed in it, making it probably the world's oldest theatre still in current use.

THE FIRST THEATRE

The auditorium of the first theatre was a simple semicircle of wooden benches perched on the steep 1 in 8 slope. Below was a round dancing area, the *orchestra*, about 25m (82ft) across. Here the chorus danced and sang and actors, first one, then two and finally more, stepped out to declaim. A plain stone wall acted as a backdrop. After the Persian defeat in 479BC, Xerxes' resplendent royal tent, 60m (200ft) wide, was used as a back-cloth for plays, according to tradition. (*Skene*, later meaning background building or scenery, originally meant tent.) Outside the theatre stood a small temple to Dionysus, the god of drama.

As the city grew, the semicircle of tiered seating was expanded further up and round the Acropolis' slopes. Pericles is credited with building the first stone theatre in the 430s BC, along with the smaller covered *odeion* but many archaeologists date the oldest stone remains discovered to after 400BC However, there definitely was a wooden skene to which scenery could be attached in the 5th century. By the mid-4th century AD the theatre had achieved the form we associate with a Greek theatre: a hemisphere of stone benches rising above the semicircular orchestra, with a long stoa behind the stone skene, on which stage 'machinery' could create sometimes elaborate special effects.

EPIDAURUS, THE PERFECT THEATRE

The most beautiful and best-preserved of Greek theatres is that of Epidaurus in the north-western Peloponnese. Although Epidaurus was not a polis of much importance, it constructed the archetypal Greek theatre on a clear, uncluttered slope. (In Athens, buildings and a cliff hemmed in the theatre.) Probably built by the architect Polyclitus the Younger about 350BC, Epidaurus' perfectly symmetrical auditorium is 118m (387ft) in diameter and very nearly semicircular in plan. It boasts superb acoustics and also allows a good view from every seat – at least of the orchestra if not of the skene. The skene probably originally rose quite high. Later a proscenium, a structure jutting out from the skene, as the name suggests, was added on which actors performed. This suited the needs of the New Comedy, which depended more on individual characters interacting, less on grand choruses.

The stone seats are 76cm (2ft 6in) wide and 43cm (17in) tall. Like many ancient theatre seats, they are surprisingly comfortable. The best seats are in the centre low down. Two tall elegant doorways allowed easy entry and exit. The theatre seated about 12,000 people, a surprisingly large number for such a small city. It was probably seldom filled.

In the Hellenistic and Roman ages, theatres became steadily grander and more elaborate. That at Pergamum, capital of the wealthy Attalid kingdom, was carved dramatically from the steep acropolis side beneath the royal palace in the 2nd century BC. More typical was the theatre of Priene, which lay further south, a city rebuilt c.300BC, which resembles Epidaurus on a smaller scale. Here the skene had two storeys and a proscenium in front.

ODEIONS

All theatres were open-aired, seating many, sometimes all, the citizens, but covered buildings were erected for musical and literary events. Around 440BC, Pericles built the first odeion (from which comes our word 'odeum'), an immense covered building next to the theatre. Its wooden roof, topped by an open-sided lantern for light and ventilation but chiefly designed with acoustics in mind, was supported on 81 columns in nine rows. Reputedly, it too was modelled on Xerxes' tent, that paradigm of oriental luxury. The odeion hosted the musical and poetry contests at the four-yearly Panathenaic Games. Originally it had wooden benches but in the 4th century BC these were replaced by stone. Many cities later copied Athens' example.

Above: Epidaurus has the best-preserved and most beautiful theatre in the Greek world. Probably built by the architect Polyclitus the Younger c.350BC, its perfectly symmetrical auditorium has superb acoustics.

Below: Begun in the 6th century BC, the Theatre of Dionysus in Athens assumed its final form by the mid-4th century BC, when its tiers of seats and skene were completed in stone. Seating 17,000 spectators, it saw the premières of works by Aeschylus, Sophocles, Euripides and Aristophanes.

STOAS AND COUNCIL HALLS

Above: The Agora of Athens, the ancient heart of the city, showing the Stoa of Attalus, the only building of its kind fully restored, with the Acropolis in the distance.

Below: The Agora at Athens under the Roman empire, when it had become almost crowded wth monuments. The oldest stoas from the 5th century BC are on the right (the Stoa Poikile housing with paintings) with the 'Royal Stoa' on the left. The bulky buildings, like the Stoa of Attalus at the top, are Hellenistic or Roman.

While temples and theatres are the Greeks' most famous public buildings, they developed many other buildings for urban life. From the 6th century BC on, increasing numbers of Greek cities built stoas: long, open-sided, pillared porticos, usually sited around the Agora. Giving shelter against winter rains or summer sun, and often carefully angled to admit warming winter sunlight, stoas sheltered many aspects of city life, from shopping or dining to philosophy. One important school of philosophy even took its name from a stoa: the Stoics.

THE FIRST STOAS

An early small stoa designed solely for shelter was at the Sanctuary of Hera in Samos from the 7th century BC. However, the first significant stoa that we know of was the Stoa Poikile (painted stoa), erected on the north side of the Athenian Agora soon after the Persian defeat in 479BC.

It took its name from the paintings on its north wall depicting heroic episodes in Athenian history. Ranging from Theseus' (mythical) war with the Amazons to the Battle of Marathon, Athens' first victory over Persia in 490BC, the panels were painted by three great artists of the classical period: Polygnotus, Micon and Panaenus. These were described by the travel-writer Pausanias 600 years later but have since vanished.

Stoas were subsequently built all round Athens' Agora. Just south-west of the Stoa Poikile was the Royal Stoa, called after the 'King Archon', by then a purely ceremonial official. Beyond that another grander stoa to Zeus Eleutherios (Zeus the Deliverer) was built in the late 5th century BC. This had Doric columns externally but used the Ionic order inside. It was divided into compartments for different activities, which possibly included law courts.

THE STOA OF ATTALUS

Further stoas were built around the other sides of the Agora, the grandest being the Stoa of Attalus, the wealthy king of Pergamum. He endowed Athens with his superb two-storeyed stoa in the 150s BC. This has been totally reconstructed in recent years, to give a good impression of how the stoa must have looked when brand new. The lower floor has Doric columns, the upper floor and the interior Ionic. This arrangement soon became very common, even canonical, not only for stoas but also for other buildings. Even the Colosseum in Rome follows this pattern.

Many cities in Greece and across Asia, such as Miletus, Ephesus, Antioch and Pergamum, built extensive stoas lining their agoras and sometimes running down their streets. An unusually long stoa was the 'South Stoa' at Corinth, built around 300BC. It was 160m (525ft) long with 71 Doric columns along its straight façade. On the gutter was a row of water-spouts in the form of lions' heads, each separated by an acanthus scroll, a common decorative device. Water gushed up from wells inside the stoa, coming from the springs of Peirene at the Agora's east end. When the Romans sacked Corinth in 146BC, they found and burnt in the stoa shops containing paint, clay, lime, along with much elaborate pottery. This suggests that workshops were located there, making stoas truly multifunctional.

BOULETERIA: COUNCIL HALLS

Although the Assembly (*ecclesia*), the sovereign body in democratic Athens, met in the open – with a quorum of 6,000 it had to – the far smaller Council did not. The Council (*boule*), of 400 or 500 councillors chosen annually by lot, discussed and shaped new proposals before they went before the often unpredictable full Assembly. But unlike the Roman Senate, the boule had little real power, at least when Athens was a full democracy.

In Athens the older Council Hall (*bouleuterion*) was a simple rectangular building on the west of the Agora, with a temple and document store attached. In the late 5th century BC a new bouleuterion was cut into the hillside behind it, with tiers of seats in a semicircle like a theatre, the old building now housing the state archives. A ceremonial porch was added 100 years later. Other cities copied Athens' example. The small island of Thasos had an almost square bouleterion, and Miletus a grand semicircular building for up to 1,500 people. This looked out on to a colonnaded courtyard in the Doric order, with a gateway with Corinthian columns beyond.

Among the largest bouleuteria was the Thersilion, built at Megalopolis in Arcadia. This new federal capital was founded late in 371BC after Sparta's long dominance of Arcadia had been ended by its crushing defeat at the battle of Leuctra. A rectangle measuring 86 by 67.7m (218 by 172ft), the Thersilion seated 6,000 people from all cities in the new confederate democracy. This meant a far bigger building than the Athenian

prototype. The centre of its front consisted of a series of doorways, but inside pillars were arranged to minimize obstruction between the speaker in the centre and his audience. The internal columns were unfluted Doric, and there was probably a lantern-type roof to admit light.

At Priene in Asia Minor a new bouleterion was built in c.200BC. Sunk into the slope like a theatre and seating 600 people – a high proportion of the tiny population – it was almost square, being 20.25 by 21m (64 by 66ft 6in).

Above: The bouleuterion (council chamber) of Priene, that model Ionian polis, was rectangular in shape, but many such chambers were semicircular.

Below: Attalus II, King of Pergamum, gave Athens a grand stoa in the 150s BC. Now totally reconstructed, it shows how such a stoa must have looked when new.

THE PRIVATE HOUSE

Above: In Delos, a thriving port in the 2nd century BC, rich merchants built fine houses with large courtyards that have survived remarkably well.

Below: The house of Diadomenus in Delos had a fine mosaic floor, a form of expensive but long-lasting decoration that would recur in many later houses in Italy.

In classical Greece, public magnificence was seldom matched by private affluence. Most houses in Periclean Athens remained modest. Citizens, who lived mainly in the open, happily spent their taxes (or their empire's tribute) on adorning their city, not their homes. But by the time Rome conquered Greece in the 2nd century BC, luxurious houses were being built in many places. These influenced Roman houses at Pompeii, that time-capsule buried by Vesuvius' eruption to give us vivid glimpses of antiquity.

Almost all Greek houses were built around courtyards with slits for external windows. Most in 5th-century BC Athens were built of mud-brick on a stone base and the windows had no glass. At first only the better houses had terracotta-tiled roofs, poorer ones using mud-tiles. Houses in Athens were crammed together without decent drainage or water supplies. For all its public splendours, classical Athens was not a salubrious city. Mud and filth clogged its narrow, mostly unpaved streets. However, some citizens always lived in markedly more lavish houses than others.

HIPPODAMUS OF MILETUS

Hippodamus (*c.* 500–420BC) is considered the first town planner and the inventor of the grid-iron plan. Although Smyrna had been rebuilt on a regular plan after an earthquake in the 7th century BC, Hippodamus produced the first coherent urban theories. He planned the Piraeus in the 460s BC, when it was growing fast, laying out regular-sized blocks for housing. An agora, approached by a wide avenue, was named after him. He then toured the Greek world, advising poleis from Rhodes to Thurii in Italy how to plan their cities. Others later copied his ideas. Sometimes, as at Priene, rebuilt around 330BC, Hippodamus' ideas were applied irrespective of the actual topography, which is steeply hilly at Priene.

ON THE ACROPOLIS' SLOPES

Demosthenes, the great orator (384–322BC), declared that luxurious houses were unknown before his time, but he exaggerated. Very comfortable houses from earlier decades have been found behind the South Stoa. All had courtyards and upper floors, with walls of mud-brick on a stone base and roofs of terracotta tiles. Halfway up the slope to the Acropolis, three houses built after 400BC have been discovered. The largest, measuring 25 by 19m (82 by 62ft) overall, had 10 ground-floor rooms and a large courtyard with a colonnade supporting a balcony. One room had a fine mosaic floor, which was clearly important because mosaics were rare. Opposite it was the *andron* ('men's room'), where men, reclining on couches, dined, drank and talked or were entertained by flute girls and dancers. Upstairs was the *gynaekeion*, the women's quarters –

women in classical Athens led segregated lives. The walls were painted with bands of colour. Similar houses have been found at the Piraeus and Megara.

FROM OLYNTHUS TO POMPEII
Olynthus, a city in northern Greece, laid out a new quarter on a rectilinear plan after 430BC. (Olynthus was destroyed by Philip II of Macedonia in 348BC.) Most houses, measuring 15.2m (*c*.50ft) square, had two floors, with cobbled courtyards at their centre and verandas on the north side to catch the winter sun. Their timber columns supported stone capitals on burnt-brick bases. Some houses had mosaic floors in the main rooms. The 'House of Good Fortune' has a superb mosaic made of 50,000 pebbles showing Dionysus driving a leopard-drawn chariot. Houses still had sun-dried brick walls on burnt-brick foundations, however.

Far grander houses were built after Alexander the Great's conquests, which enriched at least some people. At Pella, Macedonia's capital, houses 45m (150ft) square had larger rooms with peristyles (colonnades around a building) with stone columns. They also had bathrooms with terracotta bath tubs but had the same overall layout as at Olynthos.

The island of Delos, which boomed after Rome made it a free port in 166BC, saw Greek houses growing positively luxurious, but they still centred on an inner courtyard. Such courts now had peristyles all around and boasted elaborate mosaics, made no longer of pebbles but of finely cut stones. The roofs of these houses drained into the court and so into an underground cistern – Delos was chronically short of water. Comparable houses of the period have been found across the Greek world, from Dura in Mesopotamia to Saint Rémy in southern France.

Right: Most Athenian houses of the Classical period were relatively simple. On two floors, they centred around a courtyard, with colonnades supporting balconies on the upper floor and blank exterior walls.

Many of Delos' richest inhabitants were Italian businessmen. Through them, and through Greek artists or slaves imported into Italy, the 'peristyle house' spread to Italy. The best surviving examples come from Pompeii, where the peristyled courtyard of the House of the Gilded Cupids, built *c*.150BC, is so large that it is almost a colonnaded garden.

Above: The finest surviving examples of later Greek houses come from Pompeii, a city in Italy much influenced by Greek culture and preserved by Vesuvius' eruption. This is the House of the Vettii, dating from the 1st century BC.

CHAPTER II

BUILDING STYLES AND TECHNIQUES

The Greeks invented a classical language for architecture that has proved uniquely influential. The Romans later adopted and adapted the Greek style, exporting it across their own empire. The results of this artistic union, deliberately revived after 1400 in the Renaissance, shaped Western architecture into the mid-20th century. Greek architecture was trabeated, meaning it relied mainly on the column and lintel for its effect. This made the proportions of their columns, and of the entablature (the horizontal mass the pillars supported) all-important. The Greeks worked out canons (rules) for their different orders, or styles, of columns, which appear almost magically perfect. All were mathematically based, their proportions deriving ultimately from idealized versions of the human body. Classical architecture has retained its appeal because it appears supremely harmonious. It really is 'architecture with a human face'.

While Greek architectural theories and craftsmanship became sophisticated, building techniques generally remained simple. The Greeks seldom used cement, relying instead on metal clamps and precise fitting of stone, and had little machinery. But they were brilliant craftsmen in both stone and marble, working with supreme precision to create monuments of unageing intellect.

Left: The perfect proportions of the Temple of Poseidon above Cape Sunium exemplify Greek architectural skill.

BUILDING MATERIALS

Above: The Temple of Aphaea in Aegina is built of gleaming local limestone but was originally colourfully painted.

Below: The massive Temple of Athena at Poseidonia (Paestum) of the 5th century BC in southern Italy was once covered in stucco and brightly painted, creating an effect that is hard to imagine today.

While the Parthenon appears to float with effortless perfection above Athens, such excellence had taken the Greeks centuries to achieve. They started building not in marble or stone but in perishable timber and mud-brick. To create perfectly proportioned buildings, however, they needed to quarry, and work in, one of the finest if hardest of materials ever used: Greek marble.

The Minoans built their elaborate rambling palaces out of a mixture of adobe (sunbaked mud-brick), timber and rubble, usually stuccoed both inside and out. They had bases of stone or burnt brick needed to keep structures dry, and palaces built after 1600BC boasted walls of ashlar (cut stone). However, the Minoans' pillars were of wood and so combustible, as events catastrophically showed.

The Mycenaeans on mainland Greece used massive stones, often weighing 6 or more tons, to build their citadels at Tiryns and Mycenae. For these they hacked polygonal limestone megaliths ('big stones') from local hills. These were laid without plaster or cement on top of each other. This seemingly crude way of building was done so skilfully that it created the large tholos of the 'Treasury of Atreus'. Like Mycenae's cyclopean walls, it has lasted more than 3,000 years, But the knowledge and ability to build on such a scale vanished during the 12th century BC.

TERRACOTTA AND WOOD

In the Dark Ages (1100–800BC) the Greeks, when they built at all, did so in wood, making tiny temples with thatched roofs. Occasional early buildings, such as the first Temple of Hera, encouraged the use of terracotta (fired unglazed clay) roofing tiles (with wooden beams). At first these were very heavy, weighing up to 20kg (66lb). This led to the walls of the temple cella being made of stone and mud-brick, and finally also to stone columns. Well into the 6th century BC pillars were still often timber. (Later, wooden columns were widely replaced by stone ones.) Entablatures were also made of terracotta in the 7th century, before stone replaced it as a building material.

BUILDING IN LIMESTONE

The Greeks of the mainland and of Ionia were fortunate in having abundant limestone to hand when they began learning again how to build in masonry around 650BC. Comparatively easy to quarry and work, limestone can also be precisely chiselled, as the fine columns of the Temple of Aphaea on Aegina of c.500BC show.

In Sicily and southern Italy, where builders often had only much coarser materials, such as sandstone, to hand, temples were usually covered in stucco and painted, as the entablatures of almost all Greek temples across the Mediterranean always were.

The first masonry was curvilinear. Blocks fitted together like a jigsaw puzzle in the 'Lesbian style' (named after some rustic-looking fortifications on Lesbos island). By 550BC Greek temples and public buildings were being constructed of polygonal megaliths of well-cut masonry. Private houses, in contrast, were long made of mud-brick on a stone base, but increasingly had fired-clay roof tiles. These were, of course, far more weather-proof than unfired clay.

MARBLE PERFECTION

Fine though limestone was, marble was manifestly finer, requiring more skill but giving crisper outlines. In the 6th century marble was increasingly used for adorning buildings – and by the century's end also for statues – but it was expensive to build completely in it. The main sources of good marble were Cycladic islands such as Naxos and Paros. Hauling slabs over the mountains to Delphi must have made even small marble temples such as the Treasury of the Athenians expensive, although it must have been cheaper in cities like Ephesus, near the sea.

But the great source of Athenian marble was local: Mt Pentelicum, 13km (8 miles) from Athens – a fact that helped make all the Athenian architectural achievements possible. About 25 ancient marble quarries have been identified on the slopes of the mountain. The first workings had begun by 550BC, but systematic exploitation took off only early in the 5th century. It peaked under Pericles' grandiose works programme after 460BC.

The crystalline rocks of Pentelicum produced the fine white marble used for most great public buildings in Athens, including those on the Acropolis. It super-seded all other marble except that from Paros, which is easier for sculpting. The marble of the pediments was often painted or even gilded, so the effect would have been less blindingly white.

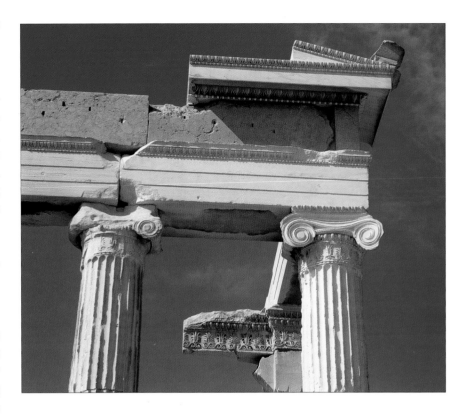

Although the rich golden tint that age alone gives to Pentelic marble could not often have been appreciated in antiquity, it was considered the world's finest build-ing material by Greeks and Romans alike. Pentelic marble long remained one of Athens' principal exports. By the 2nd century AD it was being shipped not just to Rome but also to rich African cities like Lepcis Magna. In this way too, Greek architecture spread across the world.

Above: The brilliant white columns of the Erechtheum on the Athenian Acropolis were built of marble quarried from Mt Pentelicum nearby.

Below: The quarries of Mt Pentelicum, whose crystalline rocks produced the fine white marble used for Athens' great public buildings.

Above: Columns of the Doric order, first and simplest of the three Greek orders, or types, of column.

Above: An Ionic column, the second order, with its distinctive scrolled capital.

Below: A Corinthian capital, the last and most luxurious of the three orders.

THE THREE ORDERS
DORIC, IONIC, CORINTHIAN

Greek architecture is defined by its columns. Every Greek temple was enveloped in them, every stoa composed of them, every major public building flanked by them. Today the columns' descendants adorn so many nondescript banks and government offices that we may see them as mere decoration or just ignore them. But they had vital functional roles in Greek architecture. Even when not supporting roofs and entablatures, they expressed Greek beliefs in mathematical harmony and proportion.

Harmony and proportion, of course, are central to most architecture. Unusually, Greek architecture derived these, at least in theory, from the idealized human form. (Many Greek architects wrote books on architectural theory but none has survived. Only those by Vitruvius, a Roman architect of the 1st century BC, have, incorporating earlier Greek ideas.)

The Greeks used three orders, or types, of columns, distinguished chiefly by their capitals (heads). These are, in order of emergence: Doric, Ionic and Corinthian. The names supposedly reflect the orders'

origins. But while Ionic columns certainly first appeared in Ionian cities, Athens, also an Ionian city, employed the Doric order to wonderful effect on its Acropolis. Doric became seen as suitable for masculine or official buildings, Ionic as graceful and matronly or scholarly and Corinthian as charming and feminine. (The Romans added a fourth order, the luxurious Composite, and perhaps a fifth, Tuscan, a stubby form of Doric.)

THE DORIC ORDER
First, stockiest and seemingly simplest of the orders, Doric columns had no base. Like the wooden pillars they replaced, they rose directly from the ground. Doric columns, like all Greek columns, were 'fluted', having shallow concave grooves. At the shaft's top was the capital, with

Below: The British Museum in London was built in 1823–46. Its noble Ionic columns were inspired by the Temple of Athena at Priene. They show the perennial, highly flexible appeal of the Greek orders, with their mathematically based proportions.

an *abacus* on an *echinus*, or moulding (literally 'hedgehog'). On this stood the entablature, the whole horizontal stone mass, about a quarter the height of the column. Its lowest element was the architrave, a stone beam.

Above the architrave ran the frieze, composed of triglyphs and metopes. These may derive from carpentry: triglyphs, protruding blocks scored with three grooves, originated as ends of the crossbeams of a wooden roof. (Another view suggests that the Doric order was inspired by Egypt's all-stone temples.) The metopes, the slabs between the triglyphs, were often decorated with sculptures. Above ran the cornice, the topmost ledge of stone, and above that the pediment, the low-pitched triangular gable at the end of every temple and stoa.

Triglyphs were theoretically set over the centre of every column and over the centre line of every *intercolumniation* – the space between columns measured in *modules* (column diameters). Intercolumniation was crucially important in Doric temples. Architects normally allowed for five modules, but this caused problems with thicker columns. About 20ft (6m) proved the maximum span possible for an architrave, so at times extra columns were inserted.

THE IONIC ORDER

In the mid-6th century BC, the Ionic order originated in Ionia and the Cyclades. (It is probably not linked to the earlier Aeolic order, whose volutes, scroll-like adornments, grow from the shaft of the column, enclosing a palmette.) The Ionic order was distinguished from the Doric in several ways: its shaft was more slender; the column was often taller; it always had a base; and its capitals ended in volutes that resembled either rams' horns or papyrus plants, according to the observer. The Ionian order was subdivided between 'Asian' in Ionia proper and the islands, and 'Attic', the order of the mainland, which had a more elaborate base. (The Romans favoured the latter,

which consequently become common across the Mediterranean.) The Ionic frieze has no metopes or triglyphs, so there were no problems with intercolumniation. Ionic columns were used from the late 5th century BC on, when elegance rather than power was desired, as in the Erechtheum (421–405BC) on the Athenian Acropolis.

THE CORINTHIAN ORDER

The last of the three Greek orders to emerge was the Corinthian order. Vitruvius attributed its invention to Callicrates, a 4th-century BC architect, but the order was used internally on the Temple of Apollo at Bassae in Arcadia before 400BC. A Corinthian capital is richly decorated with two rows of acanthus leaves and other pieces of vegetation. This is its chief distinction from the Ionic order, whose measurements it otherwise generally shares. One of the finest surviving examples of a Corinthian building is the Choragic Monument of Lysicrates in Athens. Dating from 334BC, this is a beautiful circular memorial.

Above, l to r: The three great orders of columns, Doric, Ionic and Corinthian, which adorned every Greek public building.

Below: The Monument of Lysicrates of 334BC. Its circular form and Corinthian columns inspired the British architect 'Athenian' Stuart.

BUILDING PROCEDURES AND TECHNIQUES

Above: To construct the Parthenon and the other temples high on the Acropolis, builders had to haul heavy cuboids of marble from the quarries of Pentelicum on rollers or in ox-carts.

The Greeks had no powered machinery of any sort and relatively few mechanisms employing human or animal muscle power. Nor did they have huge armies of slaves, as the Egyptian pharaohs had done. However, slaves certainly worked on the construction sites in small groups alongside free citizens, who might well be their masters. Records have survived detailing the payments made to the small building companies – almost all family-type businesses – who built the temples of the 5th century BC. This small scale makes the Greek, especially Athenian, architectural achievement all the more remarkable.

Instead, the Greeks relied on their intellectual powers and remarkably skilled craftsmanship to erect their buildings. Few details survive of their actual building techniques, however.

The builders of the temples on the Acropolis and other parts of Athens first had to transport their heavy cuboids of marble up to the site high above the city. The requisite blocks were cut to size at the Pentelicum quarries, but

ancones, small protruding handles, were left on their sides to allow them to be lifted by ropes. (Ancones were usually chipped off after building work was finished but some can still be seen on the Propylaea, where the outbreak of the Peloponnesian War in 431 BC prevented the work's completion.)

The blocks were then transported by unpaved roads 13km (8 miles) to Athens. Transport was presumably by ox-cart – the Greeks never used horses for haulage because they had no suitable harnesses. Alternatively, wooden discs may have been fitted to the slabs on which they rolled. Most blocks were dragged up the steep slopes of the Acropolis like this.

CRANES AND MACHINERY

Cranes were almost certainly used to help raise the masonry up to the temples during construction, although no traces of such machinery have been found. Aristotle, the encyclopaedically knowledgeable philosopher of the 4th century BC, describes complex pulley systems, with two upright timbers joined at the top with a brace and spread at the bottom. (Vitruvius wrote of very similar devices being used in Rome in the 1st century BC. Technology advanced with painful slowness, if at all, in the ancient world, so the machinery was probably much the same.) Lifting power came from a windlass attached to the back of the frame.

The 46 Doric columns of the Parthenon's pteron (outer colonnade) were made of 11 drums of marble. These were lifted into place by cranes using the ancones on each side. The column's top section, which included the Doric capital with its abacus and echinus, had its 20 flutes cut into it before being heaved into place and secured by metal clamps. Probably the fluting was cut around the base of the bottom drum to

Below: Complex pulley systems, with two upright timbers joined at the top with a brace and spread at the bottom, as described by Aristotle, were used to help build the temples.

avoid harming the stylobate's paving. The rest of the fluting was carved after the column had been assembled on site.

'REFINEMENTS'

In building the Parthenon (447–437BC), Greek architectural 'refinements' – techniques designed to make temples appear perfectly proportioned from a distance – reached their climax. Foremost among these was entasis, the thickening of columns at the centre by 2.5cm (1in) one-third of the way up their 10.4m (34ft 4in) height. Corner columns, fully visible silhouetted against the sky, were 2.5 per cent wider than the other columns and leaned inwards. Similarly, the stylobate rises by 11cm (*c.*4⅓in) at the centre on each side, giving a marginally domed effect. The west end of the Parthenon was 44cm (17in) higher than its east end.

THE LACK OF CEMENT

One of the most remarkable aspects about the Greeks' construction techniques is that they never used mortar or cement until the Romans introduced it. Instead, they fitted their blocks with such precision on top of each other that their weight alone held them in place. In this way, Greek masonry resembles that of the Incas in Peru nearly 2,000 years later, who also created majestic and enduring buildings without mortar. The Greeks did use metal ties of iron or bronze to hold their massed masonry in place. Later generations pillaged many of these ties for their metals, particularly bronze ties, which were more valuable and less perishable than iron, so weakening the buildings. One technique that the Greeks employed instead of cement was *anathyrosis*, which probably originated in Egypt. This involves leaving the centre of the surface of each block rough and gently concave, while ensuring the edges were perfectly smooth, so creating a near-vacuum to hold the stones together.

LABOUR FORCE

All these refinements meant that there are almost no true straight lines of any length in the Parthenon, Hephaistion or many other Greek temples. As impressive as the mathematical knowledge needed for such calculations is the high level of craftsmanship involved. Compared with the pyramids or even some Greek temples in Asia Minor or the west, the Parthenon is not immense – its stylobate measures only 69.5 by 30.8m (228 by 101ft), but architecturally it is supremely accomplished.

How the Athenians assembled these temples, and indeed housed and fed the large, highly skilled workforce required to build them, so efficiently is unknown. They must have needed almost every skilled mason in Greece, which may have caused resentment among other Greeks. Certainly the use of taxes from the other poleis in their empire – which were originally intended for military purposes – to build temples for Athens' benefit alone was unpopular.

Above: For the Parthenon, heavy cuboids of marble were hauled from quarries on rollers or in ox-carts.

Below: Entasis makes columns look regularly spaced when seen from afar.

GATES, WALLS, WATER SUPPLIES AND SHIPYARDS

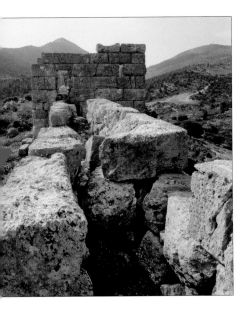

Above: The well-made but simple walls of the fort of Eleutherai, built c.400BC to defend Attica's western frontier, were typical of Greek defences for centuries.

Below: The walls built around newly liberated Messene in c.350BC were far more complex, having double gateways with enclosed courts in which enemy attackers could be trapped.

The Mycenaeans had built impressively massive and effective, if crude, walls. There was little further development in Greek city defences before 400BC, because there was no need. The Long Walls connecting Athens with the Piraeus, built in the 450s BC, baffled every Spartan attempt to take the city in the Peloponnesian Wars. The Peloponnesians had no success even when besieging tiny Plataea, having to starve the city out.

Similarly, when the Athenians attacked Syracuse in 414–13BC, they relied on building a wall to blockade the Syracusans. (Failure to complete this doomed the expedition.) Athens' own city walls, hastily rebuilt after the Persian wars, were c.2.5m (8ft) wide. A stone base of c.1m (3ft) supported upper walls of plastered mud-brick rising to c.8m (25ft). Towers c.5m (16ft) square reinforced the walls at key points.

In the 4th century BC, Dionysius I, tyrant of Syracuse, revolutionized siege warfare with his successful capture of Motya, a Carthaginian city off the coast off western Sicily, by using siege towers, causeways and catapults. Philip II of Macedonia and Alexander carried this revolution further. Alexander's capture in 332BC of supposedly impregnable Tyre, another massively walled island-city, signalled that cities must look anew to their defences. Over the next decades walls grew higher and thicker, to protect against missiles and to support catapults.

Towers, too, became larger and more frequent, with postern gates to allow sorties against besiegers. Semicircular towers, more costly to build but harder to attack, appeared in cities like Smyrna (Izmir) in the 3rd century BC. The towers of the small Ionian city of Perge were vaulted and had gabled roofs, presumably to keep torsion catapults dry.

The most famous defence of a city came in 305BC when Demetrius I, one of Alexander's flamboyant successors, failed to capture Rhodes after a year-long siege, despite assembling massive siege towers and catapults.

GATES

Athens' city walls had 15 gates. The most important, the Diplyon Gate, was elaborate, being of the 'courtyard' type. It was set back from the walls so that enemies exposed their flanks to javelins and arrows thrown by defenders on the towers and walls on either side. But the reasons for building such a grand gate like this were as much ceremonial as military. The great Panathenaic Procession entered the city by the Diplyon Gate, so it had to look impressive.

During the 4th century BC, gateways became more sophisticated. Double gateways with separated enclosed courts in which an enemy could be trapped were built at Messene c.350BC and Miletus c.300BC. The grandest such gate was at Pergamum, built c.200BC, which trapped attackers in successive enclosed courts.

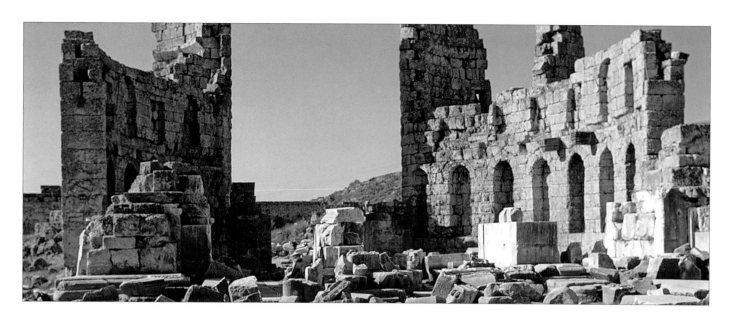

WATER SUPPLIES AND SHIPYARDS

Adequate water supplies were clearly vital for any city. The Pisistratids about 530BC first brought water into Athens through rock-cut conduits piped from Mt Lycabettus north of the city. These supplied a fountain in the Agora, which was later roofed over. It had basins about 6 by 3m (20 by 10ft) at either end of a 18m (60ft) long building. The western basin was a reservoir into which vases

Below: A water conduit in Corinth, typical of many in which Greek cities channelled water through their cities.

could be dipped, the eastern end had spouts. This served as a prototype for other spring houses known from vases.

At Corinth, another important trading city, the 'Triglyph Wall', so-called because of its decoration, was built c.500BC above a spring chamber with steps leading down through an opening in the wall. More typical was the simple fountain niche such as that built into the walls at Priene c.330BC. Wherever possible, a large fountain was placed near the agora of each city. These gave women, who fetched the household water in amphorae balanced delicately upon their heads, a rare opportunity to meet and socialize.

Among Athens' grandest buildings were the naval shipyards at the Piraeus, essential to maintaining the fleet, for long the strongest in the Aegean. This had 372 shipyards in its final and grandest form. The huge fleet kept under cover could theoretically be launched very quickly. In practice, the Athenians lacked the crews to man all their ships when war finally came in 323BC. Athens' grandest naval building was the military arsenal built by the architect Philon in the 330s BC. It was a huge hall under a single-ridged roof. The interior measured 15 by 120m (50 by 400ft) and was 8.2m (27ft) high. It had a Doric frieze around the exterior and Doric columns, unusual for the time but meant to emphasize military strength.

Above: The defences of the small city of Perge in Asia Minor in the 3rd century BC boasted semicircular gable-roofed towers in which catapults could be mounted.

Below: The massive, if crude, walls of Mycenae, dating from the 13th century BC, were not surpassed as defences until the 4th century BC.

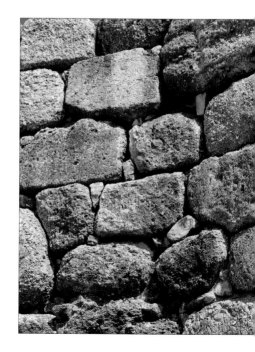

ELEMENTS OF ARCHITECTURE
GLOSSARY OF TERMS

Above: A Corinthian capital, the most ornate of the three Greek orders, has a slender column similar to the Ionian order's but its capital has two ranks of acanthus leaves over the astragal, with caules rising over the acanthus leaves and sprouting volutes.

Above: Section of a Doric frieze showing how it is separately into blocks. The metope is the square space between the triglyphs, which have two vertical grooves (glyphs) in the centre and a half-groove at each end.

Our architectural language remains predominantly Greek in origin. Some words have passed into common usage but many others may seem obscure today, so a glossary of terms used in the book follows. They should prove useful for understanding not just ancient architecture but also many more recent buildings.

ABACUS Slab on top of a capital supporting the architrave

ACANTHUS Plant with scalloped leaves used as a design on Corinthian capitals

ACROPOLIS Upper or higher city, often reserved for temples and shrines in the Classical Age

ACROTERIA Plinths for statues or ornaments at the end and top of pediments

AGORA Market, forum or meeting place at the centre of every Greek polis, often with ceremonial colonnades around it

ARCHITRAVE Beam or lintel, usually in stone or marble, forming the lowest section of an entablature

BOULETERION Council hall

CAPITAL Head or crowning feature of a column

CARYATID Sculpted, clothed standing female figure used in the same way as a column to support an entablature

Above: A volute spiral is a decorative device used on Ionic columns.

CELLA Main body of a temple containing the cult image of the deity

CORINTHIAN ORDER Third of the Greek orders, with base, slender column and capital with two ranks of acanthus leaves

CORNICE Topmost horizontal, usually projecting part of entablature

DENTIL Small square block used decoratively in cornices

DORIC ORDER First of the Greek orders, without base (Greek Doric)

ECHINUS Moulding beneath the abacus on a Doric capital

ENTABLATURE Whole horizontal upper part of a building carried on columns above the abacus

ENTASIS Slight convex curve used on columns to correct the optical illusion of concavity when seen from afar

FLUTING Shallow, concave grooves running vertically on a column

FRIEZE Middle division of an entablature between architrave and cornice

GUTTAE Small projecting pieces under each triglyph of a Doric capital

Left and far left: Caryatids are draped female figures, supporting an entablature on their heads. The photo shows caryatids on the south porch of the Erechtheum in Athens.

Left: A pediment, such as this from the Temple of Artemis on Corcyra (Corfu) of 580BC, is the triangular space created by the sloping eaves and horizontal cornice of a gabled temple or other building or ceremonial gateway.

INTERCOLUMNIATION Space between columns, normally measured in their diameters

IONIC ORDER Second of the Greek orders, with voluted capital and base

MEGARON Large rectangular hall in Mycenaean palaces, and a possible influence on early Greek temples

METOPE Square space between two triglyphs in a Doric order, often sculpted

MODULE Unit of measurement, often diameter or radius of column at its base

NAOS Innermost chamber of a Greek temple. See CELLA

ODEION Covered hall, smaller than the main city theatre, used for performances of music and poetry

ORCHESTRA Dancing floor for the chorus in Greek theatres

ORDER All the parts comprising a column and its entablature. See Corinthian, Doric, Ionic

PEDESTAL Substructure under a column

PEDIMENT Triangular space created by sloping eaves and horizontal cornice of gabled temple or other building or ceremonial gateway

PERIPTERAL Of a building surrounded by a single row of columns

Left: The slight convex curve on a column is known as entasis and makes the column appear to be straight.

PERISTYLE Continuous colonnade surrounding a temple or court

PLINTH Low plain block under the base of a column or pedestal

PODIUM Continuous pedestal with base supporting columns

PORCH/PORTICO Roofed space forming the entrance to a building, normally with columns and pediment

PROCELLA Vestibule

PROPYLAEUM Entrance gateway to an enclosure, usually of a temple

PTERON External colonnade

SHAFT Trunk or body of column

STOA Shallow long portico with colonnade on one side, wall on other

STYLOBATE Continous base or plinth on which a row of columns is set

THOLOS Domed circular building, often a tomb in the Mycenaean Age

TORUS Convex semicircular moulding

TRIGLYPH Blocks separating the metopes in a Doric frieze, with two vertical grooves (glyphs) in the centre and a half-groove at each end

VOLUTE Spiral scroll at each end of an Ionic column

Above: The entablature is the upper part of an order showing, top to bottom, the cornice, frieze and architrave.

Above: The lower part of a column showing, top to bottom, the base and pedestal.

Left: Acroteria are plinths for statues or ornaments at the end or top of pediments (seen here on the Temple of Olympian Zeus). They were often highly decorated.

CHAPTER III

CITIES OF THE GREEKS

Greek cities developed from high Mycenaean citadels, beneath which small townships huddled, to cities on the plain or coast. As Aristotle noted, aristocrats and kings preferred high places, but democracies chose lower ground, reserving the acropolis ('high city') for the gods. Nowhere illustrates this transition better than Athens, the archetypal Greek *polis*, or city-state. Above, on the Acropolis, stood the temples of Athena and other tutelary deities. Down below were all the other temples, public and private buildings, theatres, stadia, altars, gymnasia, stoas, houses, prisons, tombs and monuments. The Agora (market place) was the focus of social, intellectual and political life; around it hummed the city's turbulent life.

By 500BC Greek colonization had spread Greek *poleis* around the Mediterranean, from Egypt to southern France. After Alexander's conquests (336–323BC), there was an even greater expansion of Greek *poleis* east to the borders of India. These, too, were (for a time) self-governing cities, with theatres, agoras and gymnasia. West of the Euphrates, Roman rule ultimately saved and furthered Greek urban life, as impressive ruins attest, but some very important cities – Sparta, Thebes and Alexandria – have left few visible ruins. Ancient Thebes is mostly under modern Thebes; Alexandria's ruins are practically all under water; Sparta built relatively little. So attention turns to the sites and cities that do survive.

Left: The buildings on the Acropolis, created in the 40 years after 446BC, help to make Athens the supreme Greek polis.

THE ACROPOLIS TEMPLES

Above: The small Temple of Athena Nike, the first temple seen by visitors approaching the Acropolis, was built c.428–425BC, very probably by Mnesicles.

Below: Pericles and other Athenians admiring Pheidias at work on the frieze that decorated the Parthenon, as envisaged by the Victorian painter Alma-Tadema in 1868. In reality, women would not have accompanied the men.

In the Bronze Age, Athens was of secondary importance compared to great centres such as Pylos and Mycenae. However its Acropolis, the rock dominating central Attica, is superbly defensible. Remnants of a Mycenaean palace have been detected on its north side. The citadel was enclosed in Cyclopean walls 6m (20ft) thick, fragments of which are still visible. The palace occupied part of the Acropolis, the lower town spilling out beyond the gates to the west, protected by an outer wall.

The legendary Erechtheus, one of Athens' first kings, established the worship of Athena in the city. His descendant Theseus killed the Cretan Minotaur, uniting Attica for the first time. Athens was renowned as the 'unsacked city', the one Mycenaean stronghold to survive 12th-century BC cataclysms. This may have been due to a secret well down eight flights of stairs inside the rock, which helped the city to survive long sieges. The last king, Codrus, traditionally sacrificed himself to save Athens from invaders.

The myth cloaks the facts. By c.950BC Athens had expelled its kings, and aristocrats ruled the city, but not from the Acropolis. They did so from the nearby Areopagus (Hill of Mars), which gave its name to their council. Athens in the Dark Ages and Archaic period (at least down to c.560BC) built no more temples in stone than any other Greek city. Only with growing prosperity in the early 6th century BC did the Athenians start to build again in stone. A wave of competitive construction soon led nobles to erect splendid monuments where all could admire them: on the Acropolis.

THE FIRST STONE TEMPLES

In 566BC the massive ramp leading up to the Acropolis was constructed by Lycurgus, a leading nobleman for the Great Panathenaea, the city's main festival. Other nobles, very probably the Alcmaeonids, sponsored the building of the first proper temple to Athena Polias. Decorated with painted snakes, bulls, lions and tritons, it was built of limestone and at c.30m (100ft) was twice as long as it was wide. Inside stood an ancient statue of the goddess, the city's most sacred object, evacuated to Salamis when the Persians invaded in 480BC. (The dating – even siting – of the Acropolis' early temples remains debatable.)

The Pisistratids, in power from 546 to 510BC, gave Athens a huge boost economically and architecturally. They moved the Agora to north of the Acropolis, giving it more space, and built nine marble drinking fountains; they embellished the Temple of Athena Polias with marble and began the vast Temple of Olympian Zeus. This was left only knee-high when Hipparchus, last of the dynasty, was driven out in 510BC. (The Pisistratids seemingly lived on the Acropolis in their last years in power.)

BUILDING FOR DEMOCRACY

The democratic revolution that followed halted the building programme only briefly. Victory over the Persians at Marathon in 490BC boosted the new democracy's self-confidence. A grand gateway to the Acropolis with Doric marble columns, the Propylaea, was started and perhaps finished. Even grander but unfinished was the large temple on the south side of the Acropolis, also in marble. The Persians burnt all these temples in 480–479BC and they remained unrestored for 30 years, although the Propylaea was patched up. Themistocles, leader during the Persian wars, oversaw the city's hasty refortification and the building of the Piraeus on Hippodamus' orthogonal (grid-iron) plans, but such buildings were purely utilitarian.

PERICLES' MASTERPLAN

Pericles had the very highest conception of his city, calling it the "school of Hellas", the exemplar of democracy at its noblest if not broadest. (It was a view shared even by some of Athens' traditional enemies. "O shining city, violet-crowned… Bastion of Hellas, glorious Athens, city of godlike men," wrote the Theban poet Pindar.)

More controversially, Pericles also thought that Athens was justified in using tribute money from the Confederacy of Delos, which had originally been intended solely for fighting the Persians, to rebuild its temples, themselves destroyed by Persia. The project that he persuaded the Athenian Assembly in 449BC to approve – after a long and stormy debate – would produce the grandest, most dramatic group of buildings Greece had yet seen.

Pericles chaired the committee overseeing the project, taking a keen interest in the work. Pheidias, the sculptor in overall charge, was his friend. Beneath Pheidias worked a team of architects. Ictinus was responsible for the Parthenon, Mnesicles for the Propylaea and probably the Erechtheum and the Temple of

Athena Nike.

When completed (the Erechtheum, in some ways the most ingenious of all Athens' temples, was not finished until 405BC, the year of Athens' final defeat by Sparta at Aegospotomai), the grouped buildings, with their superb carved and painted friezes, astonished and awed contemporaries. Their feelings have been shared by most later generations.

Only in the Hellenistic and Roman periods, when absolute monarchs or emperors had far greater resources, would other architectural ensembles rival – and sometimes surpass – the Acropolis in size. None would ever surpass democratic Athens aesthetically.

Above: The Erechtheum, the last of the Acropolis temples to be completed, is really a multiple temple, housing 10 different shrines on two separate levels. It is named after Erechtheus, a legendary king of Athens.

Below: A reconstruction model of the Acropolis seen from the west, with its great staircase leading up to the Propylaea. Pheidias' statue of Athena rose just beyond this.

ATHENS' OTHER BUILDINGS

Above: The octagonal Tower of the Winds was designed c.454BC by the astronomer Andronicus of Cyrrhus. On its roof stood a large triton-shaped weathervane.

The splendours of democratic Athens were not restricted to its Acropolis. Down below, the Agora was surrounded from the 5th century BC on with increasingly fine official buildings. The old Bouleterion (Council Hall), a rectangular building about 23m (75ft) wide on the west side, was patched up after the Persian sack. It was replaced by a semicircular building better suited for meetings of the Council of 500, the advisory body, later in the century. The tholos, a domed circular building nearby c.18.3m (60ft) in diameter, was probably a clubhouse where councillors on duty ate their free dinners.

AROUND THE AGORA

On the north of the Agora the Stoa Poikile – Painted Stoa, called after paintings celebrating Athenian victories – was built c.470BC. It was the first such multi-functional structure. In the shelter of these extended porticos, citizens gathered to talk, listen and trade. Forty years later, the Stoa to Zeus Eleutherios (the deliverer) was built on the west side of the Agora. There was an altar to the 12 Olympian gods before it and the smaller Royal Stoa beside it. All had imposing Doric colonnades but were dwarfed by the huge, two-storeyed Stoa of Attalus, donated by the rich Hellenistic king Attalus II of Pergamum in the mid-2nd century BC.

Set back from the Agora, the temple of Hephaistus embodies all the principles of 5th-century BC Doric classicism, if lacking the 'refinements' of the Acropolis temples. More impressive due to its site but less well preserved, the Temple of Poseidon at Sunium is by the same unknown architect. So perhaps was the Temple of Ares, moved from Acharnae 24km (15 miles) away by the Romans. The huge Temple to Olympian Zeus, started under the Pisistratids, was half-completed thanks to Antiochus IV, the extravagant Seleucid king, with Corinthian rather than Doric capitals. Antiochus' death in 164BC abruptly ended work. Then Sulla, the Roman general who sacked Athens in 86BC for supporting Mithridates of Pontus, removed its capitals to Rome.

MONUMENTS

Athens was also a city of monuments. Most were erected not by the state but by rich individuals or families. Dozens of such monuments lined the Street of Tripods, one of the principal avenues.

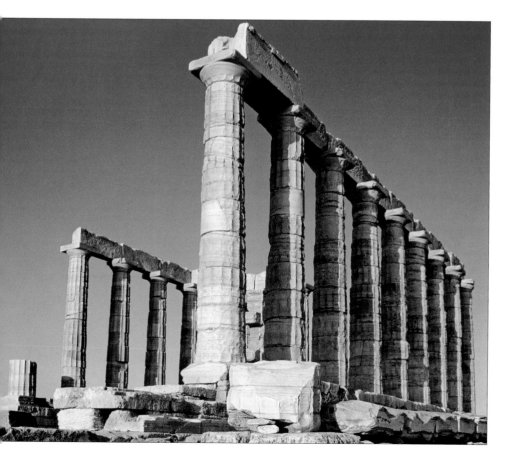

Left: Famous partly due to its spectacular site, the Temple of Poseidon at Sunium is probably by the same unknown architect who built the Hephaistion in the Athenian Agora. Both temples embody the principles of Doric classicism in the mid-5th century BC.

Right: Athens grew around the Acropolis, where the city's finest temples stood, and the Agora below, the centre of social and political life. Walls enclosed the city, and Pericles' double Long Walls later linked it to Piraeus, the port.

The most famous and elegant of these is the Choregic Monument of Lysicrates, built in 335–334BC. As a *choregos* (producer), Lysicrates had put on dozens of plays at his own expense – one of the duties expected of a rich citizen. This circular structure, with its slender Corinthian columns, proclaimed both his generosity and a victory in a theatrical contest. Its roof carried a three-branched acanthus on which stood a victory tripod. Its elegance has an almost Hellenistic air.

Yet the classical tradition remained strong in Athens, as another much later edifice demonstrates. The octagonal Tower of the Winds was designed *c.*45BC by Andronicus of Cyrrhus in Mesopotamia, a noted astronomer. Julius Caesar may have paid for it, for Athens as a city was almost destitute at the time. On its roof stood a large weathervane in the form of a triton, which pointed at the relevant wind, as personified in one of the eight wind zones. Inside was an elaborate water-powered mechanism that reputedly drove a sort of clock. Oriented due north, the tower carried sundials on each side so that passers-by could read the time on it. Like the Choregic Monument, it was made of marble and much admired by the British architect James 'Athenian' Stuart, who visited Greece in 1751.

ROMAN ATHENS

Roman rule, finally established after 31BC by Augustus, proved benevolent overall. A large new odeion was built and a new Agora, complete with Athens' first public lavatories. He commissioned a small temple to Rome and himself on the Acropolis. While admiring Greek classical culture, he stressed Rome's political authority. Nero refurbished the Theatre of Dionysus in AD61–4. But the real

philhellene was Hadrian (reigned AD117–38). He became archon (ruler), made Athens head of a Panhellenic League and built a new quarter with aqueduct and library. Herodes Atticus then restored the stadium for the Panathenaic games and built a vast new odeion beneath the Acropolis. His was the last contribution to ancient Athens.

Below: The two-storeyed Stoa of Attalus, built by the wealthy Attalus II of Pergamum in the mid-2nd century BC, is Athens' largest stoa, now reconstructed.

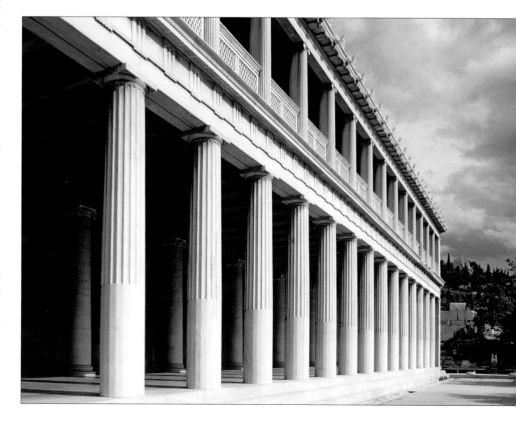

OLYMPIA AND EPIDAURUS
RENOWNED SANCTUARIES

Above: The entrance and grassy banks of Olympia's main stadium, where 40,000 spectators gathered for the great Panhellenic festival, held quadrennially for 1,200 years.

Below: A model of the sanctuary at Olympia housing the enclosure of the Altis, at the centre of which was Olympia's great Temple of Zeus. So many votive statues were erected over the centuries that the precinct became crowded.

Not every place of importance was a major polis. Some sites became famous through being the centres of particular cults. Among the greatest was Olympia in Elis in the western Peloponnese. The Olympic Games were held there quadrennially for almost 1,200 years and its Temple of the Olympian Zeus contained one of the Seven Wonders of the World: the Athenian sculptor Pheidias' last masterpiece, the gold-and-ivory statue of the king of gods. This was reputedly so huge that, even though seated, Zeus' head brushed the roof.

OLYMPIA

According to Pindar in the 5th century BC, the games were founded by Hercules, the muscular superhero. Traces of Mycenaean settlement have indeed been discovered at Olympia, but traditionally the Olympic Games were founded in 776BC. They soon became a Panhellenic event, attracting competitors from all over Greece. The games were held around the time of the second full moon after the summer solstice – meaning in practice late August or early September – the games imposed a rare truce on the otherwise constantly warring Greeks.

At the heart of the sanctuary lay the rectangular enclosure called the Altis. Three giant Doric columns of the 6th-century BC temple of Hera on its north side have been re-erected, but Olympia's main temple was that to Zeus, in the Altis' centre. One of the largest in mainland Greece, this had a stylobate made of huge stone blocks each *c.*2.75m (9ft) wide. About 63.9 by 27.7m (210 by 91ft), it was built by the local architect Libon between 470 and 456BC from soft limestone and was covered in stucco, with marble tiles, gutters and sculptures. It lacks the architectural 'refinements' of most contemporary Doric temples. This was possibly because Libon could not manage them.

The temple was destroyed by a huge earthquake in the 6th century AD. Only the drums of its columns remain *in situ*, but the well-preserved statues from its pediments rank among the finest of all Greek sculptures.

At the centre of the enclosure stood the great altar of Zeus. The area must have finally looked almost cluttered with 69 such altars. Just outside the south of the Altis lay the Bouleterion, with two wings united externally by a portico of 27 Ionic columns of the 3rd century BC. The east side of the Altis was lined with the Echo or Painted Stoa, rebuilt in the 4th century BC. Beyond that lay the Stadium, where the main Olympic events took place. It could accommodate 40,000 spectators, standing on raised banks. Its stone kerbs survive to give a vivid impression of this, the world's first great international stadium.

To the west of the Altis lay the Leonidaion, a large hostel for distinguished visitors built by Leonidas of Naxos in the 4th century BC, with an open court 30m (100ft) square. North of that was Pheidias' workshop, a tall hanger-like building where his great statue of Zeus had been made, which itself became an object of wonder. (Its ruins were later quarried for a Byzantine church.) Just north of that stood the Palaestra, a colonnaded wrestling ground, and beyond that the Gymnasium.

Olympia thrived throughout the Hellenistic period and, despite Sulla's inevitable sack in 86BC, flourished under the Romans too. Augustus favoured it and Nero took part in the games, uniquely winning every single one – as the judges prudently decided. Hadrian later restored some buildings. The games were finally banned by the devoutly Christian emperor Theodosius I in AD393.

EPIDAURUS

Sited on the Argolid plain, Epidaurus emerged as an important sanctuary only in the 5th century BC. It was the shrine of the demigod Asclepius, son of Apollo. Asclepius had many attributes, the most famous being his medical powers. He could even raise people from the dead, but was killed by a jealous Zeus for his impiety. Asclepius' symbol of a staff with a serpent coiled around it has become the symbol of medicine. Of his temple, built *c.*420BC at the centre of the sanctuary, almost nothing visible remains.

To the south stood the great altar of Asclepius. Nearby was a tholos built *c.*370–340 BC by the architect Polyclitus of local limestone with marble ornaments. (Outside the shrine, of about the same date and wonderfully preserved, is the famous theatre.) Sick pilgrims would make visits to Epidaurus as if to a Hellenic Lourdes, sleeping the night in the *enkoimeterion* (sacred enclosure).

Right: The tholos built c.*370–340BC by the architect Polyclitus at Epidaurus is the best-preserved of the site's temples.*

Healing dreams sent by the god might come to them there. Such psychosomatic cures could be very effective.

The Ptolemies of Egypt honoured the site, enriching it with offerings. Even the then-distant Romans sent to Epidaurus in 293BC asking for advice on a plague that was afflicting them. Despite the disapproval of the newly Christian imperial establishment after Constantine came to control all the empire in AD326, pilgrims in search of the god's help still visited the shrine well into the 5th century AD.

Above: The Temple of Zeus at Olympia, one of the largest in Greece, was built by the architect Libon of Elis between 470 and 456BC. It housed one of the Seven Wonders of the Ancient World: the huge chryselephantine (gold-ivory) statue of Zeus by the Athenian master-sculptor Pheidias.

THE SANCTUARY OF DELPHI

Above: The all-marble Treasury of the Athenians, built c.500BC by newly democratic Athens, was re-erected in 1906.

Nowhere was more sacred to the Greeks than Delphi. Apollo, the archetypal Greek god of poetry, reason and prophecy, had there slain (or tamed) the chthonic serpent Pytho, making the site his. To this *omphalos* ('navel', i.e. holy stone), centre of the Greek world, worshippers came for more than 1,300 years to consult the oracular priestess Pythonia.

From *c.*580BC on, Delphi was administered by the Amphictyonic Council, with representatives of several Greek states, including Athens and Sparta – the closest Greece got to a UN. However there were at least three Sacred Wars over the control of the sanctuary, the last war (356–346BC) leading to Macedonian hegemony under Philip II.

AN INTERNATIONAL REPUTATION

By the 6th century BC the Delphic oracle had gained an international reputation. Croesus, King of Lydia (560–546BC), sent to inquire if he should attack Persia. The reply, typically ambiguous – "If you cross the river Halys you will destroy a mighty kingdom" – led to his kingdom's downfall. The oracle's fame remained undimmed, however, the pharaoh Amasis also consulting it. Many Greek cities and individuals began building 'treasuries', in effect mini-temples, around the shrine.

During the Persian invasion (480–479BC), Delphi played an ambiguous role. When Xerxes sent troops to plunder the temples, the Persians reportedly were crushed by boulders hurled down by the goddess Athena Pronaia (guardian) from the surrounding crags. Probably this was a landslide, Delphi being a seismically active region.

The sanctuary is dramatically sited *c.*600m (2,000ft) up the slopes of Mt Parnassus. Approaching from the east up the Sacred Way, an Athenian would have come first to the sanctuary of Athena Pronaia, a Doric temple built *c.*500BC and damaged by the 480BC rockfall. Further up, a ravine separated the two *Phaedriades* (Shining Rocks) that reflected the light.

Here the Castalian Springs bubbled up, where Apollo had once planted his laurel tree, and here pilgrims purified themselves. Emerging, they would see the tholos gleaming above them, a round temple built *c.*375BC, with Doric columns outside and Corinthian ones within. This temple lay inside the *temenos*.

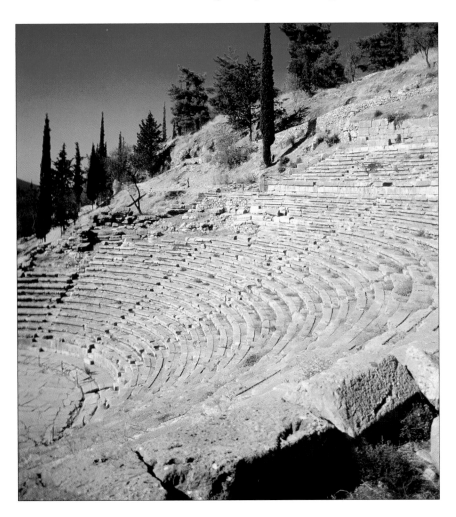

Left: The theatre at Delphi is one of the best preserved in Greece. Built in the 4th century BC, it was restored by Eumenes II of Pergamum in 159BC and again by the Romans. Its 35 tiers of seats are of white marble from Mt Parnassus.

The temenos (sacred precinct) of Apollo contained many buildings arranged to great effect against the landscape beyond. Among the treasuries was that of the Siphnians, dating from *c.*525BC, with caryatids instead of pillars. Beyond is the marble Doric Treasury of the Athenians, built *c.*500BC by the new democracy in gratitude for defeating its Greek enemies. The Treasury was re-erected in 1906. Its walls are covered with ancient inscriptions, some of which record Athenian athletes' victories in the quadrennial Pythian Games.

THE TEMPLE OF APOLLO

The largest building in the temenos was the Temple of Apollo, *c.*60m (200ft) long. The first temple, of the 7th century BC, burnt down in 548BC. It was replaced by a larger Doric temple with marble facings – then a luxury – financed by the Alcmaeonids, in exile from Athens. Wrecked in 373BC, it was rebuilt, sacked by Sulla in 86BC, and restored under the Roman Empire. The temple had six stuccoed limestone columns at the end and 15 on its sides, with an omphalos at its centre. Almost nothing remains.

The theatre above, by contrast, is one of the best preserved in Greece. Built originally in the 4th century BC, it was

restored by Eumenes II, King of Pergamum in 159BC, and again by the Romans. The 35 tiers of seats were of white marble from Mt Parnassus. The orchestra measured 18m (60ft) across, being paved with polygonal slabs. The front of the stage had a frieze depicting the labours of Hercules.

Above: The tholos, the round temple built c.375BC by Theodorus of Phocaea, has Doric columns outside and Corinthian ones inside, some of which were re-erected in 1938. It offers superb views.

Below: The stadium at Delphi of the 5th century BC. Here the Pythian Games, second only to the Olympic Games, were held every four years.

ENIGMATIC ORACLE

The oracle at Delphi retained its reputation for infallibility impressively long, partly through its excellent intelligence. Croesus tested the oracle by asking what he would be doing on a particular day. "Boiling turtles in cauldrons on a beach", came the reply, fed by inside sources.

But Delphi's real forte was its enigmatic prophecies. Pronounced in baffling verse 'interpreted' by priests, they often merely said, "Apollo thinks it better to…" This meant that, no matter how bad the outcome, the alternative would have been worse. It could pay to persevere. When the Athenians, facing Persian attack in

480BC, asked the oracle's advice, the first reply was chilling: "Fly far, far away; Leave home, town and castle, do not stay." Athens' envoys, returning for a better prophecy, were told to trust in the "wooden walls" but warned: "Divine Salamis will destroy the children of women." Themistocles spun this to mean that Athens should rely on its fleet – correctly as events proved. Julian, Rome's last non-Christian emperor (reigned AD361–3), received a depressing reply when he consulted the oracle, perhaps because it had been bribed by the Christians. Delphi was finally suppressed in AD384.

CORINTH
COMMERCE AND LUXURY

Above: The Fountain of Peirene, once a natural spring, was so built up over the centuries that it now looks like an ornamental fountain. The present façade was built under the emperor Claudius (AD41–54).

Below: The lofty citadel of Acrocorinth has been a key fortress in Greece for millennia. The present walls are mostly medieval but have Hellenic and Bronze Age foundations.

Superbly sited controlling the Isthmus, with access to sea routes east and west, Corinth was inhabited from earliest times. It took the lead in founding western colonies such as Corcyra (Corfu) and Syracuse in 734BC. Corcyra proved a disobedient daughter and the first recorded naval battle occurred in 664BC between it and Corinth. Under Periander (reigned c.629–585BC), Corinth boomed, exporting fine pottery around the Mediterranean. By the 6th century BC the city was already noted for its luxury, a reputation it never lost. The Corinthian order, most ornate of the three Greek orders, traditionally originated there, while Corinth's 1,000 sacred prostitutes, servants of the goddess Aphrodite, were renowned for their beauty and skills.

The Greeks' headquarters during the Persian invasion, Corinth was an often unhappy ally of Sparta's alliance. Later, Corinth was the site of Philip II's Congress in 338–337BC, where he proclaimed his planned crusade against Persia. It was also the last home of the philosopher Diogenes, whose world-renouncing eccentricities were the very antitheses of Macedonian megalomania.

Acrocorinth, the citadel rising 548m (1,800ft) above the city, then became one of the 'chains of Greece', garrisoned by Macedonian troops. Joining the Achaean League, which had liberated it in 243BC, Corinth was razed to the ground by the Roman general Lucius Mummius in 146BC. In 44BC Julius Caesar refounded the city as capital of the province of Achaea and it boomed again, its population reputedly reaching 300,000. St Paul preached in Corinth, appalled by its depravity but finding a readier audience among its merchants than among Athens' intellectuals. Despite recurrent earthquakes, Corinth retained its importance until the end of the Roman Empire.

Ancient Corinth lay on a rocky plateau 60m (200ft) high between Acrocorinth and its port Lechaion, connected by long walls. The ruins we see today are more Roman than Greek, however. The Lechaion Road, 12m (40ft) wide and paved under Augustus, led up past a colonnade of shops and the Peribolus (courtyard) of Apollo, toward the Fountain of Peirene. Originally a natural spring, this was so built up over the centuries that it resembled a large ornamental fountain. Water for it was stored in four reservoirs fed by a tunnel and hidden by a six-arched façade "with chambers made like grottoes, from which the water flows into a basin in the open air", according to Pausanias, writing c.AD170. This basin is 9 by 6m (c.30 by 20ft).

The present two-storied façade, built under Claudius (AD41–54), replaced a row of Ionic columns of the 3rd century BC. Herodes Atticus, a munificent multi-millionaire, remodelled the fountain into its present imposing vaulted and marble-lined form around AD150.

Above: The Temple of Apollo, north of the Agora in Corinth, is one of the oldest Doric temples. Dating from c.550BC, it has seven massive columns still standing.

A HUGE AGORA

Entered through the Propylaea, which the Romans turned into a triumphal arch, the huge Agora is itself really a Roman forum measuring 210 by 90m (230 by 100 yards). West of the Propylaea stood the Captives' Façade, an ornate two-storeyed marble structure. With Corinthian columns on the lower floor and Atlantes (giant figures) of barbarian captives on the upper, it dates from c.AD100. Nearby is the Triglyph Wall of stucco-faced limestone, reputedly built by the great sculptor Lysippus in the 4th century BC. This guards the Sacred Spring, which was originally in the open but is now underground.

Stoas and temples line the Agora, with the Julian Basilica to the east and the South Basilica on the south – both Roman buildings. Also Roman are many of the small temples on the west side – including a Temple to Tyche (Fortune) and a little square Pantheon – the public baths and latrines. The Romans remodelled the theatre, originally a 5th-century BC building, and carved the Odeion from the rock. But the Temple of Apollo on a hillock north of the Agora is wholly Greek, one of the oldest Doric temples from c.550BC, with seven austerely massive columns still standing.

ISTHMUS: CANAL AND GAMES

On the Saronic (east) side of the isthmus lies Isthmia, with the ruins of a 5th-century BC Temple of Poseidon. Here the Isthmian Games, traditionally founded by Theseus, King of Athens, and ranking just behind the Olympic and Pythian Games in prestige, were held every two years. Here also Alexander the Great was nominated leader of the Greeks against Persia in 336BC.

Just north lie the remnants of the Isthmian Wall, built against the Persians in 480BC, and beyond lies the Corinth Canal. This dates from only 1882, but the idea of a canal goes back to the 6th century BC, when Corinthians used to drag small ships across the Isthmus on rollers. At Nero's orders, work began in earnest on a canal in AD67, his engineers getting as far as the bedrock before stopping, defeated.

Below: The emperor Nero ordered the cutting of a canal through the Isthmus in AD67, a project the Greeks had long dreamed of, but his engineers stopped when they hit bedrock. Today's canal dates from the 19th century.

PERGAMUM AND PRIENE
CONTRASTING CITIES

Above: The theatre of Priene, dating from the later 2nd century BC, is a perfect example of a Greek theatre. It has a two-storeyed skene building, providing fixed architectural scenery at ground level.

Below: Pergamum developed around its Acropolis, once a citadel, whose height emphasized its architectural drama. The theatre is in the foreground.

Pergamum, once a small hilltop citadel, became under its Attalid kings (241–133BC) a marvel of Hellenistic town-planning. Its theatre, temples, palace, altars and library were dramatically arranged along the summit and sides of its Acropolis to rival Athens'. Yet Pergamum was no free polis but an absolute monarch's grand capital. In it the king's word was law, although the Attalids, who prided themselves on their philhellenism, shrewdly allowed Ionian cities under their rule autonomy. Their last monarch bequeathed his kingdom to Rome in 133BC. If smaller than the greatest Hellenistic capitals Alexandria or Antioch, Pergamum, unlike them, largely survives, although its major monuments have been mostly removed.

The first kings built only modestly, but after 200BC close alliance with the rising power of Rome meant a vast growth in Pergamene power and wealth. The upper city, broadly crescent-shaped, was spread over the southern slopes of a hill that, contracting as it rises, ends in a ridge a few hundred feet wide. Here was sited the Acropolis, necessarily irregular in shape, facing west.

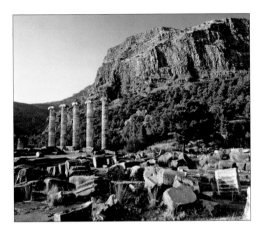

Above: The Temple of Athena Polias at Priene was a sublime Ionic temple. Designed by Pytheos, it was dedicated in 334BC by Alexander the Great.

AT THE ACROPOLIS' FOOT
Beneath the Acropolis lay the lower Agora, a large enclosed court. Beyond it, running north, was a huge Stoa 213m (c.700ft) long, supported by a retaining wall. At the Stoa's north end, a small temple was rebuilt by the emperor Caracalla in AD214. Scooped out of the hill above it was a vast theatre, partly rebuilt by the Romans. Above to the east was the imposing temple of the emperor Trajan of the early 2nd century AD – Pergamum remained important under the Romans. Behind Trajan's temple lay barracks and the relatively small royal palaces.

The small Temple of Athena, built in an old-fashioned Doric style, stood in a large colonnaded courtyard. On the court's north side was Pergamum's famous library, second only to Alexandria's in repute, housing 200,000 scrolls. Parchment, the tough writing material made from hides, was traditionally invented in, and named after, Pergamum. Parchment was intended to counter Egypt's monopoly of papyrus, then the commonest writing material. Ultimately it replaced it.

THE ALTAR OF ZEUS

Between the Temple of Athena and the lower Agora rose the melodramatic Altar of Zeus. Built by Eumenes II *c.*165BC, it was one of the grandest, most resplendent structures of its age, although large altars had been built earlier at Samothrace and Syracuse. From the front the building appeared as a U-shaped Ionic colonnade on a podium with a huge sculptured relief. A vast flight of steps led up to the altar itself, which was architecturally insignificant compared to its surrounds. Most notable was the sculpted gigantomachia (battle of giants) on the podium, symbolizing Pergamene victories over barbarous Celtic invaders. (This flamboyant altar later struck the Christian author of Revelations [II, 13] as "Satan's Throne".) The whole upper city was enclosed by stone ramparts. In the lower city, ordinary people lived in simple mudbrick houses, as they did in many other Greek cities.

PRIENE: AN IDEAL POLIS

A total contrast to opulent Pergamum was Priene in southern Ionia. A tiny polis with a population of *c.*4,000, it was slowly but completely rebuilt from 334BC on. Aristotle and Plato, those so often differing philosophers, would have agreed that Priene had the ideal size and form for a true polis. Occupying a terraced sloping site south of its almost inaccessible Acropolis 300m (1,000ft) above, Priene was laid out on the orthogonal principles of Hippodamus. This ignored the mountainous actuality of its site. Six main streets 4m (13ft) wide ran east–west on level ground, crossed at right-angles by 15 streets climbing sometimes very steep gradients.

Near the city's centre, its Agora was entered via an arched gateway of *c.*150BC. This is the first Greek ornamental arch.

Right: Pergamum's upper city, broadly crescent-shaped, was spread over the southern slopes of a hill that, contracting as it rises, ends in a ridge a few hundred feet wide.

It is far less pompous than Roman triumphal arches, which almost invariably celebrate military triumphs. Around the Agora, public buildings included a fine *dipteral* (two-rowed) stoa with Doric columns outside and Ionic columns inside. South of the Agora lay the Stadium and Palaestra (wrestling school), to the north was the theatre. The first theatre, dating from 300BC, was replaced in the later 2nd century BC with a two-storeyed scena building. This provided fixed architectural scenery at ground level with upper wooden scenery.

The Temple of Athena Polias lay northwest of the Agora. A sublime Ionic temple designed by Pytheos, it was very possibly dedicated in 334BC by Alexander the Great himself, then liberating Ionia from Persian rule. Its six by 11 columns stood on square plinths with 24 deep flutes. Capitals have the classic egg-and-dart decoration on their echinus.

The temple was designed in the proportions of a Greek human foot (which is somewhat shorter than a modern foot), on a width/length ratio of 1:2. Such perfect proportions suit so perfect a polis, creating a perfectly balanced building.

Above: The theatre at Pergamum, dramatically carved from the steep hillside beneath the Acropolis, reflected the general flamboyance of the Attalid dynasty.

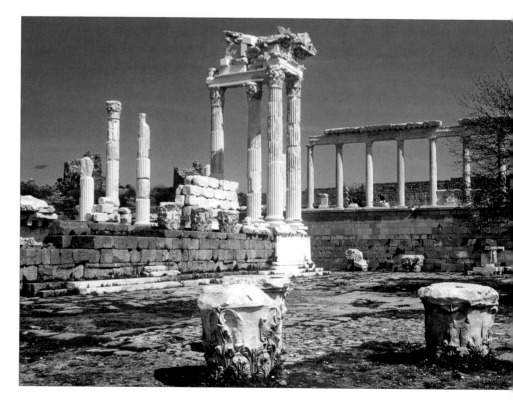

SYRACUSE AND ACRAGAS
SICILIAN CITIES

Above: The grand theatre at Syracuse, dating back to the 5th century BC. It could seat 15,000 people, revealing the city's size and wealth under its democracy.

Below: Part of the impressive fortifications around Syracuse that were brought to their peak by Archimedes, the city's most famous son, and that for long successfully defied the besieging Roman army under Marcellus in 212BC.

Ancient Sicily has been called the Greek America, for its fertile land was potentially very rich. Such wealth let the western Greeks build cities with unprecented splendour and distinction, if not always with great aesthetic subtlety. Sicilian cities' ruins are among the best-preserved in the Greek world but their politics were often ruinously unstable.

SYRACUSE
Founded in 734BC on the superbly defensible Ortygia island, Syracuse was already wealthy in the 6th century BC, as the massive if simple columns of its Temple of Apollo show. It rose to power under the tyrants Gelon and Hieron I (485–467BC). Gelon routed Carthage in 480BC and Hieron transplanted other Greek cities' populations to Syracuse. Both tyrants built lavishly. A superb Doric temple to Athena (Minerva) from their era survives, with 14 columns embedded in the walls of the current baroque cathedral. Its doors were covered in gold and ivory and on its roof a golden statue of Athena acted as a beacon to sailors. It is notable for sophisticated intercolumniation. The city's first theatre, trapezoidal in shape, was built beneath the present one. A fountain to the nymph Arethusa helped supply the city with drinking water and provided almost the only source of papyrus, the Greek paper, outside Egypt.

The city became a democracy after Hieron's death and as such repelled the Athenians' great siege in 415–413BC. But when attack by Carthage in 405BC threatened the city, a soldier called Dionysius made himself tyrant. Under his tyranny – which was truly despotic but lasted until 367BC – Syracuse attained new splendour, gaining extensive walls on the heights of Epipolae, that made it almost impregnable. But it lost not only its liberties but also part of its essential Greekness, many non-Greek mercenaries being settled there. The subsequent reign of Dionysius II (367–344BC) led to endless civil wars that wrecked Sicily.

HIERON'S GOLDEN AGE
In the 3rd century BC Syracuse regained its wealth under the steady rule of Hieron II (269–215BC). Its superb theatre was constructed then, as was its immense altar, which at 198m (650ft) was the longest ever built. Hundreds of animals were sacrificed on it at a time – Greek religion could be gory. Hieron patronized the poet Theocritus and the scientist Archimedes, who further strengthened the city's fortifications. But these did not prevent the Romans capturing the city after a long siege in 212BC when it had rashly supported Hannibal in the Second Punic War. Archimedes' accidental killing by a Roman soldier in its sack symbolized the end of Syracusan glory. Despite this, Cicero could still praise it in the 1st century BC as the elegantly Greek capital of the Roman province of Sicily.

ACRAGAS

Founded in 582BC in western Sicily from Gelon, another Sicilian city, Acragas (modern Agrigento) soon became one of the richest cities in the Mediterranean, thanks to its fertile territory and trade. In 488BC Theron became its tyrant. He continued work on the vast Temple of Olympian Zeus, one of the largest and most unusual of Greek temples, with its Atlantes, giant figures half-buried in the walls. After Theron had provoked Carthage by seizing Himera in 483BC, his alliance with Syracuse helped defeat the resulting Carthaginian attack. Victory led to an influx of slaves, allowing Acragas to expand work on the magnificent 'Valley of the Temples'.

This parade of Doric temples is now a UNESCO World Heritage site. Best-preserved of its temples is the Temple of Concord, built *c.*430BC of a local limestone so rough that it precluded many 'refinements'. With 13 by six columns, whose height equals 4.61 times their lowest diameter, it measures 39.4 by 16.9m (122ft by 18ft 6in).

After Theron died in 472BC, Acragas became a democracy, led in the 440s BC by the aristocrat, philosopher and radical democrat Empedocles. At its zenith, Acragas' population reputedly reached 200,000, rivalling Athens. Its inhabitants had luxuriously soft beds, elaborate fishponds and even pet swans. The poet Pindar praised it as the "most beautiful of cities inhabited by mortals".

But Acragas' good times did not last. When Carthage's war of revenge began in 406BC, the Acragantines, despite help from Syracuse, proved incapable of effective resistance. They had become so soft that even soldiers on sentry duty at night reputedly demanded two pillows, a mattress and quilt. In 405BC the city was

Right: A fountain to the nymph Arethusa supplied Ortygia, Syracuse's inner city, with drinking water and provided almost the only source of papyrus, the Greek paper, outside Egypt.

abandoned to the Carthaginians, who sacked but did not destroy it. Later it was repeopled by Timoleon, the saviour of Syracuse, in the 330s BC.

Acragas suffered badly again in the First Punic War (264–241BC). The Romans, capturing the city after a long siege, enslaved the whole population. Under the Roman Empire, Acragas finally regained a modest prosperity, but as a minor provincial town, not a great city.

Above: The great Doric Temple of Concord at Acragas dates from the 5th century BC, the city's golden age when it was reputedly the richest city in the Greek world, home of the mystical philosopher and statesman Empedocles.

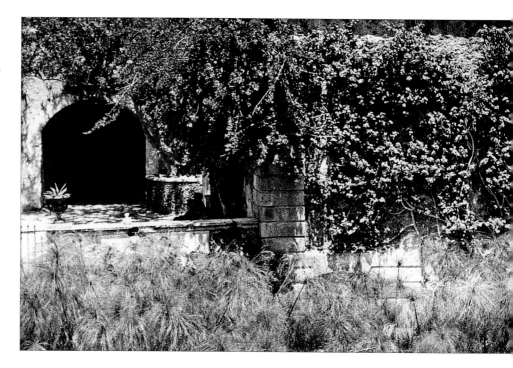

DELOS AND EPHESUS
DIFFERING FATES

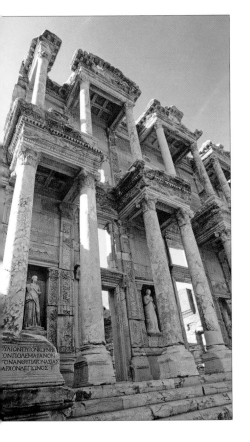

Above: The Library of Celsus at Ephesus, noted for its projecting pavilions, dates from c.AD110, when the city was thriving in the long Roman peace.

Two Aegean sites, both very closely connected with Greek life, sacred and commercial, had very different fates.

DELOS
A tiny island in the central Cyclades, Delos was the mythical birthplace of the god Apollo and his sister Artemis, among Greece's holiest shrines. 'Long-robed Ionians' with their wives and children gathered to honour Apollo at the annual *Delia* festival. At first, nearby Naxos dominated the island, donating the fine if much-weathered marble lions from c.630BC. Athens, the mother Ionian city, played a major role at Delos from the 6th century BC on and Pisistratus 'purified' the island in 543BC. Persia respected Delos' sacred neutrality during the Marathon campaign in 490BC, but in 478BC the Ionians, under Athens' leadership, based their anti-Persian League at Delos. In 426BC Athens ordered another purification, forbidding births or deaths on its sacred soil, banishing all Delians. From then on,

Athenian officials governed the island shrine. Delos became independent in 315BC after Athens' defeat by Macedonia.

Soon it was thriving as a trading centre, building a new theatre and temples. Among these the little Temple of Isis of c.170BC reveals both the persistence of the Doric style and the presence of Graeco-Egyptians resident in Delos.

THE SLAVE EMPORIUM
But Delos could not escape Roman power. In 166BC, Rome, to curb Rhodes, made Delos a free port. Soon the island filled with Italian merchants who made it the centre of the booming slave trade and built their own agora. Ever larger houses and monuments were erected. The boom ended with the sack by Mithridates' forces in 88BC, killing thousands of Italian merchants. The island then sank into obscurity. Pausanias in the 2nd century AD noted that the shrines' guards were almost the only people on the island.

The religious centre of the island was the Hieron of Apollo, the sacred precinct enclosing temples and altars. A vast 7th-century BC statue of Apollo stood on the north side, but only its base survives. The Great Temple of Apollo, begun in 477BC and completed 200 years later, had a high granite base with 13 marble columns down its sides. A Doric temple, it measured 19.5 by 13.4m (97 by 44ft). To the north lay the Sacred Lake, now dry, where Apollo and Letis were born. (Delos, now treeless, once had poplar groves.) To the south lay the theatre and around it luxurious peristyle houses with mosaics and

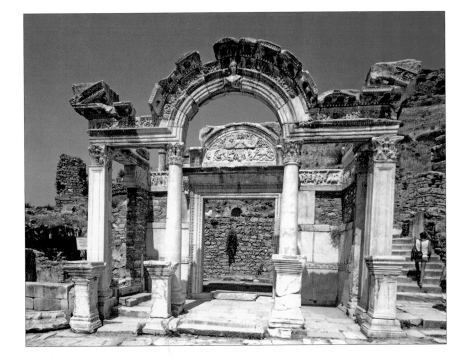

Left: In AD118 Publius Quintillius erected the monument known today as the Temple of Hadrian, dedicating it to Hadrian, Artemis and the people of Ephesus. It shows how Greek classical architecture could be adventurously enlivened with Roman arches.

fine columns, such as the 'Maison des Masques'. Similar houses have been well preserved at Pompeii.

EPHESUS

Traditionally founded by Ionian colonists on the coast of Asia Minor in *c*.1000BC, Ephesus was actually even older, having been a Mycenaean settlement. It went on to become one of the greatest of all Greek cities, a home of the Ionian Enlightenment (the enigmatic philosopher Heraclitus was born there) and a wealthy port.

Above all, it became famed for its great Temple of Artemis (Diana), one of the Seven Wonders of the Ancient World. The first temple, paid for by Croesus, King of Lydia *c*.560BC and designed by Theodorus of Samos, measured 109.2 by 55m (358 by 171ft). Originally made of limestone covered in marble, it had giant Ionic columns 20m (65ft) high. (The other Seven Wonders were the Pyramids, Alexandria's *pharos* (lighthouse), Babylon's hanging gardens, the Mausoleum of Halicarnassus, Pheidias' statue of Zeus at Olympia and the Colossus of Rhodes.)

Within its cella stood a statue of Artemis shown not as the usual chaste huntress of Greek mythology but as a many-breasted fertility goddess, suggesting possible Asian origins. The devotees of this Artemis were enraged when St

Paul, visiting the city in the 40s AD, tried to attack their profitable cult. The sellers of religious trinkets rioted, crying: "Great is Diana (Artemis) of the Ephesians."

Ephesus suffered from the depression that hit all Ionian cities after the Persian wars, but recovered in the 4th century BC. Alexander's conquests made it a terminus for traders coming down the Meander from Asia. Resited in the early 3rd century BC (the old harbour was by then silting up) it continued to flourish, whether as a fully independent polis or under Seleucid or Attalid suzerainty. A new theatre at the foot of Mount Pion seating 25,000 was built *c*.200BC. But unwilling involvement in the wars of the Roman Empire after 130BC damaged the city.

However, in the *pax Romana*, the long Roman peace following Augustus' victory in 31BC, Ephesus flourished again as the capital of the wealthy Roman province of Asia (western Turkey). From this period, when Ephesus' population reached 250,000, date many grand buildings: the colonnaded street the Arkadiane, running through the city like a huge double stoa; the Temple of Hadrian; the Library of Celsus, noted for its projecting pavilions, and the opulent marble baths by the harbour. These show cosmopolitan Ephesians happily adopting the Roman arch and vault. Ephesus remained important into the early Byzantine era.

Above: The fine theatre at Delos dates from the 3rd century BC, *when the island was enjoying a prosperous independence as the centre of an island confederacy.*

Below: The 'Agora of the Italians' at Delos dates from the 2nd century BC. *The island, by then effectively under Roman rule, became the greatest slave emporium ever known, reputedly handling up to 10,000 slaves a day.*

CHAPTER IV

SCULPTURE

In the two centuries after 500BC, Greek sculptors created an art in which gods came to look like perfect human beings and humanity like incarnate gods. This art, simultaneously naturalistic and idealized, became the paradigm to which Western artists have recurrently turned. It also influenced non-Western art as far away as India. Greek sculptors focused on depicting the human form, often nude. Until after 400BC this meant exclusively nude males. While Greek men exercised naked in public, Greek women were cloistered away fully clothed. (Only in Sparta, nearly as devoid of art as it was of freedom, could female nudity sometimes be glimpsed.) Even when artists discovered the female nude in the 4th century BC, the heroic male nude still dominated Greek art.

A common misconception is that Greek sculpture was of lifeless white marble. In fact, many materials were used: limestone, terracotta, marble, wood, sometimes *chryselephantine* (wood covered in gold and ivory) and above all bronze. All were painted in lifelike colours, with eyes, lips, teeth and hair picked out so realistically they must have looked startlingly alive. Bronze, a valuable metal, was often melted down in the Middle Ages. Few of the great bronzes mentioned by ancient writers survive, although some statues have been found underwater. Instead, we must turn to later marble copies made for Romans, or images on coins or fragmentary carvings. Only the Elgin Marbles, original sculptures taken from the Parthenon, convey fully the lithe splendour of Greek sculpture.

Left: This majestic bronze of Zeus was rescued from the sea. Idealized yet also naturalistic, it dates from c.465BC.

MINOAN AND MYCENAEAN SCULPTURES 1700–1100BC

Almost no large statues survive from the Aegean late Bronze Age, when the Minoan and Mycenaean civilizations flourished. Possibly no statues of any size were ever made in Crete and the islands. Greek-speaking Mycenaeans (Homer's Achaeans) ultimately conquered Crete politically, but Minoan Crete conquered Mycenae culturally.

BULLS WITH GILDED HORNS

Minoan influence is often so overpowering on Mycenaean art – though not its architecture – that some archaeologists once posited a Minoan mainland empire. However, we now know that the influence came from Minoan artists or artists trained in Minoan techniques. This is revealed in two carvings of bulls' heads. (The cult of the bull was clearly central to Bronze Age religion.) One, from Cnossus, dates from *c.*1500BC. Carved out of steatite with gilded horns, the bull's-head *rhyton* (ceremonial cup) has eyes of red jasper and white shell for the lines around its nostrils. It is a superb work by any standard but only 30cm (12in) high. Remarkably similar is the bull with golden horns and silver eyes found in a grave of Mycenae of about the same date.

The same style remained dominant on the mainland until the fall of Mycenaean civilization after 1200BC. How far Minoan and Mycenaean art survived or resurfaced to influence later Greek art is debatable. But the naturalism and humanism that distinguish it from grandiose contemporary art in Egypt or Babylon were also to be among the hallmarks of Hellenic art proper.

A distinctive Minoan sculpture emerged when the first palaces were built in Crete *c.*2000BC. Initially rather stiff, this had developed by *c.*1700BC into a lively and fluid art. It peaked around 1500BC just as Crete was devastated by the eruption of Thira, a blow from which it never fully recovered.

Sculptors made small figurines of bronze, clay or other materials (but seldom of marble) or in sculptured mouldings on murals and vases. Minoan artists never attempted the monumental.

ATHLETES AND GODDESSES

The Minoans and Mycenaeans anticipated later Greeks in the importance they attached to athletics, including – in Crete at least – the perilous sport of bull-leaping. A figurine from the palace at Cnossus of 1500BC of a young acrobat or bull-leaper caught in mid-air, carved in wood once covered with gold, reveals a classic naturalism. More of its time is the bronze votive figurine a mere 15cm (6in) high of *c.*1550BC. The slim young man, almost naked, has a markedly concave back, a Cretan ideal, and his right hand is raised to his forehead.

The deity he was worshipping may have been the Snake-Goddess, a frequent image in Minoan art. In a painted faience statue about 30cm (12in) high found in the temple depository of Cnossus, the goddess is shown dressed in the height of Minoan court fashion: long, flounced skirts, tight bodice with breasts exposed. The figure may, however, represent a priestess rather than the actual goddess.

Above: The Snake-Goddess, *a typically colourful painted Minoan figurine, about 30cm (12in) high, of the 16th century* BC. *Some archaeologists now think this statue has been put together from disparate pieces.*

Right: A bronze figurine of a male worshipper, with hollowed back, from Tylissos in Crete, dating to c.1600BC.

Although few court ladies carried writhing snakes in each hand, as she does, sacred serpents were common in Minoan and later religion. (The goddess Athena was portrayed 1,000 years later in the Parthenon with a great snake coiling beside her. As there are references in the Linear B tablets at Cnossus to a goddess Athena, it is even possible that this image is of Athena.)

THE *LILY PRINCE*

An equally famous image of Minoan Crete is the *Lily Prince*, an unusually large-scale figure, about 2.1m (7ft) high on a relief fresco from Cnossus Palace. Heavily – and contentiously – restored, this graceful courtier or prince, almost naked apart from his kilt and feathered headdress, probably dates from *c.*1500BC. The figure embodies Cretan gracefulness, although he is unusually stiff.

By contrast, the *Harvester Vase* has vivid relief scenes of everyday rural life. It shows farmers laughing and chatting, presumably on the way back from harvest as they are carrying farming tools. The vase shows that Minoan artists were not interested only in courtiers.

A similarly vivid brilliant art in miniature appears in seals just 2.5cm (1in) in diameter from the mainland. One, probably dating to *c.*1300BC from a tomb near Sparta, shows a priest and a griffin, a mythical creature; another from the same tomb portrays two ducks with curved necks and is a triumph of Minoan or Mycenaean artistic naturalism.

THE LION GATE

Only one example of Mycenaean monumental sculpture survives: the great stone lions flanking the Lion Gate at Mycenae itself. Built *c.*1280BC, the Lion Gate consists of giant slabs of carved ashlar,

Right: The Lion Gate at Mycenae, dating from c.*1280BC, displays Mycenaean sculpture at its most powerful. But it is the only large-scale carving to survive from the Aegean Bronze Age.*

each weighing several tons. The now-lost heads of the two stone lions once snarled down in realistic fury. The sculpture's power may derive from Hattusa, the massively walled Hittite capital in Anatolia, but the lions flank a Minoan-style column. Sculptures would frequently be incorporated in temples by Classical Greeks, but the Lion Gate seems to have been a one-off in the Aegean Bronze Age.

Above: Tiny seals, often only 2.5cm (1in) long, reveal Mycenaean art at its vivid best. This seal, showing mythical beasts carrying offerings, dates from c.*1300BC.*

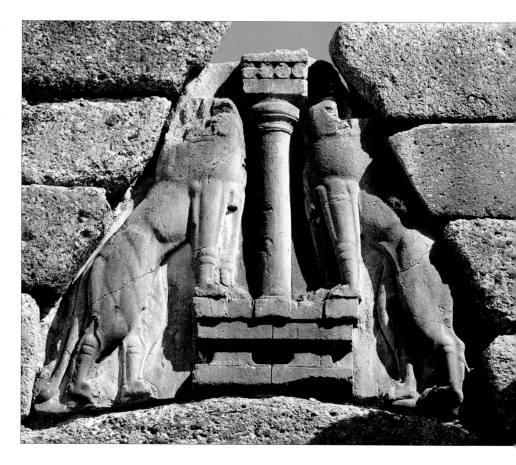

THE DARK AGES AND EARLY ARCHAIC PERIOD 1100–700BC

Above: This bronze figurine of a warrior in the Geometric style of the late 8th century BC heralds the revival of Greek sculpture after the Dark Ages. The naked human form was already the focus of interest.

The collapse of Mycenaean civilization after 1200BC led to the Greek Dark Ages. Even less is known about this period than the Bronze Age, but artistically it certainly appears to deserve its name. The end of the elaborate palace-centred culture seemingly meant a nearly complete end to almost all artistic life for at least two centuries.

Only in Athens, safe thanks to its almost impregnably high rock and perhaps to its relative obscurity, did some form of civilized life in a sub-Mycenaean spirit continue without interruption. It was in Athens also that the first signs of a new art began to emerge. Such signs are, however, generally unimpressive before 800BC. During the 8th century BC the first truly Greek sculpture hesitantly takes shape, formed by the austere contemporary Geometric style that owed nothing to Bronze Age precedents.

STATUES FROM THE DIPLYON CEMETERY

Among the ivory figurines found in the Diplyon cemetery at Athens, one has a crown decorated with a meander pattern. This probably indicates that she is a goddess. Eastern influence underlies the choice of ivory as a raw material – there were never any elephants in Greece, so the material as well as the idea must have been imported – but there is a Greek solidity even in tiny figures only 24cm (9½in) tall. (Most items that have been recovered come from cemeteries or are votive offerings made to the gods.)

STATUES FROM OLYMPIA

From Olympia come several fine small bronzes of the mid-8th century BC. One shows a deer being attacked by dogs, another shows a man with a dog fighting a lion (this is a confused piece that takes some deciphering).

Above: This head from the Diplyon cemetery at Athens reveals the highly stimulating impact of Asian art on Greek sculpture around 600BC.

Far more clearly depicted in action are the linked figurines of *The Hero and Centaur*, in which a man (or possibly a god, most probably Zeus) is shown with his arms locked around a centaur, a mythical beast shown as alternately wise and savage and long popular in Greek art. They are probably engaged in mortal combat.

Carved on a bronze tripod found at Olympia and dating from *c.*700BC, a vivid scene shows Apollo and Heracles fighting over a tripod. On a gentler note is a hind suckling her fawn.

More common than such bronze pieces as votive offerings – because they were far cheaper – are small terracotta figures

Above: Small, stiffly made bronze statues of animals dating from the late 8th century BC, the very dawn of Greek art proper.

such as that representing, rather than actually depicting, a horse of the late 8th century BC.

More realistic is the terracotta bird found in a cemetery south of the Eridanus in Athens. From such tiny, stiff, twig-like figurines, the whole grand tradition of Greek sculpture would develop.

BRONZE CASTING

Most of the greatest Greek statues were made in bronze, a material favoured because of its strength, durability and the way in which it can be easily worked.

Bronze is an alloy that typically consists of about 90 per cent copper, the rest being tin or other materials, including sometimes small amounts of lead or zinc. Bronze is easier to cast than copper because of its lower melting point. Its great tensile strength enables protruding parts – arms and legs – to be cast without supports, giving it an advantage over marble. Bronze statues' colour vary according to the amount of tin or other metals used, ranging from silverish to a rich red.

As it ages, bronze acquires a pleasing patina, although the Greeks painted all their bronze statues meticulously. Unfortunately, bronze has also always been highly valued as a metal, so most ancient statues were later melted down.

Initially, small bronze objects and tools were solid-cast in two-piece clay moulds. But by 1500BC larger statues were being

cast across the ancient world using the *cire perdue* (French: 'lost wax') method. In this type of casting, a clay core was formed in the basic shape of the statue. A thin layer of wax following the shape of the sculpture was encased within two layers of heat-resistant clay or plaster. As the wax heated up, it poured away. Wax gates let the wax out of the mould and the molten metal into the space that the 'lost wax' had created. Wax vents allowed hot gases to rise while the liquid bronze was being poured. As this cooled, it formed the statue. The master-mould could be reused many times.

The Riace bronzes of two warriors of *c.*460BC found in the sea near Reggio, Calabria in southern Italy, have almost identical bodies, although their heads are different. This suggests that their torsos were cast using the same mould, if perhaps at different times. Large-scale bronze statues were often cast in pieces no more than *c.*1m (3ft) long, for two men could only handle with ease a crucible containing *c.*9 litres (2 gallons) of molten bronze weighing *c.*68kg (150lb). Bronze must be poured quite fast or it will start to cool and not pour uniformly. If bronze is not at the right temperature to be sufficiently fluid, the casting may fail, resulting in the bronze cracking and becoming deformed as it cools.

Right: One of the Riace bronzes, statues dating from c.460BC, in the Classical period, are among the masterpieces of Greek sculpture made possible by bronze casting.

THE IMPACT OF EGYPT
DAEDALIC SCULPTURE c.700–600BC

Egypt's pharaohs had successfully repelled the invasions of the 'Sea Peoples' that wrecked Bronze Age civilizations further north. Hardly affected by a dark age, this ancient, wealthy land continued to produce superb stone sculptures in its almost unchanging millennial tradition. In the early 7th century BC, as trade revived, the Greeks began retracing Mycenaean trade routes south to Egypt and east to the Levant. Soon Greeks were settling in Egypt as traders and mercenaries, causing friction with the Egyptians at times. Naucratis in the Delta was finally established as the sole Greek city in c.570BC.

The impact of Egyptian statues, monumental in every sense, was overwhelming on the simple Greeks of the Archaic Age (700–490BC). Egyptian sculpture, carved from stone, was designed to overawe, being hieratically stiff and often massive. Such hieratic grandeur inspired Greek artists to produce the sculptures called Daedalic, after the mythical Athenian artist who had designed the Labyrinth for Minos in Crete. (If Daedalus had existed, he would of course have been a Mycenaean, but this distinction was unknown to later Greeks.) But Egypt's grand solemnity was balanced by colourful 'orientalizing' influences from Asia that often featured beasts, mythical or real.

BLOSSOMING OF ART
This fertilization led to a blossoming of Greek art from the mid-7th century BC. Among the first examples is the more than life-size statue of Artemis dedicated by Nikandre of Naxos. The goddess stands solidly imposing on her two long legs with arms flat at her side. The upper part of her body is emphasized, despite the smallness of her head, framed by the triangle of hair falling on her shoulders. The whole statue, with its unified balance of static form and dynamic force, exudes a tender calm. Smaller but equally impressive is the wooden statue of Hera from the great temple to that goddess in Samos of 650BC.

Of about the same date but in far better shape is the limestone *Auxerre Statuette*. She stands realistically, the curves of her skirt and half-naked breasts vividly carved, her long hair and facial features endowing her with feminine humanity. This statue proved influential across Greece, with similar statuettes being found at Rhodes, Corinth, Mycenae and Taranto, a colony in southern Italy.

The grandest sculptural achievement of the 7th century BC was the Lion Avenue of Delos. Nine seated lions flank the Sacred Way, each c.1.5m (5ft) high. The idea of such 'avenues' was Egyptian and they show Greek sculptors attempting, if not always achieving, monumentality. Of the gigantic statues cut from Cycladic marble quarries, some

Above: This kouros from Attica, made c.620BC, still displays marked Egyptian-inspired stiffness.

Below: The grandest sculptural achievement of the 7th century BC was the Lion Avenue of Delos. Nine seated lions flank the Sacred Way, each c.1.5m (5ft) high.

remained unfinished, clearly proving beyond their creators' powers. One such colossus that was abandoned half-hewn would have been 11m (36ft) high if it had been completed.

Lions were by then half-mythical creatures. They were probably extinct in Greece proper (though not in Macedonia), and so were treated fantastically, almost like sphinxes or chimaeras. From Corcyra (Corfu) in *c*.625BC comes a superb and quite realistic example. A mighty limestone lion, probably once part of a funerary monument, at 1.2m (4ft) long, lies menacingly on its plinth, its tail between its hind legs, forepaws extended, its fierce head expresses the dark menace of the wild.

KOUROS AND KOURE

But the focus of most Greek sculpture remained the human figure. Statues became increasingly impressive and large towards 620BC, as Greek sculptors gained confidence. The first great statues now emerge from Attica. The best-preserved is the *Kouros* by the 'Diplyon Master' of *c*.620BC. (Such naked archaic youths are called *kouros*, youth, and their female counterparts are called *koure*, maiden, the latter always portrayed fully clothed.)

Completely and proudly naked for the first time – unlike Egyptian statues – he stands more than lifesize at 1.84m (6ft 4in) tall, his long braided hair (an Archaic Greek fashion) well depicted. This kouros, imbued with Apollonian calm, probably stood on the grave of a young Athenian aristocrat, and embodies current ideals of beauty. Stylistic stiffness prevents complete realism, but anyway such statues were intended to represent, rather than depict accurately, human beings. The kouros remained a distinct type of statue down to 500BC, made according to specific rules.

A celebrated pair of kouroi are Cleobus and Biton by Polymedes of Argos of *c*.600 BC. They are bursting with muscular, youthful vigour. This is highly appropriate because, according to Herodotus the historian, these twin brothers pulled their mother in a heavy ox-cart to the Temple of Hera just in time for a ceremony, before sinking exhausted into a blessed oblivion granted to them by the gods as a reward.

Above: Found in Artemis' sanctuary on the island of Delos, with an inscription that it was dedicated to the goddess by Nikandre, this is the earliest extant all-marble statue. More than life-size, it dates to c.650BC.

Left: A celebrated pair of kouroi are Cleobus and Biton, probably made by Polymedes of Argos in c.600BC. They brim with muscular, youthful vigour.

THE 6TH-CENTURY AWAKENING c.600–490BC

The whole tempo of Greek life – political, economic, intellectual and artistic – quickened in the 6th and early 5th centuries BC. In sculpture there was no sudden revolution or great leap forward comparable to that being made around the same time by philosophers in Ionia. Instead, there was a gradually accelerating discovery of naturalism that, with hindsight, paved the way for the titanic achievements in all the plastic arts of the next two centuries.

Slowly, the stiff geometry of an art inspired by Egypt, albeit less impressive, gave way to something more vivid and human and far more inspiring. What dominated Greek art at the time and for centuries afterwards was a persistent desire to express the ideal human form. Slow, unrecorded improvements in tools, running parallel with those in architecture, also gradually enabled sculptors to develop more expressive ways of carving.

THE ARCHAIC SMILE

Typical of statues of the beginning of the century is the sublimely calm, massive kouros from the shrine to Poseidon at Sunium. (The temple itself had not yet been built.) More than 3m (10ft) high, with a typically enigmatic, frozen Archaic smile, he was one of a pair of colossal figures visible from afar to seafarers. This recurrent Archaic smile was probably intended as a sign of a free citizen, for statues were still not intended actually to portray an individual. But names and inscriptions on the base begin to appear, making the kouroi more personal.

This is apparent in the koure (maiden) commemorating Phrasikleia, originally from Paros of c.550BC, which bears the rather cryptic dedication: "I could be called koure (maiden) for ever instead of wedded by the gods thus named, Ariston of Paros created me."

The so-called Apollo of Temea of around the same date was a funerary memorial statue, like many in the 6th century, almost life-size at 1.5m (5ft). He still has the fixed smile and elaborate long hair of the "young light-hearted masters of the waves" (Homer's phrase), but his body is treated more realistically

Above: This statue of Croesus, an Athenian killed fighting, dates from c.535BC. His muscles and bones are clearly modelled and his arms hang freely from his body.

Right: This sublimely calm, massive kouros, c.525BC, from the shrine to Poseidon at Sunium, is over 3m (10ft) high. With a typically fixed, enigmatic Archaic smile, he was probably one of two colossal figures.

and smoothly. Slightly later, *c.*535BC, is the statue of Croesus, with the inscription: "Stand and grieve at the tomb of Croesus, killed in the front line by Ares (the war god)".

Croesus was a member of the powerful Alcmaeonid clan, enemies of Pisistratus who had become tyrant in 547BC. Croesus was presumably killed in inter-noble feuding. His muscles and bones are far more clearly modelled and his arms hang freely from his body. Even more realistic but badly damaged – giving it a probably unjustly brutish air – is the statue marked on its base 'Aristodicus.' He has short hair – a sign of dawning Classicism – and a natural rather than pinched-in waist, but he retains a stiff Archaic pose.

TEMPLE SCULPTURE

Equally important were the sculptures adorning temples, now being built in increasing numbers. At the Treasury of the Siphnians in Delphi, a radically new marble temple built *c.*525BC, were placed not only the famous marble caryatids but also a fine frieze showing the Council of the Gods. Like all sculptures, in bronze or marble, it was originally painted. From the Acropolis in Athens several votive kouroi still depict the maidens with enigmatic fixed smiles and stiffly elaborate robes, indicting their noble pedigree, but the shape of their bodies starts to emerge, hinting at a new realism. These date from the late 6th century BC and, like most sculptures then on the Acropolis, were damaged or sullied during the Persian invasions of 480–479BC, so that they were later jettisoned. On the metopes of the great new temple of Aphaea on Aegina some carvings are Archaic, such as the man hurrying to help a fallen comrade, and others Classical. Classicism arrived with a rush.

ON THE CUSP OF CLASSICISM

Classicism can be seen emerging in one of the rare surviving early bronzes, the *Apollo of Piombino.* Dating from *c.*490BC and found off the coast of Italy, this retains the long hair and formulaic pose of an Archaic figure but has the fully muscled torso of a Classical statue. Generally similar and thought to date from *c.*480BC – on the brink of the Persian invasion – is the *Standing Youth,* a gigantic 1.9m (6ft 3in) bronze figure. His long hair again looks Archaic but his flowing sculptural forms also show Greek art on the cusp of Classicism. He may have been a young Apollo, for his left hand may have held the god's bow.

Above: The still half-Archaic figure of a moscophoros *(calf-carrier) dating from c.580BC has increasingly realistic muscles.*

Left: The Apollo of Piombino, *found in the sea off Italy and dating from c.490BC, has the long hair and stiff pose of Archaic figures but the muscled torso is that of Classical statues.*

THE DAWN OF CLASSICISM
C.480–450BC

Right: The bronze originals of these Roman marble copies were made in 477BC by Critios and Nesiotes, honouring the Athenian tyrannicides Harmodius and Aristogeiton. Both show for the first time the 'hardness' of early Classicism, with muscles emphasized.

Below: One of the two Riace bronzes, either athletes or warriors, depicted with unprecedented realism, made in c.470–460BC.

No earlier period in history matches the phenomenally rapid development of 5th-century BC Greece. After the Persians were defeated in 480–479BC, Athens became the pre-eminent Greek city, fully democratic. In high Classicism it realized its ideal style. In sculpture, the male nude was the focus of most attention, with female figures still being depicted fully clothed. Women were long considered of secondary interest in Greek art, as in Greek life.

REVOLUTIONARY REALISM

The *Critios Boy* of c.480BC (attributed to the sculptor Critios) is a standing youth wholly freed from the kouros conventions. He rests his weight realistically on his left leg, with his right leg slack, his right thigh pushed forward. His pelvis is correspondingly tilted, his right buttock slackened, his head and shoulders slightly inclined. This revolutionary realism comes closer to depicting a 'real' relaxed figure than any earlier artwork anywhere in the world. To create such a figure required genuine understanding of the human body. However the boy is also an idealized figure. For the first time the human body is depicted as perfectly beautiful and simultaneously symmetrical. Greek artists of the time were obsessed with mathematical symmetry. The statue is, however, atypical in one important way, for most Classical statues in the 5th century BC were in bronze, not marble. Sculptors now began to think in terms of 'moulding' – for bronze

casting – rather than 'carving', even when they were actually working in marble, as in this instance.

THE RIACE BRONZES

This sculptural concern is evident in the magnificent Riace bronzes, fished from the sea near Riace in southern Italy in 1972. Dating from c.470–460BC, these two athletes or warriors have vigorous muscular bodies, depicted realistically. Their resting limbs convey the tension of recent exertions superbly. Each torso is nearly a mirror image of the other, conceivably cast from the same mould. Only their heads truly differ. They retain traces of copper on their lips and nipples, silver on their teeth and precious stones in their eyes. They were perhaps part of a group, among the many superb Greek artworks that the Romans looted. However, they are probably not by Pheidias, the great Athenian sculptor as was at one time thought, for they are not in his serenely idealizing style and are a little too early.

THE CHARIOTEER
A noble example of very early Classicism, in which traces of the Archaic style linger, is the *Delphi Charioteer*. Probably presented by Hieron, tyrant of Syracuse, as a votive offering after his victory at Cumae over the Etruscans and datable to *c.*473BC, the young charioteer has a solemnity suited to Greece's holiest shrine. He originally stood in the car of a four-horse bronze chariot with a groom standing beside him. Only this statue of the group has survived, thanks to an earthquake that dropped him down a

Below: The Delphi Charioteer *is a superb example of early Classicism, probably presented by Hieron, tyrant of Syracuse, as a votive offering after his victory at Cumae, so datable to* c.473BC.

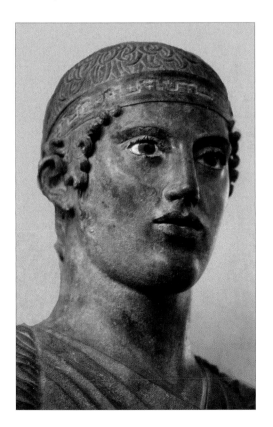

ravine into an old drain. There he was somehow overlooked by subsequent pillagers of the shrine.

The extreme verticality of the statue would not have been so marked when he was riding inside his chariot. He wears the long robes suited to his windy profession, with a diadem band around his head. His eyes are marked in coloured stones and traces remain of the gilt once on his hair, eyes and lips. This must have given his face a richness and living warmth typical of Greek statues but hard to imagine today when looking at chilly marble copies.

THE TYRANNICIDES
In Athens itself two statues made at around this time commemorate what might be called Athens' first freedom fighters: Harmodius and Aristogeiton. These famed 'tyrannicides' were two (male) lovers who killed the tyrant Hipparchus in 514BC. They did so out of sexual jealousy but in so doing unwittingly paved the way for Athens' democratic revolution soon after – hence their statues prominently placed on the Acropolis. The first statues, possibly made by Antenor who had worked at Delphi, were carried off by King Xerxes to Persepolis when he sacked Athens in 480BC. Their replacements, the bronze originals of these Roman marble copies, were made in 477BC by Critios and Nesiotes. (Alexander the Great later returned the originals when he in turn burnt Persepolis in 330BC, but they have since vanished.)

These figures may be only Roman copies, but their heroic, masculine figures incarnate determined political action. The onlooker is effectively in the position of their victim. Slightly larger than life at 1.93m (6ft 4in), they reveal for almost the first time the notable 'hardness' of the Early Classical style, with their side muscles above their thighs emphasized unrealistically to increase the impression of male strength.

Above: The Critios Boy *of* c.480BC, *the work that marks the sudden arrival of Classicism, is at once naturalistic and idealized.*

IMAGES OF THE GODS

Above: Apollo, the archetypal Hellenic god of order, reason and light, carved on the western pediment of the Temple of Zeus at Olympia, 5th century BC. He is portrayed as a calm and pitiless deity, supremely confident in his inhuman beauty and power.

The portrayal of the gods as supremely perfect but utterly realistic human beings – the greatest achievement of Classicism – was perfected in the middle decades of the 5th century BC. From the sea off Artemisium on the island of Euboea comes one magnificent bronze. (Bronze does not rust in seawater, so shipwrecks have paradoxically proved excellent at preserving such works.) Once thought to be a statue of the sea-god Poseidon wielding a triton since lost, he is now considered to represent Zeus, king of the gods, hurtling his divine thunderbolt at an unseen adversary.

A NAMELESS MASTERPIECE

This Zeus is the work of an unknown master who clearly was a genius, not just a talented local carver. The figure probably originated in northern Greece and was being transported south, perhaps like many Greek artworks to a Roman customer,

when it was shipwrecked. (If it had been travelling north, it might have been the work of Onatas of Aegina.) While attempts to identify this masterpiece with a specific statue mentioned in literary sources have failed, it is securely dated on stylistic grounds to *c.*460BC, as Classicism was approaching its peak.

Certainly Zeus' features have the Homeric majesty expected of the king of Olympus and lord of thunder. Standing more than lifesize at 2.1m (6ft 10in), as befits a god, he is complete apart from his eyes, which were once inlaid with coloured stones. His hair is tied back by a braid, usual for the time, but otherwise he is shown sublimely naked, humanity raised to divine levels. His body is powerful but not absurdly muscular. His arms are unrealistically long, but presumably this was a deliberate stylization. He is the noblest Classical bronze statue of a god to survive.

THE TEMPLE OF ZEUS AT OLYMPIA

But the chief centre of sculptural activity in Greece during the second quarter of the 5th century was at Olympia, site of the Olympic Games, a shrine second only to Delphi in Panhellenic importance. Here, in the sacred precinct around the great Temple to Zeus built in the 460s BC stood literally hundreds of statues of victors in the games. For competitors were taking part in a sacred rite, not just competing for a prize. Religion permeated athletics as it did almost every aspect of Greek life.

Unfortunately Christianity, a later religion, so detested such statues that only their bases remain. Some bronzes were

Left: One of the 12 metopes from the great Temple of Zeus at Olympia depicting the 11th labour of Hercules, carved by the anonymous 'Master of Olympia' in c.460BC.

destroyed on the orders of the emperor Theodosius I, a Christian zealot, when the Games were suppressed in *c*.AD393; others were looted or melted down for their valuable metal. The Temple to Zeus, only destroyed finally by an earthquake in the 6th century AD, was richly decorated with stone sculptures on its metopes. These have been pieced together to give a good idea of the work sometimes attributed to the 'Master of Olympia', an unknown sculptor (or sculptors) of undoubted genius, working in the severe style of early Classicism.

THE TWELVE LABOURS OF HERCULES

Hercules (Heracles) was the archetypal Greek mythical hero, semi-divine as a son of Zeus, and seen as the personification of physical strength and *areté* (excellence). Hercules was credited with founding the Olympic Games. To expiate the sin of killing his own family in a fit of madness, Hercules was ordered to carry out 12 almost impossible 'labours'. The 12 metopes of the Temple of Zeus at Olympia illustrate these in the 'severe' style, with figures about one and a half times life-size.

Among the best preserved is the 11th labour, Hercules' mission to fetch the golden apples of the Hesperides, the islands of the Blessed. Hercules passed on this particular labour to the giant Atlas, offering to carry the burden of the heavens on his own shoulders meanwhile. Atlas is shown returning with the apples in his hands to Hercules, who stands with every muscle in his body taut, upholding his titanic burden. Although the goddess

Right: The majestic face of Zeus, king of the gods, as portrayed by an unknown sculptor who was clearly a genius. Recovered from the sea off Artemisium, the Zeus *is dated on stylistic grounds to c.460*BC.

Athena, Hercules' helper in his trials, is putting a cushion on his shoulder to reduce the strain, the impression of tortured strength is overwhelming. Yet the hero's body is not that of some grotesquely over-muscled bodybuilder but harmoniously symmetrical.

APOLLONIAN SERENITY

One of the finest images of Apollo, the archetypal god of reason, comes from the west pediment of the Temple of Zeus. Apollo is shown, right arm raised in serene authority, quelling the bestial fury of the drunken centaurs. Calm, pitiless, supremely confident in his physical beauty, he is untroubled by any doubt or compassion.

Hercules' body is relatively flat and inexpressive compared to some contemporary works, but this only increases his divine yet dangerous power. Dating from *c*.450BC, this statue is the only original large-scale Apollo of the Early Classical Age that has survived intact.

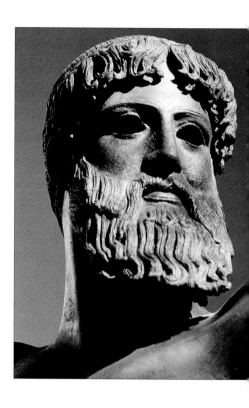

Left: The Zeus of Sunium, *c.460*BC, *fished from the sea, shown in awe-inspiring entirety. Originally the god is thought to have brandished a thunderbolt in his right hand.*

PHEIDIAS, MAKER OF THE GODS ACTIVE C.460–430BC

Above: A model of the giant statue of Athena Parthenos, *made by Pheidias in c.438BC in chryselephantine for the interior of the new Parthenon.*

Left: The Apollo of the Tiber, *a Roman copy of a bronze original from Pheidias' workshop, perhaps by the master himself, suggests something of Pheidias' idealized but monumental style.*

Considered by many the greatest Classical sculptor, Pheidias (*c*.490–*c*.428BC) was an Athenian citizen and a close friend of Pericles, the supreme democratic statesman. Little is known of his life, although he reputedly studied under Hegias. By 447BC he had become effectively Athens' Minister for the Arts as he oversaw the building of the Parthenon, that pinnacle of Greek architecture and sculpture.

Pheidias created idealized forms so realistic yet sublime that he was called 'Maker of the gods'. Infuriatingly, not one freestanding work by him survives and Roman copies are even feebler than normal. However, we have many of the superb Parthenon carvings, including the Elgin Marbles now in the British Museum. This project, far too large for one man to execute, required scores of skilled sculptors, most working to Pheidias' designs and under his supervision. Carved in high relief, many figures are depicted almost in the round, leaping from their frames with remarkable vigour.

IMAGES OF ATHENA

Pheidias was most famous for his giant statues of gods. The first was *Athena Lemnia* (made for colonists of Lemnos) of 450BC, still partly in the 'severe' style. More typical was the huge statue *Athena Parthenos* (Virgin) that Pheidias made for the new Parthenon's interior, completed in 438BC. Standing *c*.12m (40ft) high, she was of chryselephantine: her skin was covered in ivory and her robes and armour in gold, fitted over a wooden core. She carried a winged Nike in her right hand. A shield rested on the ground to her left, while a huge serpent coiled beside her. On her head was a triple-crested helmet. A pool of water in front reflected a dim sacred light on to this opulent cult image.

Outside on the Acropolis, Pheidias created another, more militant, image of the goddess *Athena Promachos* (Warrior) in bronze with shield, helmet and gilded spear, standing inside the Propylaea and immediately obvious to worshippers. The goddess was also visible far out to sea, proclaiming Athens' power and glory.

THE PARTHENON CARVINGS

The frieze running around the Parthenon, started in 447BC, is 60m (175 yards) long. More of it has survived in reasonable condition than any other sculpture of the age. However, it must have been hard to see many figures easily when *in situ*. Some may be by Pheidias himself: all reveal his spirit. The riders shown on the west frieze, young cavaliers naked apart from their cloaks, are taking part in the four-yearly Panathenaic Procession, the greatest event in Athens' civic and religious calendar. On the east frieze graceful, noble-looking gods and heroes process, also part of the festival. In thus worshipping its patron goddess, Athens also worshipped its idealized self.

Fine examples of *centauromachia* (centaur battles) from the temple's south side have been read as depicting Athenian civilization triumphing over savagery. But the centauromachia was always a popular theme, for it allowed sculptors to depict man and beast in combat. The west pediment showed Poseidon and Athena fighting for the city's loyalty – a contest Athena won by her gift of an olive tree. This central section has been lost but from the east pediment a masterly realistic study shows the wine-god Dionysus reclining wholly naked. Aphrodite, goddess of love, is also reclining but with arched, quivering body. While she is fully clothed, her clinging dress reveals more than it conceals of her beauty.

WONDER OF THE WORLD

Pheidias, unjustly accused of embezzlement by Pericles' enemies, left Athens in 432BC for Olympia. Ancient writers considered the giant statue of Zeus he made there for the Temple of Zeus in c.430BC his masterpiece. It later ranked as one of the Seven Wonders of the World. Zeus was shown on a high throne, holding a Nike in his right hand and sceptre in his left. This was also a chryselephantine statue. Although portrayed seated, at seven times life size, 13m (42ft) high, Zeus almost touched the temple's ceiling. Only coins give us any idea of this work.

One statue survives to convey something of Pheidias' monumental style: the *Apollo of the Tiber*, a Roman copy of a bronze Apollo, perhaps by the master himself. The tall, graceful god looks down

with serene, dreamy detachment. This work and the Parthenon sculptures epitomize Pheidias' High Classicism. In it the human body, perfectly understood from within, is portrayed with an idealized yet wholly naturalistic harmony.

Above: A detail of the Elgin Marbles, from the west frieze of the Parthenon showing horsemen in the Panathenaic Procession, carved to Pheidias' designs in c.440BC.

Right: A Lapith and centaur fighting, from the Parthenon's south side, a contest at times read as depicting Athens' triumphing over barbarism, carved to Pheidias' designs.

POLYCLITUS AND MYRON
ACTIVE 460–420BC

Polyclitus, a rival of Pheidias, pursued a very different approach to Classicism. Coming from Argos, he worked at times in Athens. One of the great intellectuals of Greek art, Polyclitus declared: "A well-made work results from numerous calculations, executed to within a hair's breadth." His statues did not aim to please but to incarnate the principles of mathematical beauty he had outlined in his book *The Canon*. This has not survived, nor have his original bronzes. He may have worked exclusively in bronze but we have only blockish marble copies that distort his genius. Only one marble copy, the *Theseus Diadoumenus*, is truly impressive.

SYMMETRICAL SOLIDITY
Polyclitus sought not to depict an idealized realism but to fulfil his quest for depicting symmetry in the human form. He succeeded triumphantly with the *Doryphorus* (Spear-carrier) of *c*.435BC. This shows a walking athlete/hero (he probably once held a spear). The weight of his body rests on one foot, his relaxed left leg bears no weight, his right hand hangs down freely. The sloping line of his hips resulting from his pose is carried through the torso into a correspondingly opposed shoulder line later called *contrapposto*. All his body is drawn into this movement but his torso itself is stockily solid, with the typically heavily emphasized muscles.

Polyclitus' work was much admired and copied in antiquity. A true idea of his genius emerges in the *Torso of Doryphorus*, a copy in polished basalt that resembles bronze far more closely than marble. The *Prima Porta* statue of Augustus 400 years later repeated the *Doryphorus*'s stance, although the emperor is clothed. So did images of the body-builder Charles Atlas in the 20th century.

Above: Polyclitus' Doryphorus *(Spear-carrier) of* c.435BC *shows a walking athlete, the embodiment of the artist's lifelong quest for perfect symmetry in human form. This is a Roman copy of an original Greek bronze.*

Right: The symmetrical solidity typical of Polyclitus' work marks this statue, which once again is a Roman marble copy of an original Greek bronze.

THESEUS DIADOUMENUS
This statue shows the legendary Athenian king as a victorious young athlete crowned with a diadem. The body is still solidly muscular but the youth's face reveals a softer side to Polyclitus' puritanical art, being delicately carved. Polyclitus also sculpted an Amazon, winning a competition at Ephesus with it. His wounded Amazon, shown barebreasted, is leaning against a post, the first

Amazons were, most exceptionally, portrayed half-naked even in the 5th century, when women were shown fully clothed from neck to ankle. There were good mythological reasons for this. Amazons were women-warriors who fought bare-breasted or, in some stories, after cutting off one breast to shoot better. Theseus carried off Antiope, an Amazon queen. Later the Amazons attacked Athens to revenge or regain their abducted queen but were repelled. This was often depicted as a triumph of civilization over barbarism and explains the prevalence of Amazons in Athenian art, even on the shield of Athena.

time that a figure was shown supporting itself against another object. While still more athletic than feminine in form, she reveals the sculptor's versatility. Polyclitus is credited with making the great statue of the goddess Hera in Argos, which some writers preferred to Pheidias' statue of *Zeus* at Olympia.

MYRON ACTIVE 450–430BC

The third great sculptor of the 5th century, Myron, tended to an extreme realism. This was evident in his bronze cow on the Acropolis, said to be real enough to be mistaken for actual flesh and bones. (It was of course painted.) This statue has vanished, as has his renowned statue, the *Discobolus* (discus thrower). Lucian, a writer of the 2nd century AD, describes the original as "stooping in the pose of a man preparing to throw, turning towards the hand with the discus and gently bending the knee, as ready to rise and throw." Numerous marble copies of this work exist, showing the swing of the taut, muscular body. It looks so realistic some athletes have tried to emulate it – in vain, for this is no snapshot. The support behind the *Discobolus* was needed for

marble copies but not the bronze original. (Hitler so admired a copy of this work in Rome that he persuaded Mussolini to send it to Germany. It was returned to Italy after 1945.)

Myron was also famous for his bronze *Athena and Marsyas*. This does not survive as a group even in marble copies but has been reconstructed. According to Pausanias in the 2nd century AD, it showed "Athena striking Marsyas Silenus for taking up the flute that the goddess wished thrown away". Marsyas was a satyr, one of the licentious half-goats, over-proud of his flute-playing. Athena. who disdained such vulgar music-making because it distorted the face, clutches her spear, the model of Olympian calm, looking down at the satyr. Marsyas met a ghastly end: he competed on his pipe with Apollo, lost and was then flayed alive as a punishment.

Above: A Roman copy of a part of the bronze original of Athena and Marsyas by Myron.

Left: The Discobolus *by Myron of* c.*440BC. Although a marble Roman copy, it still conveys the tension of the much-admired bronze original, which has not survived.*

Above: Paionius of Mende made this magnificent winged Nike (Victory), *which was dedicated at Olympia by the Messenians in 421BC.*

UNVEILING APHRODITE
C.420–390BC

While the male nude fascinated the greatest sculptors of the 5th century BC, the female nude was for long almost ignored. There was one exception: the *Esquiline Venus*, a marble copy of a bronze statue, showing a short but sensual figure, very realistic and completely naked, of *c.*450BC. But she was seemingly a one-off. This ignoring in part rose from the notoriously low status of women in Classical Athens. Their restricted appearance in art also reflected the tastes of a tough, heroic age, when sculptors found the muscular angularity of the male body, toned by constant exercise, more artistically challenging than the female body's curves.

By the last decades of the century, however, as the increasingly catastrophic Peloponnesian War ground on, tastes began to change. A less heroic, more sensually delighting art became appreciated

and the female form acquired – or regained – its fundamental appeal for sculptors, an appeal never since lost.

For a long time the female body was shown only under drapery. Increasingly, however, this consisted of thin clinging robes that gave almost a 'wet look'. This emphasized rather than concealed the body, until finally the female form emerged wholly naked.

THE WINGED GODDESS

The first half of the Peloponnesian War went relatively well for Athens and her allies, which included those Messenians not enslaved by Sparta. The Messenians, to commemorate their part in the victory over the Spartans at Sphacteria in 425BC, dedicated a statue of Nike at Olympia in *c.*421BC, with the inscription: "The Messenians and Naupactians dedicate her

Right: Nike Unlacing her Sandal, *from the Temple of Athena Nike on the Acropolis of* c.420BC.

GRAVE STONES

In sober contrast to such increasingly sensual statues are the tomb reliefs, particularly common in the later stages of the Peloponnesian War as Athenian casualties mounted. (Tombstones, while often found in the Archaic period, were for some reason rare in the early 5th century BC.) These usually took an architectural form with a pediment, as if the figures were outside the door of a home. Domesticity is the keynote, a reminder that even Athenians at their most public-spirited had their own families, which were the acknowledged foundation of society. The tomb of Hegeso and her servant commemorates the dead Hegeso, shown choosing a piece of jewellery from a box held by her maid. Even in this funereal carving of *c.*410BC, Hegeso's clothing reveals her body remarkably clearly.

Above: The tomb of Hegeso and her servant, commemorating a citizen's dead wife. Even in this funereal carving of c.410BC, Hegeso's light clothing reveals her body clearly.

to the Olympian Zeus as a tithe of the enemy's booty. Paionius of Mende made her." Mende was in northern Greece but Paionius worked mostly in Olympia, where he made this statue, an original work in marble, one of the masterpieces of Greek art.

Nike, winged goddess of victory, is shown at the moment of alighting to crown success on the battlefield. The wind of her flight bares one breast and presses her clothing close against her wonderfully lithe body, some 2.2m (7ft) high. Paionius has managed to convey motion at the point of being arrested with brilliant vividness. There was originally an eagle, emblem of Zeus, at her feet, and she stood on a pillar about 10m (33ft) high. Unusually at the time, Paionius signed the work on the dedication block, a sign of his pride in his achievement.

NIKE UNLACING HER SANDAL
Work on the smaller temples of the Athenian Acropolis continued despite the wars that stopped in 421BC only to restart in 415BC. Smallest and most exquisite of the temples overlooking the city was that of Athena Nike (Athena as Victory) built by Mnesicles about 428–423BC. Its frieze, which probably dates from after 420BC, shows a series of divine or mythical figures engaged in vigorous yet oddly elegant combat. One of them soon became justly famous and much copied in antiquity, that of *Nike Unlacing her Sandal*, which flanked a small staircase at the west of the temple.

For once we have the original, if without her head. Her clinging drapery, brilliantly carved, reveals a lithe but very feminine body as she bends in a marvellously fluid movement to lace up her sandal. With her breasts half-revealed, her thighs pushing against the soft fabric, this conveys as much sensuality as a nude.

APHRODITE IN THE AGORA
The true goddess of love, however, was Aphrodite (Venus), not chaste Athena or militant Nike. Aphrodite could more easily be found in the Agora, the buzzing commercial and social heart of Athens, than on the heights of the Acropolis.

One statue of Aphrodite – which suffered the indignity of being used as filling in a late Roman wall, erected in panic against renewed invasions in the 3rd century AD – reveals an almost baroque touch in her swirling robes that could slip off her at any moment. She could just be the work of Callimachus, who was one of the most famous sculptors of the late 5th century BC, although no works firmly attributed to him have survived. Callimachus was renowned for his free-flowing but fastidious grace, casting bronze 'like lace' – although some found his skills excessively ornate. He also reputedly pioneered the use of the drill in sculpture.

Below: The Esquiline Venus, *a marble copy of a bronze of c.450BC by an unknown artist, may be the first female nude in Greek art. Although not typically idealized, she emanates a gentle sensuality.*

THE 4TH-CENTURY BC REVOLUTION

Above: A marble relief copy of Timotheus' lost bronze masterpiece, Leda and the Swan. *This illustrates the myth in which Zeus, assuming a swan's form, seduced Leda, depicted here with novel sympathy and tenderness.*

The Peloponnesian War ended in 404BC with Athens' total defeat. Sparta took over Athens' empire and proceeded to misgovern it, so causing resentment and further wars. These proved inconclusive, exhausting and disillusioning. Although Athenian democracy was restored after a short-lived fascist junta and democracy even spread to other cities such as Thebes later, the *polis* (the 'citizen-state') no longer commanded the same passionate undivided loyalty from its citizens that it had. Instead, private life – or life in the secluded grounds of an Academy like Plato's founded just outside the walls of Athens – proved increasingly attractive. This retreat from the public sphere, although by no means complete, gathered pace after Alexander the Great's conquests opened up a vast new world. They made life in the old polis seem less wholly satisfying to many people.

THE TOMBSTONE OF DEXILEUS

This mood was reflected in art, as the idealized, heroic but impersonal high Classicism of the previous century gave way to a new individualism. The new era's artists discovered people's real personalities, shown by their backgrounds and deeds. The art of truly individual portraiture emerged hesitantly.

An early example of this is the Tombstone of Dexileus of Thoricus, a young Athenian killed in the Battle of Corinth in 394BC. He is shown in the act of killing his crouching enemy. His pose on the rearing horse recalls the horsemen sculpted on the Parthenon 40 years before, but he seems oddly detached from the action, rather than heroically engaged. This is fitting for what was a private tombstone rather than a public monument.

Artists also began to discover women's personalities, just as they began to depict the female nude. Although in the male-dominated world of ancient Greece the female nude was never treated as frequently as the male (in contrast to the situation today), fully naked female statues now began to engage the greatest sculptors' attention. The finest sculptors were not concerned solely with depicting their bodies but developed new ways of portraying feminine emotions.

TIMOTHEUS AT EPIDAURUS

Timotheus (active 380–340BC) may have come from Epidaurus in north-eastern Peloponnese. He is recorded as being paid 500 drachmae for work on the sculptures of the pediment of its renowned Temple of Asclepius, the healer-god, in the early 4th century BC. However, he went on to work

Left: Timotheus made some of the carvings for the immense tomb of Mausolus, ruler of Halicarnassus, around 350BC – works of dynamic drama.

in several other cities, including Halicarnassus (now Bodrum in Turkey), where he made some of the dramatic carvings on the immense tomb for its dynast Mausolus.

From the acroteria of the Epidaurus temple a *Nike* by him survives. Although now only a battered fragment, it still reveals his remarkable talent in the way her right wing is raised to catch an invisible wind. Also from the temple is the almost intact figure of Hygeia, goddess of the hearth, another half-naked figure bending gracefully. (Other more complete figures such as Aura, a deity seemingly riding side-saddle, were probably executed by Theodotus, otherwise unknown, to Timotheus' designs.)

Timotheus was also responsible for the pediments of the temple. These have not survived but it is possible to reconstruct them. The west pediment depicted the Sack of Troy. This was hardly an original subject but one that Timotheus portrayed in a highly original manner by dwelling on the sufferings of the women in the captured city.

On the right side of the pediment a female figure, possibly Hecabe, King Priam's wife, turns to help her fatally wounded son, holding him in her arms as he collapses. The sorrows of other Trojan women such as Cassandra, about to be abducted, raped or killed by the victorious Achaeans, are also movingly depicted for almost the first time in Greek art.

LEDA AND THE SWAN
The masterpiece of Timotheus' maturity is his *Leda and the Swan*, a bronze that has since been lost. However, numerous marble copies survive, most of which are approximately life-size and give a good impression of the famous original. The work illustrates the myth in which Zeus, king of the gods, assumed a swan's shape to seduce Leda. She later gave birth to the divine twins Castor and Pollux. In the myth, Zeus also sent an eagle – not sculpted – which appeared to threaten the swan, a wily tactic that persuaded the

reluctant Leda to shelter the swan. Leda is shown holding her cloak up to hide the swan nestling against her, as she cranes her head anxiously upward. Her expression conveys mingled anxiety and innocence. No earlier Greek artist had ever managed to capture female emotions so convincingly.

In an *Athena* (another bronze, which is only known in marble copies), the imposing grandeur of the goddess as depicted by Pheidias has given way to a more girlish figure, which is far less exalted and godlike.

Above: The Tombstone of Dexileus, a young Athenian who died at the Battle of Corinth in 394BC. Shown killing his cowering enemy, he lacks the aloof heroism of 5th-century horsemen, partly because this is a private memorial, partly because the exhausted post-war age felt differently about war.

PRAXITELES
ARTIST OF THE CENTURY

Praxiteles was ranked alongside Polyclitus, Pheidias and Lysippus by ancient writers as one of the supreme master sculptors. Working throughout the middle of the 4th century BC, he was renowned for the sensuous charm and grace of his art. This marked a further stage in the move away from the lofty idealism of high Classicism. Praxiteles was more concerned with portraying human emotions and creating gently beautiful objects, most famously his *Aphrodite of Cnidus*.

The master of sensual sweetness came from a family of sculptors. His father was the successful Athenian sculptor Cephisodotus, whose *Eirene* (peace) *Holding the Infant Ploutos* (wealth) was placed in the Athenian Agora in *c*.380BC. Such a prominent place for such a subject – inconceivable in earlier centuries – was a sign of the increasingly war-weary times. Praxiteles himself responded to the new mood by creating works of deliberate beauty, which may strike modern eyes as too smooth, bland and sugary. But if they fail to stir our emotions, they proved hugely influential then and long after. His son continued the family tradition after him in the same style.

Above: Praxiteles' Aphrodite of Cnidus *of c.350BC, "the finest statue in the world" according to Pliny.*

APOLLO AND THE LIZARD

One of Praxiteles' earliest works to show his distinctive genius is his *Satyr Pouring Wine* of *c*.375BC. Although we have only marble copies of this bronze, they show already the artist's hallmark of charm and beauty in this graceful youth – no trace of the bestial satyr here. (The jug and his left forearm have not survived.) Even more graceful is the later *Apollo Sauroctamus* (*Apollo Playing with a Lizard*). This shows the god as a

Left: A satyr, leaning against a tree trunk, displays to the full Praxiteles' typically languid sensuality.

Above: Despite the ravages of time that have broken her nose, this Aphrodite, carved in Praxiteles' workshop in c.325BC, has the soft beauty found in all his female figures.

smooth-limbed, beardless boy teasing a lizard crawling up a tree trunk. Instead of the sublime grandeur of earlier statues of the god, here we see the deity enjoying a languid, blissful sensuality – another key aspect of the divine from now on, but one seldom recognized earlier.

A SURVIVING MASTERPIECE

In 1877 archaeologists at Olympia discovered a marble statue of *Hermes and the Infant Dionysus* in the exact location noted by Pausanias 1,700 years earlier. This is almost certainly the famed original by Praxiteles, who often worked in marble. (His preference for doing so helped make the material fashionable again after long neglect.)

Despite being savagely over-cleaned by enthusiastic restorers, the statue still conveys an immediate sense of the splendour and glory Praxiteles could create in marble. Hermes, the messenger-god, props the tiny Dionysus, the wine god and his half-brother, on a tree-trunk to play with the child and offer him a bunch of grapes (missing from the original). Hermes was escorting the orphaned baby to Mt Nysa to be looked after by nymphs. The group shows a novel tenderness among the gods. They are still perfectly formed beings but they now exhibit less crushingly Olympian emotions.

The work was probably made around 330BC. At 2.15m (7ft 2in), it is rather larger than lifesize.

"THE FINEST STATUE IN THE WHOLE WORLD"

Praxiteles' most original and acclaimed statue was his *Aphrodite*, again made in marble. This, the first full-scale totally naked female nude of the goddess of love, was ordered in *c*.350BC by the island of Cos. The islanders were so shocked by the goddess's unprecedented nudity that they refused it. The people of nearby Cnidus happily took it instead and it became one of the most admired artworks in the ancient world. People made long journeys just to see her. One man reputedly fell in love with her. He embraced her so passionately that he could only be prised off with difficulty and left an indelible mark on her surface. Later, Pliny the Elder, the Roman writer of the 1st century AD, called her "the finest statue not just by Praxiteles but in the whole world".

Again, we have only semi-competent later copies, but they still reveal Praxiteles' great originality. *Aphrodite*, at 2m (6ft 7in) more than life-size, is depicted as a mature, shapely woman who has probably just emerged from her bath. A towel or robe is draped over a nearby vase. Her right hand covers her private parts but the rest of her body is fully exposed to the view for the first time in Greek art. She is realistically proportioned, with her hips larger than her breasts. (Ancient Greek artists were never fixated on outsized breasts.)

The copies we have, though imperfect, are often complete. They have helped create an archetype of female beauty that would later inspire Renaissance artists such as Botticelli, Raphael, Titian and Veronese, and so much of subsequent Western art. Such accepted ideals of female beauty are still apparent in almost every magazine, advertisement and film that we see today.

Above: Apollo Sauroctamus, one of Praxiteles' masterpieces, shows the god as a smooth-limbed, beardless adolescent teasing a lizard on a tree trunk. Instead of the divine sublimity conveyed by earlier statues, Apollo is shown as sensually relaxed.

Left: Discovered at Olympia in 1877, this original marble shows Praxiteles' genius at its height. Hermes, the messenger god, props the tiny Dionysus, the wine-god, and also his half-brother, on a tree-trunk to play with the child, offering him a bunch of grapes.

SCOPAS
SCULPTOR OF ECSTASY

Above: The head of a warrior, attributed to Scopas or his school, with all the master's characteristic passion still evident despite its much-battered state.

Not all art in the 4th century BC depicted the idyllic joys of gods or nymphs in Arcadia. Scopas, who worked in the middle of the century, specialized in depicting human or divine passions at their most intense. Born on the island of Paros, noted for its marble quarries, he had a famously fiery temperament. This comes through in his art, which differs radically from that of his contemporary Praxiteles, although both men preferred marble to bronze.

Scopas is recorded as working on the Mausoleum of Halicarnassus, the biggest project of the time; the great Temple of Artemis at Ephesus (then being again rebuilt); and at the Temple of Athena at Tegea in the Peloponnese. According to Pausanias, he designed this last temple.

FRENZIED BACCHANTES
The sculptures decorating the Mausoleum at Halicarnassus, later declared one of the Seven Wonders of the World, took many years of effort by some of Greece's greatest living sculptors, including Timotheus, Leochares and Scopas. Scopas, according to Pliny the Elder, the encyclopaedic Roman commentator writing 400 years later, carved the reliefs on the huge pyramidical structure's east face. Most notable were his depictions of ecstatic women, especially

Maenads or Bacchantes. (These were the female followers of the wine-god Dionysus, liberated from the normal constraints on Greek women by the ambiguously beautiful god.)

Although no originals survive of Scopas' *Maenads*, an unusually fine Roman copy in Parian marble powerfully conveys the divine madness and unleashed energy of Scopas' work. The orgiastic Maenad, with her long flowing hair and shapely body, is simultaneously a beautiful young woman and the terrifying embodiment of daemonic ecstasy. "Who carved this Bacchante?" asked an epigram of the time. "Scopas." "Who filled her with wild delirium – Dionysus or Scopas?" "Scopas." Almost naked – her short robe accentuates rather than hides her thrusting, twisting body – she is caught up in the drama of the god of wine and ecstasy.

Another less violent but equally ecstatic figure, this time totally naked, is Scopas' *Tritoness* (*Sea Goddess*), known in a copy found at Ostia. Her head is thrown back in ecstasy, her long thick hair cascades over her shoulders and toward her breasts, her flesh is modelled with remarkable vividness. Such art – "that has brought to its aid the impulse of growing life itself, so unbelievable is what you see, so invisible is what you believe", in the words of Callistratus, a near-contemporary writer – was unprecedented in Greece, probably the whole world.

AMAZONS AND HEROES

Scopas' talent for depicting emotional extremes was not restricted to Bacchantes, however. The *Amazonomachia* (*Amazon Battle*), a fragment from some part of the

Left: The Amazonomachia *(Amazon Battle), a fragment from the Mausoleum at Halicarnassus attributed to Scopas. Unarmoured in their short tunics, the Amazons show themselves equal adversaries of the male warriors. Here, Scopas ignores all Classical restraint while still working fluently in the Classical idiom.*

Mausoleum at Halicarnassus that is attributed to Scopas, shows his skills in a more military field. The fighting swirls between the helmeted warriors with their shields and helmets and the acrobatic, almost airborne Amazons. Although defenceless in their short tunics, the Amazons demonstrate that they are very much the warriors' equals. Their portrayer, Scopas, shows himself untrammelled by earlier Classical restraint but working wholly in the Classical mould.

From the middle group of figures on the west pediment of the Tegean Temple of Athena that Scopas carved, there survives a stupendous head of Achilles. Achilles was the archetypal warrior-hero of *The Iliad*, the prince with whose rising wrath the great epic poem opens and with whose sated wrath it ends. Although much battered, this surviving original stone head, with a lionskin helmet, still transmits Achilles' grimly murderous anger with chilling force. He is part of a group of warrior-heroes that originally included Hercules immediately to his left.

THE GOD OF LONGING

Less well known than his brother Eros, god of desire, Pothos was the god or personification of *pothos* (longing or yearning). Scopas made at least two statues of Pothos, one for Samothrace, mentioned by Pliny, and another for Megara. In depicting Pothos, Scopas adopted a gentler approach, suitable for an emotion less ravenous if perhaps less easily satisfied than Eros. This languid youth leans on one draped arm, with plump legs crossed and soulful eyes set in soft, effeminate features, all suggesting vague longing. In a broadly similar work, *Hypnos,* Scopas portrayed the god of sleep.

Above: Scopas did not solely depict women caught up in frenzy, as this beautifully calm, reflective head of Hygeia, attributed to him, shows. Hygeia was the goddess of health, daughter of the divine healer Asclepius.

Below: Hypnos, a bronze sculpted by Fernand Khnopff in the 1890s, was based on an original head of the god of sleep by Scopas.

LYSIPPUS
ALEXANDER'S COURT SCULPTOR

Lysippus was the most prominent, prolific and longest-lived of the great 4th-century sculptors. He was active *c*.360–*c*.305BC, reputedly making 1,500 works, all of them in bronze. Considered the most accomplished artist of his age, Lysippus suitably became Alexander the Great's favourite – in fact, court – sculptor. The world-conqueror allowed almost no one else to sculpt him. Lysippus went on to make portrait busts of many of Alexander's warring Successors, such as Cassander and Seleucus I, who founded the Seleucid Empire in 312BC. A native of Sicyon in the Peloponnese,

Above: Lysippus sculpted many bronze busts of Alexander, all since lost. This marble copy, made for the Roman Emperor Hadrian's collection at Tivoli outside Rome, captures the conqueror's ruthless determination and will mixed with his spark of romantic pothos (longing). Like most such portraits, it is probably very flattering.

Right: An ephebe *(young man) from the sea off Marathon, of* c.340BC. *It is attributed to Lysippus or his school on stylistic grounds and dated to* c.330BC. *A rare bronze original, it has a graceful sweetness very different from the severity of 5th-century art.*

THE *GETTY VICTOR*
An almost life-size bronze statue of a victorious young athlete, found in the Adriatic in 1964, has been associated with Lysippus or his workshop on stylistic grounds. It is very similar to the *Marathon Boy* also found in the sea off Marathon, another bronze original of *c*.330BC and now in Athens' National Museum. When sold to the Getty Museum in Malibu in 1977, the Adriatic bronze fetched $3,900,000, then a record sum for any sculpture. It has since become known as the *Getty Victor*. With their supple, relaxed, still half-boyish bodies and delicate features, both differ greatly from earlier tough super-masculine heroes.

Lysippus ran a workshop of almost industrial size that was continued after his death by his sons.

Ancient writers such as Pliny relate that Lysippus invented an entirely new canon, or mathematically calculated ideal of beauty, almost displacing that of Polyclitus. Lysippus' *Canon* postulated a smaller head, longer legs and a slender body, producing a generally more graceful, aristocratic air – exactly what his mostly royal or noble clients wanted.

Such new proportions also allowed Lysippus' statues to be viewed equally well from any angle, whereas Polyclitus' *Canon* only permitted a narrowly frontal approach. In this, as with his increasingly monarchical customers, Lysippus stands on the dividing line of the Classical and Hellenistic Ages.

THE *APOXYMENOS*
One of Lysippus' most famous and characteristic statues is the *Apoxymenos*, a young athlete scraping himself with a

strigil after exercising, in the usual Greek manner. A surviving Roman copy in marble gives a good impression of this smooth-cheeked, long-limbed, young man. He is shown shifting his weight from one foot to another and stretching his right arm out, while his left hand holds the strigil. His slender body is supported by long, tensed thighs, his right leg set back with only his toes touching the ground; he hardly seems to have exerted himself at all. Such effortless elegance was novel when depicting an athlete. It was made c.340BC.

The statue was brought to Rome by Marcus Agrippa (63–12BC), the emperor Augustus' first minister, and set up outside the public baths he built. Later, when the emperor Tiberius removed it to his own palace, there was such an outcry from the Roman public suddenly robbed of one of its favourite artworks that even that most parsimonious of emperors had to return it.

THE *FARNESE HERCULES*
Very different but equally illustrative of Lysippus' versatile genius is the *Farnese Hercules*, which once belonged to the Farnese family in Rome. Again this is a marble copy of a bronze. It shows the semi-divine hero, a son of Zeus, wearily leaning on a tree trunk after his labours. Hercules became increasingly seen as a human role model, for he relied almost wholly on his own strength – admittedly huge – to achieve his ends, rather than divine assistance. Alexander regarded Hercules as one of his special heroes.

If weary, the hero is massively muscled, in a way inconceivable in earlier statues, the result of obsessive body-building in the gymnasium, and far from the ideal balance of earlier Classical art. In a few years his heroic muscles could easily turn to flab. Within decades such hulks would become common in Hellenistic art.

By contrast, Lysippus' *Hermes* of c.320BC shows the messenger god – adjusting his winged sandal on a support – as a model of easy relaxation, his stance free and elegant.

Left: The Farnese Hercules, *a marble copy of an original bronze, reveals another side of Lysippus' genius. Hercules is shown massively muscled, the result of manic body-building in the gymnasium. This is very different from the balance of earlier Classical art.*

Below: The Apoxymenos, *a young athlete scraping himself after exercise, a Roman marble copy of a bronze original. This elegant, long-limbed young man hardly seems to have exerted himself at all. It was made* c.340BC.

THE FACE OF ALEXANDER
Alexander was keenly aware of the value of his royal image, as the young, handsome and unconquered hero, divinely favoured and inspired – even possibly divinely fathered, a belief that Alexander himself may have held after his pilgrimage to the shrine of Amon-Zeus at Siwah in the Libyan desert.

Alexander commissioned many portrait busts by Lysippus. All were bronzes that have since been lost, but marble copies of several survive. Among the finest are the copy made for Hadrian's collection at his Villa at Tivoli outside Rome and one that is now in Istanbul. The former especially captures the mixture of the conqueror's ruthless determination and will with the spark of romantic *pothos* that was characteristic of Alexander. Such portraits almost certainly flattered the Macedonian king, giving him uplifted eyes, sweeping hair and a heroic air. They were widely copied after Alexander's death in 323BC.

THE HELLENISTIC GOLDEN AGE 320–200BC

Right: The Winged Victory of Samothrace, *an original masterpiece in marble from the 3rd century* BC.

Below: The Apollo Belvedere, *a Roman copy of an original marble work of* c.320BC *attributed to Leochares. Its smooth beauty was once widely admired.*

The death of Alexander (323BC) conventionally marks the end of the Classical and the beginning of the Hellenistic ages, but there was no abrupt change in style. As the new Hellenistic kingdoms, often now of unprecedented size and wealth, established themselves as grand patrons, art began to explore new extremes, becoming more refined, more violent or more ecstatic.

THE *APOLLO BELVEDERE*

Typical of the new refinement was the *Apollo Belvedere*, carved *c.*320BC by Leochares. Leochares worked for Philip II of Macedonia and then Alexander and his Successors. He made gold and ivory statues of the older Macedonian monarch for a round temple, the Philippeion, in Olympia in a newly dramatic manner. But he was most noted for his representations of the gods, especially this *Apollo* (named after its present location). For centuries after its rediscovery in the Renaissance this marble was regarded as one of the supreme masterpieces of world art and the absolute summit of male beauty. It deeply impressed the German art critic Johann Winckelmann and the poet Goethe in the 18th century.

Tastes change. When the Elgin Marbles from the Parthenon revealed a new, less epicene and more dynamic canon of male beauty in the early 19th century, the *Apollo Belvedere* fell terminally out of fashion. But it remains, in its smooth, almost weightless way, a fine example of Hellenistic art at

its most exquisite. (It was, of course, originally painted.) Leochares also worked with Scopas, a very different artist, on the Mausoleum of Halicarnassus.

THE *WINGED VICTORY OF SAMOTHRACE*

The goddess Nike lands as if on the bow of a galley, her windswept drapery flying in the wind, her massive wings outstretched. An original marble work, she once stood on a marble carving of ship's prow in a sanctuary on the north Aegean island of Samothrace, where many Hellenistic kings commemorated successes. Probably she was set up to celebrate a great naval victory by one of Macedonia's kings, perhaps Antigonus II in the 250s BC. However, she could equally well date to about 50 years later and commemorate a Rhodian victory.

The sculptor's name remains unknown, but he was obviously inspired by Paionius' great *Nike* at Olympia of 200 years earlier.

THE *ALEXANDER SARCOPHAGUS*

The so-called *Alexander Sarcophagus* is the finest and most elaborate funerary monument to survive from the Hellenistic age. It has never, however, contained the body of Alexander the Great. This was interred in splendour in Alexandria by Ptolemy I but has long since vanished. This tomb was probably a commission made *c.*310BC for King Abdalonymus, a ruler whom Alexander had placed on the throne of Sidon in Phoenicia (Lebanon) in 333BC. The Phoenicians, although they rapidly became Hellenized, always preferred burial to cremation, then more common among the Greeks.

However, the Phoenicians employed sculptors from Greece to carve the friezes on the long sides. One shows Alexander fighting the Persians at the Battle of Issus in 333BC; the other depicts a hunt with both Macedonians and Sidonians together, so linking Abdalonymus' new regime firmly to Alexander. (Abdalonymus had been only the palace gardener originally. He ended up one of Alexander's Companions.) The reliefs have kept much of their colour, while the lid and chest are so richly adorned with finely carved metal mouldings that the sarcophagus resembles a giant jewel box.

He was also a genius, for this massive figure brims with tension and vigour. Originally 3m (9ft 9in) tall with her head, the *Nike*'s twisting axes and the contours of her wings and clothing are best viewed from below, as she was originally and now is once more in the Louvre. The statue shows Hellenistic art at its dynamic best.

THE *PHILOSOPHER'S HEAD*

Most statues were still made in bronze, however, and so have perished. One striking exception is the portrait bust found in the sea off Anticythera and probably dating from *c.*250BC. It has been called the *Philosopher's Head* because the face expresses such powerful intellectual energy and moral strength through the finely engraved beard, tousled locks and piercing gaze. Such qualities could only be fully conveyed in bronze, again emphasizing how much has been lost. The head was probably part of a group of

philosophers, for other fragments have been found nearby, mostly legs and feet that seem to have been torn off a plinth. They were probably *en route* to Rome, part of some victorious general's booty.

Above: A bust found in the sea from c.250BC. *It is called the* Philosopher's Head *because the face expresses such intellectual and moral energy.*

Right: The Alexander Sarcophagus *is the finest funerary monument of the Hellenistic age, packed with vigorous battle scenes, although it never contained the actual body of Alexander. It was probably a commission made* c.310BC *for King Abdalonymus, a ruler whom Alexander had placed on the throne of Sidon in Phoenicia.*

LATER HELLENISTIC ART
200–30BC

Right: Spinario, *or* Boy Pulling a Thorn from His Foot *may date from* c.200BC, *or may be a later Roman copy. It reveals the age's growing taste for sentimental genre subjects. This is a composite work, for the head and the body come from different statues.*

Below: A Crouching Aphrodite *of the later Hellenistic Age,* c.150BC. *This is typical of the works whose smooth bodies were for a long time much admired.*

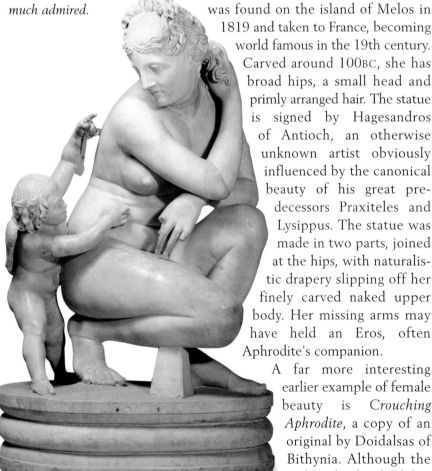

After 200BC, the growing power of Rome began to affect the Greek art market. The Romans proved enthusiasts for the Baroque styles of later Hellenistic art, shipping off many artworks, frequently without paying. The influence of Greek art on Rome, for a time overwhelming, was all one way, however, for Roman art did not at this stage affect Greek artistic development. Greece's new masters simply wanted ever more copies of existing masterworks of the most blatantly dramatic or sentimental sort.

VENUS DE MILO

Typical of the age's more serene art, which today can seem bland, is the *Venus de Milo*, an original marble. The now armless statue of the goddess Aphrodite was found on the island of Melos in 1819 and taken to France, becoming world famous in the 19th century. Carved around 100BC, she has broad hips, a small head and primly arranged hair. The statue is signed by Hagesandros of Antioch, an otherwise unknown artist obviously influenced by the canonical beauty of his great predecessors Praxiteles and Lysippus. The statue was made in two parts, joined at the hips, with naturalistic drapery slipping off her finely carved naked upper body. Her missing arms may have held an Eros, often Aphrodite's companion.

A far more interesting earlier example of female beauty is *Crouching Aphrodite*, a copy of an original by Doidalsas of Bithynia. Although the goddess has lost both her arms and the back of her head, the lovely sweep of her body as she bends, perhaps preparing to bathe, has all the naturalness of a nymph. Doidalsas' statue proved very popular and was much copied.

Among popular sculptures catering to the age's more sentimental side were small statues such as *Baby Playing with a Goose* or *Boy Pulling a Thorn from His Foot*, both of which date from c.200BC. Both these naked children, with their carefully brushed hair and almost Dickensian sweetness of manner, seem to be the offspring of good homes.

THE PERGAMUM ALTAR

But the age's real taste was for the melodramatic and exhibitionist. Nowhere was this better appreciated than in the newly rich kingdom of Pergamum in north-western Asia Minor. To commemorate his defeat of the invading Gauls in c.230BC, King Attalus I (241–197BC) erected a tremendous series of statues on

THE *LAOCOÖN'S* REDISCOVERY

In January 1506 Pope Julius I heard that some fine statues had been dug up in a vineyard near the ruins of Nero's palace in Rome. He ordered Sangallo, one of his architects, to inspect the statue. Sangallo invited Michelangelo, recently returned to Rome, along. Before they had even got off their horses, they agreed that the group must be the *Laocoön* praised by Pliny the Elder. Michelangelo later said that the discovery inspired him to portray spiritual anguish and physical torment through violent muscular movement. Many later artists, including El Greco, were influenced by the *Laocoön*. The statue is a copy of an original of *c*.180BC made probably in *c*.50BC by three sculptors: Agesander, Polydorus and Athenodorus of Rhodes, who created sensational works for the Roman market. The myth illustrated was retold in *The Aeneid* by Virgil. The priest Laocoön had warned the Trojans about the Greeks' wooden horse. His attempt to deflect the fated course of events angered the gods, who sent sea serpents to destroy him and his sons. The carving's amazing naturalism is typically late Hellenistic. (A recent theory that this is a fake made by Michelangelo himself has been generally discounted.)

Below: This Laocoön *group is a copy of an original of c.180BC made c.50BC by three sculptors of Rhodes, who created sensational works for the Roman market. The myth illustrated was later retold in* The Aeneid *by Virgil.*

Pergamum's citadel. Epigonus created the bronze *Dying Gaul*, a Gallic man propping himself up on his right arm to look at his fatal wound. Although we again have only a marble copy, it remains a brilliant study in anatomy and psychology, the wound most realistically sculpted. Epigonus also made the *Chieftain Killing Himself and His Wife*, an even more dramatic double piece showing a Gallic noble committing suicide rather than surrender.

The crowning achievement of the Attalid dynasty, and of Hellenistic baroque, was the vast Altar of Zeus, erected between 180 and 160BC, now in Berlin. Menecrates was among the named artists but many more were probably involved. The huge frieze, 121m (400ft) long, that encircles the base of the altar depicts a *gigantomachia*, a battle of the giants and gods. By casting this as the victory of Hellenism over barbarous Gauls, the Pergameme kings could justify their unpopular rule over the cities of Ionia.

The place of honour in the centre of the east frieze shows Zeus hurling a thunderbolt at Porphyrion, a serpent-footed giant. Elsewhere, Athena seizes a young winged giant by the hair, while below, sunk in the ground, Ge, mother of the giants, begs for mercy. The whole frieze surges with dynamic energy.

Below: The Altar of Zeus at Pergamum was the most spectacular work of the Hellenistic baroque, built between 180 and 160BC.

CHAPTER V

VASE PAINTING

While Greek pottery ranks among the finest in the world, vase painting was for the Greeks themselves a secondary form of art compared to painted panels and murals. These depicted events of grand historical or mythical importance. However, almost no Greek paintings before the 4th century BC have survived. By contrast, numerous vases survive from the Bronze Age on, giving fresh perspectives on the daily lives and beliefs of the Greeks.

Pottery has survived so well partly because its shards are nearly indestructible. Vases have been found in quantity over a wide area, for the Greeks seldom used glassware or other types of containers. Instead, they stored their wine, olive oil and water in vases and pots, and also exported their products, principally olive oil, around the Mediterranean in pottery of increasing splendour and magnificence. Often the container must have been more valuable than its contents, although Greek olive oil and wines were appreciated by the Etruscans, Gauls (in both France and northern Italy) and by the Romans.

At first, Corinth was the greatest exporter of vases, but during the mid-6th century BC, Athens replaced it as the chief producer of the best pottery. Athens continued to dominate the market for high-quality painted vases until the mid-4th century BC. By then, the golden age of vase-making was coming to an end, although opulent ware continued to be produced for long after.

Left: An Athenian red figure vase (on a black base) by the 'Niobid Painter' c.460BC, showing battling giants and gods.

BRONZE AGE VASES
1800–1100BC

Above: A Kamares-style cup. Pottery of almost china-like delicacy was produced in Crete at the time of the early palaces c.2000–1700BC.

The lively civilization of Minoan Crete produced colourful and vivid pottery throughout the 2nd millennium BC, the period of its great palaces. Minoan pottery styles – meticulously ranked by Arthur Evans (the archaeologist who rediscovered Cnossus Palace in 1900) into categories that not everyone, however, now accepts – show a culture reaching its peak around 1500BC. Soon after, Mycenaean Greeks from the mainland became dominant in Crete and across the whole Aegean. In their pottery, as in their other arts, the Mycenaeans essentially continued Minoan styles but in stiffer, more stylized and anthropocentric ways. But it can be hard to distinguish between the two civilizations' artefacts.

THE FIRST MINOAN STYLES
Pottery was the first art form in which the Minoan genius revealed its tremendous imaginative powers. The early style, called Kamares, probably originated in Phaestus, the main palace in southern Crete, but was discovered by archaeologists in the Kamares Cave, a burial site.

Kamares-style pottery is characterized by varied abstract spiral and curvilinear designs and dark mottled colours, combining drawings on the surface of the vase with varied relief patterns. These are mostly floral or zoomorphic (depicting animals). The human form is notably absent from this early art.

This style flourished at the time of the early palaces c.2000–1700BC, producing at its finest the so-called 'eggshell' ware. Thrown on the potter's wheel, such cups were designed to imitate the fine metal ware that has not generally survived. But they achieve a delicacy almost anticipating that of genuine china, which to many suggests a feminine influence typical of Minoan culture in general. What much Minoan art apparently lacks is the insistence on symmetry that would characterize later Greek art. Some time around 1700BC a major cataclysm, probably an earthquake, totally destroyed all the Cretan palaces. They were soon rebuilt on a grander, more systematic scale, and at the same time Cretan pottery entered its finest stage.

THE MINOAN ZENITH
Typical of Minoan vase painting at its liveliest and most naturalistic is the *Dendra Vase*, across whose curves an alarmingly lifelike octopus spreads

Left: An octopus design on the Dendra Vase, *produced c.1500BC at the apex of Minoan civilization. It reflects both the Cretans' love of the sea and their brilliantly fluid art.*

its tentacles. Similar vases are decorated with plants. They reflect both Cretan fascination with sea life – the Minoans were great sailors and fishermen – and their love of free-flowing forms. But the human image now figured also.

Three famous low reliefs, all of which would probably have been painted originally, come from Aghia Triada, a royal villa near Phaestus. They are the *Chieftain Cup*, the *Boxer Vase* and the *Harvester Vase*. All are decorated with typical serpentine patterns, giving vivid glimpses into life in Bronze Age Crete. The *Harvester Vase* in particular portrays cheerful peasants without the condescension that might be expected in an art normally geared to courtiers' tastes. A common decorative motif from Cnossus of this period is the lily, found on many vases, but the most frequent motifs feature spirals, animals, birds and fishes, depicted almost impressionistically.

All these are dated to the 'Late Minoan I' period of *c.*1550–1450BC, the seeming zenith of Minoan culture. It seems probable – although no consensus has been established – that the volcanic eruption of Thira cut short Minoan culture just as it was flowering.

THE ART OF THE MYCENAEANS

Despite their cultural debts to the Minoans, the Greek Mycenaeans favoured a markedly more militaristic art than the Cretans. This is immediately obvious in the *Chariot Krater* (mixing bowl) from Cnossus of *c.*1400BC. In the chariot, the 'tank of the Bronze Age', two tall, long-robed figures stand behind the pair of horses. The portrayal of the two horses follows Mycenaean customs in vase painting: the artist, trying to show the chariot seen head on in perspective, has painted only one horse's body, but this has two tails, two pairs of hind legs and forelegs and two heads. The whole scene has a stiffness about it

quite distinct from Minoan naturalness. So do the grandiose 'Palace-style' vases of the Mycenaean period at Cnossus.

From Mycenae itself in the 13th century BC comes the *Vase with Warriors*. This shows six helmeted soldiers with shields and helmets marching off, a woman in the background seeming to lament their parting. However, any intended pathos is undermined by the almost comically inept art.

Dating from *c.*1200BC, a terracotta vase shows an octopus, a creature loved by Minoan artists but that has here become heavily stylized. Similarly, a charging bull on a terracotta krater from Enkomi in Cyprus of *c.*1180BC retains nothing of the magnificent vitality of earlier bulls but is simply a schematic, nearly monochrome reminder of flesh-and-blood bulls. Some archaeologists think that only when Mycenaean vase painting is almost identical to Minoan does it really succeed as an art form. Others see in such simplified works the precursors of Geometric art.

Above: A Palace-style vase, made c.1400BC when Crete was under Mycenaean rule, is altogether stiffer in approach.

Below: This terracotta krater, showing a bull charging a bird, comes from Enkomi in Cyprus. It dates to the Late Mycenaean period c.1180BC.

PROTOGEOMETRIC AND GEOMETRIC ART c.1050–700BC

Right: The revival of Greek economic, social and artistic life in the 8th century BC led to the return of figurative art, albeit in a very stylized form, as the sketchy, diagrammatic figures on this terracotta vase from the Middle Geometric period reveal.

Below: The stiff, twig-like figures in this detail from the great vase opposite may depict chariot races held in honour of the dead, mentioned in Homer's The Iliad.

After 1200BC the elaborate palace-centred culture of Mycenae, with its bureaucracies, elegantly dressed courtiers, extensive trade routes and trading contacts with Egypt and the Levant, began to collapse. Traditionally this was due to Dorian invasions from the north, but other reasons, including civil wars and even climate change, have been suggested. By 1100BC Mycenaean civilization had vanished almost completely. In its place came a simpler, more parochial way of life. Art soon reflected this change, abandoning the increasingly feeble Mycenaean attempts at realism in favour of an austere style that at times approached abstraction.

Most pottery in the early centuries after 1100BC comes from Athens, the one major Mycenaean city that, according to legend, escaped total destruction. Within the shelter afforded by the walls of the Acropolis, Geometric art seems to have been born. The Diplyon Cemetery (named after the gate in the walls of classical Athens) has revealed many artefacts from this era.

PROTOGEOMETRIC: THE ART OF SURVIVORS

The first new style to emerge is called Protogeometric. Artists continued to use Mycenaean shapes, but with decorations restricted to circles, semicircles, rhombuses, crosses and hooks, arranged in bands. These designs were drawn using brushes fixed to compasses, marking a completely fresh approach to art. The ground (base colour) of the vases was generally light-coloured with decorations added in black gloss or glaze. Some Protogeometric vases may come from Cyprus, to which many Mycenaeans had fled. Such a limited range of decoration, devoid of human or animal figures, suited an age struggling for survival.

EARLY GEOMETRIC: THE FIRST AWAKENING

As Greek economic and cultural life began very tentatively to revive after 900BC, potters took to experimenting again. While they abandoned compass-controlled arcs in favour of grouped zigzags and obliques, they initially kept the mainly black base of the Protogeometric period. Decoration was increasingly organized into metopes (or panels), within which geometric patterns, especially the typically Greek shape of the *meander* (or Greek key design), were painted. Finally, artists began creating simple, silhouetted figures of animals.

An early example comes from a Cretan burial urn, which depicts some alarmingly feral creatures – possibly wild cats, but more probably creatures from some nightmarish myth. However, Athens remained the chief source of pottery. Horses, then very important in a Greek world that was strongly aristocratic, are among the first recognizable animals to appear on vases.

THE MIDDLE GEOMETRIC: THE HUMAN FORM RETURNS

By 800BC the tempo of Greek life was beginning to quicken. The century was to witness the real rebirth of Greece, with the writing of Homer's poetry, the invention of the Greek alphabet (derived from Phoenician examples), the beginnings of colonization and the establishment of great festivals such as the Olympic Games in 776BC.

This resurgence encouraged the reappearance of human forms, albeit still in rigidly geometrized form. Strange, stick-like figures gradually began to fill more and more of the vase areas. They also became freer and less rigid, although they long remained highly stylized.

Large burial urns containing the ashes of important people (cremation was then the normal form of burial, in contrast to the Mycenaean preference for inhumation) often carried scenes of mourning. One of these, a terracotta krater about 1.5m (5ft)

high dating from *c.*750BC, shows a funeral procession in the top band with a corpse lying on a bier, with identical stylized human forms on the other side. But the lower band rejoices in a multitude of figures, who seem to be wearing odd kilts or skirts. They are driving carts or more probably chariots. It is possible that they are meant to be competitors taking part in the deceased's funeral games. This typically Greek custom was by then widely established, at least according to Homer's poetry.

This grand vase is often attributed to the 'Hirschfeld Painter'. (Potters are often named after particular works, another example being the 'Diplyon Artist'). However, we know nothing at all definite about this putative potter. Even this particular vase may not have been the work of one individual.

THE LATE GEOMETRIC

By the Late Geometric period (750–700BC), decoration had spread to cover the entire surface of vases, with busy friezes of animals and humans. However, Geometric art, which had allowed the revival of decorative vase painting in a characteristically Greek form, strongly emphasizing symmetry, had by the century's end reached an artistic dead-end.

What had been necessary astringency after the collapse of Mycenaean art was in danger of becoming a straitjacket. Greek art needed a fresh direction and an injection of vitality. Both would come from Asia, then far more advanced.

Below: Standing 1.2m (4ft) high, this terracotta Late Geometric krater by the Hirschfield painter from Attica is the finest burial urn from the 8th century BC. Such urns marked the burial pits in which cremated bodies were placed. The vase actually shows a grand funeral cortège with a long row of warriors in their chariots.

IDEAS FROM THE EAST
C.720–570BC

Above: The Chigi Vase, *a very fine Corinthian-style vase with a triple tier of friezes, dates from c.620BC. It is made of terracotta with a dark and light glaze of paint, and covered in red and white figures of hoplite soldiers.*

Below: Corinth emerged as the greatest centre of vase-making c.700BC. On this skyphos (drinking cup) of c.670BC from Kameiros in Rhodes, a black dog lollops with lithe energy across a white surface – an example of Corinthian art at its vivid best.

The 7th century BC saw major changes in pottery painting. Although in some cities potters for a time retained Geometric motifs, elsewhere they began experimenting with new ways of depicting figures. They also discovered new, much more interesting subjects. (Possibly earlier artists were also illustrating myths and legends, but their starkly silhouetted forms make any narrative almost impossibly hard to discern.)

Greek artists began to borrow the flora and fauna motifs of Syria. The protypes of these may have first been introduced by the Phoenicians, then masters of the Mediterranean, and adapted by them for their own purposes.

Syrian polychromatic influence merged with the perennial Greek insistence on form to create the colourful 'orientalizing' art of the 7th century BC. The flourishing Isthmian port of Corinth, which was founding colonies across the Mediterranean, became for the next 100 years the leading centre of artistic innovation. Pottery styles are named after its innovatory use of clear-cut forms, although Athens always remained an important centre for ceramics.

Above: The Polyphemus Amphora *of c.680BC, fussily proto-Attic in style, illustrates the story of Odysseus blinding the drunken giant Polyphemus on its top frieze, while lower down animals run wild. Underneath them the Gorgons pursue Perseus, who has just killed their sister Medusa, in quite another myth.*

PROTOCORINTHIAN 720–640BC
A new interest in depicting myths and legends – which merged into religion and history – led to scenes filled with griffins, sphinxes and sirens. Homer's epics, *The Iliad* and *Odyssey*, quickly known all round the Greek world,

became one of the prime sources of myths for potters. The *Polyphemus Amphora* of *c.*680BC, found in a child's grave at Eleusis near Athens, illustrates the story of Odysseus blinding the drunken giant Polyphemus on its top frieze, while lower down animals run wild. Underneath them the Gorgons, the lethal sisters of decapitated Medusa, pursue Perseus, who has just killed the snake-headed horror, in quite another myth. Stylistically the vase is called proto-Attic. Despite its richness of detail, it lacks the purity of line of the best Corinthian work.

Much simpler in theme and artistically far more powerful is the *skyphos* (drinking cup) of *c.*670BC from Kameiros in Rhodes. The long black form of a dog lollops with superb energy across a white surface. This is a true Corinthian work, as is the *aryballos* (perfume flask) of *c.*650BC from Thebes. Its head is formed like a lion's mouth with savage fangs, while on its body hoplites are vividly depicted fighting with spears and shields. Such potent works typify the Protocorinthian style in its maturity.

THE *CHIGI VASE*
Perhaps the finest example of the Corinthian style is the *Chigi Vase*, with its triple tier of friezes. Dating from *c.*620BC, the vase, of a type called an *oinochoe* (wine-pourer), is made of terracotta with dark and light glaze paint covered in red and white figures. It comes from Formello near Veii, an important Etruscan city. The topmost frieze graphically depicts two armies approaching each other in battle formation. This vase also provides invaluable information about early hoplite warfare.

Below this scene a second frieze shows a procession of horsemen, chariots, a lion hunt and the Judgement of Paris. (The Trojan prince had had to make a perilous choice of deities: who was the most beautiful, Aphrodite, Athena or Hera? Choosing Aphrodite, the love goddess, he incurred the undying hatred of the other two, a fatal choice that

ultimately led to the fall of Troy. A sphinx meanwhile looks on impartially.) The bottom frieze shows a hare hunt. Figures are now no longer just bare silhouettes but are portrayed with a true muscular vigour.

THE 'NESSOS PAINTER'
A vase-painter known to us as the 'Nessos Painter' from his masterpiece, a huge amphora some 1.2m (4ft) tall depicting the legend of Hercules and Nessos, flourished in Attica in the late 7th century BC. Painted only on one side, this bears the names of Heracles (Hercules) and Netos (Nessos) above it for the first time. It illustrates a popular myth. Hercules, the archetypal hero, was escorting Deianeria, a princess, when Nessos, a centaur who worked as a ferryman, tried to rape her. Hercules is shown on the amphora's neck seizing the centaur by his neck and killing him. Deianeria later gave Hercules a shirt soaked in Nessos' poisoned blood, thinking it was a love potion. Maddened by the torment of the 'shirt of Nessos', the hero killed himself on a funeral pyre.

The story is painted with far more artistic verve and self-confidence than on earlier vases. So too is the lower story, again of the Gorgons chasing Perseus. Instead of the robotic figures shown on the *Polyphemus Amphora* of 70 years earlier, these monsters are depicted as horrific winged demons in hot pursuit of Perseus, who is not even present.

With masters like the 'Nessos Painter' working in Attica, Athens again displaced Corinth as the main manufacturer of vases, a position it retained until the end of the Classical Age. The potters' quarter in Athens was known as the Kerameikos, after its clay (ceramic) vase-makers.

Below: A vase-painter known as the 'Nessos Painter' produced this masterpiece, a huge amphora, 1.2m (4ft) tall, depicting the legend of Hercules and Nessos, in the late 7th century BC. Painted only on one side, this bears the names of Heracles (Hercules) and Netos (Nessos) above it for the first time.

CLASSICISM AND NATURALISM 570–480BC

Above: Among the grandest Attic vases of the 6th century is the François Vase *(named after its finder), a krater exported to Etruria. Signed by the potter Ergotimos and the painter Cleitias, its friezes brim with mythological scenes, many about Achilles, the warrior-hero.*

As Athens emerged as the chief pottery centre *c*.570BC – just when Solon's economic and social reforms were starting to have beneficial effects – its individual artists developed the black figure style (on a red or pale ground) to its effective limits. Some artists then went on to pioneer red figure vases on a black ground. Although this was technically harder, it permitted the depiction of increasingly naturalistic and powerful scenes. With this style, Greek vase painting was to reach its zenith. Artists now often signed their vases, thus demonstrating a novel self-confidence.

Among the earlier notable works is the *François Vase* of *c*.560BC, a grand krater exported to Etruria. Signed by the potter Ergotimos and the painter Cleitias, its six friezes brim with mythological scenes, many relating the story of Achilles, the warrior-hero of *The Iliad*.

Cleitias signed many other works, as did Sophilos, who was both a painter and potter. This was now an increasingly common and effective combination.

EXEKIAS THE MASTER

One of the age's greatest potter-cum-painters, some 30 pieces are attributed to Exekias. He worked between 550 and 520BC. Among his masterpieces are *Dionysus in a Ship*, a terracotta glazed *kylix* (cup) of *c*.540BC. The bearded wine god – only later was Dionysus shown as a beardless youth – lolls at ease in his ship, a drinking horn in his hands. The ship's mast is sprouting vines that bear luscious fruit above, while around cavort dolphins. The scene brims with joyful lyricism.

Different, but equally masterly, is *Ajax and Achilles*, showing the two heroes intent on a board game during a break in the Trojan Wars (not a scene mentioned by Homer). It demonstrates Exekias' skill in incised lines, which allowed greater realism in depicting armour and flesh. Also notable are his innovatory composition, with the strong diagonals formed by the spears, and the intimate subject-matter. Exekias was the first to paint such scenes from legend as complete pictures, and his work is often considered to make him the first great individual in Western art. But such black figure vases were inherently limited, for they lacked chromatic variety. To create this meant reversing the age-old formula of painting in the figures while leaving the background untouched.

Left: Ajax and Achilles, *showing the two heroes intent on a game during a break in the Trojan Wars, demonstrates Exekias' skill in incised lines, which allowed greater realism in depicting armour and flesh. Also notable are his innovatory composition, with the strong diagonals formed by the spears, and intimate subject-matter. As the first to paint such scenes as complete pictures, Exekias is sometimes considered the first great individual Western painter.*

THE RED FIGURE PIONEERS

In about 530BC Athenian painters pioneered the development of red figure vases, a truly revolutionary move. (Black figure works continued to be produced for a while as well, however.) The first such vase is attributed to Andocides, possibly a pupil of Exekias, who signed an amphora on which one side has red figures and the other has black figures, both showing Hercules reclining on a couch.

Among the best of the new painters-cum-potters, a group today called the Pioneers, was Euphronius. About 510BC he painted a kylix depicting Leagros, a beautiful youth riding a skittish horse with calm self-confidence. This shows a great advance in naturalism, as does his more elaborate vase showing the death of Sarpedon, a Trojan prince. Euphronius also depicted figures reclining at a *symposium* (party) with innovatory accuracy on a *psyketer* (wine cooler). The diners' half-naked bodies, even the pupils of their eyes, are remarkably lifelike.

There was keen competition among these painters, who must have known each other in the still small polis. Euthymides, a contemporary, inscribed a vase with his name and the boast: "As Euphronius could never have made it."

SOSIAS

One of the finest pieces of the period is a kylix by Sosias, a painter-cum-potter working in Athens around 500BC. It shows Achilles bandaging his comrade Patroclus' wounded arm (a scene inspired by, but not actually in, Homer's *The Iliad*). Sosios has painted Patroclus in such a way – his right leg bent, his left leg stretched out before him – that he fills the curve of the vase perfectly. Patroclus looks away in well-expressed pain as Achilles concentrates on his task. The faces and bodies of each warrior are shown in naturalistic perspective, marking a final break with Archaic art's frontalism.

The Dionysiac scenes painted on an amphora in *c*.490BC by the 'Cleophrades Painter' (also called Epictetus), a pupil of Euthymides, portrays the orgiastic rites of the wine god with great vigour. Dionysus, bearded and with his usual attributes of ivy and vine, is wearing long robes under which his legs move visibly, the first time that drapery was shown flowing realistically around a body. Around him, long-robed Maenads, the god's ecstatic followers, fend off impish satyrs.

The extensive use of a diluted glaze is also striking. Above, on the jar's neck, naked athletes compete. Attic potters' achievement of classical naturalism now matched that of contemporary sculptors and, presumably, panel painters.

Above: Dionysus in a Ship, *a terracotta glazed kylix of* c.540BC, *one of Exekias's 30 known masterpieces. The wine god lolls at ease in his ship, a drinking horn in his hands, while the mast sprouts vines bearing fruit and dolphins cavort around.*

Right: Achilles and Patroclus *by Sosias, a painter-cum-potter working in Athens around* 500BC. *Among the finest early red figure vases, it shows Achilles bandaging his comrade Patroclus' wounded arm (a scene not actually in* The Iliad*).*

ZENITH AND DECLINE
480–340BC

The Athenians emerged from the Persian wars (490–478BC) triumphant if battered. Rebuilding their wrecked city, they founded a new League against Persia, which soon became their empire, and completed their own progress to full democracy. This political upsurge was matched by artistic advances.

In painting, this was best exemplified by the large panel paintings of Polygnotus of Thasos. While all these have vanished, some fine vase paintings that survive are thought to be very similar in general design and approach.

Among these is a vase by an artist called the 'Niobe Painter' after another vase by him depicting the death of Niobe's children. His masterpiece of about 460BC shows Athena, goddess of the city, flanked by heroes, including Theseus, Athens' legendary king, and the muscular champion Hercules with his club. The vase probably commemorates

Above: The Pan Painter in c.450BC depicted a scene of heroic legend: Hercules killing the Egyptian king Busiris, who had intended to sacrifice him. The neat hairstyle and taut strength of the Greek hero contrast with the flabby ugliness of his opponents, perhaps reflecting Athens' aggressive new self-confidence at the time.

BURIAL VASES
One form of vase differed from the general run of black figure vases: the *lekythos*, literally an oil-flask with a white ground used for weddings or, more often, funerals. These cylindrical vases were made mostly from the 450s to the 420s BC. Among them is some of the finest Attic painted pottery. The 'Achilles Painter' is known also for his superb white-ground *lekythoi*. One shows a Muse on Mount Helicon (the rock is conveniently labelled) playing her lyre. The clear, simple lines of the young woman are timelessly classical. Other lekythoi could be more colourful but all remained relatively simple.

the Battle of Marathon, Athens' first victory over the Persians in 490BC. In that battle, Theseus and other long-dead heroes were rumoured to have returned to fight alongside living Athenians. The figures are not painted in perspective or as part of a whole narrative but are isolated around the vase, as was probably then the style in mural painting too.

HEROES AND AMAZONS
More dramatically interesting is the *Amazonomachia* (Battle of the Amazons) on a resplendent krater 75cm (2ft 6in) high. This popular legend – of the defeat of the attack on Athens by the Amazons, those warrior-women who so inverted Greek ideas about women's proper role – gave artists the licence to depict

Left: A detail from the large red figure vase opposite above, showing the goddess Demeter, the goddess of wheat and agriculture, in her chariot with Triptolemus, a prince. Red figure painting allowed much clearer lines against the black ground.

THE 'ACHILLES PAINTER'

During the period of Pericles' dominance of Athenian politics, in the high noon of Athenian democracy – around 450–430BC when the Parthenon with its superb sculptures was being built – an artist known as the 'Achilles Painter' also brought vase painting to its peak. He is so-called because of an amphora attributed to him showing *Achilles and Briseis*, the Homeric hero and the slave girl, another scene inspired by *The Iliad*. His compositions are simple, usually with just a couple of isolated but serene figures who radiate the same graceful nobility as Pheidias' great sculptures of the same period. Because of this, the 'Achilles Painter' is often considered the most deeply classical vase-painter of the High Classical period. About 200 surviving vases have, with varying degrees of certainty, been ascribed to him. Many lesser painters were reputedly his pupils. With him, Attic vase painting reached its peak.

DECLINE AND DECADENCE

Although fine vases continued to be made in the late 5th century BC in Athens, the 4th century BC saw a general decline in standards. In Athens artistic interest now increasingly focused on making vases in metals, including silver and even gold. But in Greek cities in southern Italy, lavish pottery vases such as the *Alcestis Vase* continued to be made.

Increasingly, these vases were floridly decorated with often flabby designs. Only when illustrating low-life scenes from theatrical comedy – as on a vase from Paestum, which shows actors with grotesque masks – can these painters be considered really successful.

half-naked women. It also served as a parable for the recent defeat of Persia, another non-Hellenic invader. The scene is crowded with violent action as armoured Athenians spear and hack at the Amazons, who are dressed as lightly as Scythian archers.

Above, on the vase's neck, in contrast, diners are shown peacefully drinking and listening to flute girls. *The Pan Painter* around 450BC depicted another scene of heroic massacre, Hercules killing the Ethiopian king Busiris, who had intended to sacrifice *him*.

A rather different scene of legendary violence on a *skyphos* or drinking cup shows Odysseus, home from his long wanderings, shooting his mighty bow at the suitors who had long been plaguing his wife Penelope. The Homeric hero is depicted on one side of the skyphos while the terrified suitors, one with an arrow sticking into him, cower from the returning king on the other. Dating from *c*.450BC, this piece achieves its impact with notably simple, uncluttered forms.

Left: A grand example of an Athenian red figure vase from the 5th century BC, the golden age of Athenian pottery, by the 'Niobe Painter', one of the master-potters. It shows the battle of the giants and gods above and Demeter and Triptolemus below.

Below: A lekythos, an oil-flask with figures on a white ground, was used for weddings and especially funerals. The clear, simple lines of the woman playing her lyre are very classical. Other lekythoi could be more colourful but all remained relatively simple.

CHAPTER VI

WALL PAINTINGS AND MOSAICS

The Greeks admired their painters as much as their sculptors. This may not now be apparent from artworks in museums, where statues predominate, but no real Greek painting before the mid-4th century BC survives. Instead, we must rely on descriptions by later writers such as Pliny, and what can be guessed from contemporary vases. We would have even less idea of Greek painting were it not for the eruption of Vesuvius in AD79, that preserved Pompeii and Herculaneum so well.

Pompeii is hugely important because, although never a Greek colony, it was very open to Greek cultural influences. Many of its houses were decorated with copies of Hellenistic masterpieces, often made by actual Greek artists. These works provide vivid examples of Greek painting in its illusionistic prime. Helped by recent discoveries from royal tombs in Macedonia and examples from houses in Rome, we can now see what master painters the Greeks were, even though they never fully grasped the principle of single unitary perspective that has underpinned realist Western art since the Renaissance. However painting in the Greek world starts far earlier with Minoan murals, some preserved by the volcanic eruption at Thira.

Left: Among the greatest of ancient paintings, The Finding of Telephus *at Herculaneum copies a work from Pergamum.*

MINOAN AND MYCENAEAN PAINTING 1700–1200BC

Above: Typical of Minoan art, this c.1550BC mural of a woman with big eyes and hair is now called La Parisienne. *She was probably a courtier, possibly a priestess.*

Below: The Prince with the Lilies of c.1500BC, a superb relief fresco, shows a young noble in an elaborate gold headdress of great courtliness.

The art of the Bronze-Age Aegean Minoans and Mycenaeans forms a prelude to Greek art proper. While it is uncertain how much, if any, influence their paintings had on later Greek art, one convention certainly survived: that of depicting women as white-skinned and most men as tanned brown.

Minoan paintings have been found in Crete and southern Aegean islands. In the Second Palace period (c.1700–1400BC), the Minoans produced wonderfully vivid and free-flowing, if hardly naturalistic, art. (Their colouring was not realistic and they gracefully elongated the human form, while the whole eye is often visible on faces painted in profile, an anatomical impossibility.) Minoan art also showed a keen awareness of non-human nature.

In all this it differed radically from the monumental art of contemporary Egypt and the Near East, areas that the Minoans knew. Cretan artists, uninterested in attempting to overawe spectators, delighted in celebrating life's fleeting pleasures. They generally painted frescoes, that is they applied pigment directly onto wet plaster, as did many Greek and Renaissance artists later. This technique, feasible only in dry climates, is well suited to painting quickly.

PALACE FRESCOES

Among earlier frescoes is a mural called *The Saffron Gatherer* from the palace at Cnossus of c.1600BC. Restored originally by Arthur Evans to represent a human being, it is now thought to depict a monkey picking saffron in a field. Larger and livelier at 80cm (2ft 8in) high is the *Bull-leaping Fresco* from the east wing of the great palace of c.1500BC. With its border painted to imitate marble, this grand mural illustrates a rite at the heart of Cretan life, the bull game, played by girls as well as boys, both sexes wearing kilts.

THE PRINCE WITH THE LILIES

A courtly, even decadent, note is struck by the superb relief fresco *The Prince with the Lilies*, showing a young noble with a huge golden headdress in almost hieratic pose. More typically Minoan in its vivacity is the *Running Officer*, showing a man leading a row of African guards, all sprinting. Typical also is the woman with big eyes and elaborate hair called *La Parisienne* (*The Parisian Woman*) who was perhaps a priestess.

In the room Evans called the Queen's Bathroom, dolphins leap gracefully around the royal bathtub – the sea was always important to the Minoans. There are few signs of war or warriors until the palace's very last phase, when it was under Mycenaean rule. From that period date the griffins, noble if stylized beasts flanking the throne of Minos.

THE THIRA MURALS

The volcanic eruption at Thira around 1500BC (some geologists prefer an earlier date) has kept the murals in houses on that once wealthy island dazzlingly fresh. These provide different views of the Bronze-Age world from the Cretan palace murals, although painted in the same style: two boys (judging by their brown colouring) are boxing; blue monkeys (unmistakeable simians, this time) clamber up rocks, fleeing pursuing dogs; butterflies and swallows flit among tree-tops; a woman, elegant in Minoan dress with small waist and puffed sleeves, is gathering saffron; antelopes brush against each other's flanks – all are scenes pulsing with vitality. The inhabitants of Thira were presumably merchants, not kings, but many murals rivals those of Crete itself. There is nothing provincial here.

Nor were they always as peace-loving as the Cretans have been assumed to be. Other frescoes show the fleet – of Thira, or admired his painter that when Apelles fell in love with Pancapse, then the current royal mistress whose portrait he was painting, Alexander gave her to the artist. Or so the story goes. Apelles worked mostly in the eastern Aegean when he was not following Alexander's conquering path across Asia.

About 30 works by Apelles are mentioned by ancient writers, among them a *Calumny* (of which Botticelli made a Renaissance version) and an *Aphrodite Anadyomene* (*Aphrodite Rising from the Foam*) later taken to Rome by the emperor Augustus. Apelles was said to excel all other painters in grace and to be a master of chiaroscuro. The *Zeus Enthroned* in the House of the Vetti at Pompeii may be a copy of Apelles' work.

THE ROYAL TOMBS

Excavations at Vergina (Aegae, the ancient Macedonian capital in the hills above Pella) have recently produced remarkable murals. One, possibly from the tomb of Philip II himself and so dating to *c*.338BC, shows a dramatic and complex hunting scene in which for the first time landscape contributes to the picture's depth. The frieze, though much pitted, presents a panoramic view of the hunt, in which the young Alexander is shown on horseback.

Even more vivid is *The Abduction of Persephone*, a mural in a nearby tomb sketched with quick, light strokes that aptly capture the despair of the goddess Demeter. She is shown seated on the right as the shaggy-bearded god Hades carries off her terrified daughter Persephone in his chariot to the underworld. Nicomachus, an artist praised by Pliny, may have created this novel depiction of human emotion.

THE FIRST MOSAICS

Mosaics, that far more laborious and costly, if also far more enduring, form of art than murals or panels, were initially made in pebbles. *Lion Hunt*, dated *c*.320–300BC is from Pella, the

Macedonian capital, and is signed by Gnosis, a famous artist. It depicts two naked youths, one perhaps being Alexander and the other his friend Craterus, who with a hound are attacking a lion. It is a dynamically dramatic scene, the muscular bodies and flying cloaks of the naked hunters and the animals shown with convincing foreshortening and shadowing.

In the Hellenistic and Roman eras, mosaics became commoner and grander, but painted *tesserae* (glass or marble cubes) replaced pebbles. Tesserae were easier to work in than pebbles, which encouraged the spread of mosaics.

Above: The Birth of Venus *from the House of Venus, a mural from Pompeii that probably copies a lost Hellenistic original – a reminder that not all such paintings were masterpieces.*

Below: Botticelli's Calumny of Apelles, *painted in 1495, was a Renaissance attempt to recreate a lost masterpiece by Apelles. Often considered the greatest artist of antiquity, Apelles became Alexander's court painter in the 330s* BC.

THE EVIDENCE OF POMPEII
THE *ALEXANDER MOSAIC*

Above: A detail from the Alexander Mosaic *showing King Darius panic-stricken in his chariot at Alexander's sudden advance.*

Below: The Alexander Mosaic, *the grandest copy of a Greek masterpiece, was made in Pompeii around 100BC. It shows Alexander charging at King Darius. Reproducing a mural probably painted by Apelles c.328BC, it keeps to the original four-colour palette.*

Originally an Etruscan settlement, and so, like many other Etruscan cities, very receptive to Greek culture, Pompeii later became an Oscan town. It prospered on the fertile if, as it finally turned out, perilous lands beneath Mt Vesuvius. Only Romanized properly after Sulla had planted a military colony there in 80BC, Pompeii then expanded further, acquiring a permanent amphitheatre long before Rome did. But at its peak in AD79 its population reached only *c*.15,000, making it quite small even by the standards of the age.

But there was nothing pettily provincial about Pompeii culturally. It not only had all the trappings of a Graeco-Roman city – temples, baths, a forum, elected officials – it also had long been attracting fine artists from around the Greek world. They produced often excellent copies of renowned Hellenistic paintings that decorated royal palaces in Hellenistic kingdoms such as Pergamum. The quality of the murals and mosaics uncovered at Pompeii and nearby Herculaneum are rivalled only by those excavated from Rome's largest houses and palaces.

THE *ALEXANDER MOSAIC*
Grandest of Pompeian paintings is the *Alexander Mosaic*, the most faithful full-size copy of a Greek masterpiece known. This intensely dramatic battle scene was made for a wealthy – and clearly philhellenic – Pompeian around 100BC and displayed in its own special *exedra* (recess) in his mansion, now called the 'House of the Faun'. The picture shows Alexander powering through the fighting towards his opponent, a terrified King Darius, who is about to flee in his chariot. (Whether the battle shown is the Issus in 333BC or Gaugamela two years later remains debated. The same dramatic incident occurred in both.) The mosaic

in Pompeii reproduces an earlier work that was almost certainly a mural due to the generally free style of its painting.

The mosaic meticulously follows the original work's restricted four-colour palette – red, yellow, black and white – employed by many of the greatest Classical artists from Polygnotus to Apelles. The picture uses highlights, deep-cast shadows and recession in depth to heighten its realism. More recent innovations are the three-dimensional modelling in black (of some of the horses) and the extreme foreshortening of a horse right in the centre, whose rear quarters are seen from behind. The reflected face of a fallen Persian in the burnished shield in the centre marks another advance in dramatic realism.

Very large at 2.7 by 5.1m (8ft 10in by 16ft 9in) and ringing with the tumult of battle, the picture rivals in its emotional impact the grandest works by later Renaissance and Baroque masters. Many archaeologists think that the original was painted by Apelles in *c.*328BC, soon after the battle depicted. Others attribute it to Philoxenos of Eretria, another famous artist of Alexander's age.

THE VILLA AT BOSCOREALE

Very different in tone is the cycle of fresco paintings made *c.*50BC for Publius Fannius Synistor, who owned a large villa at Boscoreale just outside Pompeii. These also copy Hellenistic royal pictures painted nearly 200 years earlier. There are five panels, each with one or two static, almost life-size figures. One shows a craggy philosopher leaning on a stick. In another, a woman personifying Asia is seated looking intensely at a pensive man with a shield opposite her, who has been identified as symbolizing a Macedonian king. Another panel shows a draped women in a gold headband playing a golden cithara, with a girl standing behind her high-backed chair, a contrasting scene of domestic tranquillity. The unknown creator of these pieces was clearly a highly adaptable artist.

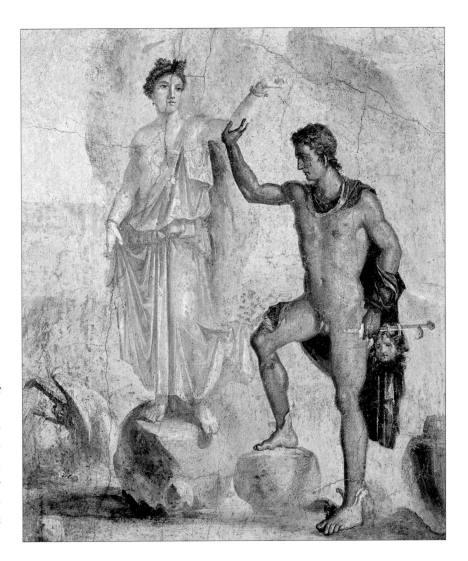

Above: A mural from Pompeii of the 1st century BC *copying an older Hellenistic work. Depicting the hero Perseus, it shows remarkable illusionistic skills.*

Below: This mural of c.*50*BC *from a villa at Pompeii copies a work of* c.*240*BC *for a Macedonian royal palace.*

THE FINDING OF TELEPHUS

From Herculaneum comes one of the finest paintings of antiquity, a copy of *The Finding of Telephus*. The original was made for Eumenes II of Pergamum in *c.*190BC. Telephus was the son of Hercules. Hercules, flanked by the royal lion and eagle, looks down at his son, being suckled by a doe in the foreground. The boy and deer are masterpieces of tenderly depicted realism. Behind the child sits a female figure personifying Arcadia. She is so majestic, massive and calm that she could have been painted by J.A.D. Ingres (1780–1867), the French Neoclassical master.

IDYLLIC LANDSCAPES
THE GRAECO-ROMAN FUSION

Above: Dionysus riding a panther, a mosaic from a rich merchant's house on Delos made c.120BC.

Below: The great Nile Mosaic from Praeneste near Rome decorated a public building. It gives a bird's-eye view of the Nile in flood, with temples, boats and animals, copying a Ptolemaic original of c.100BC.

Landscape painting, seemingly unknown to Classical artists, emerged during the Hellenistic period as often idyllic illustrations of mythical scenes. The genre may have reflected a nostalgia for rural life among people in vast new cities such as Antioch, Alexandria and Rome itself. But it revealed, too, artists' growing skills in suggesting depth and recession, which were at times used to depict cityscapes too. One of the first such scenery painters, generally called *topographoi*, was Demetrius, who worked in Alexandria in the 2nd century BC.

At the Boscoreale Villa near Pompeii the murals of imaginary cities in the main *cubiculum* (bedroom) make superb examples of architectural *trompe l'oeil*. They copy stage scenery from Ephesus painted *c.*150BC and later described by Pliny. Like most original paintings described by writers, the Ephesus works have not survived.

THE ODYSSEY LANDSCAPES
The second more romantic Homeric epic about the wanderings of its homesick hero, *The Odyssey*, was a popular source of stories for painters in the Hellenistic and Roman worlds. (Educated Romans understood Greek.) Unearthed from a house on the Esquiline Hill in Rome in 1848–9, a cycle of eight magnificent murals, painted *c.*50BC but copying earlier Hellenistic work, depicts Odysseus' adventures in sketches done with an almost impressionistic lightness.

The landscapes gain a romantic, indeed menacing air from the huge boulders overshadowing the tiny figures, and from the great vistas of sea and islands opening up beyond them. Such backgrounds add to the drama of the stories. In the first panel Odysseus and his men have innocently arrive in the land of the Laestrygonians. They make inquiries of a graceful woman carrying an amphora descending a path. The tone is pastorally idyllic.

It changes abruptly in the next panels as the Laestrygonians attack Odysseus' men with rocks and trees. The Laestrygonians, who are really cannibals, then destroy many of the Greeks' boats, dragging off the slaughtered Greeks to eat them. Odysseus' ship alone escapes as he sails off with a few companions for Circe's island. Other scenes show Odysseus' descent to the Underworld. The unknown artist radically reduced the size of figures as they recede deeper into the landscape. To identify some of the men dwarfed by the landscape, he helpfully added labels.

THE 'HOUSE OF THE TRAGIC POET'
In the 'House of the Tragic Poet' at Pompeii an unknown painter created a masterpiece in *Achilles and Briseis*, illustrating a scene from *The Iliad*. Achilles smoulders with barely suppressed rage as

Left: From the Villa at Tivoli of the emperor Hadrian (reigned AD117–38) comes this mosaic of drinking doves, a copy of an original made by Sosus of Pergamum in about 150BC. Its realism approaches trompe l'oeil.

Briseis, his favourite slave girl, is forcibly carried off on King Agamemnon's orders. Behind the pitifully weeping figure of Briseis stand a line of threateningly armoured soldiers. The fresco copies a Hellenistic original of *c*.300BC.

In sober, dignified contrast the stucco panel from a villa in Herculaneum shows an exhausted actor resting in his dressing-room. His sceptre and sword indicate that he is playing a royal role. A woman crouches in front of a female tragic mask. (She is not an actress, because men played women's roles in Greek theatre and this painting copies a Greek original of *c*.300BC.) The work may portray the psychological tension between actors' grand roles and their low social status.

MOSAICS EAST AND WEST

The art of mosaic continued to develop, being carried west to Italy. In Delos, booming after Rome made it a tax-free port in 166BC, wealthy Roman or Italian merchants commissioned fine mosaics for their luxurious houses. One of the most striking comes from the 'House of Dionysus', named after its vibrantly

coloured mosaic made *c*.120BC. It shows the wine-god on a panther, looking debauched and riding curiously side-saddle. His panther or leopard snarls with feral power, its claws painted with almost alarming realism.

Approximately contemporary is the great *Nile Mosaic* from Praeneste (Palestrina) near Rome made to decorate the apse of a public building. It shows a bird's-eye view of the Nile in flood, with temples, boats, soldiers and animals. Everything is teeming with life and colour. It probably copies a Ptolemaic royal original, but makes no attempt at using perspective.

From the Villa at Tivoli of Hadrian, that most philhellenic of Roman emperors (reigned AD117–38), comes a brilliant copy of a mosaic by Sosus of Pergamum, originally made *c*.150BC. It shows doves drinking from a burnished bowl, whose surface is disturbed by the beak of one sipping bird. This marvel of realism marks the climax of Graeco-Roman cultural fusion as the Roman empire itself passed through its zenith.

Below: From the 'House of the Tragic Poet' at Pompeii comes an anonymous masterpiece illustrating a scene from The Iliad. *It copies a Hellenistic original of* c.300BC.

PART TWO

GREEK SOCIETY

The Greeks were the pioneers in so many fields – athletics, astronomy, biology, philosophy, theatre, geography, medicine among others – that it is easy to take them for granted, to see their achievements as simply part of the human make-up. But what makes us *modern* today frequently stems from the Greek experience. With the Greeks, Western literature began on an unparalleled high with Homer, still being translated anew today. With the Greeks, Western medicine, with its Hippocratic oath, began, as did Western theatre (and so, by extension, cinema). With the Greeks, formal mathematics, astronomy and geography emerged for the first time. Competitive sport, too, first sprang up in recognizable form in ancient Greece.

The Greeks were not omniscient or infallible. In early years they borrowed what they needed from their older, often richer neighbours. They were certainly not the richest or most powerful people in the ancient world, but they influenced those who were, including the Romans later. Greek life, which centred on the *polis*, the often tiny city-state, was simple but lived with passionate vigour in a spirit of keenest competition. "Nothing in excess", the god Apollo's famous maxim, was needed in a turbulent world in which men often sought everything in excess. The Greek world had its dark sides. Women were excluded, at least in the Classical period, from all public life. And male citizens' frugal leisure depended on the labour of slaves, whose status was seldom questioned even by philosophers. But women and slaves were no freer in many comparable societies, at the time or later, that have never begun to rival the Greeks' contribution to human achievements in so many spheres.

Left: The 4th-century BC theatre at Epidaurus. The Greeks created the world's first true drama, for Greek plays are still performed in theatres to this day.

CHAPTER VII

RELIGION AND MYTHOLOGY

For the Greeks, the world was filled with gods and mythical beings. Greek religion underlay all society to a degree unimaginable today in the West, but it was very different from monotheistic faiths. As polytheists, the Greeks revered many different gods. To the Olympian deities worshipped by the polis, newer gods were often added. Greek gods were anthropomorphic – having human forms, faces, virtues and foibles – even when they personified natural forces such as the sun (*helios*).

If perfect in form, most gods were far from perfect in behaviour. Homer and Hesiod, whose poems shaped Greek views of the pantheon, recounted the gods' amorous, sometimes dishonest, exploits. This divine amorality later upset philosophers but hardly worried ordinary Greeks. Religion was not a matter of dogma or revealed truth, but of the correct rites performed in public. Gods had to be honoured and placated, usually by sacrifices, or the whole polis could suffer. The gap between gods and men was not wholly unbridgeable, as the cult of the heroes (semi-divine beings) reveals. Alexander the Great was worshipped as a god even in his lifetime. Greek religion flowed into myth, but *mythos* meant not 'falsehood' but 'story' or 'tale'. Greek mythology remains among the world's richest, open to many interpretations.

Left: Three of the principal Olympian deities – Poseidon, Apollo and Artemis – from the Parthenon in Athens.

THE TWELVE OLYMPIANS

Above: The wedding of Zeus, king of the gods, to Hera, queen of heaven, guardian of marriage and an often murderously jealous wife, 470BC.

Below: Zeus and Thetis, memorably painted by the 19th-century French artist Ingres. Zeus, always highly susceptible to female charms, is being urged by the sea-nymph Thetis to help her son Achilles in the Trojan War.

The cloud-capped peak of Mt Olympus, Greece's highest mountain, was the mythical home of the Twelve Olympians. Here the deities feasted, drank and slept with each other – or with mortals abducted from below – in palaces built by Hephaestus, the blacksmith god. Although Zeus, the thunder-wielding king of the gods, was their acknowledged lord, they were a querulous brood. In this they fittingly resembled the Greeks quarrelling and fighting on earth.

The Olympians, often called sky-gods, because they roamed through the skies (although Poseidon lived in the sea) were probably introduced by Indo-European invaders who over-ran the Aegean world c.2000BC. Tablets in early Mycenaean Greek of c.1200BC seem to show that some of the Olympians, including Zeus, Poseidon and Hera, were already being worshipped in the Late Bronze Age.

However these divine newcomers seldom displaced the older deities totally. Some of the latter were *chthonic* gods, living beneath the earth. As the myths vaguely indicate, the Olympian deities soon became the unchallenged rulers of the heavens but not always of the earth. Paganism's basic tendency anyway was to incorporate other gods into the pantheon, not to exclude them.

THE 'INHERITED CONGLOMERATE'

This inclusive tendency produced what has been called the 'inherited conglomerate', with cults superimposed on each other. Such an elastic pantheon suited popular and official needs remarkably well. Gods had different titles, depending partly on their locality but chiefly on their function.

Athena, patron goddess of Athens, was called Promachos (warrior) when depicted as a warrior outside on the

---

GREEK AND LATIN NAMES

Greek gods today are often known by their Latin names in Western countries, for the Romans came to equate their deities with the Greek ones. Below on the right are the Roman names for the most common Greek gods.

Aphrodite	Venus
Ares	Mars
Artemis	Diana
Athena	Minerva
Demeter	Ceres
Dionysus	Bacchus
Eros	Cupid
Hades	Pluto
Hephaestus	Vulcan
Helios	Sol
Hera	Juno
Hermes	Mercury
Pan	Faunus
Persephone	Proserpine
Poseidon	Neptune
Zeus	Jupiter

(Apollo and Orpheus had the same names in both Latin and Greek.)

Acropolis but Parthenos (virgin) inside the Parthenon. Hera, Zeus' wife, was similarly patron goddess of Argos. All Greeks revered Zeus, one of whose many titles was Panhellenios (god of all the Greeks). Another was Horkios (oath-keeper). For the king of the gods, who was a gentleman despite his repeated lechery, always insisted on the sanctity of oaths.

SACRIFICES AND ALTARS

In large cities such as Athens most important gods had their own temples, shrines and altars, but in a small city such as Priene in Ionia there might be only two or three shrines. Individuals chose a god for their particular purpose at the time,

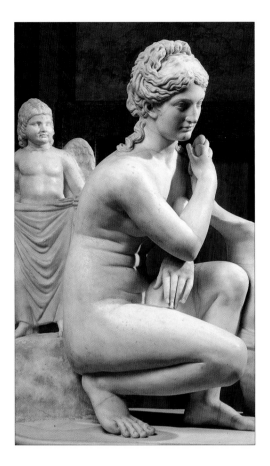

OTHER GODS

If the Olympians were the city's official gods, honoured in great festivals, other gods or cults offered individuals personal consolations. Among these was salvation beyond the grave, for mainstream religion promised no afterlife worth the name. The Orphics and the Eleusinian Mysteries were the chief mystery religions, the details of which remain to this day mysterious. But Greek religion was generally concerned with this life, not the next. Typifying Greek this-worldly attitudes were the *herms* – phallic fertility figures that stood outside many people's homes.

A god of another type was the rustic Pan, originally the god of Arcadian shepherds who became increasingly popular in Athens and several other large cities. Dionysus, only a minor god in Homer, grew during the 6th century BC into a major deity. He was patron of the newly emerging theatre, and his cult offered ecstatic and rare release to women. Otherwise much repressed, they could run wild on the mountainside every spring.

Such bacchic ecstasy was exceptional. But religion was usually a cause for celebration, be it solemn for a great deity such as Athena or Zeus, or ribald for a minor rustic god such as Pan or Dionysus in his less awesome aspects as the god of wine.

but whole cities were involved in their collective public festivals. These were as much civic as religious rites.

Of these the Panathenaea, a religious festival honouring Athena, is the most famous and became the grandest. Religious rites centred on prayers – made standing up, not kneeling – libations (offerings of wine) and sacrifices. This involved domestic animals from cockerels to bulls, but only rarely fish or game and never human beings. (Even in myth, human sacrifice was always considered an abomination by the Greeks.) Bloodless offerings – the first fruits, grains, cakes and cheese – were acceptable from poorer citizens who could not afford even a cockerel. For them, public sacrifices meant a chance to eat meat, which was a luxury for most Greeks.

The altar was the focus of worship, assuming grandiose architectural forms in rich cities like Syracuse or Pergamum. The temple itself, which housed the god's statue in holy gloom, was less important if architecturally striking. Some country shrines never had a temple.

Left: Aphrodite, the love-goddess, emerging from her bath attended by Eros, god of desire. According to Homer, she was the daughter of Zeus, but Hesiod gave a gory picture of her origins. This is a Roman copy of the bronze by the 3rd-century BC sculptor Doidalsas of Bithynia.

Below: A Roman copy of a statue of Artemis. The virginal hunter-goddess roaming the woods was associated with wild animals and girls' transition to womanhood.

ZEUS, HERA AND ATHENA
THE OLYMPIAN ROYAL FAMILY

*Above: A copy of Pheidias'
giant chryselephantine statue
of Athena that stood inside the
Athenian Parthenon. Goddess
of wisdom, the arts and crafts,
she was the patron goddess of
Athens but was worshipped
in many other Greek cities.*

Three deities made up the 'royal family'
of Olympus: Zeus, king of the gods; his
consort Hera, goddess of marriage; and
Athena, born directly from his head, goddess of the arts, wisdom and handicrafts.

ZEUS
The archetypal skyfather, whose name
echoes that of Sanskrit Dyaus-Pita and
Latin Jupiter, Zeus was the supreme ruler
of gods and mortals, almost omnipotent.
Embodying power, wisdom and majesty,
he lived on Mt Olympus, from which his
thunderbolts might blast his enemies.
Zeus was also the father of justice and
mercy, hailed as *Xenios*, protector of
strangers and ultimate guarantor of law,
human and divine. His own record was,
however, no model of good behaviour.

The youngest son of Cronus (Saturn)
who had devoured his older children
fearing that they would usurp him, Zeus
was hidden by his mother Rhea on Mt Ida

*Above: Hera, patron goddess of Samos,
shaking hands with Athena, a carving made
in 403BC to celebrate the loyalty of the island
of Samos to Athens even in her defeat. At
Samos, the Heraion, the goddess' temple,
was one of the greatest in the Greek world.*

in Crete. There he was brought up by
nymphs. Later, Zeus made his father
vomit up his siblings, then deposed him,
crushed the giant Titans and established
his own rule. He divided the world with
his brothers, Poseidon taking the ocean
and Hades the underworld. Zeus married
Hera, who was his sister, but he
constantly seduced women, both divine
and mortal, fathering many children.

ZEUS' CONQUESTS
Among his conquests were Leto, mother
of Apollo and Artemis; Europa, whom he
seduced in the form of a bull, producing
Minos of Crete; Danae, to whom he
appeared as a shower of gold; Leda,

*Left: Reconstruction of the massive statue
of Zeus made by Pheidias that was once
housed in the Temple of Zeus at Olympia.*

whom he seduced as a swan, fathering Helen, whose incomparable beauty started the Trojan War; Semele, who was burnt up by Zeus revealing himself in his full glory, but whose baby Dionysus was saved; and (with Zeus in the form of an eagle) Ganymede, a beautiful Trojan princeling, who became his catamite and was cup-bearer to the gods on Olympus.

Zeus was worshipped at sites throughout Greece, especially at Olympia in the Peloponnese, where the games were held in his honour. A giant chryselephantine (gold/ivory) image of Zeus by Pheidias filled Olympia's main temple. Dodona in Epirus in the north was another major sanctuary of Zeus, famed for its oracle, which Alexander and the future emperor Augustus consulted. Some poets and playwrights spoke of Zeus in tones of almost monotheistic awe, overlooking the god's more picaresque exploits.

HERA

The sister and unwilling wife of Zeus, Hera was portrayed as enthroned beside him, the queen of Olympus, majestic rather than beautiful. She often wore a triple crown, which reveals her links with the pre-Greek Great Goddess, and was accompanied by a peacock. Her temper was famously fiery – understandably so, considering Zeus' endless love affairs. Hera did not take these calmly, constantly threatening the lives of Zeus' mistresses.

At one stage Zeus, in exasperation, hung his wife upside down from Mt Olympus. But usually Hera held her own, intervening to great effect against the Trojans in war after Prince Paris had snubbed her.

Hera was the mother of Ares, the irascible war-god, and Hephaestus, the ingenious blacksmith of Olympus. Widely revered as the goddess of childbirth and marriage, Hera was particularly honoured in Argos and on the island of Samos, where one of the largest of all Greek temples was built in her honour.

ATHENA

Born fully formed from Zeus' forehead, Athena Parthenos, the Maiden, was Zeus' most brilliant child. She was often shown with shield and spear as a warrior-goddess (*Promachos*) in Athens, whose patron she became after winning a contest with Poseidon. He had offered a spring, while she produced an olive tree, symbol of peace and plenty. Athena was goddess of wisdom, learning and the arts, but she inherited her father's pride. She intervened actively on the Achaean side in the Trojan War after being spurned by Paris, who preferred the erotic Aphrodite to her own chilly beauty. Often shown with the chthonic earth snake coiled beside her and an owl symbolizing wisdom, she also sported the hideous snake-haired aegis of Medusa, whom her protégé Perseus had slain.

The Athenians celebrated Athena as the personification of their city at their great Panathenaic Festival, but she was also worshipped in many other places. At Syracuse in Sicily a particularly fine Doric temple to Athena survives inside the existing cathedral.

Left: Reconstruction of the huge statue of Athena that once stood in the Parthenon.

Below: A statue of Zeus made in Pergamum in the 2nd century AD during the Roman Empire, copying a presumed Greek original.

APOLLO AND ARTEMIS
THE TWINS OF DELOS

Apollo and Artemis were twins, born on Delos. Their father was Zeus, their mother Leto, a titaness driven by Hera's jealousy to hide on the island. The twins proved to be very different deities.

APOLLO

Apollo is the archetypal Greek god, epitomizing reason and civilization. Called Phoebus (bright/radiant), he was later identified with the sun-god Helios. But he had many titles and attributes, including Lysios, deliverer, for he was generally a beneficent deity. Typically he was portrayed as a noble, handsome, beardless young man. His cult, very strong in Sparta, spread across the Greek world and beyond, both the Etruscans and Romans welcoming him into their pantheons. Augustus built a temple to Apollo near his palace on the Palatine in Rome.

Fed with divine nectar, Apollo when only four days old strangled (or tamed) the serpent Pytho attacking his mother. He renamed the site of the attack Delphi. It became his principal shrine, its fame surpassing even that of Delos. The serpent itself became the Pythoness priestess, uttering prophecies. For Apollo was the god of prophecy, although the answers his oracle gave were famously obscure. His own motto was "Know thyself" (*gnosi seauton*), which Socrates took to heart. Apollo's other famous injunction was "Nothing in excess", a warning few Greeks heeded. Apollo promised another oracle, the Sibyl of Cumae in Italy, immortality if she loved him. When she rejected his advances, he damned her with eternal life but not youth, for she aged horribly through the centuries.

Apollo was the god of science, medicine, music and poetry. He is often shown with his lyre or bow, being called 'far-shooting'. Every winter Apollo went north to the land of the Hyperboreans, returning with spring in a gold chariot drawn by swans or griffins. Apollo's calm, remote yet sometimes perilous divinity is illustrated by his contest with Marsyas, a satyr proud of his flute-playing who rashly competed with the god of music. Judged the loser by the muses, Marsyas was tied to a tree and flayed alive.

APOLLO'S LOVE AFFAIRS

Apollo had many, sometimes unhappy love affairs, most notably with Daphne, a nymph and daughter of the river-god

Above: Apollo, god of medicine, prophecy, science and poetry, was often portrayed naked, like most male gods, as in this rare original bronze of c.490BC.

Right: The Apollo of the Tiber *showed the god as perfectly proportioned and almost dreamily aloof. This is a marble copy of the Greek original by the Athenian sculptor Pheidias.*

THE NINE MUSES

Apollo was at times called Apollo Musagetes (Apollo of the Muses). Seated on Mt Parnassus above Delphi by the Castalian spring of inspiration, he was shown flanked by the muses. Daughters of Zeus and Mnemosymene, these nine goddesses of poetic inspiration had, according to Hesiod, been begotten on nine successive nights. They are with their respective arts: Calliope (epic poetry); Clio (history); Erato (lyric and love poetry); Euterpe (music); Melpomene (tragedy); Polyhymnia (heroic hymns); Terpsichore (dancing); Thalia (comedy, pastoral poetry); and Urania (astronomy).

Peneus. Apollo pursued her passionately but in vain, for she prayed to her father who turned her into a laurel tree just as the god was grasping her. Another lover was the princess Coronis. When Apollo discovered she had left him, he killed her with an arrow, repenting of his anger too late. Their son Asclepius, saved by the centaur Chiron, grew up to be a divine healer. Apollo also loved Hyacinthus, a beautiful young Spartan prince, whom he taught to throw the discus. When Hyacinthus was killed by a flying discus, the hyacinth flower first sprang from the ground where his blood fell.

ARTEMIS

Apollo's twin sister, Artemis (Diana), was a paradoxical goddess. In one avatar she was the chaste hunting-goddess of the woods carrying a bow, attended by nymphs (ever-youthful and divine) whom she swore to celibacy. When a nymph Callisto, succumbing to Zeus' advances, became pregnant, Artemis changed Callisto into a bear and let the hunt dogs savage her. The hunter Actaeon, surprising Artemis and her nymphs bathing, was transformed into a stag and killed by his own hounds. As a hunting-goddess, Artemis is portrayed as tall and slim in a short skirt and carrying a bow. She had a chariot drawn by stags in this virginal woodland guise.

But Artemis was also revered as the many-breasted fertility goddess worshipped in her great temple at Ephesus, whose cult St Paul later attacked. Here she revealed a far older Asian ancestry, as the mother-goddess and Mistress of the Animals. In Classical times she presided over women's changes, most notably their transition from virgin (*parthenos*) to married woman (*gyne*). Artemis was later identified with the moon-goddess Selene, for a crescent moon was one of her symbols. The Spartans revered her as Artemis Orthia, connected with their *agoge*, their brutal education. Boys were ritually beaten at her altar in Sparta's savage initiation rites.

Below: Apollo fell in love with Daphne, but she escaped him by turning into a laurel tree. This dramatic sculpture is by Bernini (1598–1680).

POSEIDON, HERMES AND ARES

The other major Olympian gods had less in common with each other but all were larger-than-life in their power, splendour and, very often, their anger.

POSEIDON

One of Zeus' older brothers, Poseidon was swallowed by his paranoid father Cronus and then regurgitated. He fought alongside Zeus against the Titans. Subsequently allotted the sea as his realm, he ruled it with his trident, riding through the waves in a chariot drawn by *hippocampi* (sea-horses) and dolphins. Poseidon had non-marine attributes too, as the god of horses, earthquakes and springs. Like his brother, he was normally portrayed as a powerfully built, bearded older man. Like the sea, he was given to unpredictable rages. Sailors and fishermen prayed to him for a safe voyage – hence the great temple to Poseidon on Cape Sunium, visible for miles – with rich sailors sacrificing a horse. In Mycenaean times he may have been more important than Zeus, judging by tablets from Pylos, but in Classical times he was inferior to his brother.

Homer calls him *enosichthon* (earth-shaker), a potent epithet in a land as seismically active as Greece. Poseidon, who hated Odysseus for blinding his son the Cyclops Polyphemus, sealed off the port of the Phaecians with massive rockfalls for helping the wanderer. Failing to win Athens' affections in a contest with Athena, he flooded half Attica in revenge, for he was a vengeful god.

His love life was happier than many gods'. He successfully courted the Nereid (sea nymph) Amphitrite. He had seen her dancing with her sisters on Naxos when she had run away from him in alarm, but he sent dolphins to persuade her to accept him. Amphitrite then became his aquatic consort, riding beside his chariot on a dolphin or in a cockle-shell drawn by dolphins, with a retinue of other Nereids and Tritons (mermen). He rescued Amymone, a Danaid, one of the 50 daughters of King Danaeus of Argos, from a satyr pursuing her. The Isthmian Games, one of the most important in the Greek calendar, were sacred to Poseidon.

HERMES

One of the Twelve Olympians, a son of Zeus, Hermes was the eloquent messenger-god, young, graceful and swift-footed, memorably depicted by Praxiteles. Born

Above: Poseidon was Zeus' brother and a formidable god, as this bronze of the 6th century BC suggests.

Below: Poseidon, god of the sea, rides through the waves in a chariot drawn by hippocampi (sea-horses) and dolphins. From a late 2nd-century AD Roman mosaic at La Chebba, Tunisia.

Above: Hermes was the ingenious messenger-god, ferrying messages from Mt Olympus to mortals. He was also the god of shepherds, here shown as a kriophoros (carrying a ram).

Left: Aphrodite, goddess of love, fell in love with Ares and they had a passionate affair – until Hephaestus, her jealous husband, trapped them in an iron net. This mural comes from Pompeii.

Below: Ares, god of war, as depicted in this statue copying an original by Polyclitus of the 5th century BC. Ares was one of the lesser Olympians, more irascible than formidable.

to the nymph Maia in a cave in Arcadia, he was only hours old when he stole some cattle belonging to his half-brother Apollo. He managed this thanks to his divine winged sandals. By his quick wit and the timely gift of the lyre that he had invented, Hermes then saved himself from Apollo's wrath. He normally wore a broad-rimmed winged hat and carried a magic wand with two snakes entwined round it that could send people to sleep.

His ingenuity led him to be regarded as the inventor of many things, among them the alphabet, numbers and weights and measures, while his eloquence made him the patron of merchants and of thieves. As *diactoros* (messenger-god), he was constantly ferrying messages from Olympus down to earth, and he went farther down still. As *psychopompos* he led the souls of the dead down to Charon, the boatman to Hades. As the patron god of travellers, herms were set up in his honour on doors and road posts, while as *agonios* he presided over games. The Roman god Mercury took on many of his attributes.

ARES

Even his parents, Hera and Zeus, disliked Ares, the irascible red-haired god of war. The other Olympians generally shunned him too. Attended by his sons Phobos (terror) and Deimos (fear), Ares roamed the battlefields in a chariot, killing for pleasure. He was seldom victorious on the battlefield, often being outwitted by Athena or by heroes like Hercules. Nor was Ares luckier in love, with one notable exception: Aphrodite, unwillingly married to the blacksmith god Hephaestus, fell for the dashing war-god and slept with him. But their affair proved brief, for Hephaestus forged a net, which he dropped over the sleeping lovers. Ares traditionally was of Thracian origin. Despite the fact that the Greeks were often at war, and that the Areopagus, the hill facing the Acropolis in Athens, was named after him, Ares' cult was insignificant outside Thebes. But he often received sacrifices on the battlefield.

APHRODITE, EROS AND HEPHAESTUS

Above: Aphrodite, the divine embodiment of beauty and desire, here kneeling with her long hair in her hands as if she has just been bathing.

Below: Aphrodite was, according to Hesiod, born from the foam (aphros). Emerging perfectly beautiful, she was blown to land on a seashell by zephyrs, and there attended by the Horae. The myth was sublimely painted by Botticelli in c.1486.

No two deities have been less alike than Aphrodite, the beautiful goddess of love, and Hephaestus, the lame blacksmith, yet they married each other. It did not prove a match made in heaven, nor one blessed by Eros, the god of erotic love.

APHRODITE
The goddess Aphrodite, who embodied beauty, glamour and erotic allure, had disconcertingly foul origins, according to Hesiod. She was born from the foam (*aphros*) bubbling around the severed genitals of Uranus that Cronus had thrown into the sea after castrating his father. Emerging radiantly beautiful, Aphrodite was blown ashore on a seashell by zephyrs, landing at Paphos on Cyprus, which became a centre of her worship. There she was attended by three goddesses known as the Horae ('hours'), who adorned her divine nudity with jewellery and fine clothing. But Homer thought that she was simply – and more honorably – the daughter of Zeus and the minor goddess Dione.

Whatever her genesis, Aphrodite was the most desired deity on Olympus, a source of potential strife, as Zeus soon realized. He accordingly married her off to the sober Hephaestus, who made lavish jewels for her, including a magic gold girdle. But the pleasure-loving goddess, soon bored with being the wife of the industrious blacksmith god, had an affair with Ares and later with many others, both mortal and divine.

APHRODITE'S LOVE LIFE
Among her lovers was Adonis, in Greek myth the offspring of the incestuous union of King Cinyras of Paphos with his daughter Myrrha. Aphrodite fell in love with the handsome youth, but Adonis, a passionate hunter, was killed by a wild boar. Where his blood fell to earth, anemones sprouted.

Of greater legendary importance was her affair with the Trojan prince Anchises. Aeneas was their son, the Trojan who escaped from burning Troy and who, after many vicissitudes, landed in Latium to found the precursor of Rome. Julius Caesar and his imperial heirs claimed descent from Aeneas and so from the goddess.

Aphrodite won the fatal beauty contest of the Judgement of Paris. Hera, Athena and Aphrodite paraded before the dashing Trojan prince. The first two

---

EROS, GOD OF DESIRE

The god of desire, Eros, was the son of Hermes (or Zeus) and Aphrodite, whom he often accompanied. Shown as a boy with a bow that shot arrows of desire at his victims, Eros was thought a dangerous deity, sexual passion being considered more a sickness than a joy. Homer did not regard Eros as a proper god, but later poets such as Sappho recognized his 'bitter-sweet' powers. In contrast, Plato saw erotic desire as potentially helping to power the soul in its ascent towards the impersonal Good.

offered him respectively glory and victory but Aphrodite offered love. Paris chose love and later eloped with Helen, queen of Sparta. So started the Trojan War, in which Aphrodite provided feeble support for the Trojans, unlike Hera and Athena who vigorously helped the Greeks.

Aphrodite in origin was related to Babylonian Ishtar and Syrian Astarte, fertility goddesses, but her worship spread around the Mediterranean in Hellenized form. Aphrodite's attributes are the dove, swan and pomegranate. Besides her shrine at Paphos, she was especially worshipped at Cythera, Eryx in Sicily and at Corinth, where her devotees reputedly prostituted themselves in her temple precincts.

HEPHAESTUS

The god of fire and metal-forging, Hephaestus, could be considered the odd god out among the Olympians, being lame and ugly. His lameness came from intervening in a quarrel between his parents

Zeus and Hera, who threw him from Olympus. Falling into the sea, he was rescued by Thetis, a sea-nymph. In revenge he devised a gold throne for Hera that trapped her. Only Dionysus could persuade him to leave the sea's depths and free his mother.

In return, Hephaestus demanded the hand of Aphrodite, loveliest of goddesses. When she fell in love with Ares, the dim war-god, Hephaestus was madly jealous. He secretly forged a net of gossamer-light iron that he draped over the sleeping adulterers. They awoke trapped in it as the other Olympians gathered to laugh at them.

More usually, however, Hephaestus was kept busy at his furnace, sited beneath Mt Etna in Sicily or on Stromboli island – both active volcanoes, his Latin name being Vulcan. He built palaces for the other gods and made Achilles a magnificent shield and some armour, so memorably described by Homer, at the request of Achilles' mother Thetis. Although Hephaestus was not the most popular Olympian, the best-surviving temple in Greece is the Hephaestion on the Athenian Agora.

Above: Aphrodite emerging from the sea attended by the Horae in an Ionian carving from the early 5th century BC.

Below: Hephaestus, the stocky god of fire and metal-forging.

Left: 5th-century BC *amphora showing the god of sexual desire. Eros was often shown shooting arrows of desire at his victims. He was thought to be a more dangerous than delightful deity.*

DIONYSUS
THE TRANSGRESSIVE OLYMPIAN

Above: Krater showing Dionysus as an effeminate youth holding a thyrsus, a wand tipped with a pine cone.

Below: Dionysus rescuing Ariadne, abandoned on the island of Naxos, lavishly painted by Titian in 1523.

Homer hardly mentioned Dionysus, although the god's name appears on some Mycenaean tablets. But in the 6th century BC the god of wine, drama and ecstasy became one of the most important in the Greek pantheon, playing a major role in public festivals. Dionysus also offered a rare release for Greek women. One of his epithets was *eleutherios*, the liberator, for his great invention, wine, dissolved social bonds.

Dionysus thus stood in marked contrast to aristocratic Homeric gods. One of his names, Bacchus (his Roman name) was Lydian but he was no foreigner in Greece. In legend, Dionysus was the son of Zeus and Semele, a Theban princess. Urged by ever-jealous Hera, Semele rashly asked Zeus to reveal himself in his glory. When Zeus did so, she was incinerated by his intolerably manifest godhead. Zeus rescued the child she was carrying and

---

BACCHAE AND MAENADS
One of the most distinctive aspects of Dionysus' cult was the wild behaviour of his (mostly) female followers. Freed briefly from domestic drudgery, Greek housewives left the city for the mountains and woods to participate in Dionysiac *orgia* (secret rites or mysteries). What exactly happened in these orgies remains unclear. According to Euripides, still our best source, women known as Bacchantes got drunk and roamed the hills. Attacking wild animals with their bare hands, they daubed themselves with the blood, putting on skins torn from the still-warm beasts. In doing so they became like Maenads, Dionysus' ecstatically intoxicated worshippers. Any man who met them in their divine madness might suffer the horrifying fate of Pentheus, who was dismembered by his own raving mother.

Dionysus was brought up by nymphs on Mt Nysa, taught by satyrs and Maenads how to make wine. When he had recovered from a fit of madness sent by Hera, he set off for India in a chariot drawn by leopards, making laws, planting vineyards, founding cities. Reurning, he married Ariadne, abandoned by Theseus on the island of Naxos. Dionysus could be a benevolent, consoling god to those who acknowledged him. To those who did not, he could be lethal, as Euripides demonstrates in his last play, *The Bacchae*.

DIONYSUS IN THEBES
When Dionysus returned from India to his native Thebes, he was welcomed by the city's people but not by its puritanical king Pentheus. The king locked up this effeminate-looking youth whose orgiastic rites affronted him. But the god mocked the

Right: Pompeii fresco of Dionysus' keenest followers, the Maenads, women intoxicated by his worship and wine who took part in secret orgia, *ecstatic rites held outside the city.*

uptight king, but sacred ivy burst through the prison walls to free him. Then Pentheus, demented by Dionysus, dressed up as a woman to spy on the Bacchantes, the god's drunk followers celebrating on the mountains. Among them was the king's mother Agave. Also maddened by the god, Agave saw in her son a wild animal and tore him to shreds.

The moral of *The Bacchae* was that Dionysus, incarnating the forces of nature, was as unstoppable as the rising sap or melting snows. His attributes were the *thyrsus* (wand), ivy, snakes, panthers, tigers and leopards, beautiful but dangerous creatures. Usually portrayed beardless and long-haired, he was a transgressive deity, dissolving boundaries – between male and female, animal and human, man and god, one individual and the next – in mass intoxication. On Olympus, Dionysus always remained an outsider.

GOD OF THE THEATRE
Dionysus became the god of Greek theatre in the 6th century BC. Theatre started as stylized re-enactments of the god's life and death on stage. It developed into wide-ranging but still (usually) legend-based dramas. Encouraged by the Pisistratid rulers of Athens, this led after 500BC to the world's first true tragedy. Athens' three greatest playwrights, Aeschylus, Sophocles and Euripides, raised tragedy to unsurpassed heights.

There were two festivals of Dionysus in Athens. The rural Dionysia was held annually in December, a jovial procession behind a giant phallus, followed by theatrical competitions. The main event was the Greater Dionysia held in the city late in March. On this grand public holiday, the god's statue was carried in a procession to his temple on the southern Acropolis where bulls were sacrificed. Four days of dramatic competition

followed, with tragedies, comedies and satyr plays. Each playwright presented one new work in each genre, the winner receiving a crown of ivy. As patron of Athenian drama, Dionysus must rank among humanity's most beneficial deities.

Below: This mosaic from Delos shows Dionysus riding a leopard and dressed seemingly in drag, suggesting both his wildness and his sexual ambiguity.

MYSTERY CULTS
ORPHICS AND PYTHAGOREANS

Official Greek religion lacked two things central to many religions: a belief in the afterlife and a body of sacred writings. In the 6th century BC two mystery cults, the Orphics and Pythagoreans, emerged to half-fill these gaps with private rituals and beliefs. The latter derived from a real man, the former from a mythical figure, the archetypal poet. Both preached vegetarianism and personal immortality, influencing Platonism, Neoplatonism and finally Christianity.

ORPHEUS

Considered by Greeks as their first poet, Orpheus predates even Homer. Mycenaean frescoes from Pylos of c.1250BC depict an Orpheus-like figure; Pindar around 480BC called Orpheus the "father of song". Orpheus was credited with inventing the lyre, inspired by Apollo, his father. His mother was the muse of poetry Calliope. Some Theogonies (creation myths) attributed

Above: Orpheus Mourning Eurydice, *a painting by Gustave Moreau of 1875 showing the poet lamenting the loss of his beloved wife.*

Below: Orpheus charming *the wild beasts with the magic of his lyre, from a mosaic at Tarsus. Orpheus became and remains the archetypal poet.*

to him show Hesiod's influence, but the oldest extant full poems date only from after 400BC.

In legend Orpheus was born in Thrace, a land of wild mysteries to Greeks. Apollo endowed the budding poet with magical powers so that the music he played on his seven-stringed lyre entranced wild animals, who gathered around him to listen. His music could even move rocks and trees and divert rivers. Like other divine heroes, Orpheus fostered the arts of civilization, including agriculture, which he had learnt in Egypt. Although he accompanied the Argonauts on their quest for the Golden Fleece, his music lulling the Sirens and refloating their ship, he generally avoided war, unlike most heroes.

Orpheus fell in love with the nymph Eurydice, but their joy together was short-lived. Eurydice, chased by Aristaeus who had tried to rape her, was bitten by a snake and died. Overwhelmed with grief, Orpheus descended to the underworld. There his music so charmed Hades, king of the dead, that he was allowed to lead Eurydice back to the living – provided he did not look back at her until regaining the upper world. But Orpheus turned to look at his beloved at the last moment, and she was doomed.

After her final death, Orpheus lost all interest in women, preferring boys or, in most accounts, celibacy. This so outraged the Maenads, Dionysus' followers, that they tore him to pieces. His dismembered head, thrown into the River Strymon, floated, still singing, on the seas to Lesbos, where it later became revered as an oracle. Orpheus himself was then reincarnated as a swan.

THE CULT OF ORPHISM

Orphism as a cult spread around the Greek world, but it often had a dubious reputation, probably due to its secretiveness.

(Plato in *Republic* dismissed its contemporary peddlers as spiritual quacks.) Orphics believed that the soul existed separately from the body. Of divine origin, it could best return to the godhead through ascetic practices such as celibacy and vegetarianism. Some tablets recently unearthed give very detailed instructions on how to cope with trials in the afterlife.

PYTHAGOREANISM

Pythagoras was the first man actually to be termed a 'philosopher'. He was also the founder of an esoteric mystical cult of which very little is known. (None of his writings survive.) This second aspect was the more important during and after his lifetime, for adherents to his secretive cult wielded real political power in southern Italy. Pythagoras had fled there in *c.*532BC to escape Polycrates' tyranny in Samos.

Pythagoreans believed in the magic of numbers, which, manifested in music, governed the universe. Such a concept appealed to the Greeks. Pythagoreans also believed in reincarnation, even as animals. They were vegetarians, aiming to liberate the soul from the body in progressive re-embodiments. The religious community Pythagoras founded at Croton was open

to men and women, then very unusual. Among its many odd taboos were prohibitions on eating beans.

Pythagoreanism died out or merged with Platonism after the rule of the Pythagorean Archytas at Taranto in the 4th century BC. Under the Romans the cult revived in a magical form as Neopythagoreanism. Apollonius of Tyana, born *c.*4BC, was a noted Neopythagorean who reputedly visited India. His life of miracle-working resembles that of Jesus.

Above: Pythagoreans hymning the rising sun from a 19th-century painting by Russian artist F.A. Bronnikov. Adherents of Pythagoras' mystical philosophy were vegetarians who believed in reincarnation. Pythagoreans wielded great political power in southern Italy in the early 4th century BC.

Left: Orpheus, the son of Apollo, was credited with inventing the lyre and being a wonder-working ascetic from the legendary past. His followers regarded his reputed poetry, much of which actually dates from the 5th century BC, as holding cosmic secrets. From a painting of 1618 by the Italian Marcello Provenzale.

HADES AND PERSEPHONE
GODS OF THE UNDERWORLD

Above: Demeter, Persephone and Triptolemus in a relief of the 5th century BC. Triptolemus was a prince of Eleusis to whom the goddess Demeter and her daughter Persephone, the unhappy queen of the underworld, revealed their mysteries.

In the three-part division of the universe that Zeus made with his brothers after they helped him to power, Hades seemingly came off worst. He got only the underworld. But what his infernal realm lacked in appeal, it made up for in horrific power. Hades, the underworld which took its ruler's name, was mentioned by the living only with huge reluctance. Hades himself was also known as Pluto, meaning wealthy, because he owned the earth's precious metals. He also grew rich on the misery of the dead, as Sophocles said. But Hades was a dim passive ruler, not an actively malevolent being.

Most Greeks anticipated a colourless, bloodless afterlife in Hades, as if in a particularly dismal retirement home. While only the notoriously wicked were actually punished by being imprisoned in Tartarus in one corner, very few even among the heroes were allowed into the delightful Elysian Fields in another area. When in *The Odyssey* Odysseus visits the underworld – making a most rare return trip – the ghosts who appear can only talk to him after he has made a blood sacrifice to give them physical substance. As Achilles' shade says, he would rather "be the most wretched slave alive on earth than a prince among the dead".

THE UNDERWORLD

Hades' realm was located underground and approached via deep caves or subterranean rivers. At its entrance lay a grove of gloomy poplars, the Grove of Persephone, and gates guarded by Cerberus. With 50 heads, each dribbling black venom, Cerberus made a formidable watchdog. Only

Orpheus managed to charm the beast with his music, although Hercules overcame him by force. Once past Cerberus, the souls of the dead faced the black waters of the River Styx (or Acheron). The boatman Charon demanded an *obol* as payment. Those buried without this small coin in their mouths were left wandering forever on the desolate shores.

The Greeks were unclear about the geography of Hades, but various figures were noted there. Minos, the legendary wise king of Crete, was thought to judge the dead, but this was no Last Judgement on Christian lines, more a reckoning of accounts. Around Hades flowed the River Lethe. All who drank from its icy waters forgot their former lives.

THE ABDUCTION OF PERSEPHONE

Hades seldom left his gloomy kingdom, although he had a helmet that made him invisible when he did. His most famous

Right: Hades, god of the underworld, violently abducting Persephone (Proserpine), the beautiful daughter of Demeter, goddess of corn, as passionately sculpted by Bernini in 1621.

THE ELEUSINIAN MYSTERIES

The legend of the annual abduction and return of Kore ('maiden', as Persephone was first known) was central to the Eleusinian Mysteries, held in that small town near Athens. Open to everyone – male and female, free and slave – who spoke Greek and was not guilty of murder, they took place every September. A grand procession along the Sacred Way from Athens to Eleusis was accompanied by dancing and chanting. At Eleusis the neophytes bathed in the sea at nightfall and then crowded into the darkened Hall of Mysteries, the Anactorum or Telesterium. What exactly happened there is unknown – only hostile and blatantly distorted Christian accounts survive. But the rites certainly culminated in the entry of the *hierophant* (hereditary high priest) carrying a golden wheatsheaf in a blaze of light. This, symbolizing Kore's life-giving return to earth with the spring, also promised salvation after death of some sort to those initiated. The mysteries remained very popular until suppressed by the intolerant Christian emperor Theodosius I in c.AD395.

Finally Zeus sent Hermes down to make Hades release Persephone. Hades grudgingly agreed, but before she went back he offered Persephone a magic pomegranate. Eating it, she became bound to Hades and had to stay underground for four months each year. The other months she spent with Demeter, alongside whom she was worshipped. This division explained the earth's barrenness during winter.

As goddess of the underworld, Persephone's attributes were the bat, narcissus and pomegranate. She fell in love with Adonis, competing with Aphrodite. Zeus decreed Adonis should spend four months of the year with her in Hades.

Above: Hades carrying off Persephone in his chariot to become his unhappy queen in the underworld, as depicted on a red figure vase of c.400BC.

Below: Hades enthroned with his reluctant queen Persephone. Around them swirl the bloodless shades of the dead, forever doomed to this gloomy realm. The monstrous hound Cerberus, who guarded the gates of Hades' kingdom, can be seen just below the royal couple. From an amphora found at Canosa.

excursion led to the abduction of Persephone. The daughter of Zeus and Demeter, who was goddess of the harvest and vegetation, Persephone was so beautiful that everyone loved her, even the under-sexed Hades. One day, when Persephone was picking narcissi on the fields of Enna, Hades burst up out of the earth to carry her off in his chariot. Unwillingly Persephone became his consort, queen of the underworld. No one but Zeus and the all-seeing sun, Helios, had noticed her disappearance.

Broken-hearted, Demeter wandered the earth looking for her daughter until Helios revealed what had happened. Demeter became so angry that she withdrew her cornucopic gifts, inflicting endless drought and sterility on the earth.

PAN, HELIOS AND HERCULES

Above: Pan and nymphs for once portrayed in an urban context at Pompeii, although the rustic god generally shunned cities.

The Greeks worshipped many gods besides the Olympians. Some were rural gods like Pan. Others such as Helios (the sun) flourished during the Hellenistic period (322–30BC). Closest to most people, however, was the cult of heroes, often worshipped in their own villages.

PAN

Originally an Arcadian shepherds' god, Pan always retained his rustic air. He had the legs, horns and cloven hooves of a goat but a man's head and body. Arcadia was considered a backward part of Greece (which it was), but it was also increasingly seen as a pastoral 'arcadia' of nymphs and centaurs. Pan, son of Hermes and a nymph, was worshipped by shepherds in caves. In return he made their flocks fertile. He cavorted with nymphs, who were often alarmed by his hairy appearance but usually won over by his persistence. One exception was the nymph Syrinx. Praying for help to her father the river-god Ladon, she was changed into a reed. Pan, left clutching a bunch of reeds, consoled himself by making a flute from them, the origin of pan pipes. He also joined the wild retinue of Dionysus, seducing every Maenad he could.

"GREAT PAN IS DEAD!"

The Athenian messenger Philippides, returning through Arcadia after begging the Spartans for aid against Persia in 490BC, had a vision of Pan. The god promised to help Athens. The panic that hit the Persian forces in the Battle of Marathon was therefore

Left: Pan crouching on a rock, an unusual statue of c.200BC. Pan was said to haunt the woods and hills, especially in the deep stillness of the noonday sun.

ascribed to Pan, whom the Athenians began worshipping. (However 'panic' was originally the terror that strikes flocks in the midday heat.) Pan's name, which can mean 'all' in Greek, later led to his being worshipped as a universal deity.

His cult produced the one reported death of a pagan god. A ship sailing from Greece to Italy in the reign of the emperor Tiberius (AD14–37) heard lamentations and a voice crying: "Great Pan is dead!" However, a century later Pausanias found Pan's worship still flourishing, so reports of his death were clearly much exaggerated. Pan, quite harmless despite his appearance with horns and hooves, became for Christians the very image of the devil.

HELIOS

Although the Greeks considered Apollo the god of light, the sun had its own deity: Helios (sun). Helios was the son of the Titans Hyperion and Theca and brother of the goddesses Selene (moon) and Eos (dawn). Every morning he emerged from the eastern ocean to drive his golden chariot, pulled by dazzlingly white winged horses, across the sky, giving light to gods and men alike. At noon Helios reached his zenith and began his descent towards the west, where he appeared to plunge into the encircling Ocean. There a barque waited to carry him back east again. Zeus gave Helios the island of Rhodes and the sun-god also owned herds of oxen on the island of Thrinacia. When Odysseus' men slaughtered the 'oxen of the sun', Zeus blasted them with lightning. The Rhodians, who worshipped Helios, in the 3rd century BC raised a huge statue 30m (100ft) high to him, the Colossus of Rhodes, one of the Seven Wonders of the World. Under the Romans, Helios became generally identified with Apollo.

HERCULES, THE SUPERHERO

Midway between gods and men were the heroes. These were men, sometimes with divine parents (often Zeus and so in effect demigods), who had won undying fame. Sometimes their exploits were recounted in epic poetry and legends across the Greek world. More usually they were famous only locally, but there they were often worshipped for centuries. In Attica alone over 300 minor heroes had shrines. Only a very few, notably the muscular superman Hercules (Heracles in Greek) were Panhellenic gods.

Fathered by Zeus on the princess Alcmene, Hercules was harassed from birth by the ever-jealous Hera, who sent two snakes to kill him in his crib. The infant hero easily strangled both, however. Still madly jealous, Hera afflicted Hercules with a fit of madness, so that he killed his wife Meagre and his family. To atone for this fearful crime, Apollo ordered Hercules to perform his renowned Twelve Labours.

These tasks, regarded as utterly impossible for any normal human being, included killing the Nemaean lion, whose skin Hercules then wore, this making him almost invincible; slaying the huge Erymanthean boar and the Hydra of Lerna, a many-headed dragon; getting rid of the Stymphalian birds, which were iron-clawed man-eaters; cleaning the Augean stables fouled by 3,000 oxen; stealing golden apples from the Hesperides, the islands of the blessed; and, lastly, descending to Hades to seize Cerberus, its monstrous watchdog. All missions accomplished, Hercules became the archetypal conquering hero.

Hercules' end, however, was truly horrific. He was persuaded to wear a tunic soaked in the blood of Nessus, a centaur he had killed for trying to rape his second wife Denaira. Hercules became tormented by the poison it contained. He finally immolated himself on a pyre, but his soul ascended to Olympus. There he was deified as a constellation, like other demigods.

Right: Hercules shown wearing the skin of the Nemaean lion, one of the many creatures he had to kill as part of his Twelve Labours, in an original bronze from the 3rd century BC.

Left: The apotheosis (ascent to Olympus and deification) of the soul of Hercules the muscular superhero. From an 1813 engraving by Alexander de la Borde of an ancient Greek vase.

FESTIVALS, SACRIFICES, PRIESTHOOD AND ORACLES

Above: Consulting the oracle of Apollo at Delphi, the most revered of Greek oracles, from a vase of the 4th century BC.

Below: Sacrificial sheep being led up to the Acropolis for the Panathenaea, the great quadrennial festival, in part of a carving from the Parthenon.

Most Greek religion, closely connected with the political life of the polis, centred on festivals and sacrifices performed in public, except for mystery cults such as that at Eleusis. Public religion was generally a cheerful occasion. By celebrating their gods, citizens were celebrating their city and themselves, while public sacrifices gave poorer citizens a rare chance to eat meat. Gods were deemed content with sniffing the burnt skin and bones of sacrificed beasts.

THE PANATHENAIC FESTIVAL

Panhellenic festivals, such as the Isthmian or Olympian, were linked with their respective games attracting contestants from across Greece. More significantly,

ORACLES

Through oracles the gods spoke to men and through oracles men could ask the gods for advice and solace. The oldest known oracle in Greece was that to Zeus at Dodona in Epirus, mentioned by Homer and consulted 700 years later by the future emperor Augustus. The oracle of Zeus at Siwah in the Libyan desert later became famous, after being consulted by Alexander the Great. But Apollo was the chief oracular deity, with oracles at Didyma and Claros. All were eclipsed, however, by Apollo's oracle at Delphi, which emerged in the 8th century BC as the great Panhellenic oracle. After sacrificing a goat and paying a fee, the inquirer was admitted to the temple. There the Pythian priestess, crouched on a stool over a chasm, would enter a drugged trance. Her responses, transmitted by attendant priests, were usually in verse and always so ambiguous that they could never be proved wrong. Delphi's prestige lasted through the Roman era, the last pagan emperor Julian (AD361–3) consulting it with typically ambiguous results. It was suppressed in *c.*AD390.

each polis had its own special festivals. The Carnea was Sparta's greatest while Argos' was the Heraea, in honour of Hera, the city's tutelary goddess.

In Athens, the main festival was the Panathenaea in July. (Every four years a 'Greater Panathenea' was held.) Competitions – in music, poetry and sports – began five days before the main feast, with singing and dancing on the last night. At dawn, a sacrifice was offered to Athena and Eros, then a torch race with 40 runners carried the sacred flame to Athena's altar, high on the Acropolis.

Above: Athenians carrying vases in the great Panathenaic festival, from part of the Parthenon's renowned frieze.

At this the crowds, gathering since before dawn at the Diplyon Gate, set off in a grand procession. In front went the new *peplos* (tunic) to clothe the ancient statue of Athena Polias, the city's protector. It was carried by *arrephoroi*, four little girls chosen each year, and Athena's priestesses. More than 100 sacrificial oxen and sheep followed, with those leading them. Then came *metics* (resident foreigners), musicians, old men, military commanders and cavalry, marching in formation and carrying olive branches, and finally the rest of the city, *deme* by *deme*.

The procession moved on through the Agora and up the Acropolis, singing and chanting. In front of the little temple of Athena Nike, the best oxen were sacrificed. Only full Athenian citizens now entered the Acropolis, passing through the Propylaea to the great altar before the Erechtheum. There the little girls handed the *peplos* to the *ergastinai*, the women who had woven it, and the remaining animals were sacrificed to Athena. The ergastinai later entered the chamber of Athena Polias to change her peplos. The ceremony ended in a feast at which chosen members of each *demos* ate the sacrificed animals' meat.

This is the procession eternalized on the Parthenon carvings by Pheidias and his workshop. Here, god and heroes join idealized citizens, creating the archetypal image of Athens at its zenith in *c*.430BC. (Many sculptures are now in the British Museum.) Every fourth year from 566BC the Greater Panathenaea was celebrated with pomp as a Panhellenic festival.

PRIESTHOOD

There was no priestly caste or profession in ancient Greece. Instead, priests and priestesses were appointed from full citizens of good repute – i.e. free from blood guilt but not usually celibate. Priesthood was generally unpaid and not full-time, except at Eleusis where the priestess lived in the sanctuary. Women played an important role, serving the goddesses. Many priesthoods were normally reserved for members of noble families. The hierophant at Eleusis was chosen from the Emoulpidaie family, for example. At Sparta, the two kings took the chief priestly roles. But for local cults, the head of a local household would officiate.

Below: The theatre at Dodona in north-western Greece, dating from c.300BC. Here, Zeus' oracle, which claimed to be the oldest in Greece, spoke through a sacred oak tree.

Above: The Tholos, the circular sanctuary at Delphi dating from c.375BC. The Greeks regarded Delphi with awe as omphalos, the navel of the earth.

FUNERAL RITES AND BURIALS

Above: The Kerameikos, the main cemetery of Athens in the Classical Age, had superb funerary monuments. The city of the dead complemented the city of the living.

Below: An Athenian red figure vase depicting mourners. Dating from c.440BC and found in southern Italy, it was among Athens' many fine pottery exports.

The proper conduct of their funeral rites was always a matter of huge importance to the families concerned or, for those Greeks killed in battle, to comrades-in-arms or friends. Funeral rites determined what happened to the soul after death.

The souls of those left without the proper funeral rites were depicted by Homer in *The Iliad*, whose epics shaped all subsequent Greek religious beliefs, as forever roaming the desolate banks of the River Styx that flowed around Hades. Because of this, one way that a beaten Greek army conceded defeat was to ask permission from the victors to retrieve their dead for proper burial – a permission only rarely and most shockingly refused. (The Greeks also revered old age, and sons had by law to look after their ageing parents. But very old and infirm people were exceptional, although Sophocles lived to 90, Iscocrates to 94.)

In the Bronze Age, inhumation (burial) was apparently universal on both the islands and the mainland. The great grave-shafts of Mycenae were often superbly built structures, their many-corbelled chambers housing different members of a dynasty, the richer ones endowed with splendid grave goods. Such posthumous affluence suggests that the Bronze Age Greeks' beliefs about the afterlife may have been influenced by Egypt, as their grave architecture was.

By Homer's time, cremation had replaced burial as the normal way to dispose of the dead. In Classical times this preference for cremation continued, although inhumation was common too. In later antiquity, perhaps partly due to the rise of Christianity, inhumation once more became the norm.

FUNERALS
Relatives of the dead, usually women, carried out the elaborate three-part burial rites: the *prothesis* (exhibiting or laying out of the body), anointing the corpse with oil and dressing it in clean garments. The body was then bound in waxed cloths and put in a coffin, leaving the face uncovered. A coin was placed in the corpse's mouth to pay Charon, the ferryman who transported the dead across the River Styx into the shadow-world of Hades. The body was then placed on a

Below: For long after the funeral, women mourners made regular visits to the grave with offerings of small cakes and libations.

bier in the entrance of the house for a day before the funeral. Mourning for the dead followed, being vividly depicted on vases as early as the Geometric period.

Before sunrise the next day the body was taken out of the city in the *ekphora* (burial procession), with male relatives carrying the bier. The procession normally was led by a woman holding a libation jar. Immediately behind her came the male mourners and then all the female relatives, all wearing black or dark colours.

At times professional mourners were hired to add grandeur to the procession, with flute-players following the mourners. Aristocratic funerals could become so ostentatiously opulent that sumptuary laws were passed in many democracies, including Athens, to restrict the amount of money spent on them.

After cremation, the ashes and bones were collected in a cloth and placed in an urn, or the body was placed in a grave. Very few objects were by Classical times interred with the body, unlike the burial rites of the Bronze Age. Libations of wine and oil were then poured on to the deceased and the procession returned home. Mourners had to undergo lengthy purification ceremonies, the house itself being cleansed with sea-water and hyssop, for the Greeks believed that corpses were spiritually polluting. Later, women in mourning used to make regular visits to the grave with offerings of small cakes and libations.

FUNERAL MONUMENTS

Lavish funerary monuments were erected from the sixth century BC on by richer Athenian families in private burial grounds along the roadsides near Athens, especially on the 'Street of Tombs' in the Kerameikos quarter. This area was used for such purposes for many centuries. Relief sculpture, statues and tall *stelai* crowned by capitals marked the numerous, often sculpturally impressive, graves.

Funerary monuments often had bases inscribed with epitaphs in verse commemorating the dead. A relief depicting the dead sometimes recalled aspects of the person's life, with a favourite slave or dog. Young men killed in action were often shown fighting, idealized as heroic nudes. Many of these stelai have survived to provide vivid pictures of ancient life.

Above: A fresco of a funerary banquet from the 'Tomb of the Diver' at Poseidonia (Paestum) of c.480BC. Funerals could be scenes of ostentatious consumption.

Below: Lavish funerary monuments were erected from the 6th century BC on by richer Athenians along the 'Street of Tombs' in the Kerameikos quarter. Relief sculpture, statues and tall stelai marked many graves. Funerary monuments had inscribed bases with epitaphs commemorating the dead. Young men killed in action were depicted as fighting.

CHAPTER VIII

THEATRE

The Greeks produced the first tragedies and comedies still performed on stage today. Greek theatre had emerged in Athens shortly before 500BC, but its golden age lasted only 100 years. Although other dramatists wrote later, even the Greeks considered their plays relatively unimportant. Greek theatre originated in the rites of the god Dionysus, and long retained a religious aura. Highly stylized, with masked actors declaiming in verse, while a chorus chanted and danced, tragedy combined elements of opera and ballet and was normally set in a mythical past. Aristotle thought that true tragedy involved the downfall of a hero, humanly fallible, caught in a conflict with the laws of gods or men that reveal fatal character flaws. But such tragedy was never remotely mawkish. It showed adversity heroically endured or overcome, leading to resignation, even serenity. In contrast, Greek comedy offered a ribald view of the world.

Most works by the three great Athenian tragedians – Aeschylus, Sophocles and Euripides – and by Aristophanes, master of Old Comedy, are lost. Plautus and Terence, Rome's main comic playwrights, reworked Greek comedies for Roman audiences, but Roman tragedians wrote only for private readings. Roman theatre had mostly become a place of brutal thrills long before Christianity banned it. Only in the Renaissance did theatre regain its scope and humanity in the plays of Shakespeare and company. Greek theatre is the under-recognized ancestor of Western theatre, opera, musicals and even television.

Left: A red figure volute krater depicting actors preparing for a satyric drama about Dionysus and Ariadne.

PHRYNICUS AND AESCHYLUS
THE RISE OF TRAGEDY

Above: Actors on the Greek stage always wore masks, which were often very lifelike. This mask, unusual in being of gold, was perhaps made for a god's face.

Below: Tragedy was born in Athens in the 6th century BC. It reached its climax in the next 100 years with performances at the Theatre of Dionysus below the Acropolis.

Tragoidia (tragedy) originally meant 'goat-song'. It reveals Greek theatre's rustic origins in the ecstatic rites of Dionysus, who was, as god of dance, also the god of dramatic performances.

The first actors either wore goatskins or were given goats as prizes. In the mid-6th century BC, *tragoidia* came to town under the enlightened patronage of Pisistratus, Athens' tyrant or unconstitutional ruler. In 534BC Pisistratus established the Festival of the Greater Dionysia in late March, when the god's statue was carried to his temple beneath the Acropolis. There men dressed as satyrs, those mythical creatures who were half-goat half-man, danced and sang in *chorus* about the god's death and life. Soon rudimentary plays developed from these rites and drama was presented for the first time in Greece.

In 534BC the actor Thespis had made theatrical history by stepping out of the chorus and, by donning various different masks, taking different roles. Drama itself had been born. By *c*.500BC two actors were performing alongside the chorus, each one playing many parts.

PHRYNICUS c.540–c.470BC
The earliest known playwright – who also acted, like most playwrights – was Phrynicus. He won first prize for tragedy in 511BC and again for the last time in 476BC. He expanded drama by introducing female characters (played by men in masks) and by choosing serious legendary themes, not ribald subjects.

Only fragments of his plays survive. Among them are *Alcestis*, a mythical play, and two topical plays: *The Fall of Miletus* about the Persian sack of Miletus in 494BC, which proved such a painful subject for his audience (Athens had lent support to Miletus against Persia but only ineffectually) that he was fined; and his prize-winning *Phoenician Women* of 476BC. Phrynicus was most famed for his beautifully melodic verse.

AESCHYLUS c.525–456BC
Widely known as the father of Greek drama, Aeschylus was the first to write plays in trilogies, so making them suited for drama on the grandest scale. He is credited with introducing dramatic suspense, letting one character remain impressively silent, and with first employing special effects. Aeschylus himself, however, was proudest of having fought at Marathon in 490BC, according to the inscription on his tomb. (He probably also fought at Salamis.) He came from an aristocratic family, which explains this military pride, but he was no reactionary. *Eumenides*, one of his last plays, may contain radical democratic propaganda. He died in Sicily.

Aeschylus wrote 90 plays in all, winning 13 first prizes, but only seven works survive. (Some scholars doubt that

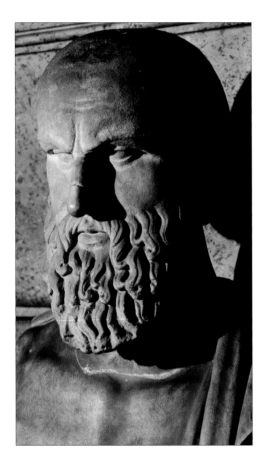

he wrote *Prometheus Bound*.) *Persian Women*, his first surviving play of 472BC, deals with the recent Persian defeat at Salamis. The play is unusually topical, not mythological, although set in the far-off Persian capital of Susa. The theme is Xerxes' despondent return, but Aeschylus does not gloat. The viewpoint is Persian and mostly female. Xerxes is the tragic hero, belatedly realizing that his own *hubris* (excessive pride) has caused his defeat.

THE ORESTEIA TRILOGY

Aeschylus' one extant trilogy is *The Oresteia*, dealing with legends of the royal house of Atreus linked to the Trojan War. It starts with *Agamemnon*, whose majestic opening lines are spoken by a watchman: "I ask the gods for relief from these pains, as I watch from one year's end to another's, Hunched on the palace roof like a dog. I have come to know the crowds of the night stars, Bright kings glimmering in the upper regions, bringing winter and summer to the earth.

I wait for the beacon light to burn, to blaze the news that the city of Troy has fallen." Troy has indeed fallen, but King Agamemnon's final homecoming brings only disaster. Clytemnestra, his wife, has long been planning his murder. Agamemnon's murder occurs offstage – the iron rule in tragedy broken only once by Euripides. The chorus, horrified, emerges finally to cry for vengance over the royal corpse.

Revenge is the theme of the next play, *Suppliants*. Orestes, Agamemnon's son, helped by his sister Electra, revenges his father by killing his mother. For this, among the worst crimes imaginable, Orestes is pursued by the Furies (*erinnyes*), hideous supernatural hags, seeking sanctuary in Delphi. In the trilogy's last play *Eumenides* (*Kindly Ones*), Orestes finally flees to Athens. There Athena judges and acquits him. She founds a new court, the Areopagus, for homicide cases, turning the Furies into the Kindly Ones, benevolent guardian spirits. (This bit may be partly propaganda for Ephialtes' democratic reforms of 458BC.)

Aeschylus called his plays "mere crumbs from Homer's table". But deep, if unconventional, religious views underlay his bold imaginative attempt to give what were often gruesome myths a firm moral basis. With him, tragedy attained an eloquent richness and simple grandeur that rival the work of Homer.

Left: Greek bust of Aeschylus. The 'father of Greek tragedy'. He was the first to write plays in trilogies, so making them suited for the highest drama.

Below: Orestes and Electra in a sculpture of the late 4th century BC. In Aeschylus' Suppliants, the central play of The Oresteia trilogy, Orestes, Agamemnon's son, helped by Electra, revenges his father by killing his mother.

SOPHOCLES
MASTER TRAGEDIAN c.496–406BC

Above: Sophocles, the most prolific and arguably greatest of the three classical tragedians, in a Roman copy of an original bust of the 4th century BC.

Below: A modern performance of Sophocles' Philoctetes *in the theatre at Epidaurus. Most Greek plays were performed in such open auditoria – but never at night.*

To contemporaries, Sophocles' tragedies approached perfection, a view shared by many later commentators. Aristotle thought Sophocles' *Oedipus the Tyrant* the most sublime of tragedies, the summit of all Greek drama. Sophocles' language is clearer than Aeschylus' often heavy grandeur, lacking bombast or self-conscious grandeur but retaining an epic note. His characters are roundedly human but always noble. They certainly have their faults – there would be no tragedy otherwise – but generally they conform to Aristotle's formula that tragic characters should be "like us, only finer".

Dominating Athenian theatre for almost 50 years, Sophocles had just one real rival, Euripides. Only 11 years Sophocles' junior but very different in temperament and style, Euripides wrote romances and tragicomedies besides tragedies of shocking realism. Sophocles said: "I portray men as they ought to be, Euripides shows them as they are." Sophocles' long, productive life spanned the rise and fall of the Athenian Empire, to which he contributed in many ways.

SOPHOCLES THE MAN
Born to a wealthy family at Colonus near Athens, Sophocles was a handsome youth who led the boys' chorus in victory songs after Salamis in 480BC. Although not a politician, he had a successful public career as a Treasurer of the Athenian Empire in 442BC, and in 440BC served as *strategos* (general) with Pericles, his friend. Later in 412BC, he was one of the 400 Councillors charged with drawing up a new constitution. He was markedly pious, helping introduce the cult of the healer-god Asclepius to the city in 420BC – in effect founding a public hospital – for which he was honoured posthumously.

But Sophocles was no prig, being notorious for his love of both boys and girls. On campaign once, Pericles had to rebuke him for ogling a handsome young recruit, saying "a general must keep not only his hands clean but also his eyes". Later Sophocles joked about his declining sexual urges: "I thank old age for delivering me from a cruel master." His last public appearance in 406BC was leading the chorus on stage in mourning for Euripides, who had just died in Macedonia.

THE PROLIFIC PLAYWRIGHT
Sophocles wrote 128 plays, winning first prize in 468BC against Aeschylus, and on 23 later occasions. But only seven of his tragedies survive. His early style continued Aeschylus' grand manner; his middle style was more austere; his last richly expressive and dramatic. The cycle of legends connected with the Trojan War and the ill-starred royal house of Thebes supplies the material for much of his plays.

His *Ajax*, his first datable surviving play, was staged in 440BC. In *Antigone* the heroine ignores a ban by King Creon on burying her dead brother (who had attacked Thebes), claiming a higher moral authority than the city's. This clash of

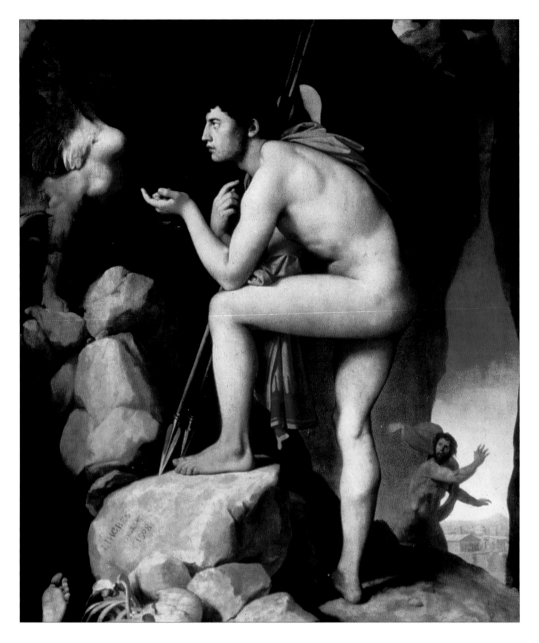

Left: Oedipus and the Sphinx painted by the French artist J.A.D. Ingres (1780–1867). The myth of Oedipus and the Sphinx has recurrently fascinated artists, writers and psychoanalysts, from Sophocles to Sigmund Freud.

Below: Oedipus being questioned by the man-eating Sphinx near Thebes. Answering the creature's riddles correctly saved his life but led to his doom later in Thebes. Oedipus the Tyrant is perhaps Sophocles' greatest tragedy. From a vase of the 5th century BC.

principles leads finally to her death. *Electra* treats the same myth as Aeschylus' *Libation Bearers* but positively, for Electra's recognition of her long-lost brother Orestes brings her joy, not grief. The play is more melodrama than tragedy. In *Oedipus the Tyrant* Sophocles turned to another Theban legend. Oedipus, king of Thebes, married to Jocasta, vows to discover which god's displeasure is behind the plague ravaging the city. He consults the Delphic oracle and finally discovers that *he* is the cause. He has unwittingly killed Laius, his father, the previous king, and, married his mother. Jocasta, hearing the news, kills herself. Oedipus, learning the intolerable truth, stabs out his eyes and leaves the city. "Call no man happy until he is dead!" are the play's last lines.

A FINAL MASTERPIECE

Oedipus at Colonus, Sophocles' final masterpiece of 406BC, takes up the same story. Oedipus, now a blind, tormented vagrant, rejected by all for his horrendous crimes, arrives at Colonus in Attica. There he retells his fate to Theseus, king of Athens. Theseus accompanies Oedipus to his apotheosis, where, amid divine thunder, the old king vanishes from earth. This final play was first staged in 401BC by his grandson, Sophocles the younger.

EURIPIDES
THE LAST TRAGEDIAN C.485–406BC

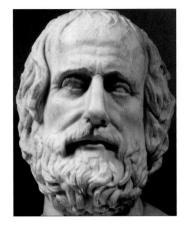

Above: Euripides, last and most controversial of the great Athenian tragedians, in a Roman copy of a Greek bust.

Below: 4th-century BC krater of Orestes with his sister Iphigenia in a scene from Iphigenia in Tauris, *a fantastical tragicomedy written in c.412BC.*

Euripides was the last and most controversial of Athens' three dramatists. The least successful in his lifetime – he won only four first prizes – he became the most popular after his death. This is revealed by the high ratio of his plays to survive: 18 out of 90. Athenian captives, slaving in the mines at Syracuse after being defeated in 413BC, reputedly bought their freedom by reciting lines from Euripides' plays. With Euripides, Greek drama explored novel realms of tragi-comedy and romance before returning to the savage myth at its heart in *The Bacchae*. This, his final play, proved tragedy's stupendous epitaph. Aristotle called Euripides "the most tragic of poets" and he is still the most performed today.

> **THE DEATH OF TRAGEDY**
> Friedrich Nietzsche (1844–1900), the great iconoclastic philosopher and classicist, blamed "Socratic scepticism" for killing Greek drama. In his *Birth of Tragedy* of 1872, Nietzsche claimed rationalism had undermined the communal myths that alone made Greek drama possible, turning theatre from collective rite into mere entertainment. Socrates and Euripides were the villains. While Nietzsche was the first to reveal the importance of the irrational and Dionysiac in Greek life, this view is not widely held today. Euripides knew Socrates – many Athenians did – and his plays *are* more complex than his precursors'. But Athenian society was becoming more complex and Euripides' last play, *The Bacchae*, proclaims the triumph of the irrational and Dionysiac. Tragedy in fact died a natural death just before the brief eclipse of Athenian democracy. The two were intertwined.

EURIPIDES THE MAN
Born on the island of Salamis (part of the Athenian state) to a respectable family, Euripides had an excellent education. He attended the lectures of Anaxagoras, Prodicus and Protagoras, three leading Sophists (itinerant teachers). A fellow-student was Pericles, who became a friend. Euripides also came to know Socrates. Aspects of Socrates' unsettling heterodoxy perhaps colour some plays.

Euripides himself was a recluse, at least by the standards of his age, retiring to Salamis to write, allegedly in a cave. More certainly, he built up one of the first book collections worth calling a library. He took almost no part in public life, unlike other playwrights. Such behaviour, unusual at the time, was mocked by

Right: A mosaic from Pompeii of the princess Medea about to kill her children before flying off in a dragon-drawn chariot in Medea, *a tragedy that won Euripides second prize when it was premièred in 431BC.*

Aristophanes. So were his radical views that portrayed women and slaves sympathetically. He was married twice, each time unhappily, and had four children.

THE INNOVATORY PLAYWRIGHT

Euripides' earliest surviving play, *Alcestis*, won second prize in 438BC. Based on folk tale, not heroic myth, it is a piquant tragicomedy, a form that the playwright made his own. *Medea*, a tragedy, also came second when staged in 431BC. It portrays the fiery barbarian princess Medea killing her rival and her own children before flying off in a dragon-drawn chariot.

His *Hippolytus* of 428BC innovates in depicting a tormented heroine. Queen Phaedra develops a disastrous passion for Hippolytus, her stepson sworn to celibacy (then most unusual). In beautiful verse, Hippolytus prays to Artemis: "Goddess, I bring you what I have created/A wreath picked from pure meadows/Where no shepherd ever pastures his flocks/Nor iron has touched, only the bees in spring…"

If reclusive, Euripides was not apolitical and *Trojan Women*, staged in 415BC after Athens had unprovokedly destroyed little Melos, highlights the fate of a captured city's women. It won him few friends in Athens at the time.

Electra in 413BC combined bitter pathos, romantic melodrama and farce in ways that still divide critical opinion, but Euripides' brilliant language captivated Athenian audiences. After the Syracusan disaster, he wrote fantastical semi-comedies such as *Helen* and *Iphigenia in Tauris*, plays with happy endings.

EXILE IN MACEDONIA

Euripides' last, and arguably greatest, play *The Bacchae* was written in Macedonia in 406BC, where he had gone at the invitation of its king, Archelaus. Returning to

the sources of Greek tragedy, the play is at once beautiful in its lyric power and horrifying in its revelation of the savagely irrational in human nature.

Dionysus, god of wine and often murderous ecstasy, returns to Thebes, whose uptight king Pentheus tries to arrest him – in vain, as he breaks free. Bewitched in turn by the god, Pentheus dresses in drag to spy on the Bacchantes, which include his own mother, Agave, who, seeing in her son only a wild animal, tears him to bits, brandishing his head in gory triumph. The chorus sings chillingly at the end: "Gods have many shapes/Gods bring many things to pass./What was most expected/Has not been accomplished./But the god has found his way/For what no one expected."

Below: A Roman mosaic showing Iphigenia, daughter of Agamemnon, about to be sacrificed to Artemis in a scene from Iphigenia in Tauris.

GREEK COMEDY
ARISTOPHANES AND MENANDER

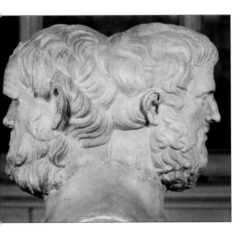

Above: The Athenians' huge respect for Aristophanes, their greatest comic playwright, was shown by pairing his head with that of Sophocles, the master-tragedian, in a double bust of the 4th century BC.

Komoidia (comedy) – another Greek word for a Greek invention – emerged around the same time as tragedy. Officially introduced to Athens' Great Dionysia in 486BC, its rustic origins are far older, going back to the seasonal ribaldry of Dionysiac fertility cults. Greek comedy divides into two phases: the Old, the often savagely topical satire of the 5th century BC; and the New, the more romantic, relaxed comedy of manners that followed. Aristophanes was the greatest but not first exponent of Old Comedy, as Menander was of the New. One of the early comedians, Cratinus (*c.*484–420BC), was Aristophanes' greatest rival, winning first prize nine times, but none of his work survives.

ARISTOPHANES C.450–385BC

Little is known of Aristophanes' early life but, although born in Aegina, he was an Athenian citizen. He wrote about 40 plays of which 11 survive. His first play, *The Banqueters*, won second prize in 427BC; his last appeared in 388BC. Although winning first prize only four times, Aristophanes aimed primarily to

Below: Terracotta figurines of Greek comic actors. As in tragedy, all actors in comedies wore masks and all roles were played by men.

> ### SATYR PLAYS
> In the 5th century BC the day's performance of tragedies was followed by a short satyr piece, offered by a tragedian as light relief. The play was named after the chorus dressed as satyrs, those lascivious creatures with goat legs and feet who follow Silenus, the fat, jovial and very drunk elderly companion of Dionysus. Aeschylus' satyr plays were much praised but are all lost. We have only one complete satyr play by a great dramatist: *Cyclopes* by Euripides. The overall tone of such pieces was humorously exuberant, not satirical.

make his audiences laugh. This meant catering to its often conservative feelings, but his own views were probably more liberal. He appears in Plato's *Symposium* as a friend of Socrates, whom he ridiculed in his plays. Several of his plays show unusual sympathy for women.

Aristophanes' first extant play, *The Acharnanians*, won first prize in 425BC perhaps because it voiced general war-weariness. (The Peloponnesian war had lasted six years already.) *The Knights* next year also gained first prize. It attacked Cleon, a politician whom Aristophanes portrays as an unscrupulous demagogue outwitted by an even greater scoundrel, a sausage-seller. *The Clouds* of 423BC famously depicts Socrates as an intellectual charlatan running a school of spin where young men learn to make the bad cause appear good to escape their debts. The school is finally burnt down. Seemingly unperturbed by this attack, Socrates stood up to be identified among the first audience. In *The Wasps* of 422BC Aristophanes went on to lampoon the jury courts that were supposedly filled with buzzing old men.

Above: Grotesque comic figures from a 4th-century BC vase in southern Italy.

ARISTOPHANES THE PEACEMONGER

When war resumed after 415BC, Aristophanes produced *The Birds*, an escapist story about two Athenians who, disgusted by war, go off to find somewhere better. They join up with the birds to form 'Cloudcuckooland', a fantastic utopian state hung between heaven and earth. In 411BC, as the war turned catastrophically against Athens, Aristophanes wrote *Lysistrata*. Lysistrata persuades all Greek women to refuse their husbands sex until they make peace. This has a potent effect. Finally, the Spartan envoys, similarly frustrated, arrive with peace proposals. The humour, often obscene, scarcely hides the playwright's own longing for peace. It too was to be frustrated.

Women at the Themophoria contained attacks on two tragic playwrights, the effeminate Agathon and Euripides, who had reputedly offended the women of Athens. Aristophanes' last play, *Women in Parliament*, produced in 392BC, toys with ideas of feminism and communism but his satire now lacked topical bite. Much of his wit is lost in translation – the rest is often too obscene to quote – but certain passages of pure poetry are remarkably beautiful.

Right: A Greek vase painting of a scene from Lysistrata, *Aristophanes' most political comedy, where the women of Athens refuse their husbands sex unless they make peace.*

MENANDER c.342–290BC

An Athenian of good family and friend of the eccentric tyrant Demetrius of Phalerum, Menander founded the New Comedy. After Aristophanes' death, comedy had stagnated. By adding fantastical elements from Euripides, Menander developed a new escapist form. Politics was now too grim a business for laughter, so he turned to domestic sitcoms and romances. Of his 100 plays only one, from an Egyptian papyrus, survives complete: *Dyscolus* (*The Misanthrope*). Presented at the Lenaian festival in 317BC, it won Menander first prize. In the play, a bitter but wealthy recluse violently rejects the peasant girl his son wants to marry until he falls down a well and believes he is dying. The play ends with dancing and song. Such simple plots were what now appealed. Roman comedians copied Menander so closely that New Comedy survives chiefly through their works.

Above: A Pompeii fresco of Menander, chief playwright of the New Comedy, who had a huge influence on Roman comedians and modern sitcoms.

INSIDE THE GREEK THEATRE

In Athens, birthplace of Greek theatre, the main dramatic performances took place during the Great Dionysia festival of late March. For four days citizens flocked to see the latest plays, with ten judges, one from each Athenian tribe, allotting prizes. In the 5th century BC plays were always new productions. But judges in the 4th century BC, realizing that newer playwrights could not compete with the great trio of tragedians – Aeschylus, Sophocles, Euripides – permitted revivals and so a classical canon emerged. While entrance cost 2 obols, an unskilled worker's daily wage, a fund provided free entry for the poorest. In the 4th century BC, women citizens too were admitted to the theatre, very probably for the first time.

Performances lasted all day, spectators sitting motionless on unpadded benches in the open, even though March can be chilly in Greece. They brought refreshments

Above: A vase showing actors holding up their masks – the one prop vital for any Greek play.

with them, eating and drinking during plays – doing so especially, Aristotle noted, if the play was poor. But theatre generally was as popular as football is today, with 15,000 or more in the audience. It was also very expensive, being closer with its masks, costumes, dancers and musicians to opera or musicals than modern theatre. In classical Athens, richer citizens, *choregoi*, were chosen to fund and put on productions personally – an onerous but honourable duty.

THE THEATRE'S STRUCTURE
By 500BC the slope below the Acropolis by the Temple of Dionysus was the site of Athenian theatre, but at first there was no theatre building. The theatre's shape derived from the orchestra (circular dancing area) for the chorus, about 25m (82ft) across, with tiers of wooden benches rising in a semicircle.

At first there was little to distract the spectator's eye from the actors and chorus, but after Persia's defeat in 479BC,

Above: A bronze bust of Sophocles from the 3rd century BC. By that time, the canon of the three great Athenian dramatists – Aeschylus, Sophocles and Euripides – was already firmly established.

Below: A mosaic of the 3rd century AD from Antioch, the great Hellenistic city in Syria, showing an architecturally imposing skene needed to support the scenery.

the first *skene* (background building) appeared. Xerxes' luxurious tent, captured at Plataea that year, reputedly provided the first skene (the word can mean 'tent'). Some of Sophocles' plays needed scenery, but by his debut in 468BC Xerxes' tent may have been replaced by wooden structures.

Traditionally, Pericles built Athens' first stone theatre in the 430s BC, but the oldest parts excavated are now considered 4th century BC. By 330BC, Athens' theatre had a stoa 62m (200ft) long with a colonnade facing south, away from the theatre. It served to support the skene behind it on which scenery was raised and lowered. The semicircular auditorium was now built in stone and marble.

THE PERFORMERS

All actors wore masks and were male. Women were not allowed on the Greek stage. Masks were elaborate and often realistic, being made of strips of linen moulded on to the actors' faces. Some masks were horrific – one for Oedipus showed his gouged-out eyes bleeding. Aristophanes also insisted on realistic masks for the characters he was mocking, such as Socrates.

Most actors were men of good repute. A maximum of three actors played all speaking parts, making lightning-quick changes of mask and costume. Most costumes were simple, based on everyday dress. The most extravagantly dressed person on stage was the *aulos*, flute-player, who accompanied the chorus. This consisted of 12–15 actors who danced, recited and sang, but the importance of the chorus faded in the 5th century BC.

DEUS EX MACHINA

The Greeks used cranes to introduce gods from on high on to the stage and then to whisk them up again. Such cranes had

Right: Actors wearing comic masks representing a slave, a peasant and an idler respectively. In comedies, broad caricature was the norm.

to be strong. In Euripides' *Medea* the queen flies across stage in a chariot with the bodies of her dead children. Socrates in *The Clouds* goes up in a bucket to view the stars. The Greek phrase for this was, *theos ek mekhane* (Latin *deus ex machina*, god from the machine). A wheeled platform also displayed events that had occurred offstage, perhaps in a palace. It was moved into view bearing, for example, the corpse of the just murdered king Agamemnon. Greek theatre could be startlingly realistic – so much so that women in the audience were said to faint at times.

Above: An archetypal Greek theatre in the form that emerged after 400BC, with a stone-built auditorium exploiting any natural slope, and a solid skene or background with some grand architectural features.

ΟΜΗΡΟΣ

ΑΝΔΡΩΝ ΗΡΩΩΝ

ΚΟΣΜΗΤΟΡΙ

ΙΛΙΑΣ   ΟΔΥΣΣ

ΕΙ ΘΕΟΣ ΕΣΤΙΝ ΟΜΗΡΟΣ, ΕΝ ΑΘΑΝΑΤΟΙΣΙ ΣΕΒΕΣΘΩ·
ΕΙ Δ ΑΥ ΜΗ ΘΕΟΣ ΕΣΤΙ, ΝΟΜΙΖΕΣΘΩ ΘΕΟΣ ΕΙΝΑΙ·

MODESTE TAMEN ET CIRCVMSPECTO IVDICIO DE TANTIS
VIRIS PRONVNCIANDVM NE QVOD PLERISQVE ACCIDIT
DAMNENT QVAE NON INTELLIGVNT   AC SI NECESSE
EST IN ALTERAM ERRARE PARTEM OMNIA EORVM LEGENTIBVS
PLACERE QVAM MVLTA DISPLICERE MALVERIM

ΕΝΔΕΙΚΝΥΤΑΙ ΗΜΙΝ Ο ΠΛΑΤΩΝ ΕΙ ΒΟΥΛΟΜΕΘΑ
ΜΗ ΚΑΤΩΛΙΓΩΡΕΙΝ ΩΣ ΚΑΙ ΑΛΛΗ ΤΙΣ ΠΑΡΑ ΤΑ
ΕΙΡΗΜΕΝΑ ΟΔΟΣ ΕΠΙ ΤΑ ΥΨΗΛΑ ΤΕΙΝΕΙ ΠΟΙΑ
ΔΕ ΚΑΙ ΤΙΣ ΑΥΤΗ Η ΤΩΝ ΕΜΠΡΟΣΘΕΝ ΜΕΓΑΛΩΝ
ΣΥΓΓΡΑΦΩΝ ΚΑΙ ΠΟΙΗΤΩΝ ΜΙΜΗΣΙΣ ΤΕ ΚΑΙ

CHAPTER IX

LITERATURE

Greek literature begins on an unsurpassed high. Homer, the first and grandest of Greek poets, opened *The Iliad*, his epic about the Trojan War, with the "wrath of Achilles", the archetypal warrior-hero. The poem is mainly about war, heroism and killing, described with sometimes overwhelming vividness. But the violence is balanced by passages of tenderness and humour, especially on Mt Olympus, home to oddly human gods. His second great poem, *The Odyssey*, is very different, an account of Odysseus' picaresque adventures on his slow journey home from Troy. In contrast to Homer's life-affirming gusto, Hesiod, a grumbling farmer, gave the Greeks a detailed genealogy of their gods – portrayed much less glamorously – and some sound advice, mostly on farming.

Greek literature never regained Homer's epic poetic heights, but it had no need to. Instead, it branched out over the centuries into almost every other genre, from lyric poetry to travel writing. One of the finest lyric poets was a woman, Sappho, whose fragments burn with love's bittersweetness. Many lyric poets took a lighter note, writing most unheroic verse. Others praised the triumphs of aristocratic athletes and the deeds of tyrants. The Greeks also pioneered the development of libraries. The greatest, at Alexandria, held up to 600,000 volumes. The library's destruction symbolizes the loss of Greek literature, of which only a fraction has survived. Even this has inspired later writers from the Romans to the 20th century.

Left: The Apotheosis of Homer *by J.A.D. Ingres, showing the poet honoured by other writers from Plutarch to Molière.*

HOMER, THE MASTER OF EPIC
C.730BC

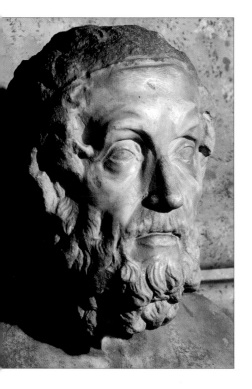

Above: A bust of Homer, made long after his death in c.700BC. No actual portraits exist of the first and greatest Greek poet.

Below: Phoenix, the tutor of Achilles, being served by Briseis, the slave girl – an apocryphal scene not in The Iliad. Homer's great epic inspired many later Greek vase-painters.

Homer's two great epics rank among the grandest tales, in prose or verse, ever written. Although he was the very first Greek poet – or at least the first we know anything about – he is astonishingly accomplished. There is nothing crude or unformed about his two great poems: *The Iliad*, about the siege of Troy (Ilium); and *The Odyssey*, about the wanderings of Odysseus on his long journey home.

Written in hexameters (lines of six metrical feet), they were learnt by heart by every Greek school boy and frequently quoted by every adult. Homer occupied the same authoritative role as the Bible and Shakespeare once did for all English-speakers. His poetic world – of gods, heroes, beautiful women and truly regal kings – had the larger-than-life glamour and danger that Hollywood has today.

Almost nothing is known of Homer himself. He probably lived in the mid-8th century BC. He may have been " a blind man living in Chios", as the poet Semonides suggested *c*.650BC, or he may have lived in Smyrna (modern Izmir), on the Ionian coast, for his poems are in Ionian Greek, mixed with some Aeolian phrases. At one time it was questioned whether the same man had written both poems, but today most scholars think that almost certainly one man compiled both epics. Both poems make recurrent use of Homeric epithets such as "wine-dark sea", "rosy-fingered dawn", "Mycenae rich in gold" and "grey-eyed Athena". Both are huge (15,689 and 12,110 lines respectively) and depict life as seen by the age's aristocracy.

The age was Homer's own and the generations just before him (*c*.900–750BC), but garbled memories of the Mycenaean world survive. Homer incorporated fragments from much earlier poems, but his genius alone created the majestic epics of compelling drive and power. He probably wrote down nothing himself, but the revival of literacy in Greece meant that others soon did. Homer's poetry was too good to be forgotten. A definitive 'Homer' was compiled in 6th-century BC Athens.

THE ILIAD
Paradoxically, *The Iliad*, the grandest war-exulting poem, brims with life, although it starts with a murderous quarrel and ends in a funeral. The "wrath of Achilles", the finest warrior in the Achaean army besieging Troy, is stirred when Agamemnon, High King of Mycenae, demands Briseis, Achilles' favourite slave girl. From their quarrel spring the events described in this, the siege's tenth year. Achilles, sulking in his tent, refuses to fight despite disastrous Greek defeats.

Finally, Achilles' friend Patroclus goes out in his place and wearing his armour, to be killed by Hector, the Trojan prince, King Priam's eldest son. Maddened by grief, Achilles takes to the field to kill Hector in turn. Triumphing, he drags the corpse behind his chariot until Priam comes to beg in person for it. Achilles, moved, gives way, knowing that he too is doomed to die soon. The poem ends: "And so the Trojans buried Hector, tamer of horses." Still to come, as Homer's audiences knew, were the death of Achilles and the bloody final sack of Troy.

Throughout, the gods frivolously intervene to help their favourites, adding to the massacres, but the poem's carnage is tempered by other scenes. Some are tender, such as that between Hector and land of Phaecia. At one stage Odysseus descends to the underworld to question the ghosts who flit bat-like through it.

Odysseus survives his travails more by his wits than his strength – though that is immense, as he often shows. The book culminates in his return home to Ithaca after 20 years' absence, where understandably he is not recognized at first by some of his subjects. There follows his reunion with his wife Penelope, heroically faithful to him after 20 years' absence, and meeting his now grown-up son Telemachus. Then comes his bloody reckoning with the suitors. These have long been pestering Penelope to marry one of them, for the kingdom will go to whoever marries the seemingly widowed queen.

The Odyssey ends in connubial joy in the great bed that Odysseus long ago built for Penelope. Women, human and immortal, play prominent roles throughout *The Odyssey*, which is not, like *The Iliad*, so dominated by blood-mad heroes. But the fast-moving gusto and magnificence of the poem as a whole remain truly Homeric.

Left: Odysseus blinding the giant Polyphemus, a scene from Homer's second poem The Odyssey *on a 5th-century BC black-figure vase.*

Below: King Agamemnon's envoys arrive to demand the slave girl Briseis from Achilles, so firing the latter's implacable wrath, which forms the central theme of The Iliad. *From a 5th-century BC vase made by the potter Hieron.*

his wife Andromache, with their little boy screaming in fright at the sight of his tall father in armour; some are resplendent, such as the description of Helen, as breathtakingly beautiful as ever, or of Achilles' elaborate god-forged shield: "Here youths and girls…danced and danced, arm in arm…the girls wore light flowing robes, crowned with fresh garlands, the youths had golden knives swinging from silver belts." However, such peaceful interludes are rare.

THE ODYSSEY

The second great epic opens with Odysseus, the Greek leader "who excels all men in wisdom", held captive by Calypso, the "bewitching nymph", until Athena, his champion, intervenes to liberate him. Very different in theme, it relates Odysseus' wanderings around the limits of the then-known world, and his encounters with cannibalistic giants, lethal sirens, shipwrecking monsters and finally an enchanting princess in the delightful

HESIOD'S DARK GODS
C.700BC

Above: Athena's birth from the head of Zeus shown on a 6th-century BC vase. A story told in Hesiod's poem Theogony.

Below: Hesiod's Works and Days *includes the tale of Pandora, whose box released sorrow into the world. Painted by Jean Cousin, 1540.*

Hesiod is traditionally seen as Homer's opposite as a poet and man. He has been considered a hide-bound peasant who wrote gloomily about the gods' gory origins in his *Theogony*, and a farmer's almanac interspersed with moralizing in *Works and Days*. Certainly Hesiod could be pessimistic. He describes his home near Mt Helicon in Boeotia, central Greece as "a bad place in winter, sultry in summer, good at no season of the year".

Yet Hesiod was not just a parochial old grumbler. He seems to have ended life as a substantial farmer, while his father had migrated from Cyme in Ionia. However, Hesiod totally lacks Homer's aristocratic splendour and range. His gods are not all-too-human immortals living in palaces on Mt Olympus, but ominous, sometimes inchoate creatures of the night. But his view of the underside of creation, and detailed accounts of the gods' origins, exercised an influence on later Greek religion second only to Homer's. Hesiod's dark gods aptly complement Homer's sublime deities.

Hesiod claimed to have become a poet after an encounter on Mt Helicon with the Muses, who breathed divine inspiration into him. He then went on to win a tripod in a poetry competition on Euboea. Like Homer, Hesiod wrote in hexameters but his have been called "hobnailed" by comparison.

Hesiod probably lived around 700BC but scholars remain divided as to whether one man wrote both major poems. Stories that he met and competed with Homer can be discounted, but he too wrote in Ionian if with some Boeotian phrases.

EVA PRIMA PANDORA

THEOGONY

Hesiod's first poem, *Theogony*, on the genealogy of the gods, runs to 1,022 lines. After invoking the Muses, he starts by describing "Chaos" – meaning empty space, not disorder – from which sprang night and Gaia, earth. Uranus (Heaven) emerges next – there is no creator god – and his coupling with Gaia produces more gods, including Cronus and inchoate figures called simply Night and Dreams. Encouraged by his mother Gaia, Cronus castrates his father and devours his own children to avert a prophecy that they will overthrow him. But his wife Rhea tricks him by giving him a stone to swallow instead of Zeus, their youngest son. Zeus, after growing up in Crete, forces his father to disgorge his siblings. The divine brothers then join in war against the Titans and establish the Olympian hierarchy.

After listing at a length that soon becomes tedious the other gods and demigods – including Athena, born directly from Zeus' head, and Aphrodite, the love-goddess born from the foam of Uranus' severed genitals – Hesiod ends with another invocation of the Muses. Zeus is the real hero of the poem, whose omniscience, power and justice are repeatedly stressed. Babylonian and Akkadian creation myths possibly influenced Hesiod's cosmogony.

WORKS AND DAYS

The "works" of the title of this poem are the operations of the farmer's working year; the "days" are the astrologically lucky or unlucky days of the lunar month. The poem starts by berating his feckless and greedy brother Perses, who wants more than his due share of their inherited land. It continues by describing the descent of the world from the first Age of Gold under Cronus, when men lived peacefully, to the current Age of Iron, marked by endless strife. This explains why human life is now so cursedly hard. It must, however, be born with dignity. Above all, men must work hard all their lives.

Below: Aesop's fable of the fox and grapes from a French 15th-century woodcut. Aesop's fables, once thought of minor merit, remain very popular.

Hesiod continues with farming advice that can be both sensible and poetic. "When the Pleiades, Atlas' daughters, start to rise/Begin your harvest; plough when they go down." He discourages Perses from trying to better his lot by trade, emphasizing the perils of the seas and the shortness of the sailing season – which amounts to only 50 days in his not very well informed view.

Among such brotherly admonitions come surprisingly beautiful versions of the tale of the Hawk and the Nightingale and Pandora's Box. The poem ends with a list of auspicious or lucky days.

OTHER POEMS

Some poems once attributed to Hesiod are now attributed to other writers, probably from the 6th century BC. *The Catalogue of Women* continues the *Theogony* in five books, with extensive genealogies with frequent notes, some of them on papyrus fragments recently found in Egypt. *The Shield* is a short narrative poem about Hercules' fight with Cycnus, so-called because of the detailed description of Hercules' shield with which the book starts.

Below: Cronos Devouring his Children, one of Hesiod's darkest myths, painted by Francisco de Goya (1746–1828).

DRINK, LOVE AND WAR
LYRIC POETS C.650–550BC

Above: A girl with a writing tablet and stylus from a mural in Pompeii, once thought to be a portrait of Sappho.

Below: Sappho and Alcaeus, the two great poets of Lesbos, shown on a 5th-century vase.

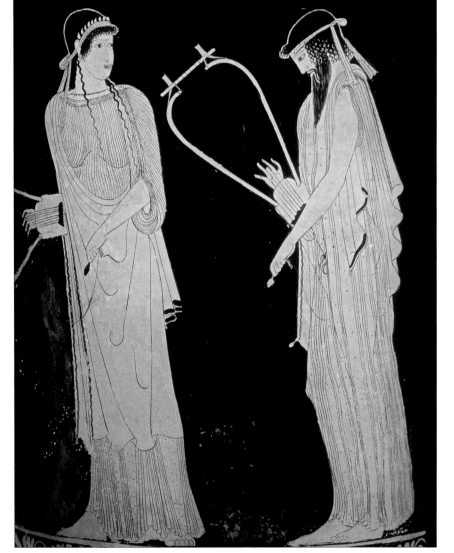

Tiring of heroic epics, poets of later generations took a very different view of life as the Greek world revived culturally and economically. This led to new types of poetry in the Ionian or Aeolian cities and islands of the east Aegean, then probably the most developed parts of Greece. The poetry written about life in these cities was humorous, passionate and personal, very seldom heroic. Only a few of these lyric poems – intended to be sung to a lyre at *symposia* (dinner parties) – have survived, but these give us glimpses of an aristocratic, debonair yet passionate life.

ARCHILOCHUS (C.680–630BC)

The illegitimate, penniless son of a nobleman of Paros and a slave girl, Archilochus had to leave home young. He became a mercenary, finally dying in battle against the Naxians. But his was hardly a tragic life, as his poems attest. "Some lucky Thracian has my fine shield./ I had to flee and dropped it in a wood./But I got right away, thank God!/Damn the shield, I'll find another just as good." Such insouciance, unthinkable for a Homeric hero (or a Spartan), typified the carefree aspect of the new age. Writing in a vernacular version of the Ionic dialect, he turned a keenly satirical eye on the aristocrat-ruled world. Unlike earlier poets, he freely expressed his own views, often using metaphors drawn from folklore. His sometimes savage but always original genius was recognized in antiquity.

SAPPHO (BORN C.630BC)

The first – and only – Greek woman poet of note, Sappho was born into the aristocracy of Mytilene on the island of Lesbos. Exiled to Sicily as the result of a coup, she returned to establish not so much a school as a circle for young girls, which she dominated by her personality, anticipating Socrates' circle later in Athens. For some girls she wrote poems about the love that she may well have felt for them, giving rise to the (modern) term Lesbian.

All Sappho's poems, which survive only in the briefest fragments, concern erotic passion, although Sappho was married and had a daughter herself. Some of her poems celebrate her girls' forthcoming marriages. (The tale of Sappho leaping to her death from a cliff after being rejected by Phaeon, a male lover, is a later fiction.) Sappho wrote in the relatively obscure Aeolic dialect, not the canonical Ionic, which may explain her subsequent neglect by Hellenistic and Byzantine scholars. (Some further fragments were discovered on papyrus scrolls in Egypt in the 1920s. Papyrus is well preserved in the desert sands.)

Whatever their subject, the intensity of Sappho's feelings fires her imagination to a white-hot passion never since surpassed. She wrote with deceptive simplicity, often in 4-line verses, couplets or even single lines. About one girl she wrote: "She outshines all the women of Lydia/As sometimes the rosy-fingered moon outshines all the stars, When its light spreads over the salt sea/ And over the many flowered fields, where the roses are blooming." Or, writing even more simply, perhaps about her own romantic loss: "The Pleiades are set/And here I Sappho lie alone."

Such poetry, despite so much being lost in translation, often has something of the heart-piercing beauty of Mozart's most lyrical arias. Catullus in the 1st century BC wrote poems that are almost exact Latin renderings of Sappho. Through his verse, which has mostly survived, Sappho came to influence the mainstream of European love poetry.

ALCAEUS (BORN C.620BC)

Another aristocratic poet of Mytilene who wrote in the Aeolic dialect was Alcaeus. A friend or acquaintance of Sappho, he fought as a young man for his city against Athens at Sigeum. He then became actively involved in factional politics, first as an ally and then as an enemy of Pittacus, the reforming "tyrant" who finally exiled Alcaeus and other nobles. Alcaeus visited Egypt and probably became a mercenary in the Lydian army. He was finally allowed home by 580BC, but was never reconciled to the new regime – for snobbish reasons as much as anything, it seems.

Alcaeus lived, fought and drank hard. He seems to have been better at hating than loving. This is reflected in his scathing political poetry. He wrote love poems – not just about his own affairs, which were mostly with boys, but also as the dramatic monologues of a lovesick girl – and cheerful drinking songs such as: "We should not abandon our hearts to despair/ For we gain nothing by groaning./ Bycchis, the best cure for us now/ Is to pour out the wine and start drinking".

Left: Sappho playing her lyre, theatrically imagined by the artist Léopold Burthe in 1849. Lyric poets are so-called because they accompanied their recitals on the lyre.

Below: Much lyric poetry celebrated symposia, here recalled on the funerary stele of Menelaus from Demetrias in Macedonia.

TYRANTS AND ATHLETES
THE LATER LYRIC POETS C.570–C.440BC

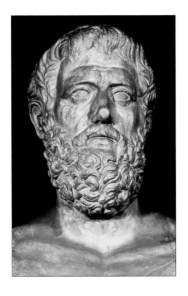

Above: Pindar of Thebes (518–438BC), the greatest poet of his age, in a Roman copy of a bronze Greek original.

Below: Anacreon (with Dionysus and Eros), as pictured by Jean-Léon Gérôme in the 19th century. A versatile poet, Anacreon wrote for Sicilian tyrants as well as Athenian democrats.

The advance of Persian power to the Aegean in the 540s BC meant the loss of Ionian liberty, but it did not harm lyric poets, who proved very adaptable. Most were happy to write for (Greek) tyrants and democracies. Some, like Pindar, preferred aristocratic oligarchies.

ANACREON C.570–485BC

Typical of the adaptable poet was Anacreon. Born on the small island of Teos, he followed other Teans who migrated to Abdera in the Hellespont (Dardanelles) rather than accept Persian rule. Soon much in demand as a poet and entertainer, Anacreon did accept an invitation from Polycrates, tyrant of Samos, in 532BC. Tyrant and poet became close friends and Anacreon wrote songs celebrating love and wine. After Polycrates' capture by the Persians in 522BC, the poet moved to the court of the Pisistratid tyrants in Athens. The fall of the Pisistratids in 510BC only briefly disconcerted Anacreon. He was soon back in Athens praising the new democracy, which returned his regard. A statue to him was even erected on the Acropolis. His poetry is written in simple yet vigorous Ionic that conceals a detached ironic wit. It appealed to Romans like Horace.

SIMONIDES 556–468BC AND BACCHYLIDES 516–450BC

Poetry is seldom a family business, but Simonides managed to gain an entrée at court in Syracuse for his nephew Bacchylides. Born on Ceos, Simonides gained the patronage of Hipparchus the Pisistratid ruler of Athens. After the fall of the Pisistratids, he moved to Thessaly. He then returned to Athens to beat Aeschylus in the contest to write an epitaph on the dead after the Battle of Marathon in 490BC. A friend of Themistocles, the leading democratic politician, Simonides left Athens in 476BC as Themistocles' political power waned.

In Sicily he resolved the conflict between Hieron I, tyrant of Syracuse, and Theron, the ruler of Acragas, as a result becoming effectively Syracuse's court poet. Simonides was famed for his epigrams, especially his epitaphs, and also wrote hymns, elegies and drinking-songs. His style, always graceful, gained in power as he grew older.

Bacchylides, also a native of Ceos, first wrote poems in praise of local athletes but soon connections with Thessaly led to successes there and later on the wealthy island of Aegina. Gaining a post in Syracuse through his uncle, Bacchylides wrote odes praising Hieron's sporting victories at Olympia in 468BC.

After the death of Hieron in 467BC, Bacchylides found no other court post and had to return to Cos, where he praised his countrymen's athletic successes. His style was often compared to that of a nightingale.

PINDAR 518–438BC

Arguably the greatest poet of his age and the first notable Boeotian poet since Hesiod, Pindar came from an aristocratic family. Despite being educated in Athens and later travelling widely, Pindar remained essentially Boeotian – narrowly conservative – in outlook, devoted to his class and also to tyrants. Above all, he praised aristocrats' athletic victories, a field where they long remained supreme.

His first odes praised the Aleuad nobles of Thessaly. Soon commissions from Aegina and Sicily spread his fame, but, like many Boeotians, he faced an agonizing dilemma during the Persian invasion of 480–479BC about whether to "medize" i.e. support the Persians. How Pindar himself behaved is unclear. After the Persian defeat in 479BC, his Sicilian connections led to a welcome opening at Hieron's court in Syracuse and so to useful commissions from Syracuse and other tyrants. But Simonides and nephew were too well established at court to be dislodged, as Pindar sourly noted.

Back in Greece, Pindar's reputation as master of odes and hymns continued to grow, both in mainland cities such as Athens and Corinth and in the islands. Yet towards the end of his life, with the seemingly unstoppable rise of Athenian power and of democracy, Pindar felt increasingly out of tune with the age.

About 45 of Pindar's poems survive, nearly all odes about sporting victors. Four books of *Epinician Odes* (so-called because they were sung celebrating victories in the Games) are extant. Greatest of these is his Fourth Pythian Ode of 462BC. Very long (12 pages in translation), it contains some of his grandest poetry, full of mythical resonance and invocations, with complex, varied metres. His style has been called eagle-like, but he has also been called a scholars' poet.

Right: Many Greek poets celebrated athletes' victories in the Panhellenic games, of which the greatest were those held quadrennially at Olympia.

Whatever the judgement, Pindar had a high opinion of his calling: "Muse you have raised me up/To be your chosen messenger of fine words/To the fine dancing-places of Hellas."

Above:
A fine dekadrachm (ten-drachmae coin) of Syracuse, celebrating the defeat of Carthage in 480BC, which heralded a long peace.

LATER POETS AND OTHER WRITERS c.310–80 BC

Above: Roman fresco of Jason with the Golden Fleece and Medea, the subject of Apollonius' 6,000-line epic.

Below: Theocritus created the pastoral, poems about arcadian idylls in the country. His dreamy eroticism inspired Renaissance artists like Giorgione who painted Concert Champêtre *(Pastoral Concert). Titian probably completed this work after Giorgione died in 1510.*

The great literary achievements of Athens in the 5th century BC were in drama and history, with lyric poetry for a time becoming less popular. After Alexander the Great's conquests (334–323BC) over-turned the Greek world, new audiences emerged for poetry in the new cities. Their increasingly urbane citizens enjoyed witty sophisticated poems, along with romantic pastoral verse tinged with nostalgia for country life. Poets were now often also scholars in royal libraries, some-times feuding bitterly with one other. All now wrote in the *koine*, the common Greek dialect based on Attic (Ionian), the lingua franca of this wide new world.

THEOCRITUS c.310–250BC
Born in Syracuse, Theocritus' poetry was rooted in his early memories of Sicilian rustic life. The idyllic – in truth idealized – life of Sicilian shepherds figures so prominently in his verse that it is called 'pastoral'. Theocritus wrote poems to Hieron II, the new ruler of Syracuse, in 275BC but by 272BC he was writing a panegyric praising Ptolemy II king of Egypt. For the next few years Theocritus lived at the glittering Ptolemaic court at Alexandria, but he finally settled on the island of Cos. There he wrote his famous pastoral poems. These are set in imagi-nary landscapes but contain accurate observations of plant life, especially that of the eastern Aegean. Theocritus' wit spices his nostalgia in a way that was very appealing at the time and proved hugely influential on later poets from Virgil in the 1st century BC to Shakespeare and Milton in more recent times.

APOLLONIUS RHODIUS c.300–247BC
Despite his name, Apollonius was a native of Alexandria, the booming metropolis. He became at one stage head of its famous Library. He had an (almost equally) famous blazing row with Callimachus, a rival poet who insisted that epic poetry was obsolete in the new era. To prove him wrong, Apollonius wrote a huge (6,000 line) epic, *Argonautica*, about Jason and the Argonauts. Seen in its totality, this is an over-detailed antiquarian failure, but it has fascinating and beautiful passages. Apollonius was especially good at portraying romantic love from a woman's viewpoint – a rarity among Greeks, which influenced the Latin poet Ovid's love poetry nearly 300 years later.

CALLIMACHUS c.305–240BC
Born in Cyrene (today in Libya, then part of the Ptolemaic Empire), Callimachus became a leading figure among the intel-lectual elite of Alexandria in its heyday. Like many other literary men, he was a polymath. Callimachus worked in the great Library – although he was twice passed over for the post of Head Librarian – and compiled its first huge catalogue in

120 books. His other prose works include a chronology of the great dramatists, a book on the Seven Wonders of the World and many books on topics ranging from the winds to nymphs, birds and rivers. He reputedly wrote 800 slim volumes of poetry, but only fragments survive. However, as he aimed at – and often achieved – perfection on a very small scale (hence his quarrel with Apollonius), this has not harmed his reputation. His elegant wit emerges in the fragment *The Lock of Berenice* praising the Ptolemaic queen Berenice. Judging by most of his love poems, though, Callimachus was mainly attracted to boys.

PAUSANIAS c.AD120–180

Living through the Roman Empire's peaceful zenith in the 2nd century AD, Pausanias was probably the first man who can be called a travel writer. But he was far more than a mere tourist guide, being encyclopaedically knowledgeable. Born in Lydia (western Turkey), he travelled around Asia Minor, Syria, Palestine, Egypt and Greece. His ten books about Greece have survived and kept him famous.

Pausanias wrote primarily for wealthy philhellenic Romans visiting what were already ancient cities. His books combine archaeology, history, art, religion, architecture and folklore. He not only wrote lengthily and intelligently about all the major sites – Delphi, Athens, Sparta, Olympia – but also sought out, and was genuinely interested in, the most obscure places and the rituals and legends connected with them.

Although he shows little interest in natural beauty, many sites give him an excuse for a historical digression. For example, in mentioning the statues of the

Above: The palaestra *(wrestling-school) of Olympia, one of the many sites vividly described by Pausanias.*

Ptolemies and Lysimachus in Athens, he launches into a detailed account of the wars of the Successors, the dynasts who carved out rival kingdoms at Alexander's death. His viewpoint is that of a patriotic Greek although he admired the emperor Hadrian. His books have proved invaluable for later historians and can be seen as forerunners of modern guide books.

Right: The statue of Zeus at Olympia, made by Pheidias in c.428BC, *was so huge that, even though he was seated, the god's head brushed the temple roof. Long destroyed, it is known to us chiefly through writers like Pausanias. This 18th-century engraving by J.A. Deisenbach is wildly imaginative.*

LITERACY, LIBRARIES, SCHOLARS AND SCROLLS

A	B	Γ	Δ
Alpha	Beta	Gamma	Delta

E	Z	H	Θ
Epsilon	Zeta	Eta	Theta

I	K	Λ	M
Iota	Kappa	Lambda	Mu

N	Ξ	O	Π
Nu	Xi	Omicron	Pi

P	Σ	T	Y
Rho	Sigma	Tau	Upsilon

Φ	X	Ψ	Ω
Phi	Chi	Psi	Omega

Above: The Greek alphabet from which our present Roman (Latin) alphabet derives. The Greek alphabet had fewer letters than ours.

Below: An ostrakon *(pottery fragment) with the name of Aristides, the Athenian statesman ostracized in 482BC. Pottery supplied a cheap writing material for such actions.*

Around 700BC the Greeks adopted the Phoenician alphabet, adding vowel symbols to the consonant signs adequate for Phoenician. In doing so they created a simple, flexible way of writing that was to help make mass literacy possible. Our own Roman (or Latin) alphabet derives from the Greeks'. Inscriptions in Greek are widespread on monuments – on tombs, temples, walls, gateways – and as graffiti, scratched even on the statues of Abu Simbel in Egypt by Greek mercenaries. By 500BC most Greeks, at least in the major cities, were half-literate i.e. they could read if not always write.

This limitation is revealed by the story about the Athenian politician Aristides. Facing ostracism (temporary exile) by popular vote in 482BC, he was stopped by a citizen and asked to inscribe his own name on an *ostrakon* (the pottery shard used for such votes). Aristides did, so meriting his nickname the Just but also indicating that citizens could generally read if not write names. The material used shows something else: the lack of a cheap and convenient writing material. Paper, today so common, was unknown.

PAPYRUS AND PARCHMENT

In antiquity the main writing material was papyrus, which comes from the papyrus plant – our word paper derives from it – grown almost exclusively along the Nile

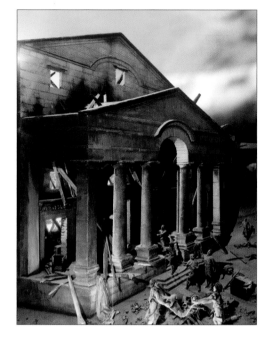

Above: An imaginary painting of the great Library at Alexandria in one of the frequent fires that threatened it. It survived, however, until the end of the Graeco-Roman world.

in Egypt. A tiny amount was also grown in Syracuse. Papyrus, a royal monopoly in Egypt, was expensive, but provided a fine writing material when made into scrolls.

Text was written in vertical columns, which the reader slowly unwound from one roll and wound on to another. As many texts were 8m (25ft) long, this made reading a cumbersome business, requiring two hands. Also, papyrus was fragile. For daily use, other forms of writing material were used, from *ostraka* (discarded after use) to wooden boards rubbed clean of chalked messages.

In the 2nd century BC the kings of Pergamum, great rivals of the Ptolemies of Egypt, pioneered the development of parchment, made from treated animal hides. Parchment (vellum) was tougher than papyrus, though less easy to write on. When parchment sheets began being sewn together into a *codex* (bound book)

Right: A Ptolemaic schoolboy's workbook from Egypt, made of wood and showing Greek writing. Even in the land where papyrus grew, it was too expensive for schoolboys to use.

in the 3rd century AD, parchment slowly displaced papyrus. By the 6th century AD this process was almost complete.

LIBRARIES AND LIBRARIANS

Euripides, the Athenian dramatist, built up the first library in the 5th century BC. However Aristotle, the encyclopaedic philosopher, started the first proper library in the 4th century for his school, the Lyceum, in Athens. After his death in 322BC, scholarly studies moved to the richer city of Alexandria, where Ptolemy I founded the great Library in c.295BC. Attached to the Museum, which was more university than museum, the Library became the greatest in the ancient world, holding up to 600,000 scrolls. Scrolls were wrapped round sticks, identified with tags and stacked like loose rolls of wallpaper in numbered cupboards, boxes and barrels. The index alone came to 120 scrolls. Outside this "chicken coop of the muses", were cool, open colonnades beneath which scholars could work.

Many great literary or scientific men became head librarians: Apollonius of Rhodes, Eratosthenes and Aristarchus of Samothrace. The Library was concerned as much with science as the humanities.

Only slightly damaged in fighting between Julius Caesar's troops and the Alexandrians in 47BC, the Library thrived under the Romans. But the emperor Aurelian's brutal reconquest of Egypt in AD275 may have started its decline, which was accelerated by Christian attacks on Hellenic learning. By the time the Arabs captured the city in the 7th century AD, the Library had almost ceased to function.

Below: A terracotta figure found in Thebes dating from c.500BC of a man writing. By that time literacy was common among Greeks, at least in the major cities.

READING WITH MOVING LIPS?

It was once thought that the Greeks read only with their lips moving, suggesting they read with some difficulty. More recently, scholars, on re-examining ancient literary sources, have realized that many Greeks could indeed read silently. In Euripides' play *Hippolytus*, Theseus, confronted with his wife's corpse, silently reads the letter containing Phaedra's false accusation against his son Hippolytus. Then he bursts out saying that "the letter shrieks, its howls horror insufferable...

a voice speaks from the letter." Plutarch related that Alexander was silently reading a confidential letter from his mother when Hephaestion "quietly put his head beside Alexander's and read the letter with him. Alexander could not bear to stop him but took off his ring and placed the seal on Hephaestion's lips", reminding his closest friend that such letters are indeed confidential. All of which suggests that at least some of the Greeks could read without moving their lips.

CHAPTER X

PHILOSOPHY AND SCIENCE

Philosophy 'begins in wonder' – and it began with the Greeks. The Greeks were the first to think systematically, almost free of constraints, about the universe and humanity's place in it. Ethics, logic, metaphysics, philosophy itself – Greek words for concepts the Greeks originated. Western philosophy stands so firmly on Greek foundations that to call it "footnotes to Plato" (as the 20th-century philosopher A.N. Whitehead did) seems only an exaggeration. The freedom that Greek city-states gave their intellectually more daring citizens was not unlimited. There was the odd backlash against free thought, most famously in Athens with Socrates, but there was far more intellectual freedom in a polis than in any earlier (and most later) states. This freedom continued for almost 1,000 years even under Roman rule, although after 320BC many philosophers ignored politics, seeking instead inner happiness and freedom (*eudaimonia*).

Philosophical enlightenment affected the physical sciences. Early philosophers were often also scientists. Astronomy, biology, geography, maths and zoology are all Greek words. Although Socrates concentrated mostly on ethics, and Plato spurned the natural world, Aristotle was hugely knowledgeable about the natural world *and* human affairs. There were significant advances also in technology, too often under-rated. Medicine under the Greeks first became a field for rational inquiry, reaching levels unsurpassed for 1,500 years.

Left: Raphael's vision of The School of Athens *of 1510 shows Plato and Aristotle flanked by other philosophers.*

THE IONIANS: THE WORLD'S FIRST PHILOSOPHERS 600–500BC

Above: Thales (c.625–547BC), the first known philosopher and natural scientist, came from the great Ionian city of Miletus. He predicted the solar eclipse of 585BC.

Philosophy began in the small cities of Ionia on the west coast of Asia Minor around 600BC. There some men first had the freedom and audacity to ask fundamental questions about the universe. Their answers, if sometimes inaccurate, were never absurd. However most of our knowledge of them comes only through Aristotle, writing 200 years later.

THALES C.625–547BC

A native of Miletus, then the richest Greek city, Thales is considered the founder of natural philosophy. He foretold the solar eclipse of 28 May 585BC, which stopped a battle between the Lydians and Medes, both being superstitiously terrified. Such accuracy – about its exact place more than time – suggests that Thales knew of astronomy in Babylon, whose records went back centuries.

Traditionally Thales also visited Egypt to learn geometry from its priests, but his speculations about the nature of things owed nothing to priestly precedent. Observing that at low temperature water becomes like rock and at high temperature vaporizes, that land is surrounded by water and water falls from the sky, Thales deduced that water is the primary principle of everything.

He probably also regarded the Earth as spherical, a truly radical idea. Crucially, he reached his conclusions not through divine revelation or scripture but by observing and *thinking*. Although poor, Thales showed commercial acumen once by cornering the market in olive presses before a bumper harvest he had foreseen. He also urged the disparate Ionian cities to unite against the Asian empires rising in the east – in vain. He was later revered as one of the Seven Sages of Greece.

ANAXIMANDER C.610–C.540BC

A pupil of Thales, also from Miletus, Anaximander rejected his master's belief in the primacy of water. He thought instead that this world, and countless other worlds beyond our knowledge, came into being out of the *apeiron* – infinity, the basis of existence. From this have split off 'innumerable worlds'. He was the pioneer of geometrical (if mistaken) astronomy, suggesting the Earth was a huge cylinder, floating unsupported in space, equidistant from all else, and that the planets (counting the Sun and Moon as such) moved in orbits. Anaximander is also credited with making the first map and *gnomon* (sundial), of huge importance

Left: A Roman mosaic of Anaximander, the second Milesian philosopher, is credited with making the first gnomon (sundial). He also suggested theories about the evolution of animals from the sea after studying fossils.

in an age without clocks, and speculating about the evolution of living creatures from the sea after studying fossils.

His cosmological views were so radical that they were rejected by his own pupil Anaximenes, who thought the Earth was flat and the stars were fiery leaves. The cosmos consisted of air of differing densities. Anaximenes' views at the time proved more acceptable than his master's.

PYTHAGORAS C.570–C.497BC

The first man actually to be called a philosopher (lover of wisdom), Pythagoras was a philosopher/mathematician, conjuror and mystic. Born on the island of Samos, he left to escape the rule of its tyrant Polycrates. Settling at Croton in southern Italy in c.530BC, he founded a secretive community where his disciples long remained. Said to wear white robes and a gold coronet, Pythagoras declaimed (supposed) poems by Orpheus. Like the Orphics, he believed in an immortal soul that might be reincarnated as an animal. This made him a vegetarian.

Pythagoras' great mathematical discovery was that the sum of the squares on the two shorter sides of a right-angled triangle equals the sum of the square on the remaining side, the hypotenuse. He also discovered the harmony of octaves and had a mystical belief in Number, which he saw ruling the universe. Astronomy and harmony were, he said, sisters. Bertrand Russell considered him "one of the most important men that ever lived", for in him the perennial conflict in Greek thought between the rational and the mystical first surfaces. Although he left no writings, Pythagoras greatly inspired Plato.

XENOPHANES OF COLOPHON
C.570–C.480BC

Xenophanes quit his small native city after it fell to the Persians in 545BC to spend life in Sicily. He attacked Homer for his frivolous and immoral depictions of the Olympian gods, and poets for their anthropomorphic concepts of deities in general. "Thracians depict gods as

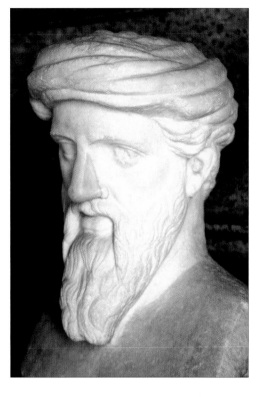

Left: Bust of Pythagoras of Samos, the first man to be called a 'philosopher', united mysticism and maths in an esoteric mixture. Reputedly he believed in reincarnation, but no writings by him survive. He and his followers settled in southern Italy.

Thracians, Africans as Africans. If horses or cattle had hands and could draw, they would create gods like horses or cattle," he claimed, a startlingly novel viewpoint that found few followers at the time. As a natural philosopher he oddly assumed that the earth was flat and the sky extended indefinitely upward. From this he concluded that each day a totally new sun rose in the east, expiring at sunset.

Below: Thales believed that the fundamental principle of the whole cosmos was water – a reasonable belief for a Greek living by the sea.

PRE-SOCRATIC PHILOSOPHERS OF THE 5TH CENTURY BC

Above: Raphael's portrait of the enigmatic Heraclitus, another philosopher from Miletus, who proclaimed that "all is flux".

After the defeat of the Ionian revolt against Persia in 494BC, intellectual life moved to Athens. The booming, usually liberal city for centuries attracted thinkers from around the Greek world. Those living before Socrates are called Pre-Socratic.

HERACLITUS
FLOURISHED C.500–490BC

A native of Ephesus, Heraclitus was renowned both for his personal arrogance and the obscurity of his philosophical aphorisms. About 120 of these survive. Heraclitus rejected earlier quests for a single imperishable entity beneath the constant flow of phenomena, proclaiming: *panta rei, ouden menei* (all is flux, nothing is stable). He saw the world as the unending conflict of opposites, governed by the unchanging Logos (principle, order, word). He believed that the world consisted of three cosmic elements – earth, water and fire – forever changing into each other. The greatest was fire, linked to Logos: "Fire is the underlying element, the world is everlasting fire." Although he ridiculed Xenophanes, he too believed in relativism, pointing out that the way up a mountain is also the way down. Many of his more radical aphorisms shocked contemporaries. Dead bodies, he said, smell nastier than excrement.

PARMENIDES C.510–C.430BC AND ZENO C.490–C.430BC

Parmenides, said Plato, had "magnificent depths". He is increasingly seen as the most significant Pre-Socratic, for with his thinking consciousness becomes aware of itself. This led to the human mind first recognizing its unique cognitive powers, an intellectually vital step.

Parmenides was an aristocrat from Elea, a Greek city in Italy, who visited Athens in *c*.440BC. His work survives in a three-part poem in hexameters of 150 lines. The *Prologue* is a mystic revelation by a goddess who explains two ways. *The Way of Truth*, expounded with rigorous logic, concludes by showing that all that truly exists must be one, eternal, undifferentiated and changeless. Whatever is cannot come into being or cease to exist. Conversely, that which is *not* cannot come into being. Change, therefore, is impossible. As this is clearly not the phenomenal world our senses reveal, our senses are somehow wrong. In *The Way of Opinion* he restated conventional views but only to rebut them. By confining truth to the realm of an unchanging One, Parmenides' ideas deeply influenced Plato.

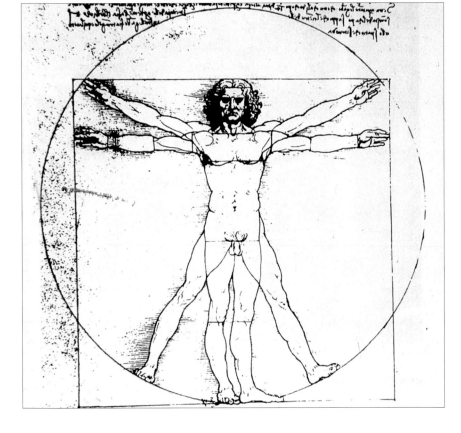

Left: Leonardo da Vinci's drawing of a perfectly symmetrical 'Vitruvian Man' illustrates Protagoras' belief that "Man is the measure of all things."

Zeno of Elea, Parmenides' main follower, defended his master's teachings against pluralist critics by extending their arguments *ad absurdum* in "Achilles' Paradox". Though Achilles runs much faster than a tortoise, if he gives the tortoise a head start in a race he will never *logically* catch up with it, because at each distinct stage the tortoise will still be an ever-reducing stage ahead.

ANAXAGORAS C.500–428BC

Born in the tiny Ionian city of Clazomenae, Anaxagoras moved to Athens in *c.*480BC. He lived there for nearly 50 years, becoming a teacher and friend of Pericles. He tried to refute Parmenides' logical monism by postulating a plurality of eternal, qualitatively different substances. His version of cosmic history began, rather like the Big Bang, when *Nous* (Mind) 'the finest and purest of all things', started a rotatory process that formed the stars and other bodies from air, separating dark from light, wet from dry. All creatures, not just humans, have minds but *Mind* is separate and infinite. Anaxagoras was nicknamed 'Mind' for stressing this but he was essentially a materialist. He was also a perceptive astronomer. He realized that the Moon shines with the Sun's reflected light and considered the Sun a "fiery rock larger than the Peloponnese." Such observations struck many Athenians as impious – the heavenly bodies were thought divine – and Anaxagoras had to retire to Lampsacus in 430BC when Pericles lost office. There he was honoured and died.

PROTAGORAS C.485–C.415BC

A native of Abdera on the Hellespont, Protagoras was probably the greatest Sophist. Sophists ('wise men') travelled around Greek cities teaching and charging fees. Protagoras taught *areté* (virtue, excellence, valour, goodness) not as an abstract virtue but as a form of life skill. Rhetoric (public eloquence) formed an important part of his training. Plato portrays him hostilely in the dialogue

Above: Athens became the centre of philosophy after the Ionian revolt was crushed by Persia in 494BC. Many Ionian thinkers found a welcome in its (usually) liberal democracy. It kept this reputation until the very end of the ancient world.

named after him, attacking his then novel concept of moral relativism, but Protagoras was widely admired. He was asked by Pericles to draw up a constitution for Thurii in Italy, and was Abdera's ambassador in Athens. In *On Truth*, one of his extant works, he famously proclaimed: "Man is the measure of all things!" Such exultant humanism led him to disregard theology. "Of the gods I know nothing, whether or not they exist nor what they are like. Many things prevent such knowledge: the obscurity of the subject, the shortness of human life." Instead, Protagoras concentrated on imparting areté in Athens at its Periclean noon.

Below: Black-figure amphora of runners. Zeno of Elea produced the argument ad absurdum *of "Achilles' Paradox". Although he runs faster, if Achilles gives the tortoise a start he can never logically* catch up with it.

SOCRATES: THE ARCHETYPAL PHILOSOPHER C.470–399BC

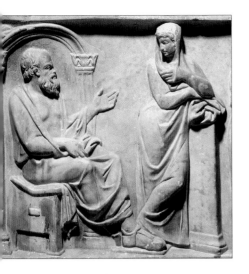

Above: Greek bas-relief of Socrates talking to Diotima, the priestess sometimes called his muse, who revealed to him the potentially transcendent nature of eros *(desire).*

Below: The Death of Socrates, painted by J.L. David in 1787. Condemned to death for his unorthodox religious views, Socrates swallowed hemlock while debating with his disciples. He thus became a model martyr for free speech.

The first Athenian-born philosopher, Socrates changed the focus of philosophy from speculation about the physical world to ethical issues. In doing so, he also became the archetypal philosopher in his disdain for worldly riches, his intellectual curiosity and his bravery. Socrates likened himself to a gadfly, stinging people into thought. Like a fly, he was finally squashed. He has often been considered an intellectual martyr. Like Christ and the Buddha, he wrote nothing, so we must rely on others' conflicting accounts of his life and thought. But the bare facts of his life are clear.

SOCRATES THE MAN

The son of a stonemason of the hoplite middle-class, Socrates fought bravely in the army, notably at Delium in 424BC. By then he was well-known enough to be ridiculed by Aristophanes in *The Clouds*, where he is portrayed as a charlatan teaching young Athenians to lie and study godless astronomy. If a travesty of the truth – although Socrates may have been interested in natural science for a time – this was an accurate enough portrait to amuse citizens.

Socrates was already attracting a circle of followers, mostly leisured young aristocrats, but anyone could listen to him debating in the Agora or street. Charging no fees, unlike the Sophists, Socrates became impoverished on abandoning his mason's trade, going around in rags. His wife Xanthippe objected to this neglect but Socrates had set his mind on higher things. This made him seem indifferent to wealth, sex and drink. The handsome young aristocrat Alcibiades tried to seduce Socrates – who was notably ugly if charming – but got nowhere, to his amazement. Equally amazing was Socrates' indifference to cold, shown on northern campaigns. He also was unaffected by alcohol, no matter how much he drank. However he was governed by his *daimon*, an inner guide that often forbade him to do things but never urged him on.

THE SOCRATIC METHOD

According to Plato's *Apology*, a prime biographical source, Socrates' intellectual quest began when the Delphic oracle declared that there was none wiser than him. Amazed, he declared himself ignorant but determined to find wise men by the Socratic method. (This is also called *elenctic*, refuting an argument by proving the contrary of its expected conclusion).

Such an approach led Socrates to question ordinary Athenians about fundamental, usually unchallenged concepts. "What is courage?" "What is justice?" "What is areté?" he asked, subjecting those who thought they knew the answers to probing inquiries that revealed their ignorance. This seldom made him loved, especially when he asked: "Who is truly fit to govern?" The answer appeared to be: no one.

But Socrates, despite a sharp-edged irony, was not playing word games. When he asked "What is justice?" he believed that, although laws might differ with different peoples, there was an underlying reality called 'justice'. Everyone could recognize it if they saw it clearly. Socrates wanted to demolish misconceptions to reveal the essence of justice, or of bravery or of areté. While he never claimed to have the final truth, he believed that no one knowingly does wrong. Wrong-doing stems from ignorance about man's real good. A man of true areté cannot be harmed by external factors such as imprisonment or death. Personal ruin comes from inner corruption.

TRIAL AND DEATH

Socrates did not seek public office but this was thrust on every Athenian at times by the city's direct democracy. In 406BC he was a member of the Council of 500 during the trial of the generals after the Battle of Arginusae, a pyrrhic victory with the generals blamed unfairly for the high losses after it. Amid demotic hysteria, the Council illegally tried and executed the generals collectively. Only Socrates protested against this injustice.

Two years later, with Athens under a fascistic junta, he showed equal courage by refusing its orders to arrest a prominent man whose wealth the junta wanted.

Democracy was restored in 403BC under a general amnesty, but memories persisted. Many recalled Socrates undermining old certainties, and that two of his ex-disciples had led the junta. Both reactionaries and democrats had reason to dislike him. In 399BC Anytus, a noted democrat, accused Socrates of "not recognizing the city's official gods and introducing new ones" and "corrupting the young" – strange charges superficially, for new gods were at times welcomed to Athens. In fact, both were ways of attacking Socrates for his views and associates. His self-defence was ironic and oddly jejune. The standard 501-strong jury found him guilty by a small majority.

He was not expected to remain for the death sentence but to go into exile. Instead, claiming he could not abandon his post, he stayed, discoursing on the immortality of the soul until his end. This came in a dose of hemlock – not a dignified death, involving convulsions and vomiting. "I owe a cock to Asclepius," were his last enigmatic words. Asclepius was the healer-god. Did Socrates mean he was freed at last from the disease of life?

Above: Socrates Snatching Alcibiades from Sexual Lures, *painted by J.-B. Regnault in 1791. In fact, Socrates failed to persuade the flamboyant aristocrat, once his star pupil, to devote himself properly to philosophy.*

Below: A Roman copy of a Greek bust of Socrates. The philosopher, although charming, was seen as shabby and ugly by contemporaries.

PLATO: THE GREATEST PHILOSOPHER? c.429–347BC

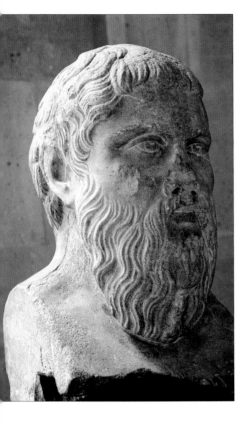

Above: This bust from the 4th century BC is probably the most accurate portrait of Plato, suggesting his physical as well as intellectual strength. When young, he had been a noted wrestler.

Plato, Socrates' most brilliant student, was arguably the greatest philosopher ever. Most of his work (c.500,000 words) survives, on subjects from cosmology to politics. Plato had a novelist's gift for portraying people vividly and wrote superb prose. His own views can be unclear because he usually wrote in dialogues, not verse as earlier thinkers had done, to stimulate discussion. His use of dialectic was to be very influential, in the 19th century G.F. Hegel and Karl Marx employed dialetic to great effect. Yet Plato considered all writing inferior to live debates.

Plato, although an aristocrat, rejected politics because of events early in his life: the junta of 'Thirty Tyrants' and the trial and execution under the restored democracy of his revered teacher in 399BC. Plato then left Athens, visiting Italy, where he stayed with the Pythagorean philosopher-ruler of Taranto and Sicily where he fell foul of the tyrant Dionysius I. Returning to Athens in c.387BC, he founded his Academy outside the city, for a select few to study philosophy.

Plato's 25 extant *dialogues*, along with several long letters, form the finest body of Greek prose ever written. Early dialogues, such as *Euthyphro* and *Crito*, and *Apology* (a rare monologue), give a vivid portrait of Socrates. They explore ethical, political and religious issues, with Socrates the genial, ironic, open-minded inquirer. In later dialogues Socrates the real person fades, as Plato's own ideas develop.

EROS HIGH AND LOW

In the *Symposium* (Banquet), the nature of eros (desire) is discussed. The comedian Aristophanes explains that, as once parts of a circular whole, we are forever seeking our divided selves. After the incursion of Alcibiades, very drunk, Socrates propounds what may be Plato's own view, relating a purported talk with Diotima, a priestess. She declared that physical sex of any type is the lowest form of eros. Higher is spiritual procreation, with souls uniting to create intellectual beauty. But eros at its highest transcends individuals, as the soul grasps the impersonal *idea* of beauty. Erotic desire is only the springboard for this ascent. (From *Symposium* comes our muddled concept of 'Platonic love'.)

THE MYTH OF THE CAVE

Central to Plato's philosophy is his Theory of Ideas (or Ideal Forms), propounded in the Myth of the Cave in *Republic*. (*Republic* also describes Plato's utopia, an austere society governed by an elite of Guardians, with poets and artists banned. While most people live lives of

Left: The myth of the prisoners chained in the cave, from which only philosophy can help them to escape. From a Flemish painting of the 16th century illustrating one of the crucial sections of Plato's Republic.

Right: Plato's Academy outside Athens, where the philosopher taught via dialectical debates. From a Roman mosaic.

unenlighted drudgery, women Guardians are men's equals – as revolutionary as the proposal to raise children communally.)

Imagine, says Plato, a row of prisoners in a cave, chained together facing inward, all unable to move. A great fire blazes behind them, separated by a parapet on which men walk carrying statues. Firelight casts the statues' shadows onto the inner wall. Prisoners, knowing only these shadows, take them for reality.

One day a prisoner, somehow escaping his shackles, turns round. He is at first blinded by the real fire. Even more overwhelming is the sunlight when he reaches the surface. Once over his shock, he is astonished by the beauty of reality. But, on returning to the cave, he cannot convince his fellow-prisoners of the real world above. *We* are those hide-bound prisoners, chained by our stupidity and desires to this world of shadows. Only through philosophy, grasping the eternal world of Ideas behind the transient sensual world, can we escape.

In *Phaedrus*, Plato related a complementary myth: that of the Charioteer with two horses, a savage black animal filled with base sensual desires, and a white one, its spiritual opposite. The charioteer must master the black horse or it will drag him to ruin. Plato believed that our souls must strive to control or transcend our carnal desires.

THE PHILOSOPHER-KING

In 367BC the 62-year-old Plato sailed to Syracuse to be adviser to its new ruler, Dionysius II. He had been invited by Dion, a former Academy student and Dionysius' cousin, who said that the young tyrant was interested in philosophy. Despite misgivings, Plato could not ignore this chance to turn Greece's most powerful ruler into a 'philosopher-king' guided by virtue. But Dionysius, although he had intellectual interests, proved more interested in wine and women than the tough

philosophical course grounded in maths that Plato proposed. Plato himself proved useless at court politics. Soon jealous courtiers turned the tyrant against Dion, who went into exile. Plato finally left Syracuse ignominiously. Yet he returned five years later at the pleading of Dionysius. He found that the tyrant now considered himself a philosopher. Plato was imprisoned and only managed to leave with great difficulty. Then Dion returned to Sicily and the island was engulfed in civil war. All seemed to show that politics and philosophy never mix.

Plato died in Athens working on *Laws*, his last, grimmest blueprint for an ideal society, based on Spartan models. This is truly authoritarian – even homosexuality is banned, although Plato himself was homosexual – and there is no religious or intellectual freedom at all. But Plato the man apparently could still laugh. After he died at a wedding-feast, Aristophanes' comedies were found by his bed.

Below: Plato disputing with Aristotle, his most brilliant pupil, who evolved a very different philosophy. Carved by Luca della Robbia in the 15th century.

ARISTOTLE: THE MASTER OF KNOWLEDGE 384–322BC

Above: This bust, possibly based on an original by his contemporary Praxiteles, may portray Aristotle accurately rather than flatteringly.

Below: Aristotle contemplating a bust of Homer, from a painting by Rembrandt. Aristotle was as knowledgeable about literature as he was about the natural world.

Aristotle and Plato, the twin giants of Greek philosophy, are often seen as polar opposites, the former systematically examining this world, the latter gazing mystically upward to the next world. In fact they complement almost as much as they contradict each other. Aristotle studied for decades at Plato's Academy and his work shows Plato's influence, which he only gradually rejected or modified. Aristotle himself said: "Plato is dear to me, but dearer still is truth."

THE COURTLY OUTSIDER

Aristotle was born at Stagira, a small Ionic city in northern Greece, so he was a foreigner in Athens. His father was court physician to the Macedonian king Amyntas II, and Aristotle grew up in a strange royal court, not as a citizen of a polis. All his life he was notably well-dressed but remained always an outsider.

After his father died in 367BC, Aristotle joined Plato's Academy in Athens, the "city hall of wisdom" in his words. He remained there for 20 years, his genius being recognized by Plato, but the Academy's increasing emphasis on maths did not suit its most brilliant student.

When, on Plato's death, his mediocre nephew Speusippus took over the Academy, Aristotle left to found a philosophical community near the Hellespont. There he fell in love with and married Phyllis (also called Pythias), niece of a local Greek ruler. In 342BC he returned to Macedonia, the rising superpower, as tutor to Alexander, Philip II's son. Alexander, headstrong and romantic, was very unlike his tutor. However Aristotle imparted to the prince a love of Greek culture – Alexander especially liked Euripides' tragedies, although Homer was his idol – if not, it appears, his contempt for 'barbarians' (non-Greeks).

THE LYCEUM

By 335BC Aristotle was back in Athens. There he founded his school: the Lyceum. Open to all, unlike the Academy, it had wide interests, becoming the world's first research institute, with library, museum, collections of natural objects and ultimately 2,000 students, then a huge number. Initially Aristotle taught while walking around its half-built colonnade, hence his school's traditional name: Peripatetic.

Aristotle systematically classified the natural world – botany and biology begin with his studies – from shellfish to stars. He dissected animal and human corpses, making notes and illustrations (since lost). Alexander sent his ex-tutor specimens during his world-conquest. When, after Alexander's death in 323BC, war broke out between Athens and Macedonia, Aristotle fled to Chalcis "to prevent Athens repeating its mistake with Socrates", i.e. executing him. When he died in 322BC, he left 18 household slaves, indicating remarkable wealth for a philosopher.

THE GREAT CATEGORIZER

Aristotle was one of the most systematic thinkers known. He mapped out many still basic fields of inquiry, including biology, economics, logic, law, physics, metaphysics, politics, meteorology, ethics – probably no one else has ever *categorized* so many things as he did. Dante Alighieri, the medieval poet, called him *il maestro di color che sanno* (the master of those who know). However, Aristotle's writings survive only as dense, dry lecture notes, which restricts his wider appeal.

Unlike Plato, Aristotle accepted the material world, thinking it the only world we can investigate, but he was no crude materialist. While Plato believed that worldly objects are mere shadows of ideal forms, Aristotle asked: What *are* objects in this world? He thought that *form* is what give an object its purpose. A house is more than a jumble of building materials, necessary though they are. Similarly, Socrates was not just his physical constituents. An object's form exists within it, and could no more exist independently from it than a man's shape could exist apart from his body.

Aristotle's logically deduced views on form differed radically from Plato's mysticism. He posited four distinct but complementary Causes of form, which explains why a thing is what it is: the material, efficient, formal and final causes.

POETRY AND POLITICS

Aristotle's major works include *Poetics*, *Nicomachean Ethics*, *Politics*, *Rhetoric*, *Physics*, *Metaphysics* (so-called because it came *meta* [after] physics in the library).

Right: Aristotle (right) gestures toward the ground while Plato points to the heavens, indicating the former's less idealistic philosophy. From Raphael's School of Athens *in the Vatican, Rome.*

In *Poetics* Aristotle proclaimed poetry and tragedy superior to history because they portray noble actions that "rouse pity and fear, so achieving emotional cleansing (*catharsis*)." He posited a divine Unmoved Mover beyond the universe but was ambivalent about immortality.

In *Politics* (the last major Greek work on the topic), he wrote: "Man is by nature a political animal... Men come to the city to live, they stay to live the Good Life." Instead of the excellence/virtue (areté) sought earlier, he offered happiness (*eudaimonia*). Like Socrates, he saw virtue and happiness as connected. Happiness could be found through the Golden Mean. For example, bravery is the mean between cowardice and rashness. He was more realistic (or conservative) than Plato about his ideal society, accepting slavery and women's inferiority as natural, but still saw it as based on a medium-sized polis. While Alexander was overturning the political world, Aristotle was laying the groundwork of a logical philosophy that would dominate much of Western and Islamic thought in the Middle Ages.

Above: Aristotle being 'ridden' by his wife Phyllis. Aristotle, who had married for love, was reputedly later henpecked by Phyllis. From a drawing by Hans Baldung of c.1540.

IN SOCRATES' FOOTSTEPS
CYNICS AND SCEPTICS

Above: Diogenes, a bust of the 3rd century BC showing this most original philosopher in a sombre mood, unusual for someone normally so cheerful.

Below: Diogenes was noted for his ascetically minimalist life. Seeing a boy drinking without even a mug, he threw his away his own. From a painting by Etienne Jeurat of the 18th century.

Socrates' followers varied from the high-minded Plato to the hedonistic Aristippus of Cyrene (435–356BC). Aristippus thought undeferred pleasure the one worthwhile goal, preferably the "smooth motions of the flesh". He practised what he preached, but his school, perpetuated by his grandson, impressed few Greeks. In contrast, two other schools at odds with mainstream thinking flourished: Cynicism and Scepticism.

DIOGENES THE CYNIC c.404–325BC
Plato in irritation called Diogenes "Socrates gone mad". Certainly the great Athenian thinker inspired Diogenes, but for Diogenes life finally proved a comedy, not a tragedy.

Diogenes came from Sinope, a Greek city on the Black Sea, where his father was imprisoned for currency-forging. Diogenes, also implicated, was exiled, moving to Athens. There he became a follower of Antisthenes (*c.*445–360BC),

once a student of Socrates. Antisthenes dressed like a poor labourer, rejecting public affairs, private property, marriage and established religion. (That he could spurn religion publicly shows that Athens, after Socrates' trial, had regained its normal tolerance.) Antisthenes generally discouraged followers but Diogenes was his most persistent disciple, who would not be dissuaded even by a stick. With Diogenes the Cynics became a school – if dropouts can be said to form a school.

LIVING LIKE DOGS
Cynic (*cynicos*), meaning dog-like, was an insult happily accepted by Diogenes. He flouted social customs in an ultra-Socratic quest for truth and virtue, but was not remotely 'cynical' in today's negative sense. Once asked why he was carrying a lantern in daylight, he replied that he was looking for an "honest man".

Diogenes had no house but lived in a barrel. He had one ragged cloak for the day that was his blanket at night. He begged for his food, having one bowl and one mug. But when he saw a boy drinking from his cupped hands, he threw away even his mug as superfluous.

Diogenes satisfied all his bodily functions in public, even masturbating. When rebuked for this – the Greeks admired heroic nudity, not sexual exhibitionism – he simply said: "Ah, if only I could satisfy my hunger by rubbing my belly."

Effectively stateless, having no polis, he claimed to be a *cosmopolitan*, a "citizen of the universe". Captured by pirates and put up for sale as a slave, Diogenes was asked if he had any special skills. "Governing men," he replied, and pointed to a well-dressed man. "Sell me to him, he needs a master." He was freed by friends. Finally dying from eating raw octopus – to show that cooking is unnecessary – he ordered his corpse thrown in a ditch.

Ignoring these last wishes – which outraged the deepest religious beliefs – Athens erected a marble monument with a dog to this most original of thinkers.

Diogenes' aim was not to win fame by crude sensationalism but to show that almost all material wants can be discarded. Like many later philosophers, he sought not areté (virtue) but eudmamonia (happiness) and ataraxia (freedom from worry or care). His successor Crates of Thebes (c.365–285BC) renounced great wealth to live a similar wandering life. Crates' wife Hipparchia, who was famous for her beauty, was among the few noted female philosophers. Cynicism survived under the Roman Empire. It in some ways anticipated the Stoics, Christian ascetics and even, much later, the hippies.

PYRRHO THE SCEPTIC C.365–275BC

Among the Greeks who followed Alexander to India was Pyrrho of Elis. He was so impressed by the diversity of customs and beliefs that he saw, especially among Indian fakirs, that he became the founder of scepticism. He argued that the reasons for a belief are never better than those against, and that the only wise approach is to suspend judgement and accept the world as it seems. His goal was ataraxia, like Diogenes. Pyrrho often pointed to animals as living enviably undisturbed lifes. He retired to Elis, where he lived out a long and peaceful life amid admirers.

Pyrrho's chief pupil, Timon of Phlius, (c.320–230BC) took scepticism further, showing that every argument proceeds from premises not already established. To demonstrate those premises' truth by other arguments, they must be based on other undemonstrated premises, a potentially infinite and so absurd regression.

Timon's follower Arcesilaus (315–240BC) became head of Plato's Academy in 275BC, making it a bastion of scepticism for about 200 years. Timon's successor Carneades caused a stir when visiting Rome by arguing both sides of a cause on successive days. Cicero was later influenced by the Academy's scepticism. The best account of scepticism comes from Sextus Empiricus' summary of its arguments in the *Pyrrhoniarum* of c.AD200. David Hume, the great 18th-century Scottish philosopher, was inspired by Pyrrhonic scepticism.

Above: Bion of Olbia (c.325–255BC) was an eclectic philosopher, intellectually closest to the Cynics. He lived by wandering around the major cities teaching, but finally gained the patronage of Antigonus II, king of Macedonia.

Left: Alexander the Great and the barrel-dwelling Diogenes reputedly met in Corinth in 335BC. When Alexander asked what he could do for the thinker, Diogenes replied: "Get out of my sunlight."

RIVAL SCHOOLS
STOICS V. EPICUREANS

Above: A copy of an original statue of c.240BC of Chrysippus, the second great Stoic teacher, who emphasized ethics over logic and physics in a way that proved very appealing.

Two rival schools of thought, Stoicism and Epicureanism, emerged around 300BC in Athens to become the main forms of philosophy for centuries.

STOICISM

Stoicism was founded by Zeno of Citium (333–262BC). Zeno, reaching Athens in 311BC, attended the Academy, listened to Crates the Cynic and studied Aristotle before evolving his own philosophy. He taught in the Stoa Poikile (Painted Stoa) from which his school takes its name. His courses were tripartite: logic, physics and ethics. His teachings were refined by his successors Cleanthes and Chrysippus (c.280–207BC). Chrysippus downplayed logic and physics in favour of ethics, creating an appealing philosophical package.

The essence of Stoicism was that nothing happens by chance, all things being predetermined by the laws of the cosmos. There is nothing higher than the natural universe, of which we are part. We must live in harmony with it, accepting everything that happens. Stoics proclaimed a "brotherhood of man" that included slaves and non-Greeks. Although they raised a god (called Zeus) to quasi-pantheistic primacy, they did not believe in individual afterlife. Nor did they forbid suicide.

Left: The stern nobility of Epicurus is apparent in this bust. Far from advocating sensual indulgence, as his enemies said, Epicurus thought most pleasures were not worth the effort. He abjured politics, fame and – guardedly – any real belief in the gods, valuing friendship above everything.

Poseidonius (c.135–51BC), a polymathic Stoic, travelled widely before establishing his school at Rhodes, where important Romans, including Pompey and Cicero, visited him. Cicero later translated Greek philosophical ideas into Latin and Stoicism became the favoured philosophy of the Roman elite, who found its noble austerity appealing.

ROMAN STOICS

Seneca (2BC–AD65) was a playwright and courtier, the emperor Nero's tutor and then minister. Retiring from the increasingly paranoid emperor's court, Seneca turned again to philosophy until, implicated in a conspiracy against Nero in AD65, he committed suicide. He wrote (in Latin) essays, plays and 124 letters on varied subjects, especially the humane treatment of slaves. "Remember, the man you call your slave is of the same species and breathes, lives and dies under the same skies as you." His work, if unoriginal, inspired many later generations unable to read Greek.

Epictetus (AD55–135) also suffered from imperial paranoia, being among the philosophers exiled by the emperor Domitian in AD89. He accepted this as calmly as earlier maltreatment while a slave, settling in western Greece. There he taught an austere yet compassionate philosophy, attacking easy cures for human misery that ignored the "wisdom of God". Epictetus wrote in Greek.

So did the emperor Marcus Aurelius (reigned AD161–80). Antiquity's one philosopher-king. Marcus was brought up to rule as a sage but in practice had to spend much of his reign fighting invading barbarians on the Danube frontier. His *Meditations*, written on campaign, are the private records of an exhausted if great-souled man. Tinged with Platonism, they were the last true Stoic writings.

Right: An original – and very rare – bronze statue of Marcus Aurelius, the philosopher-emperor (reigned AD161–80). The last great Stoic, he wrote his Meditations *while campaigning on the Danube. They were not meant for publication.*

EPICUREANISM

Although Epicureanism was often damned by its enemies as encouraging gross sensuality, this was a travesty of the real aims of its founder Epicurus (341–270BC). The son of Athenian colonists on Samos, Epicurus settled in Athens in 307BC. He established his Garden – literally, it was a vegetable garden – near Plato's Academy, but with very different aims: to seek human happiness, not mystical truth.

Epicurus believed the chief causes of human misery were fear of what happens after death and frustrated desires for the superfluous while alive.

He set out to demolish fear of death by showing that the soul, like the rest of the universe, is composed of constituent atoms, which simply dissolve at death. Here he was echoing the thinking of Democritus (*c.*460–370BC), an earlier atomist. There is nothing to be feared or expected after death.

Contentment in this life is best achieved by intelligent frugality, Epicurus' extant maxims suggest. "Value frugality not for asceticism's sake but because it minimizes worries… It is better to sleep without fear on a straw mattress than trembling on a gold bed … No pleasure is bad in itself but certain pleasures incur drawbacks far greater than the pleasure gained."

Epicurus shunned public life, seeing in the polis only a source of strife – an understandable reaction to the turmoil of his age, if one that marked the withdrawal of philosophers from society. Instead, he valued friendship above everything else. Never marrying, he made his Garden a refuge for the like-minded, be they citizens, slaves or women. Admitting slaves and women to his school – something Plato had only contemplated – caused a

scandal even greater than denying the afterlife. (Epicurus tactfully accepted the gods' existence but denied they were at all interested in humanity.) The Garden, emulating the Academy and Lyceum, had a communal life, with regular debates and monthly *symposia*. Often ill in later years, Epicurus lived mostly off bread and cheese and died in great pain with cheerful, indeed Stoical, fortitude.

Epicurus wrote more than 300 books on philosophy but none has survived. While his teaching proved popular in the Greek world, his greatest disciple was the Roman Lucretius (94–55BC). In *De Rerum Natura* (*About the Nature of Things*), Lucretius wrote a brilliant philosophical poem. Although Lucretius called his poetry just "honey round the edges" of his beliefs, Cicero was much impressed by this philosophy expounded so lyrically.

Below: Zeno of Citium, who settled in Athens in 311BC and founded the Stoic school of philosophy. This stresed acceptance of the universe as reflecting the divine will.

THE PLATONIST REVIVAL
PLOTINUS AND NEOPLATONISTS

The last great philosophical school of antiquity was Neoplatonism. Its founder was Plotinus (*c.*AD204–70), an Egyptian Greek. Plotinus saw himself not as founding a new school but as reviving true Platonism. However, he gave Plato's thinking a deeply mystical, overwhelmingly monistic turn by positing a superexistent *One* as the source of all being, far beyond sensory perception.

Plotinus first studied under Ammonius Saccas, an obscure figure who wrote nothing. He then joined the Persian expedition of the emperor Gordian III in AD243, apparently hoping to learn about eastern religions in India. After Gordian's murder by his troops, Plotinus moved to Rome. There he started his own school.

Among his aristocratic students was Gallienus, who became emperor in AD253. Gallienus so admired Plotinus that he offered to found Platonopolis, a city for philosophers in Campania, but court intrigues aborted this utopian project. After Gallienus' death in AD268, Plotinus withdrew from public life. He had never been a worldly man. Plato, while spurning Athenian democracy, had remained interested in politics. By contrast, Neoplatonists ignored the world falling into ruin about them. Instead, they turned to the mystical *Monos* (the One).

FLIGHT OF THE ONE TO THE ONE
Porphyry (AD232–305), Plotinus' biographer and most important follower, recorded the last words of his teacher as: "Strive to bring back the god within yourselves to the God in the Universe." This injunction lies at the heart of Plotinus' philosophy, simultaneously rational and mystical. His thinking incorporated Pre-Socratic, Aristotelian and Stoic ideas, creating a novel, moving philosophy.

Plotinus saw the One as the supernatural, ineffable basis of all being, resembling Plato's idea of the Good. Below this ineffable summit are tiers of being. The first is *Nous*, or Mind, the second *Psyche*, or Soul, a projection of Mind. Soul looks up to Mind but down to Nature (*Bios*), but the tiers are interdependent. Even at the lowest corporeal level, all things seek *epistrophe*, a return to the One. Plotinus' dynamic vision has been compared to an inexhaustible fountain of light whose waters constantly descend before returning to the source. He believed human beings can, via philosophy, attain ecstatic visions of the One as *fuge monou pros monon*, the "Flight of the One to the One". He claimed to have achieved this three times.

As a man, Plotinus was self-effacing and ascetic, so ashamed of bodily functions he did not even like to be seen eating. He never married, eschewing sex, but freely admitted women to his classes. These could be tortured sessions, the philosopher falling silent in his attempt to express the inexpressible. He wrote little and then only in his last years.

THE FOLLOWERS
Porphyry, born in Tyre, came to Rome in *c.*AD262 and joined Plotinus' classes. Soon the master's favourite, he recorded Plotinus' teaching in nine books, *Enneads* (*Ninths*). Like his master, Porphyry rejected Christianity because of its belief in a personal god and salvation by faith – the One is not a person, superficial resemblances to the Christian Trinity are accidental. Porphyry amended Plotinus' thought by positing the importance of

Above: The spiritual nobility of Plotinus, the ancient world's last great original thinker who founded the Neoplatonist school, shines through this bust of the 3rd century AD. *This might well be a portrait from life.*

Left: Julian, the last significant non-Christian Roman emperor (reigned AD361–3*), was also a Neoplatonist philosopher. His attempts to revive Hellenism as an organized religion died with him, but Greek philosophy itself survived for a time.*

astrology. Plotinus, however, to whom the stars shone with the universe's divinity, always rejected astrology's basic premises.

Porphyry's successor Iamblichus (*c.*AD250–326) added *theurgy*, magical rites derived from Neopythagoreanism – more a religion than philosophy – to Neoplatonism. His synthesis shaped Neoplatonism as it spread around the Roman Empire. Schools sprang up at Alexandria, Pergamum and Athens. The last pagan emperor Julian studied this semi-magical philosophy at Athens and Pergamum. During his brief reign (AD361–3), Julian tried to revitalize paganism along Neoplatonist lines.

THE END OF GREEK PHILOSOPHY

In Alexandria one of the last Hellenic philosophers was a woman, Hypatia (*c.*AD370–420). A fine mathematician as well as a Neoplatonist, beautiful but celibate, Hypatia devoted her life to philosophy until one day she was dragged from her coach and murdered by a fanatical Christian mob. Despite her murder, Neoplatonism lingered on in Alexandria, but its last bastion was, appositely, Athens. There, Proclus (AD410–85) fused mathematics and mysticism to expound the interconnectedness of all things, arguing that time itself is a circular dance. Finally in AD529 the Byzantine emperor Justinian ordered the closure of the schools of Athens.

This marked the end of ancient Neoplatonism, but it had deeply influenced St Augustine (AD354–430), among the greatest Christian thinkers. Other early Christian writers, from the Roman patrician Boethius in the 6th century and Dionysus the Aeropagite (suposedly an Athenian converted by St Paul in the 1st century AD but actually a Greek

Right: Percy Bysshe Shelley (1792–1822) was one of many Romantic poets influenced by Neoplatonism, most notably in Adonais. *Here he sits writing amid the ruins of the Baths of Caracalla, Rome. From a posthumous painting by Joseph Severn.*

Right: Hypatia of Alexandria, one of the few women philosophers in Hellenic tradition, was traditionally very beautiful but celibate. A mathematician as well as a mystic, she was murdered by a mob of fanatical Christians in C.AD *420.*

contemporary of Boethius) to Eriugena in the 9th century, were also profoundly affected by Neoplatonism. (How far the last two thinkers are really Christians, rather than mystical pantheists, remains debated.)

In Renaissance Italy, Neoplatonism re-emerged fully, first inspired by Greek thinkers fleeing the fall of Constantinople to the Turks. Marsilio Ficino translated the *Enneads* while Pico della Mirandola tried to reconcile Christianity, Platonism, Judaism and even Chaldean paganism in a mystical synthesis. His heroic efforts landed him briefly in a papal prison, but Neoplatonism spread north to England. Reviving again with the Romantics, its perennial philosophy underlies much of the poetry of S.T. Coleridge, P.B. Shelley, Ralph Waldo Emerson and W.B. Yeats.

THE FIRST MATHEMATICIANS
600BC–AD200

Above: Thales, visiting Egypt in the 6th century BC, was asked by the pharaoh to calculate the height of a pyramid. He waited for the time when his shadow equalled his own height and thus calculated the height of the pyramid itself.

Below: A monument built in Samos in 1989 to Pythagoras. The mystical mathematician, born in Samos, traditionally discovered the theorem that bears his name.

Mathematics as a proper discipline began with the Greeks in the 6th century BC. The Egyptians had long been brilliant at practical calculation and measuring and the Babylonians had first divided the circle into 360 degrees, but neither had developed a series of theories based on definitions with axioms and proofs. It took Greek intellectual passion and precision to do this. Maths became so central to Greek thinking that Plato stipulated that only the numerate should enter his Academy. But Greek maths had its limits. For example, it had no term for – or concept of – zero, unlike Indian maths.

EARLY MATHEMATICIANS
Thales is considered the first Greek mathematician. Visiting Egypt in the 6th century BC, Thales was reputedly asked by the pharaoh to calculate the height of a pyramid. He waited for a time when his shadow equalled his own height and then calculated the pyramid's height. He also worked out how to calculate a ship's distance from the shore. Around 520BC, Pythagoras traditionally discovered the theorem that bears his name: that in a right-angled triangle the square of the sum of the opposite side equals the squares of the other two sides. Pythagoreans also knew that the sum of all three angles of a triangle equals two right angles. They had a mystical belief in number, being the true (if secret) unity behind the universe, manifested in musical octaves. But their discovery of incommensurability – that some ratios could not be expressed as whole numbers, a seemingly insoluble problem already encountered in Babylon – led them to concentrate on geometry.

Eudoxus of Cnidus (*c.*408–347BC) studied with the Pythagoreans at Taranto and also in Egypt. In geometry he discovered the general theory of proportions

Above: Euclid (c.330–270BC), the greatest mathematician before the late 19th century. From a portrait by the Renaissance artist Girolamo Mocetto.

applicable to both incommensurable and commensurable magnitudes, later shown by Euclid in Book 5. He also showed by the "method of exhaustion" that the cone and pyramid are one third the volume respectively of the cylinder and prism with the same base and height.

EUCLID THE MATHEMATICAL MASTER
The greatest Greek mathematician was Euclid (*c.*330–270BC), who taught at the Museum/Library of Alexandria. His famous work is his *Elements* (*Stoichea*) in 13 books. The most influential book in mathematical history, it formed the basis of

Western maths until the late 19th century. Although not all the contents are original – Plato in *Timaeus* had anticipated the treatment of regular geometric solids – Euclid added a new logical structure of such elegant clarity that Bertrand Russell called *Elements* "the most perfect monument of Greek intellect". By deducing the geometrical objects' properties from a few axioms, Euclid in effect founded the axiomatic method of mathematics. Book 1 begins with definitions followed by the famous 5 postulates. Euclid then gives a list of common notions. The first definitions are:

1.1. *A point is that which has no part.*
1.2. *A line is a breadthless length.*
1.3. *The extremities of lines are points.*
1.4. *A straight line lies equally with respect to the points on itself.*

The common notions are axioms such as: *"Things equal to the same thing are also equal to one another."*

LATER MATHS AND ARCHIMEDES

Archimedes (287–212BC) was a brilliant mathematician as well as famed inventor. His achievements in maths were prodigious, as a list of even his surviving works suggests: *On the Sphere and the Cylinder; On the Measurement of the Circle; On Conoids and Spheroids; On Spirals; On the Equilibrium of Surfaces* where the theory of the lever is propounded, enabling him to boast "Give me somewhere to stand and I will move the Earth!"; *On the Quadratura of the Parabola* and *The Sand Reckoner.* This last work deals with the problem of expressing huge numbers. It demonstrates that the number of grains of sand in the universe, far from being infinite, may on some asumptions be reckoned as 10^{63}.

Archimedes also calculated a far closer value for Pi. He designed his own tomb incorporating a sphere inside a cylinder, to record his discovery that the sphere occupies two-thirds of the space. His most famous discovery, 'Archimedes' principle', states that a body immersed in fluid loses weight equal to the weight of

Above: Reconstruction of the lighthouse at Alexandria. At c.115m (383ft) tall, its light both guided shipping and symbolized the city's intellectual brilliance.

Below: Archimedes, the great mathematician of the 3rd century BC, portrayed by José de Ribera (1591–1652).

the amount of fluid it displaces. Archimedes traditionally realized this on stepping into his bath, crying out "Eureka" (I have found it!).

Only two of 12 works attributed to Apollonius of Perge (*c.*260–190BC), the 'Great Geometer', survive. In *Conics*, he pioneered terms such as ellipse, parabola, and hyperbola describing various types of orbit. *Conics* distilled 200 years of earlier thinking. It remained canonical even for 17th-century revolutionaries such as Descartes, Fermat and Newton.

Later Greek maths continued to develop but less vigorously. Ptolemy summarized much of it in the 2nd century AD. Diophantus (*c.*AD200–80) was the one noted Greek contributor to algebra, although only six of his works survive. He influenced the Arabs, who later proved far more original at algebra.

ASTRONOMY
MAPPING THE COSMOS 600BC–AD150

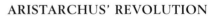

Above: Ptolemy (Claudius Ptolemaeus), the last great Hellenic astronomer, who worked in Alexandria in the 2nd century AD. From a portrait by Pedro Berruguette and Justus of Ghent c.1475.

Below: The constellation of Hercules with Corona and Lycra, from Atlas Coelestis *of 1729 by John Flamsteed, painted by James Thornhill. Viewing the cosmos scientifically and mythologically is one of the Greeks' lasting achievements.*

The Greeks were not the world's first astronomers. Egyptians and Babylonians had compiled detailed star charts to predict eclipses, but their knowledge remained tied to their religions. Soon after 600BC, the Greeks began to observe and speculate boldly and rationally. Thales probably used Babylonian records to predict the solar eclipse of 585BC. But his other astronomical feat, suggesting the Earth was spherical, was unprecedented. Inspired by him, Anaximander pioneered geometrical astronomy. He posited that the Sun, stars and Moon are rings of fire, respectively 27, 18 and 9 times the Earth's diameter, encased in tubes. Through holes in these tubes their light is seen. His concept of the Earth floating in space was too radical for his first successors, who reverted to cosier ideas.

CLASSICAL ASTRONOMY
In Periclean Athens (*c.*460–430BC), Anaxagoras daringly posited that the sun was a fiery stone "larger than the Peloponnese", the moon shining with its reflected light. (These were such novel ideas that Anaxagoras left Athens to escape impiety charges. These were really political, aimed at Pericles his patron.)

Pythagoreans living in Italy went much further. Restating Thales' idea of a spherical Earth, they suggested that the Earth itself is one of the planets, not the centre of the universe. All planets, including the Sun, move around the "central fire" whose light, in Pythagorean cosmogony, the Sun only reflects. The Pythagoreans also first realized that the morning and evening stars are the same planet: Venus.

Aristotle in the 4th century BC put the Earth solidly back at the centre of things, with the planets circling it. But he was an unoriginal astronomer, just restating the views of Eudoxus of Cnidus. Eudoxus had posited homocentric orbits for the planets to explain their *retrograde motions* (when seen from Earth, planets can appear to move backward). Around 330BC Callipus elaborated this system, adding further spheres for the lunar and solar orbits and calculating the year accurately at 365.25 days. Heraclides Ponticus (*c.*390–310BC) reputedly suggested that Mercury and Venus rotate around the Sun, which itself circles the Earth, pointing towards the heliocentric theory.

ARISTARCHUS' REVOLUTION
At Alexandria, whose new Library/ Mausoleum attracted Greece's brightest minds, Greek astronomy reached its climax. Its boldest thinker was Aristarchus of Samos (*c.*310–230BC). He posited the full heliocentric theory: that the Earth and other planets revolve around the Sun, the Earth itself turning every 24 hours on its own axis. To avoid the parallax (apparent movement) of the fixed stars, he placed them unimaginably far off. This solved all problems of retrograde motions. It proved too radical, however, for Aristarchus

Right: The geocentric universe as envisaged by Ptolemy, with 27 concentric circles describing the orbits of the heavenly bodies from the Moon to Saturn, the farthest planet visible to the naked eye.

united other scientists against him, one trying to indict him for impiety in uprooting the Earth. Archimedes also rejected Aristarchus' ideas – without calling for his trial. Aristarchus had just one Greek follower, Seleucus, his ideas lying dormant until Copernicus in the 16th century.

THE ALEXANDRIAN ACHIEVEMENT

While sticking to the geocentric theory, Alexandria's astronomers made impressive contributions to science. Most were polymaths, such as Eratosthenes of Cyrene (275–194BC), who became Librarian in 235BC. He is renowned for calculating the Earth's diameter. Eratosthenes knew that on 21 June at noon in Syene on the Tropic of Cancer the Sun would be at its zenith. He also knew that in Alexandria the angle of the Sun's elevation would then be 7.2 degrees south of the zenith. He calculated the distance from Alexandria to Syene as 7.2/360 of the total circumference of the Earth. The distance between the cities was a known 800km (500 miles), so he worked out the Earth's circumference as 39,690km (24,663 miles), within 98% of the real figure. Like other Greek astronomers, he relied wholly on observations made by the naked eye, as they had no lenses.

Hipparchus of Nicaea (*c.*190–126BC) was probably the greatest Alexandrian astronomer. He discovered the precession of the equinoxes; estimated the length of the lunar month and catalogued 850 fixed stars, giving their longitude and latitude, and improved the theory of epicycles invented by Apollonius *c.*220BC. He based his theories both on observation and on tables going back to Babylonian records. He also noted a *nova* (new star).

Most of Hipparchus' work survives only in the *Almagest* of Ptolemy, the last Greek astronomer, living in Alexandria in the 2nd century AD. Ptolemy perfected the geocentric theory of the universe, providing detailed mathematical theories supported by observations. His belief that the same divine harmony resonated in the stars and the human soul passed to the medieval and Renaissance worlds.

Below: Syene (Aswan) in Egypt. Eratosthenes calculated the distance from Alexandria to Syene as 7.2/360 of the Earth's circumference, so giving him a remarkably accurate figure for it.

GEOGRAPHY
MAPPING THE EARTH C.550BC–AD170

Above: The Stoa at Miletus, the wealthy Ionian city where Hecataeus drew up the first known map of the world in the 6th century BC.

Below: Ptolemy of Alexandria's map of the Middle East, from Phoenicia (Lebanon) across to Babylonia (southern Iraq), drawn up in the 2nd century AD. His maps are both beautiful and functional.

The Greeks were the first geographers in the full meaning of the word. Their researches were linked to astronomers' theoretical findings – which led to the idea of the Earth as spherical – and to reports from navigators and other travellers. Greek geographical knowledge continued growing under the Romans.

THE FIRST GEOGRAPHERS (C.550–420BC)

The first geographers were also historians – *historia* meant originally any inquiry or research. Hecataeus (*c.*560–490BC), born in Miletus, travelled widely around the Mediterranean, possibly venturing into the Atlantic. He was involved in the abortive Ionian Revolt against Persia of 499–494BC, despite initially opposing it because hostile to its leader Aristagoras.

Hecataeus' great work was a map of the whole world, possibly inspired by an earlier map by Anaximander. He saw the Earth as a disc surrounded by the all-encircling Ocean, divided into four

PYTHEAS, THE GREAT EXPLORER

The classical Greeks were seldom adventurous sailors, preferring to stick to known routes and landmarks. The Carthaginians, anyway, had long barred Greeks from the western Mediterranean and Atlantic. But Pytheas (*c.*380–310BC), a native of Marseilles, the largest Greek colony in southern France, managed somehow to break out to the Atlantic. He sailed up the west coast of Gaul (France) to Cornwall, then commercially very important due to its tin mines. He continued on up past the "Bretannic Isles" – as he is the first recorded person to call them – and reached a northern land called Thule. This could have been Iceland or Norway. It baffled Pytheas, who wrote of places where "land properly speaking no longer exists, nor sea nor air, but a mixture of these things, in which earth and water and all things are suspended… on which no one can walk nor sail." This sounds like pack ice and heavy fogs, both unknown to Greeks. Pytheas returned safely home but his account survives only through Strabo's summaries.

quadrants, east–west by the Mediterranean, and north–south by the rivers Ister (Danube) and Nile. Europe filled the northern half and Africa/Asia the southern half. If ridiculed for inaccuracies by Herodotus (*c.*484–420BC), his better-informed successor, Hecataeus' map was the first to state accurately the continents' relative positions.

In *Periegasis*, Hecataeus described many countries' customs, religions, fauna and flora. (In Egypt, he boasted to a priest that his ancestry went back 16 generations.

The priest replied that his own went back 345!) Hecataeus' map influenced many later generations' worldview. Herodotus, although fascinatingly informative about much of Asia and Europe, was not a cartographer.

Aristotle realized that the Earth was a globe, dividing it into zones, and his pupil Dicecarchus made a new map incorporating his changes. Otherwise geography had advanced little by the mid-4th century BC. Aristotle was uncertain whether the Caspian Sea opened on to the Ocean that Greeks thought encircled the Earth, and he confused the Caucasus with the Himalayan mountains. All changed radically with the philosopher's other pupil.

AFTER ALEXANDER

Alexander the Great's conquests (334–323BC) opened up a vast new world. Alexander himself reached the Punjab in northern India, and the voyage by his admiral Nearchus from the mouth of the Indus to the head of the Persian Gulf provided a flood of new information for geographers. This was collected and analysed at Alexandria's great Library/ Museum. Eratosthenes in the 3rd century BC worked out not only the Earth's

Below: Herodotus the great historian was also an intrepid traveller.

circumference but also longitudes and latitudes for many places – suggesting that he deserved more than his nickname of Beta, or second best. Hipparchus in the 2nd century BC and Posidonius in the 1st continued this work.

GRAECO-ROMAN GEOGRAPHY

Under the long *pax Romana* (Roman peace) after 30BC, geography remained primarily a Greek affair. Strabo (64BC–AD21), who came from the Greek city of Amasia on the Black Sea, travelled widely and wrote 17 books on geography. He held the view that the Earth was a sphere with all the continents, Europe, Asia and Africa, forming a single mass surrounded by the Ocean. Although Strabo claimed to have travelled as far as Ethiopia, his knowledge derives in fact mostly from Eratosthenes, whose works he thus helped to preserve.

The last great Hellenic geographer was Ptolemy of Alexandria. In the mid-2nd century AD he wrote his *Geography* in eight books. By then Rome's invasion of the British Isles, expeditions into the North Sea and trade links with India had vastly extended geographical knowledge. The map Ptolemy drew up reflected this, showing India and even, hazily, China. But he still imagined the three (known) continents as encircled by one ocean. His map remained canonical until 1492.

Above: The Earth as mapped by Ptolemy of Alexandria, who was a great cartographer as well as astronomer. Showing the three known continents, with even China hazily recognized, his ideas remained canonical until the discovery of America in 1492.

Below: Alexander's conquests led to a vast widening of Greek geographical knowledge. From an Indian Mughal painting of the 16th century.

TECHNOLOGY
THE FORGOTTEN ACHIEVEMENTS

Above: Archimedes, the most polymathic of Greek geniuses, inadvertently killed by a Roman soldier in the fall of Syracuse in 212BC. From a Roman mosaic.

Below: Found in the sea near Antikythera, dating to c.80BC, this complex bronze mechanism has 31 gear wheels. It was probably both an astronomical and a navigational device.

The Greeks were once thought to have neglected technology because they had no wish to dirty their hands with science's practical applications. Maintained by their myriad slaves, the argument ran, the Greeks saw science as a gentlemanly pursuit of no practical value. Plutarch, the 2nd-century AD historian, has been quoted to support this view: "Thinking mechanics and all utilitarian arts fit only for vulgar craftsmen, he [Archimedes] concentrated only on things where the beautiful and are not mixed with the necessary." No or little machinery meant little economic advance, and ultimately Graeco-Roman civilization's failure.

Plutarch's view is now seen as misleading, reflecting only the prejudices of his class. (Similar sentiments were frequently voiced by British aristocrats during Britain's Industrial Revolution.) If the Greeks could not match even medieval and early modern Europe's technological achievements, let alone

THE ANTIKYTHERA MECHANISM

A discovery from beneath the sea near the island of Antikythera has revealed Greek technological sophistication. Dating from c.80BC, this remarkable bronze mechanism has at least 31 gear wheels, making it a rival of any such mechanism, in Asia or Europe, before the 19th century. With orbits for the Sun, Venus and other planets, it was probably intended both as a clock and as an astronomical device, incorporating discoveries made in the Hellenistic period. It is the sophisticated ancestor of both computers and clocks, therefore. Although the only such device known today, it is unlikely to have been the only one made. Most bronze objects have been lost, however, melted down for their metal content in the Dark Ages, be they computers or clocks.

China's massive inventiveness, they made many useful inventions. Only the ancient world's political and economic limitations, and its general decline after c.AD200, precluded further technological advances by still creative polymaths. That the word *machine* comes from Greek *mekhane* is no coincidence.

One of the earliest known applications of machinery was in the theatre. Here large cranes lifted scenery and actors, usually representing gods (but once Socrates) on and off stage. These cranes, described by Aristotle, must have used a weight and pulley principle of some complexity but no remains have been found.

Similar machinery was probably used to build many of the great Greek temples, including the Parthenon in Athens, where massive blocks of marble had to be lifted high into place.

Above: The waterwheels of Bihiyat on the Orontes River. Known to the Greeks by the 4th century BC, watermills spread in the Hellenistic and Roman periods. A watermill can grind 150kg (330lb) of grain per hour, compared to 7kg (15lb) ground by a slave.

ARCHIMEDES' SCREW

A mathematician, astronomer and inventor of genius, Archimedes (287–212BC) was born in Syracuse. He worked in Alexandria before returning to become Hieron II's chief scientist. He devised for the powerful Syracusan king many military devices, including formidable walls, cranes that could pull ships from the sea and possibly solar mirrors to burn ships, besides a planetarium and star globe. Archimedes was killed accidentally by a Roman soldier in the capture of Syracuse, but the Romans took over his devices. He is deservedly best known for a utilitarian invention, his screw that helps irrigation.

Archimedes' Screw consists of a screw inside a hollow pipe. The lower end is put in water and the screw then turned, usually by manual labour. As the bottom of the tube turns, it scoops up water. This water slides up a spiral tube as the shaft is turned, until it finally pours out from the top of the tube to feed the irrigation systems. A cruder screw may have been used earlier by the Babylonians to water their Hanging Gardens, but Archimedes definitely developed the screw as used since.

An important labour-saving development that the Greeks adopted was the watermill. Known by the 4th century BC,

watermills spread slowly across western Asia, under Roman rule becoming popular around the Mediterranean. A typical watermill could grind 150kg (330lb) of grain per hour, compared to only 7kg (15lb) by a slave.

HERON OF ALEXANDRIA

A mathematician and engineer, Heron, who lived in Alexandria in the mid-1st century AD, was another remarkable polymath. He listed more than 80 different devices in his numerous books, mainly about hydraulics, pneumatics and mechanics. Among them are drinking fountains, self-filling wine goblets, self-trimming lanterns and self-opening temple doors – all ingenious toys. But in his *Mechanics* he dealt with utilitarian devices such as cranes, hoists (lifts) and presses. Another book, *Stereometrica*, gave useful advice on measuring the contents of ships and *amphorae* (jars).

However, Heron perhaps remains best known for his prototype steam engine, a device that was probably of no use at all. In its developed form this was an *aelopile*, a sealed metal cauldron under a hollow metal sphere. Steam funnelled in tubes from the cauldron made the sphere spin, creating the world's first steam turbine Lack of accessible fossil fuels and crude metallurgy may have kept this steam engine a toy, despite legends that it carried fuel up Alexandria's giant *pharos* (lighthouse).

Above and below: Archimedes' most useful invention was his screw. Turned usually by manual labour, it lifted water for irrigation.

MEDICINE
FROM SUPERSTITION TO SCIENCE

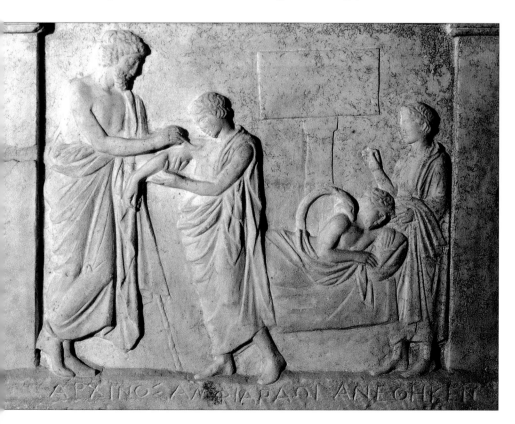

Above: Hippocrates (c.460–380BC), the 'father of medicine', was the first to study medicine systematically and scientifically.

Below: Asclepius, the divine healer, treating a patient. Greek medicine never wholly lost its religious connections. From a relief of the 4th century BC.

Both the Hippocratic oath that doctors traditionally swear, and the snake-entwined staff of their profession, reveal medicine's Greek roots. The oath recalls Hippocrates, the 'first doctor', the latter Asclepius and medicine's religious origins. The Greeks pioneered the move from a religious to scientific approach in medical matters, the invention of rational medicine being among their finest deeds.

In Homer's time, Greek attitudes to sickness and medicine mirrored those of Egypt and Babylon. Treatment involved incantations, magical amulets, spells and prayers to Apollo, god of medicine, and his son Asclepius, the divine healer. These customs long persisted, as did *incubation*, sleeping in precincts at Cos sacred to the god, when healing dreams might come in the night. Such psychosomatic methods helped suggestible sufferers. From the 6th century BC, both attitudes and practice began to change, however.

Above: Galen, the great 2nd-century AD physician, believed that human health was governed by the balance of the 'Four Humours'. From a medieval drawing.

HIPPOCRATES, THE 'FATHER OF MEDICINE' (c.465–c.380BC)

Almost nothing is known of the first true physician, Hippocrates. Traditionally he was associated with the famous medical school on Cos, but surviving buildings there date from after his time and his very existence has been doubted. He probably lived about the same time as Socrates.

Hippocrates first made careful observation of the body the basis of medicine. Though he never practised dissection – which religion discouraged – prayers and sacrifices held no place in his theories. Instead, changes in diet, drugs, rest and keeping the body 'in balance' were key elements of his cure. This rational approach was his greatest single contribution to medicine. About 60 treatises, the *Hippocratic Corpus*, are attributed to him. In *Sacred Disease* he demolished the idea that epilepsy was a god-sent sickness; in *Airs, Waters, Places* he examined the effects of climate and locality on illnesses. Other treatises cover diagnosis, epidemics, paediatrics, nutrition and surgery.

In the 4th century BC Aristotle made a few significant discoveries. His pupil Diocles first practised dissection, so essential to discovering anatomy, and wrote a book on the subject. Dissection of animals was subsequently practised at the Lyceum, Aristotle's school.

ANATOMY IN ALEXANDRIA

In the rich new city of Alexandria, protected by a dynasty of powerful kings with scientific interests and freed from religious taboos, physicians could at last freely practise dissection and even, it is thought, vivisection. Foremost among the bold anatomists of the mid-3rd century BC were Herophilus from Chalcedon and Erasistratus, who had studied at Cos and Athens. Their discoveries about the importance of the heart, brain, vascular and nervous systems were carefully recorded and formed the basis for almost all subsequent medicine for 1,500 years in the Islamic and Christian worlds.

GALEN, THE GREAT SYNTHESIZER (AD129–200)

Galen was a native of Pergamum in Asia Minor. He studied philosophy and rhetoric before switching to study medicine at Pergamum, Smyrna and Alexandria. He began his career treating wounded gladiators at Pergamum. Going to Rome in AD162, he practised as a physician and a medical writer. As the former, he found himself in demand in the highest circles, treating Commodus, the emperor's son, the empress herself and later rulers. Despite fleeing the plague-stricken city in AD166, Galen remained very popular all his life.

As a writer, Galen was prolific. About 350 works are known to be by him. Galen sometimes lectured in public and even dissected pigs' corpses, but original research was not his chief interest. Instead, he tried to synthesize not only earlier findings but also his ideas on philosophy, derived from both Plato and Aristotle, with medicine. A revealing title of one work is *The Ideal Physician is also a Philosopher*.

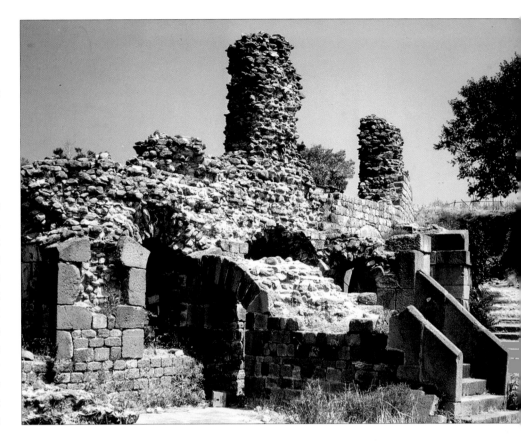

Galen took a holistic view of health, stressing the importance of exercise, a balanced diet and general hygiene. Among his most vital ideas was the theory of the Four Humours, the four bodily fluids of blood, phlegm, yellow bile and black bile that must be kept in balance. Illness arose when they were out of balance, and might require bloodletting. The overall result was an integrated, comprehensive system summarizing all medical knowledge, canonical until the 17th century.

Above: The Asclepium at Pergamum, in whose sacred precincts patients slept, hoping for healing dreams from the healer-god Asclepius. Such incubation could be very effective with the right person.

Below: Galen's theory of the Four Humours was accepted in Europe and the Arab world for almost 1,500 years.

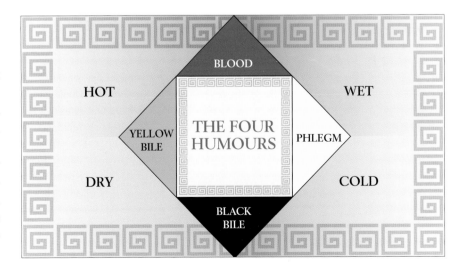

HOT

WET

BLOOD

YELLOW BILE

THE FOUR HUMOURS

PHLEGM

DRY

COLD

BLACK BILE

CHAPTER XI

ATHLETICS AND SPORT

Athletics, which culminated in the great sporting festivals, were central to Greek life. The *agon* (contest) was crucial to the Greek desire of 'striving always to be best'. Games were important in Homer in the 8th century BC and were still important 1,000 years later under the Romans. While Greek athletic contests are the ancestors of modern sporting events, the differences are as great as the similarities. Greek sports were long dominated by aristocrats, who alone could train properly. Only after 320BC did athletics become professionalized. Contests were between individuals, for there were no team sports. Each polis took intense pride in its victors, honouring them almost as demi-gods.

Excelling in athletics was an expected part of public life for an aspiring aristocrat, as was excelling in oratory or drama. Musical and poetry contests featured in many games, although professional musicians were not admired. Among aspects distinguishing Greek games from other cultures were the nudity of all contestants, which was extremely important – for the gods were shown naked — and the restriction on eligibility to freeborn Greeks from around the Greek world. (Romans were later admitted too, however.) As Greek culture spread around the Mediterranean and Black Sea coasts, and then thinly but widely across Asia after Alexander's conquests, the gymnasium, along with the theatre and agora, became a vital part of urban life.

Left: Two men in the palaestra (wrestling ground), naked like all Greek athletes. From an Athenian carving of c.500BC.

THE GREAT FESTIVALS
THE OLYMPICS AND OTHER GAMES

Above: The starting line of the stadium at Olympia, the site of the most important games in the Hellenic sporting calendar, for which all cities observed a rare truce.

Below: Spartan girls shocked and fascinated other Greeks by exercising only in skimpy tunics, like this girl from the 6th century BC. But they took no part in the main games.

Oldest and most important of Greek festivals, the Olympic Games in honour of Zeus traditionally date from 776BC. Significantly, this was the year at which most Greek cities later chose to start their calendars. According to myth, Hercules was the Games' founder. Olympia's location in the south-western Peloponnese meant that it was distant from major wars (although there were minor local ones) if vulnerable to earthquakes.

The Olympic Games were held quadrennially at the time of the second full moon after the summer solstice. This usually meant late August, not the coolest time of year. Over the centuries Olympia became filled with treasures and fine buildings, the greatest being the Temple of Olympian Zeus. This contained the sculptor Pheidias' last masterpiece, the gold-and-ivory statue of the king of gods, so huge that even seated Zeus' head brushed the roof, making it one of the Seven Wonders of the World. In AD393 Theodosius I banned the Games, whose paganism offended many Christians. (In 1896 the modern Olympics were founded by Pierre de Coubertin.)

THE OLYMPIC TRUCE
A distinctive feature of the Olympics was the proclamation of *Ekecheiria*, the Olympic Truce. Surprisingly, this was almost universally observed and the games were held regularly despite wars and invasions. For their duration, contestants, whether Athenian, Spartan, Theban or Syracusan, recalled they were *all* Greek. To stress this Panhellenism, the ten judges were called *Hellanodikai* (judges of the Greeks). An Olympic prize – a simple olive crown – was the supreme accolade for an athlete.

WOMEN ONLY GAMES
If women could not compete in the main Olympic Games, they had the consolation of holding their own games, the Heraea, honouring the goddess Hera. These too were quadrennial. According to Pausanias writing in the mid 2nd century AD: "The games are footraces for unmarried girls of varying ages. First the youngest run; then come the girls next in age, and the last contestants are the oldest. As they run, their hair falls free and their tunics do not even reach to the knee, while they bare their right shoulders as far as their breasts. The Olympic stadium is reserved for their games but shortened for them by about one-sixth. The winners receive crowns of olive leaves and part of the ox sacrificed to Hera. They may also dedicate statues with their names inscribed upon them." Men were not allowed to watch these games.

Competitors at the games were divided into three age groups: boys, adolescents and grown men. The games were only open to freeborn male Greeks, though from cities all over the Greek world. (Women were barred even from watching). However, there were exceptions. The kings of Macedonia, who claimed Hercules as their ancestor, could participate, but ordinary Macedonians, not classed as Greek, were excluded until after Alexander's conquests.

Later, Roman citizens were also permitted to enter. The most notorious Roman contestant was the emperor Nero, who won *all* the prizes in AD66. Nero introduced Hellenic games to Rome but with little success. The emperor Domitian also failed to interest the Romans in competitive athletics.

Above: 4th-century BC *amphora of runners. The foot races were the oldest and most prestigious games, divided into several types. The original race was for one* stadion *(185m/ 202 yards), giving its name to the stadium.*

FESTIVALS AND GAMES

Other Panhellenic games emulated the Olympics. The most important were the Pythian Games held in honour of Apollo at Delphi – originally every eight years and then, after a reorganization in 582BC, every four years. There were the usual athletic and equestrian events but poetry and music were also important contests. The prize was a wreath of bay leaves, a link to poetry.

The Isthmian Games near Corinth were founded – according to different legends – either by Sisyphus, king of Corinth or by Theseus, king of Athens. A less mythical founder was the Corinthian tyrant Periander in *c.*600BC. The games were held every two years. At the Isthmian Games in 336BC Alexander declared his plan to conquer Persia and there, in 196BC, the Roman general Flaminius proclaimed "liberty for the Greeks", to tumultuous applause. Unfortunately, Roman and Greek ideas of liberty proved very different, leading to prolonged wars.

The Nemean Games, again held every second year, were staged in honour of Zeus at Nemea in the Argolid. They became part of the Panhellenic circuit in 573BC and in the 4th century BC were moved to Argos. The games were similar to those at Olympia.

There were also many local festivals. The grandest were the Panathenaic Games, held every four years as part of the Panathenaic festival in Athena's honour. They included the usual contests but were solely for Athenians.

Above: Aerial view of part of Olympia showing the central Temple of Olympian Zeus and, in the top left corner, the Temple of Hera or Heraion.

Below: The ruins of the covered palaestra (wrestling school) at Olympia date from the 3rd century BC. *The site slowly filled with temples, monuments and other buildings donated by kings and cities.*

RACES ON FOOT AND BY CHARIOT

Above: An Olympic athlete sprinting for one stadion. From a vase painting of the 4th century BC.

Below: Chariot racing was the most glamorous, expensive and dangerous of the contests. It brought huge glory to the victor, although he often employed a driver who might be a slave. From a red figure vase of the 6th century BC.

The oldest and most prestigious of the games was the foot race. The word *stadion* (stadium), meaning race course, comes from *stade*, a Greek measurement of 185m (202 yards), the length of the first race on foot. The winner of this inaugural sprint at Olympia gave his name to the Olympiad.

Other foot races developed from this. The two-stade race was traditionally introduced at Olympia in 724BC. The *dolichos* (long race) was introduced in 720BC. Its actual length is uncertain but was probably about 20 stade or 4.8km (3 miles). As in a modern marathon, runners began and ended the race in the stadium, but ran through Olympia itself before returning.

THE HOPLITE RACE

The last running contest added to the Olympics was the *hoplitodromos* (hoplite race), in 520BC. Contestants ran around the stadium for 1.6km (1 mile), carrying a shield with greaves (leg guards) and helmet. As their armour weighed up to 24kg (60lb), runners often dropped their shields or tripped over fallen competitors, making onlookers laugh. In vase paintings, runners are sometimes shown leaping over the fallen shields of their collapsing competitors as they pass them.

This race flaunted each polis' military strength. As in hoplite warfare, stamina counted for more than speed, the Spartans being particularly good at the hoplitodromos, as was to be expected from Greece's best hoplites. The link between sport and military training was always acknowledged by the Greeks.

CHARIOT RACING

The most expensive and dangerous Olympic contest was chariot racing, which only rich aristocrats or kings could afford. Chariots had long been used for racing – Homer describes chariot racing at Patroclus' funeral in *The Iliad*.

The sport was introduced to the Olympics in 680BC and soon eclipsed horse racing. Chariots were very light wooden two-wheeled vehicles, drawn by two or four horses. They were difficult to control but the glory and prize went not to the skilled and courageous charioteer, who might be a slave, but to the owner.

This was the one race in which the contestants were not nude but wore a long robe. Falling to the ankles, it fastened high at the waist with a plain belt. Two straps crossing high at the back prevented this from ballooning during the race. Like modern jockeys, charioteers were chosen for their light build.

Arcesilaus IV, king of Greek Cyrene (in Libya), won the chariot race at the Pythian Games at Delphi in 462BC. His slave driver was in fact the only one to complete the whole course. In 416BC the flamboyant Athenian aristocrat Alcibiades had seven chariots in one race at Olympia, which came in first, second and fourth. Philip II of Macedon entered and won an Olympic chariot race in 356BC, a victory that helped prove his true Hellenic credentials.

DANGEROUS GLAMOUR

Chariot races were notoriously dangerous, sometimes lethal. Each race began with a procession into the hippodrome, a herald proclaiming the drivers' and owners' names. About 550m (600 yards) long, the course at Olympia could take

60 chariots but normally fewer entered. The four-horse race – run anticlockwise – had 12 laps, with sharp turns around the posts at each end.

A vivid, perhaps eyewitness, description of the Pythian races comes in Sophocles' play *Electra*, in which the exiled Orestes takes part: "As the bronze trumpet sounded they were off, all shouting to their horses and urging them on… The clatter of rattling chariots filled the arena, the dust flew up as they raced along in a dense mass, each driver goading his team mercilessly trying to draw clear of rival axles and panting horses, whose steaming breath and sweat drenched the flying wheels with foam…

"Orestes kept his horse near the pillar at each end so skilfully that his hub just grazed the turning-post by a hair's breadth each time… But at the last bend he misjudged it, slackening his left rein before the horse was safely round, and so hit the post. The hub was smashed across and he was hurled over the chariot rail, entangled in the reins. As he fell, his horses ran madly on around the course… he was dragged along the ground, his legs pointing at the sky, until other charioteers stopped his horses and released him, so bloody that none of his friends could have recognized him."

Chariot racing, unlike most Greek sports, proved hugely popular in Rome The Circus Maximus, the largest building in Rome, reputedly held 250,000 people. Later, chariot racing was transplanted to Constantinople, capital of the Christian Byzantine Empire, somehow escaping Christian censure. The emperor's palace had a passage leading directly into the hippodrome, so central was chariot racing to Byzantine life. But the rioting mobs who supported the rival Green and Blue factions in Byzantium had long forgotten the ideals of the Classical agon.

Left: The hoplitodromos (hoplite race) was added to the Olympics in 520BC. Contestants ran around the stadium for 1,600m (1 mile) in full armour.

Below: The Charioteer of Delphi, *a rare surviving bronze masterpiece of serene beauty, from c.473BC.*

LIGHT AND HEAVY SPORTS

Above: Athletes wrestling, from a red figure vase attributed to the Euergides painter, an Attic artist of the 5th century BC. In wrestling, a contestant tried to immobilize his opponent, either by getting him in a hold or pinning him to the ground in a 'fall'. A victor won by getting three out of five falls.

Other sports included boxing and wrestling, both classed as 'heavy' sports, and the long jump and throwing the javelin or discus, considered 'light'. The pentathlon, which was considered by Aristotle the best of sports, combined all five. But all were individual contests. This was the one major difference between ancient and modern athletics: team sports of any sort, were quite unknown in Greece, that land of herocially ultra-competitive individuals.

BOXING AND WRESTLING

In wrestling (*pale*) the aim was to immobilize your opponent, either by getting him in a hold or pinning him to the ground in a 'fall'. The victor was the man who won three out of five falls. 'All-in' wrestling (*pankration*) was popular but could be brutal. Almost anything was allowed, including punching, kicking and strangleholds, only biting and eye-gouging being banned. A referee or judge stood by with a stick to enforce these minimal rules. In both sports the defeated person signalled submission by raising his hand with the index finger extended. Beforehand, contestants rubbed themselves down with oil and sprinkled sand over their naked bodies. They also tried to soften the sun-baked earth by breaking it up or, in the case of the pankration, soaking it in water. This made the resulting bout a mud bath.

Boxing was even more dangerous. There were no 'Queensberry rules' to restrict where blows might land, and most were aimed at the head. Rabbit punches and blows with the butt of the hand were common. Boxers wore leather thongs around their hands, which later were iron-weighted.

Bouts were decided by a knockout, and often lasted hours. On rare occasions this could lead to the death of one contestant. In that case, however, the prize went to the dead man and his opponent was banned from contests for life. Boxers with their battered faces were notoriously ugly, and therefore not so widely admired as most other athletes.

'LIGHT' SPORTS

The long jump, which seems to have been the only Greek jumping contest, differed radically from the modern long jump. Contestants carried weights of up to 4.5kg (10lb), which they swung forward to increase their mid-air momentum. They reached lengths of 16.6m (54ft), possibly not in one single leap but in a series of rabbit-like jumps. Running remained one of the events at the Panhellenic games such as the Pythian, but the other 'light' sports were performed only as parts of the pentathlon.

The discus thrown by Greek athletes varied considerably in its weight, but as all competitors at a particular festival used

Left: A statue of Apollonius, a famous boxer. In the Hellenistic period (322–30BC) successful professional athletes could become celebrities.

FAMOUS ATHLETES

The cult of the victor was a striking aspect of the Panhellenic games. Winners were hailed as godlike heroes in their home towns. Statues were raised to them, poetry written in their honour – some of it, such as Pindar's, very fine – breaches were even made in the city walls to welcome them on their return. Down to c.400BC most victors were aristocrats because they alone could devote themselves to almost full-time training. From the 4th century BC athletes who were not nobly born began to rival these blue-blooded sportsmen. Later still, professional athletes in the modern sense became common.

Typical of an early victor was Milon of Croton in southern Italy. He won the Olympic wrestling prize several times in a career that began with winning the boys' contest in 540BC and lasted 26 years. When finally defeated by a younger man, he was carried shoulder-high around the stadium to cheers. Renowned for his strength, Milon was also known for his immense appetite. The boxer Melancomas of Caria became famous not only for his powerful body but also for his unusual technique. He preferred not to hit his opponents but instead to wear them out by dodging their blows.

Above: A youthful discobolus (disc-thrower). From a black figure vase attributed to the 'Epeleius Painter', c.480BC.

the same one, this did not matter. Surviving examples, made from marble, bronze or lead, weigh between 1.5 and 6.5kg (3 and 14lb), with diameters ranging from approximately 17 to 35cm (6 to 14 inches).

Javelins for athletes differed from the military javelins, being made of an extremely light elder-wood. They had throwing loops that made them spin in flight, keeping them on course. Throws of up to 92m (100 yards) were achievable, sources suggest.

THE PENTATHLON

The pentathlon combined all five sports: discus and javelin throwing, long jump, running and wrestling. It was considered the supreme test of an athlete, for it tested stamina, strength and speed. It was added in 708BC to the 18th Olympiad.

According to legend it was invented by Jason (who had earlier led the Argonauts on the Quest for the Golden Fleece). He combined the five contests, awarding the first prize to his friend Peleus, the father of Achilles, Homer's super-hero. The historical order of events is uncertain, as is how the prizes were awarded. Probably the winner of at least three parts of the overall contest won the pentathlon.

The Victorian British, with their ideals of fair play and the 'game being the thing', on looking at Greek athletics, fondly imagined they had found like-minded precursors. In reality most Greek athletes competed with the obsessive determination of modern professional athletes, although they seldom became rich by doing so.

Below: Athletes with a discus and a javelin. From a red figure vase of the 4th century BC. Both discus and javelin-throwing were considered 'light sports'.

THE GYMNASIUM AND PALAESTRA

Above: The 'Gladiators' Gymnasium' at Pompeii in Italy. The gymnasium, central to true Hellenic life, was adopted by many non-Greek cities too, if for different ends.

Below: Athletes being presented with victory tokens, from an Athenian red figure cup of the 5th century BC. Victorious athletes received only symbolic prizes but gained immense prestige.

The *gymnasion* (gymnasium) and the *palaestra* (wrestling ground) were as central to Greek life as the agora or temples. They were far more than modern gyms or fitness centres, serving as clubs and centres of social and cultural life.

In the gymnasia and palaestras of Athens, Socrates discoursed to Athens' brightest youth in the 5th century BC. Later, Plato and Aristotle founded their schools, the Academy and Lyceum, near gymnasia. These were built outside the city because they needed so much land. (Plato himself had been a wrestler in his youth). The ruins of the gymnasium at Ai Khanum in Afghanistan, a Greek city founded by Alexander the Great or his successors (perhaps originally an Alexandria), bear as quotations from Aristotle the maxims for the Five Ages of Man. Dating from *c.*200BC, these show that, even here, thousands of miles from Greece, the link between mental and physical exercise remained strong.

THE IMPORTANCE OF NUDITY
The word *gymnasion* comes from *gymnos*, naked, for all athletes exercised and competed nude. Athletes at the Olympics and other games always participated nude, the perfect state in which Greek artists depicted gods and heroes. This stress on nudity distinguishes Greek culture from all others. Even the Romans, in so many ways the Greeks' heirs, did not share this love of idealized nudity (although Romans at times exercised naked). Male nudity, openly admired, probably increased the general homoerotic aura of athletics.

THE PERFECT MALE BODY

The gymnasium was essentially a public sports ground open to all citizens. Usually stoas were built around the sanded area, originally a running track, where those not exercising could talk or ogle the athletes. In classical Athens there were private gymnasia, some socially exclusive. The politician Themistocles, mastermind of Persia's defeat in 480BC, had to join an un-smart gymnasium, but this suited his democratic instincts well.

Most cities established and maintained at least one public gymnasium. Citizens' physical fitness was seen as vital to the health of the city itself – unsurprisingly, as a polis relied for its existence on the fighting abilities of its citizen army. Socrates, in a dialogue written by Xenophon (a soldier), chided Epigenes, another disciple, for not keeping in good shape, for shirking his duty as a citizen: "You've got the body of someone who just doesn't care about public matters… You should care for your body like an Olympic athlete." In Athens, gymnasia were supervised by boards of ten *gymnasiarchs* (superintendents), one from each tribe. In smaller poleis an honorary gymnasiarch hired professional trainers. Lucian, writing in the 2nd century AD, summed up the Greek ideal: "The young men have a tanned complexion from the sun ... they reveal spirit, fire and manliness. They are in fabulous condition, being neither lean and skinny nor excessively fat, but have perfectly symmetrical bodies." This perfectly describes the *Doryphorus* statue made by Polyclitus 650 years earlier, long a canon of male beauty.

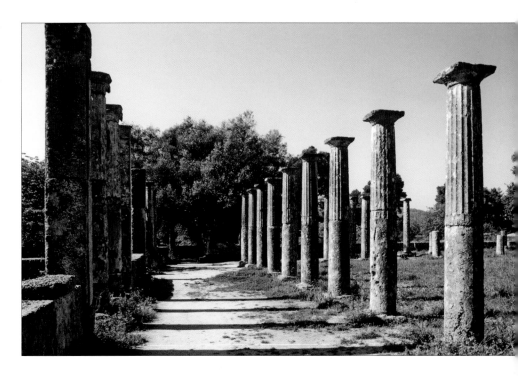

PALAESTRA AND BATHS

Sometimes adjacent to the gymnasium but often separate, the palaestra or wrestling ground was similarly laid out as a rectangular court surrounded by stoas, often thicker on the north side to protect against winter winds. More compact than a gymnasium, a palaestra might be found inside the city, which increased its attraction as a social and intellectual centre. Before wrestling or boxing, athletes covered themselves with olive oil – a costly procedure, at times subsidized by public funds – and dusted themselves with fine sand. This gave some protection against the sun or wind. Younger men who could afford to spent much of the day toning up their bodies and, sometimes, their minds. Boys received most of their physical education in the paleastra's stoas, ogled by older men and watched over by their tutor (usually a slave), who was intended to deter would-be seducers.

After exercising, athletes scraped off their sweat, oil and dust with a strigal, a metal object, or a sponge. The Greeks had public baths that, if not luxurious like the Romans' opulent structures, had hip baths, a hot room and a communal plunge pool.

Above: The palaestra at Olympia, the most prestigious in the Greek world. Here contestants for the great quadrennial games did their final training.

Left: Polyclitus of Argos's Doryphorus (Spear-carrier), incarnating the perfectly honed, symmetrical Greek ideal. A Roman copy of the bronze original by the great 5th-century BC sculptor.

CHAPTER XII

WORK AND LEISURE

Greece's cultural brilliance rested on a very limited economic base. Greece has few fertile valleys. Much land is rough hill terrain, although Sicily and some other colonies were more fertile. Later, Alexander's conquests opened up wide new territories but widened the gap between rich and poor. Life for most Greeks, if frugal, was lived with passionate intensity. The Greeks celebrated marriages, funerals and other events with ceremony, almost always in the open. The idea of a private life was considered eccentrically antisocial – a charge levelled against the playwright Euripides when he retreated to Salamis Island. Women, however, remained at home most of the time, especially in Athens. Closeted in cramped houses, they enjoyed little freedom except in religious roles. Such seclusion may partly explain the prevalence of male homosexuality, which in Classical Greece enjoyed a status probably unique in history. But the monogamous family was the basis of society.

Not unique to ancient Greece, but hard for the modern world to accept, was the prevalence of slavery. Slavery in the Greek world lacked any racist element – one source of slaves was other Greeks – but it alone made possible the leisured life, whether devoted to athletics, politics, art, drama or philosophy. The Greeks' achievement in these fields distinguishes them from other, often richer, slave-owning societies such as Carthage, which is famed for little beyond its wealth.

Left: 6th-century BC cup of a man embracing a woman, probably a hetaera *(courtesan). Greek artists celebrated all aspects of life.*

FARMERS, SHEPHERDS AND FISHERMEN

Above: Two men threshing wheat by hand. Farming in Greece was traditionally small-scale, providing small surpluses even in good years.

Below: Despite most Greek cities' proximity to the sea, fish remained something of a rarity – if one much enjoyed, as this exuberant marine mosaic from Pompeii suggests.

Paradoxically, while Greek life was urban and focused on the polis, most citizens remained farmers, except in the rare trading city such as Corinth, which had little hinterland. Most farmer-citizens lived inside their polis for reasons of security and entertainment, commuting out to their fields. However, some built solid shelters in the countryside for the busy summer months. Land always retained its unique social, political and symbolic status as the basis of wealth.

SKILLED FARMERS

Greek farms were mostly very small, with a typical plot being only 6ha (15 acres). Technically, farming always remained simple, but within these limits Greek farmers exploited their land to the full. They multi-cropped their fields, mixing many different crops – vegetables including pulses, fruits, figs, vines and olives – and

FISH, A RARE DISH

Most Greek cities were near the sea, so fish might be thought to have been a staple food. But although authors mention fish-eating, and fishbones have often been unearthed, fish usually remained a relative luxury. The Mediterranean is not a particularly rich area for fishing. Without modern means of transport and storage, fish had to be eaten right away. This meant that the Greeks only ate fish occasionally and in small amounts, often only to add flavour to otherwise monotonous meals.

also letting fields lie fallow. They normally grew fruit and vegetables in plots close to town, while up on the hills shepherds tended flocks of sheep and goats. Transhumance was practised: moving animals up to mountain pastures in summer and back again in winter, so that their dung fertilized the land. Owners of such flocks were among the wealthier minority of farmers, however.

HARD TOIL

Greek rural life was far from idyllic. Described in *The Iliad* and more fully in Hesiod's *Works and Days*, it was for most people a daily grind. Better-off farmers had oxen, which could pull carts as well as ploughs but needed feeding and watering year round, plus a slave or two. Slaves provided more skilled muscle-power but needed feeding *and* clothing all year round. Both human and non-human livestock represented major investments.

In the 6th century BC Greek farmers – except those in poor backwoods like Aetolia – were pulled into a 'market economy', a process speeded up by the introduction of coinage. Because early coins were high-value pieces, barter

Left: Greek sheep-farmers often practised transhumance, moving flocks up to the mountains in summer and back to the lowlands in winter, where they multi-cropped with olive groves. Sheep dung is a valuable fertilizer.

remained the norm for daily purposes, but wealth could now be measured and amassed. While the rich grew richer, the poor became ever more indebted, often being forced to make their own persons surety for debts, so losing their liberty along with their land.

To protect poorer farmers, in 594BC the Athenian reformer Solon banned enslavement for debt and the export of wheat from Attica. This led to an enduring enthusiasm for cultivating olive trees. It needed to endure, for olive trees take 15 years to start bearing fruit and about 40 to become fully productive. Attic olive oil was valued across the Mediterranean as a perfume as well as for cooking and lighting. The vases in which it was sold encouraged the phenomenal growth of Athenian pottery. Wheat was now imported to Attica from the Black Sea area or Egypt.

THE STAPLE CROPS

Barley and wheat were the main cereals grown in Greece. Olive groves allowed intercropping, i.e. land could be cultivated beneath or between the trees, but olives cannot stand much frost. Vines, tougher and thriving on very rocky slopes, were even more widely planted. Wine was the main drink after water, a useful (if unrecognized) source of sugar and vitamins. Pulses formed a key part of the diet, and helped fix nitrogen in the soil. Cabbages, onions, garlic and lettuce were grown widely, but tomatoes, rice, peppers and potatoes were unknown. Figs, apples, grapes, plums and quinces were common

fruits, but meat was an expensive rarity for ordinary people. Cheese, from sheep, goats and cattle, was eaten more often.

PERENNIAL SHORTAGES

The Greek climate is hard for farmers. Rainfall, mostly concentrated in the winter months, can vary dramatically from year to year and place to place. As Aristotle noted in his treatise on *Meteorology*: "At times drought or flood can affect large areas of the country simultaneously, but sometimes it has only local effects. Often the country overall has the normal rainfall for the season or even more, but one part suffers drought. Occasionally the opposite happens, when the country all around has only light rainfall or even a drought, one particular part is deluged in rain." Farming produced small surpluses in good years, and in bad years there were acute shortages.

Below: The olive harvest from a black figure vase. Olives were vital to Greek life, providing oil for cooking and lighting and serving also as a soap-substitute.

TRADERS AND TRADE ROUTES

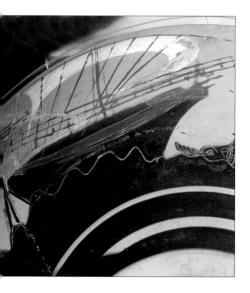

Above: Most merchants ships remained small with one mast. Despite this, Greek traders criss-crossed the Mediterranean and the Black Sea. From a vase of c.500BC.

Mycenaean traders had crossed the Mediterranean from Sicily to Egypt, but they disappeared after 1200BC. By the 8th century BC, Greece's modest trade was dominated by Phoenician ships. Yet soon after, as growing populations pressed on limited land, Greek poleis began to found colonies around the Mediterranean and Black Sea. Trade was seldom the chief reason for this expansion – Naucratis in Egypt was one of the few colonies founded for trade – but good harbours were always sought. Even colonies founded as agricultural settlements initially needed goods from the homeland. Transport was always far cheaper by sea than land for heavy goods.

Pottery, at first mostly from Corinth but by the mid-6th century BC overwhelmingly from Athens, was Greece's main export. Black and red figure vases containing olive oil from Attica and fine wines – from Chios, Samos, Thasos and Lesbos, where the poet Sappho's brother was a wine merchant – went to Egypt, Italy and Gaul (France). But the Greeks also made other, even grander containers.

A PRINCESS'S TOMB

Herodotus in his *Histories* mentioned a *krater* (bronze jar) holding 300 amphorae of wine, made by Laconian smiths for Croesus of Lydia (560–546BC). He was thought to have exaggerated until the discovery in 1953 of a vessel at Vix in an Iron Age tomb in central France. The *Krater of Vix*, the largest known ancient bronze vessel, is 1.5m (5ft) high and could have held about 1,089 litres (240 gallons) of wine. Along with Athenian silver cups c.530 and 520BC, it was buried in the tomb of a Gallic princess around 500BC. It shows how Greek trade had already penetrated distant lands.

Massilia (Marseilles), founded c.600BC by settlers from Ionia, became the chief entrepôt for this trade. Gaul, on the overland routes north, was by 500BC very important to the Greeks as Carthage had closed the south-western Mediterranean to monopolize trade with northwest Europe.

THE GRAIN TRADE

During the course of the 6th century, Athens, growing fast, became critically dependent on grain imports from the Black Sea. The fertile Ukrainian and

Left: The Krater of Vix, *the largest known ancient bronze vessel, which can hold c.1,089 litres (240 gallons), shows the extent of Greek exports. Unearthed in Burgundy, central France, it dates from c.520BC.*

Left: Greek trade routes
spread right across the
Mediterranean and the Black
Sea, exchanging Greek
artefacts usually for wheat.
After Alexander the Great,
these routes extended far
across central Asia and then
down the Red Sea to India.*

Russian steppes were then ruled by
Scythian princes. Fortunately, they proved
fond of the Greek wine, oil, pottery and
other artefacts sold them in return for
their exports of hides, timber, slaves and
grain. Safeguarding the wheat route
became a prime concern of Athenian
politics from the time of the Pisistratids
(545–510BC). Hence the importance of
controlling the Hellespont and Bosphorus.

The Piraeus, rebuilt on the gridiron
pattern after the Persian wars (490–
478BC) by Hippodamus, became the
greatest port in the eastern Mediterranean,
secured to Athens by the Long Walls. An
import-export tax of just 2 per cent made
it an attractive place to do business,
including banking, and many Greeks from
ravaged Ionia settled there.

ROUTES ACROSS ASIA

After Alexander's conquest of the Persian
Empire, new overland routes east opened
up. In great Hellenistic cities such as
Antioch or Alexandria, the rich
demanded luxuries: perfumes, silks, drugs,
spices and precious stones. Spices came
from India and Arabia Felix (Yemen).
Silk from China remained a great luxury
even in the Roman Empire, as China
jealously guarded its monopoly of seri-
culture. A rougher 'wild silk' came from the

island of Cos. Caravan routes along the
valleys of Asia Minor made coastal cities
like Ephesus and Miletus wealthy.

The Ptolemaic rulers of Egypt encouraged exploration, sending expeditions up
the Nile in search of gold and ivory and
down the Red Sea looking for spices. This
second route led to a lucky discovery in
116BC, when a sea captain in their service
found the sea-route to India via the Red
Sea port of Berenice. Utilizing the regular
monsoon winds that blow across the
Indian Ocean, he set sail in July, returning
home blown by reverse winds in
December. The routes east were outlined
in the *Periplus Maris Erythrae*, a handbook
for sailors of the 1st century AD.

*Below: After 550BC Athens
became increasingly dependent
on grain imports from the Black
Sea region. Safeguarding the
wheat route through the Hellespont (Dardanelles), here shown
at Gallipoli, became very
important in Athenian politics.*

TRADES AND PROFESSIONS
FROM POTTERS TO BANKERS

Above: Storage jars for olive oil from the Bronze Age. Oil was always one of the Greeks' main tradeable commodities.

Below right: Vase painting of a smith at work. Whether free or slave, all smiths worked in small forges, mass production being unknown.

Below: Marble stele (gravestone) of Sosinos of Gortyna, a bronze founder of the late 5th century BC. Classical Athens attracted many such specialized metal-workers.

Although Greek society always remained mostly agricultural, craftsmen had a recognized role by classical times in large cities such as Athens and Corinth. Even in the Bronze Age, Cretan potters and goldsmiths had produced fine artefacts exported around the Aegean and sometimes farther afield. A bronze tripod made in Crete is mentioned by the tablets in Linear B, an early form of Greek. One was found in the palace at Pylos, dating from *c*.1200BC. The ensuing Dark Ages ended such trade, which revived only after 700BC. Athens most notably then became, and long remained, noted for making goods of superb quality.

POTTERY
The most common Greek artefact is pottery. Pottery shards have the advantage (for archaeologists) of being almost indestructible. When reassembled, vases make a valuable guide to dating because styles changed fairly quickly and consistently. Olive oil and wine from Greece were almost always exported in pottery amphorae. The superb vases, often signed by their makers or found intact in Etruscan tombs, such as the *Chigi Vase* with its triple tier of friezes from *c*.620BC, were certainly regarded as artworks, not just as containers. However, with plastic unknown and glass rare and expensive, most storage vessels and domestic appliances, from cookers to hip-baths, were made of fired clay.

Corinth, which initially dominated the important carrying trade west, was home to the first great ceramicists. Then, in the mid-6th century BC, Athenian potters almost totally displaced them. From the late 5th century BC on they, in turn, faced rivalry from Boeotian and southern Italian potters. But booming demand kept all Greek potters busy. Other cities specialized in different products: Chalcis and Corinth in metalware, Miletus in textiles, Pergamum later in parchment. Potters in Athens originally worked in the Kerameikos, the potters' quarter (our word ceramic comes from Greek *keramikos*) south-west of the Agora. The hill on the west of the Agora, the Kolonos Agoraeus, was known for its concentration of blacksmiths and bronze-workers. The whole area must have rung with the sounds of hammered metal, with smoke from their charcoal forges forming a mini-smog. Appropriately, the temple on the low hill nearby was dedicated to Hephaestus, the blacksmith god.

CEPHALUS, SHIELD-MAKER EXTRAORDINARY
Later, the Piraeus, which became after 480BC the economic heart of Athens – indeed soon almost of the eastern Mediterranean – attracted numerous merchants and workshops. Many different types of craftsmen, free or slave, including bronze-, silver- and goldsmiths, cobblers, carpenters, and arms and armour makers, lived and worked there.

Left: The Temple of Hephaestus, the god of metal-workers, overlooked the Agora, the centre of Athens' social and economic life. Nearby was the smiths' quarter.

Below: A potter of the late 6th century BC, *the period when Athenian ceramic products became pre-eminent around the Mediterranean.*

One of the largest workshops known in the Piraeus belonged to Cephalus, a wealthy metic (resident foreigner) from Syracuse. He appears in the opening passages of Plato's great dialogue *Republic*. Cephalus was a historical figure, the owner of 120 slaves who specialized in making shields – an essential part of the Athenian war effort, the dialogue being set during the Peloponnesian War. However, these slaves were probably not all under one roof and certainly were not working on a production line. Instead, each would have made a whole shield himself. Cephalus was among the richest men in Athens. Socrates, Plato's protagonist in the dialogue, treats him with respect, so clearly tradesmen as such were not despised even by aristocrats such as Plato. Most workshops had a maximum of five or six workers.

BANKERS AND MONEY-LENDERS

Banking in Greece was originally a monopoly of the temples. People would deposit and borrow money on interest from priests, and temples remained important safe deposits for major sums until the end of paganism. But, when coins became common in the 5th century BC, money-lenders called *trapezitae* set up their 'tables' in public places such as the South Stoa in Athens, displacing most temples. (Greek *trapeza*, bank, comes from *trapeza* 'table', just as bank comes from Latin *bancus*, 'bench'.) This banking system operated primarily on letters of credit, not coinage. Pasion, an ex-slave, was one of the richest bankers of the 4th century BC. Another system was later developed by Ionian cities such as Miletus, where financial transactions became so complicated that they required professional managers. Often these worked with the city authorities to create an effective bank monopoly.

In Ptolemaic Egypt, where commerce on a grander scale required larger funds, a central state monopoly bank was established in Alexandria. It opened branches across the kingdom and continued in operation under Roman rule after 30BC.

DRINKING TOGETHER
SYMPOSIA AND BARS

Above: Diners at a symposium from a mural in the Tomb of the Diver, Poseidonia (Paestum), Italy, c.480BC. Symposia were among the highlights of Greek life, where conversation and entertainment, high or low, accompanied the wine.

Below: A scene from a symposium, where two diners, sharing a couch as was usual, seem drunk and mutually attracted. From a red figure Attic vase of c.500BC.

For Greek men, a symposium was the great occasion for socializing. *Symposion* means literally 'drinking together', and wine (the only alcohol the Greeks drank) flowed at these events. They could be celebrations – of an athletic or artistic victory – but many seemed to have just involved people dropping in uninvited. A true symposium was more than a mere booze-up. It offered, besides food, entertainment by dancers and flute girls, who were enjoyed as much for looks as their music. At the best type of symposium, wine-fired conversation was what finally counted.

A symposium took place in a house's *andron* ('men's room'), a special windowless room on the ground floor. Its floor was raised at the walls, against which couches were arranged. Greeks always dined reclining on couches, a custom copied by Etruscans and Romans. Guests on arrival had their sandals

Above: Pompeii fresco showing Ariadne seduced by Dionysus, the re-enactment of which myth in Xenophon's Symposium *fired onlookers with heterosexual lust.*

removed by slaves and might be garlanded with flowers and anointed before being shown to their couches. Two men shared one couch, reclining on their left sides. Finger bowls were placed on tables beside them – the Greeks ate chiefly with their fingers, throwing bones to the floor for the dogs.

THE SYMPOSIARCH
A crucial figure at a well-run symposium was the *symposiarch*, master of ceremonies, elected for the evening. He decided the proportion of wine to water. This varied, but about two parts of wine to five of water was usual. (Drinking wine undiluted was thought barbaric if not insane. Conversely Demosthenes, the great orator, was thought a prig for preferring plain water.) The two were mixed in a krater, a large elaborate bowl, snow sometimes first being used to cool

the wine in a *psykter* (wine-cooler). Guests decided how many kraters of wine to prepare, as all drank the same amount. At most symposia, three kraters were thought enough. In the words of Eubulus, a playwright, "One krater is for health, one for love, one for sleep."

Wine circulated 'from left to right', i.e. anticlockwise, the symposiarch setting the pace. Libations – sprinkling wine on the floor – were made to Dionysus, the wine god, Zeus and to the special *agathon daimon*, the good spirit presiding. As wine flowed, diners might debate agreed topics, but there were other entertainments too.

FLUTE GIRLS AND PHILOSOPHY

In an atmosphere as enclosed as a modern nightclub's, with wine flowing ever more freely, diners played games such as *kottabos*, flicking wine at a target. Sex – with other guests, or more usually with dancing girls and serving boys (both often slaves) – might follow. Illustrations show some symposia degenerating into orgies.

But two famous dinner parties ended very differently. In Plato's novel-like *Symposium*, the guests – among them Aristophanes and the tragedian Agathon, the host – solemnly if not soberly discuss the nature of *eros*, sexual desire. Alcibiades bursts in drunk, takes over the symposiarch's role and falls asleep after wailing that Socrates seems as impervious to sex as he is to the effects of drink. The crux of the dialogue comes in Socrates' report of a talk with Diotima, a priestess, about the higher eros, ideally homoerotic, that engenders ideas, not bodies.

In *Symposium* by Xenophon, another of Socrates' disciples, an evening ends with an "imitation of the wedding-night of Dionysus and Ariadne... When the guests saw that 'Dionysus' was attractive and 'Ariadne' gorgeous, and the actors were not playing but really kissing, they

Right: Playing kottabos, a game in which wine was flicked across the room at small statuettes by diners. From a late 5th-century BC krater (drinking cup).

became fired up... When they finally saw the actors apparently going to bed together, the bachelors swore they must get married and the married men rode off on their horses to their wives with but one purpose in mind." The eroticism here is wholly heterosexual.

BARS AND TAVERNS

Poorer citizens could not afford such festivities and had to socialize elsewhere in a bar or tavern called *kapeleion*. If some *kapeleia* were only stalls, others were many-roomed buildings. Citizens could eat snacks and buy wine in flasks to take away along with torches to light their way home through Athens' unlit streets.

Kapeleia were often condemned as sources of popular disturbance and riots, rather like pubs in modern Britain.

Above: A flute girl entertaining men at a symposium, a typical entertainment. From a red figure vase of c.450BC.

GREEK SEXUALITY
ACTS AND ATTITUDES

Ancient Greece was once seen as a sexual arcadia where happy pagans, free from Christian restraint, enjoyed sex in ways damned by the Bible or law. In particular, homosexuality, male and female, was openly celebrated. Such views of Greece as a homosexual paradise owe as much to

Left: 6th-century BC herm, a phallic good luck sign placed outside houses and at street-corners, originally dedicated to the god Hermes. Male nudity in all its forms was much celebrated by Greek art, encouraging or reflecting Greek homoeroticism.

Below: A man embracing a boy. Such paederastia (pederasty) was thought acceptable, even admirable, if the relationship was between social equals and suitably conducted. From a red figure cup by the 'Briseis Painter'.

fantasy as to reality. The Greeks had no words for, or concepts of, 'homosexual' or 'heterosexual' (terms coined in the late 19th century), nor for 'gay', which gained its current meaning even more recently. They would have thought people who so defined themselves as odd, bisexuality being the unspoken norm.

The Greeks did, however, have a word for *paederastia*, pederasty, the love of an adult man for boy – usually an adolescent. Far from regarding this as a crime, classical art and literature celebrated an idealized paederastia. This fact, which so embarrassed Victorian scholars, must be seen in the context of the Greeks' general attitudes to love and sex.

CONCEPTS OF 'LOVE'

For us 'love' means romantic love in the St Valentine's Day sense: couples – mainly if not always heterosexual – love each other physically and spiritually and aim to live 'happily ever after' together. Tragedy arises when requited love is blocked, as in *Romeo and Juliet*. Things were very different in antiquity.

Greek men were often fond of their wives. Certainly they felt a duty and responsibility to them. But they did not usually marry for love, marriages being arranged for social reasons. (Spouses presumably felt sexual desire for each other – the Greek birth-rate was certainly high enough.) Families were the acknowledged bedrock of any polis, essential to sustaining Greek society.

In contrast, eros, overwhelming sexual desire, was seen as a 'bitter-sweet' disruptive force, at times terrifyingly destructive, especially if it afflicted women. When eros strikes women in Greek myth and tragedy, the results are often catastrophic: the Trojan War was caused by the headstrong love of Helen for Prince Paris; Queen Clytemnestra, for the

Right: Red-figure painting of a man being served by a naked youth – perhaps a slave – at a symposium. Symposia could end with the diners having sex with the slaves, male or female.

sake of her lover, murders her husband Agamemnon on his return from Troy, before being killed by her son Orestes; Phaedra, King Theseus' wife, conceives an unrequited passion for her stepson Hippolytus that leads to the deaths of both. No happy endings here.

Philosophers attempted self-control to gain *eudaimonia* (contentment) or *ataraxia* (stoical indifference) to escape sexual turmoil. Others, less high-minded, tried to possess the object of their desire, male or female, as swiftly as possible.

A HOMOEROTIC WORLD?

Every Greek city boasted a second marble and bronze population of athletes, heroes and gods. These statues portrayed idealized men with superb bodies, mostly naked. Balancing this Olympian idealism were statues of herms, phallic symbols topped by heads. While the city overflowed with male nudity, female statues, naked or clothed, were far less frequent, although beautiful nude goddesses were sculpted from the 4th century BC.

This possibly roused any latent homoerotic feelings. More crucially, unmarried Greek women were so secluded that young men hardly ever met them. Young girls, being uneducated, may have been uninspiring company. Nor were married women a better prospect. Adultery, according to an old Draconian law, was a capital offence. Unsurprisingly, many men turned to prostitutes, but some preferred other males, usually teenaged boys.

LOVER AND BELOVED

In the ideal homoerotic relationship, the *erastes*, a lover in his twenties, courted an *eromenos*, the beloved, a boy in his teens of similar social status. The gymnasium was a common meeting place, where each could admire the other working out naked. A boy received small gifts from his admirer – a hare or cockerel – but was expected to behave with suitable modesty, rather as 'respectable' girls being courted in the West were once expected to behave. Any hint of effeminacy on either side was strongly deplored.

How much actual sex occurred remains debatable. Ancient authors tend to discretion, modern ones to speculation. But one thing is clear: such relationships were not viewed by either partner as degrading, for soon the eromenos would become a fellow citizen, fighting in the army and voting in the Assembly beside the older man. They would then no longer be lovers, because sex between grown men was thought a little absurd in Athens. In Sparta, predictably, pederasty was a rougher, compulsory affair. Only in Thebes was adult homosexuality fully accepted, being epitomized in the 'Sacred Band', the elite corps of 300 lovers.

However, affections could long persist, most notably in Sparta but also in Athens. The reformer Solon when young loved the teenaged Pisistratus. Years later, when Pisistratus had become tyrant, he ignored his aged ex-lover's loud criticisms of his regime for old time's sake.

Above: 2nd-century AD statue of Antinous, the youth loved by Hadrian, who was of reputed royal descent and so almost the emperor's social equal.

THE HETEROSEXUAL MAJORITY

Above: A stele commemorating marital affection. Monogamous marriage remained the bedrock of Greek society, whatever men did in their youth.

Below: A man and woman exchanging sexually significant glances. Heterosexual affairs between equals could be hard in classical Athens, as women were kept so secluded. From a red figure krater c.460BC.

Most men and women in ancient Greece were predominantly heterosexual, however. In Homer, *all* erotic passion is between men and women. *The Iliad* is the archetypal book of love and war – of love because, although war predominates, the Trojan War originates in Paris' love for Helen. The epic itself starts with Achilles and Agamemnon quarrelling over Briseis, a slave girl. In *The Odyssey* Odysseus on his wanderings has many affairs with women, divine and human – the shipwrecking sirens who lure him so strongly are prototypical *femmes fatales* – before returning to his ever-faithful wife Penelope. Connubial affection rather than erotic passion marks their reunion in the marriage bed, but then neither is young.

In classical Athens Pericles lived for years with Aspasia, his mistress. He enjoyed her company not just in the bedroom but also at symposia, where she entertained Athens' best minds. While Pericles and Aspasia were exceptional, the comic playwright Aristophanes often voiced the feelings – erotic and political – of the Athenian man-in-the-street.

LESBIANISM: A HIDDEN LOVE
While the male half of the population was amusing itself with hetaerae or each other, Greek women cloistered in small, dark houses sought what consolations they could. Sex with another man was so risky that they presumably turned at times to each other. Their love has remained unrecorded except for Sappho, whose incandescently lyrical poetry has immortalized her passions. In Sparta, where women paradoxically enjoyed considerably more freedom, often exercising half naked, lesbianism was almost openly accepted.

WIVES ON STRIKE

In *Lysistrata*, one of Aristophanes' typically outrageous plays, staged in 411BC, the women of Athens, tired of the endless Peloponnesian war, follow Lysistrata's advice. They organize a sex-strike, denying their husbands their beds until the men agree to make peace. The strike is exported to Sparta and Thebes, Athens' enemies. The women have to seize the Acropolis and treasury to make the strike effective, but Sparta's ambassadors arrive with tales of similar strike action by their wives – and their own similar frustration. If Greek husbands never enjoyed having sex with their wives, the comedy would have lacked all point. But heterosexuality also found many extramarital outlets.

COURTESANS AND PROSTITUTES

Aspasia was originally a *hetaera*, a word meaning (female) 'companion'. In a notoriously misogynistic speech *Against Neaera*, Apollodorus in c.340BC said: "We have *hetaerae* for pleasure, *pallakae* (concubines) for physical needs and *gynaekes* (wives) to bear us legitimate children and be faithful guardians of our households."

This neat division of womankind into three types owed more to Apollodorus' wish to pigeonhole women than to social reality. While married women were distinct from hetaerae, prostitutes ranged from glamorous courtesans to '2-obol' streetwalkers, 2 obols being a third of a workman's daily wage. Grand hetaerae, who might became great men's lovers, charged hundreds of drachmae not for specific sexual acts but for their 'company'– hence their name. They also retained the crucial right to refuse anyone, so retaining some independence.

For those at the bottom of the scale, things were starkly different. The Kerameikos quarter was a red-light district notorious for streetwalkers of both sexes. These could be brutally treated, for the streets of Athens at night, unlit and unpoliced, were dangerous. The fate of prostitutes locked up in brothels was little better, however, for they were often foreign slaves, perhaps speaking only a little or no Greek.

Above: A man caressing a woman playing a lyre, probably a professional entertainer who sold sexual favours with her music. From a red figure cup of c.510BC.

GRAND HETAERAE

Neaera was in fact an expensive hetaera from Corinth, a city famous for its prostitutes, but she was also originally a slave, bought by two former clients. She was not, therefore, exactly the independent, cultured lady that romantic historians once thought. But the orator Lysias had his hetaera initiated at Eleusis, obviously caring for his lover's (assumed) fate in the next world too.

Thais, an Athenian hetaera, accompanied Ptolemy, one of Alexander's generals, on the conquest of Persia. At a banquet after the capture of Persepolis, she demanded the Persian capital be torched in revenge for the Persians burning Athens 150 years earlier. Persepolis duly went up in flames. The episode reveals that when courtesans attended wild Macedonian symposia, their voices were at times heeded. Later Ptolemy, on becoming king of Egypt, settled Thais and their three children comfortably. Then he married someone dynastically suitable.

Left: A 19th-century statue by Claude Rame of Sappho, the supreme women poet who was reputedly 'Lesbian' in the modern sense. Lesbianism presumably flourished unrecorded.

FOOD AND WINE

Above: Ritual sacrifice of animals, such as this pig, followed by a democratic public banquet, gave poorer Greeks their best chance of eating meat. From a red figure vase of c.500BC.

Below: Seafood always supplemented meat across Greece, as this fresco from Thira of c.1550BC attests. Fish was seldom particularly cheap, however.

The ancient Greeks could never be accused of being gourmands or gluttons. Even among the rich, food usually remained simple to the point of repetitive frugality. The Greek diet, focusing on olive oil, bread, fish and vegetables, appears at first glance like the precursor of the Mediterranean diet so recommended today. In fact it was far plainer, being a product of general poverty, not health-consciousness.

However, the Greeks compensated for their gastronomic austerity by being enthusiastic, even excessive, drinkers. Greek wines were valued around the Mediterranean not only by the Greeks but by Etruscans and later the Romans of the imperial period. This has led some historians to the suspicion that either tastes or Greek wine-making must have changed considerably since then.

DIETARY STAPLES

Although Greeks ate more than "a sort of porridge followed by another sort of porridge", in the words of one unimpressed researcher, their diet was based on cereals. Bread was made from wheat when they could get it or afford it, and from barley or millet when they could not. Olives and olive oil, along with cheese – from sheep and especially goats, far more often than cows – pulses, beans and vegetables such as cabbage, onions and garlic supplemented bread.

A thick soup made chiefly from beans and lentils was a standard Greek dish. The Spartans, as ever unique, lived mostly off a 'black broth' reputedly made partly from blood and so disgusting that other Greeks gagged on it. Before setting off on their military expeditions, large quantities of this repellent mixture would be mixed up and carried by helots, to give their masters the consolation of home cooking while in foreign parts.

Fruits, including apples, plums, figs and grapes, were eaten, fresh in season and dried out of season. Sugar was unknown, honey being the only sweetener. Also unknown in the ancient world were rice, potatoes, tomatoes, (bell) peppers, citrus fruits, bananas, chocolate and many other now common fruits and vegetables, since introduced from around the world.

THE LUXURY OF MEAT

Meat was a luxury enjoyed by most Greeks only following the public sacrifice of a chicken, sheep, pig or bull. The priest would, after killing the animal, butcher it, removing the thigh bones and covering them with a little fat that was burned on the altar as an offering to the god invoked. While gods were deemed content with the mere smell of the beast, their human worshippers tucked into a communal feast eaten in the open. The meat was grilled (broiled) or boiled in cauldrons, each portion being conspicuously fair.

Little meat found its way to the market except for pork. This was relatively inexpensive, a suckling pig costing about three drachmae or three days' average wages. Some pork was also made into sausages. (Homer's heroes ate meat daily, but then they were really superhumans and not to be judged by normal standards in any way.) Athletes, especially those taking part in 'heavy' sports such as the pentathlon, might occasionally be put on a high-protein diet, even eating meat on a daily basis.

Fish was a useful supplement to the Greek diet, some species being much prized. Exactly what types of fish ancient names refer to is not always known. But fish too was relatively expensive, and not part of most people's daily diets. Nor was game, which, like fish, was never sacrificed. Interestingly, the Pythagoreans, almost the only vegetarians in the ancient world, especially avoided fish, while they occasionally would eat sacrificed meat to conform to a polis' religious customs.

In classical Athens most shopping for food was done by men. This might seem strange in a male-dominated society where cooking and food had such a low status, but it followed, logically enough, from women's seclusion. Cooking was a different matter, however. There were no celebrity chefs in the Greek world. Instead, anonymous slaves and/or women cooked in small dark kitchens. Over open fires, meat was boiled or grilled, cooking being generally very simple.

WINES FAMOUS AND ORDINARY

Wine was drunk by Greeks wherever they lived – indeed, it was a mark of a true Hellene that he drank wine rather than beer, a drink fit only for barbarians. Wherever Greeks settled, they planted vines, and in so doing spread viticulture from the Black Sea to Gaul. (Tea, coffee and other non-alcoholic drinks were unknown, as were spirits.) Wine was strong, probably around 15 per cent alcohol, but was universally diluted, so that it would be no stronger than beer is today.

The Greeks recognized three colours of wine: 'black', 'white' and 'amber' (*kirrhos*). White and amber wines could be sweet or dry, black wines could be dry or

'medium'. Most wines were drunk young and rough, with half-fermented pieces of grape floating in them. Such wines would have tasted strongly of wineskins or resinated barrels.

The best wines came from Chios, Lesbos, Thasos and Mende in the Chalcidice in the north. They were bottled in distinctive clay amphorae, sealed airtight, that have been found around the Greek world. Although classical Greeks did not date wines by vintage – unlike the Mycenaeans and Romans – they understood the need to age the best wine.

Above: Families did, if rarely, eat together for festivals such as weddings, as this relief from Cyzicus on the Sea of Marmara of the 3rd century BC shows.

Below: Grapes and wine were always vital parts of the sparse Greek diet. This sarcophagus from Alexandria shows a grape harvest.

CITIZENS AND FOREIGNERS

Above: In 451BC Pericles introduced a law restricting Athenian citizenship to those with two full Athenian parents. This showed the value Athenians put on their citizenship but would have excluded Themistocles, the strategist behind victory at Salamis, whose mother was not Athenian.

Below: Ostraka (pot shards) with the name of Aristides, the politician ostracized in 482BC for opposing Themistocles' naval policy. Ostracism provided a useful safety valve.

In 451BC Pericles introduced a law that restricted Athenian citizenship to those with two full Athenian parents. This measure, meant partly to encourage Athenian colonists to wed Athenian women, would have disenfranchised Themistocles, Athens' saviour in the Persian wars, who had a non-Athenian mother. The law reveals the high value placed on citizenship by the classical polis.

Although we translate polis as city-state, 'citizen-state' would be a closer description, for a polis consisted of its citizens. (The word 'politics' comes from this Greek root.) Citizenship could be restricted under oligarchies. In Sparta, only the Equals, who had helots to till their land for them, counted as full Spartiates. (Their number, originally set at around 8,000, had declined to only 1,500 in the 4th century BC.) More numerous were the *perioeci* ('dwellers-around'), who lacked a Spartiate's rights and obligations but provided much of the army and revenue.

In Athens after Solon's reforms in 594BC, all free men ranked as citizens, despite the poorest being excluded from important posts until the 5th century BC. By 432BC there were *c.*60,000 adult male citizens in Attica, although plague and war soon reduced their number. In 404BC the junta of the Thirty Tyrants restricted citizenship to the 3,000 richest citizens, but the revived democracy at once restored the full franchise.

DUTIES AND PRIVILEGES
The most demanding duty for an adult Athenian citizen was military service, which he had to undertake at any age between 18 and 61. Although Athens' hoplite army remained amateur and part-time compared to Sparta's – and later to Thebes' – military service was a recurrent, often dangerous burden. In contrast, the

Above: An Athenian citizen-soldier saying goodbye to his family, from an Attic vase of c.440BC. Military service was demanded of every citizen between the ages of 18 and 61.

Athenian fleet of *c.*300 triremes rowed by the *thetes*, free but poor citizens, rapidly became a semi-professional force after the Persian war. However triremes were usually laid up in winter.

Citizens also had to serve on the huge juries, typically 501 men strong, selected by lot from a roster of 6,000 men. At least once in their lives most also served on the Council of 500. Modest pay for these offices – as for fighting in the fleet or army – was introduced in the 5th century, but was no more an inducement for an able-bodied citizen than jury pay is today. Richer citizens also faced the extra burdens and honours of the *liturgies*, such as the choreogia (the financing and staging of plays).

Although the Athenian state had no real welfare system, it did provide modest support for the arts. By the 4th century BC, free tickets for the theatre, the greatest public entertainment and an occasion for the whole polis to manifest its collective identity, were available for poorer citizens. The orphans of citizens killed fighting for Athens also received state support as children.

METICS: TRADING PLACES

Foreign-born permanent residents of Athens were known as metics (*metoikoi*), meaning literally those who have changed their home. After the Persian wars (499–478BC), many Greeks from Ionia migrated to Athens to make their living. They had to pay a special poll tax (*metoikon*) of one drachma per month, as well as normal taxes. Failure to pay the metoikon promptly could mean enslavement.

While metics were liable for military service, they were not allowed to vote or hold office. Nor could they own land – a severe disadvantage in a society where land was still the safest form of wealth. They had, however, access to the courts, although they had to post bail, unlike citizens. Occasionally, citizenship, or citizen rights, were granted to exceptionally worthy metics such as Pasion. In 338BC, after Athens' defeat by Macedonia, it was proposed to enfranchise all metics to boost the citizen body, but the measure was not carried out.

Despite their disadvantages, the number of metics in Athens grew rapidly in the 5th century, reaching about 20,000 men by 431BC. These metics lived mainly in the Piraeus, where they played leading roles in commerce and banking. Many distinguished, wealthy men, including the shield-maker Cephalus, the philosopher Aristotle and the orator Lysias, were metics. Lysias had strongly supported the exiled democrats in 404BC. Granted citizenship at their triumph, he made cogent speeches before being disenfranchised again by the grudging Athenian demos.

The Roman emperor Claudius (reigned AD41–54) later compared Greek cities' parsimony in granting citizenship with Rome's generosity. This winning of conquered people's acquiescence and often their active support was seen as a secret of Rome's imperial success. But a Greek

polis was inherently a small, autonomous unit in which citizens took active part. Roman citizens, by contrast, fought but seldom voted for their city, as Rome's empire grew. By AD212, when Caracalla gave all free men Roman citizenship, it had lost much of its value anyway.

Right: Marble bust of Lysias (c.455–380BC), a metic who was made a citizen for his services to democracy, only to be later demoted again.

Below: A cobbler, either a poorer citizen or a metic (a resident foreigner). From a black figure vase of the early 5th century BC.

SLAVERY
FACTS AND MYTHS

Above: A shaft in a silver mine at Laurium, where Greek slavery was at its worst. Tens of thousands of slaves worked and died there in appalling conditions that no free man would have accepted but which almost no one at the time condemned.

Right: A man using a strigil (scraper) after exercising while his slave boy holds a jar of olive oil for him, c.400BC. Most slavery in classical Greece was small-scale. Many slaves came from the Black Sea area or Asia Minor, often being sold as children. War was another source of slaves, for captured cities' inhabitants were normally enslaved.

Greek civilization depended on slavery. This fact – which is indisputable but one that has made many Greek scholars uncomfortable – can mislead. To begin with, slavery in antiquity had no racial connotations. Although most slaves were foreign-born in the Classical period, Greeks themselves always risked being enslaved if they were captured. The Cynic sage Diogenes – and even Plato reputedly – suffered this philosophy-testing fate, although both were soon freed.

The Greeks did not pioneer what has been called 'chattel slavery', meaning buying and selling enslaved persons as objects. It was already common among other seafaring peoples like the Carthaginians and Phoenicians, while absolute monarchies such as Persia, Egypt and Babylon had long been accustomed to controlling vast armies of slaves.

Nor did owning slaves make most Greeks rich, for slavery in the Greek world was normally small-scale. Slaves were, like cars today, generally thought of as useful, even essential, to everyday life.

Slaves worked in the house or workshop or on the farm alongside free labourers. Contrary to myth, slaves almost never rowed Athens' or other cities' galleys, a job done by poor citizens – who wanted the modest wages, and became highly professional oarsmen. (In the Hellenistic era, when fleets and ships grew massively larger, slaves were at times used.) Nor did slaves labour in great gangs on large estates. Most Greek farms were tiny.

An unskilled slave cost c.200 drachmae (a drachma was a skilled worker's daily wage) and the same to clothe and feed each year. Demosthenes, whose wealthy father had owned skilled metal-worker slaves, said each cost 500–600 drachmae. Neaera, the beautiful slave-prostitute, cost 3,000 drachmae, but she was exceptional. There was very seldom a quick profit to be made in owning a slave.

As most Greeks strongly disliked working for their fellow citizens, slave labour could be easier than employing free men. Slaves and free men worked side by side in small groups building the Acropolis temples, doing exactly the same work in the same conditions. The difference, of course, was that the free workers kept their modest pay while the slave workers saw it all go to their masters.

ASPECTS OF SLAVERY
The numbers of slaves in Athens, the best-documented as well as richest city, is estimated at c.80,000–100,000 in 431BC, about 25 per cent of the population. Most were in domestic service. The affluent Aristotle, who defended slavery, had 18 household slaves. More typical, however, is the disabled citizen for whom Lysias

Left: Bust of Aristotle, who defended slavery, saying some men were born so naturally brutish they were better off belonging to a master. He practised what he preached, finally owning 18 domestic slaves.

made a speech claiming public support. He claimed his client was too ill to work himself but not yet able to buy a slave to work for him.

Female slaves worked in the house as servants and nurses, some becoming almost part of the family. However, they had no redress against their masters beating or sexually abusing them, although killing slaves was a crime. When slaves were witnesses in legal cases, they were routinely tortured first. Otherwise it was thought they would never dare testify against their masters.

Skilled male slaves were often set up in their own workshops. This was called 'living apart' and some earned enough extra money at their trade to buy their freedom. Freedmen had the same limited rights as metics. Pasion, a freedman probably born in Syria, became a rich banker and manufacturer – using slaves – in the 4th century BC. For donating armaments to Athens during a crisis, he was granted citizenship, a rare honour for anyone.

Pasion was exceptional, however. The real feelings of most Athenian slaves were shown by how many ran away to Deceleia, the fort occupied by the Spartans after 413BC: 20,000, according to Thucydides. Although the nearest source of slaves was Greek war-captives, growing demand meant that slaves came from many areas. The Balkans, Asia Minor, Syria and the Black Sea were prime sources. These slaves often came through trade, not raids or conquest, i.e. other peoples sold the Greeks slaves, including often their own children.

HELOTS: SPARTA'S SERFS

Sparta, as always distinctive, had its own form of slaves in the helots, native Greeks of Messenia. Their forebears had been enslaved by Spartan conquest and they were tied to the land they cultivated, i.e. they could not be bought or sold, unlike slaves in Corinth or Athens. Although sometimes called serfs, helots were as unfree as any slaves. But, retaining their national identity, they were unusually prone to revolt. Spartans, Xenophon noted, always went around fully armed because of this threat. Every year Sparta formally declared war against the helots, allowing possible ringleaders to be murdered. Yet at times helots fought bravely for Sparta even abroad – for example under Brasidas in 424BC.

MINES: INFERNAL LABOUR

One form of slavery stands out for its sheer horror: the mines. Slave labour was the norm here, for few free men would work underground in poor conditions. About 20,000 slaves were employed at the peak of the silver mines at Laurium, revenues from which underpinned Athenian power. Nicias, the politician who led the Syracusan expedition to disaster, owned 1,000 slaves at Laurium, a fact not thought remotely shocking at the time. Slaves also laboured in the gold mines at Mt Pangaeus in Macedonia.

During the Hellenistic and Roman periods, slaves – including children who were small enough to crawl through very low tunnels – were employed in Egypt's gold mines on a massive scale. Many were literally worked to death underground, where tiny skeletons have been found.

Below: Neaera, an exceptionally beautiful slave-prostitute from Corinth, as pictured by the Victorian artist H.J. Hudson. She cost 3,000 drachmae but most slaves were much cheaper.

WOMEN
A VARYING STATUS

Above: Women, left on their own as their men went out into the city, turned to entertaining themselves, here making music. In Plato's Symposium *it was suggested that the auletris, the female flute-player, should go upstairs to entertain the house's women.*

The traditional picture of Greek women is bleak. Excluded from politics and culture, never owning property in their own right, always dependent on a male relative, they seem hardly freer than slaves.

Aristotle's generally misgoynistic views provided intellectual support for female subordination. Women were, he thought, too emotional and passionate to act rationally, even if they could *think* clearly. Even their role in child bearing was only as passive receptacles for male seed. If his views reveal women's oppressed status in classical Athens, the fate of women elsewhere in Greece possibly differed markedly over the centuries. It appears, though firm evidence is lacking, that other Greek women at times had far more freedom.

MINOANS TO MACEDONIANS
In Minoan Crete women probably played a prominent role in religious and social life. Whether they had any political power is unknown, although the idea of a matriarchy is implausible. Mycenaean Greece was a militaristic society, but its women were probably not cloistered away. The prominent role of women in myth and tragedy may reflect memories of their Bronze Age importance.

In Homer, women have significant roles. In *The Iliad* Helen is less condemned for her adultery than admired for her imperilling beauty. In *The Odyssey* women are often active players: Calypso the nymph entraps Odysseus while the princess Nausicaa helps his final return. However, the patient cunning of Penelope, epitomized by her unravelling the tapestry she has woven every night to put off suitors wanting her hand and fortune, was probably far more typical of a woman's role.

In the Archaic Age (700–500BC) Sappho enjoyed enough freedom to write and love, traditionally setting up her own female academy in Lesbos. As she went into exile for a while, she presumably had an active interest in politics too. In Sparta, women always enjoyed unusual freedom. To help produce tough soldier-sons, they exercised half-naked, shocking if fascinating other Greeks. By the 4th century BC they could inherit land and choose husbands, with disastrous consequences, as wealth became concentrated in ever fewer hands. In Doric Crete, culturally half-Spartan, women in Gortyna could inherit half their brothers' share of land.

Left: A Maenad dancing to flute music. The orgiastic rites of Dionysus, celebrated outside the city, gave some women a rare break from their usual life of domestic drudgery. From a red figure kylix of c.510BC.

In Macedonia, still half-reminiscent of the Homeric world, women at times had crucial roles. Olympias, Alexander's tempestuous mother, had furious rows with her husband Philip, going into exile once. After Alexander's death, she became a major player in dynastic politics. In the Hellenistic age, queens at times ruled, the most famous monarch being Cleopatra VII of Egypt (69–30BC), who tried to revive Ptolemaic power through her affair with Mark Antony, the Roman general.

SECLUSION IN ATHENS

In Athens, women could hope for no such potential glory. Married off young, at best half-educated, women in theory had to content themselves with domestic duties in their houses. This included weaving, for most clothes were home-made – even Penelope, queen of Ithaca, wove. (Poorer women had to work in the fields or in shops as well.)

As men or slaves did most shopping, women's best chance to socialize was collecting water from the fountains, as private water supplies were almost unknown. Even this was denied rich women, whose slaves fetched the water.

Respectable women did not attend symposia. Only flute girls, dancers and prostitutes entered the andron, the men's room. Instead, women were restricted to the gynaeikon, their rooms upstairs. But they may at times have been entertained there. In Plato's *Symposium* it was suggested that the *auletris*, the (female) flute-player, should go upstairs and entertain the women. Women also seem to have attended the theatre after *c.*400BC; some are reported to have fainted at alarming performances. This exception to their seclusion emphasizes their high status as Athenian citizens, albeit unenfranchised female ones.

PRIESTESSES AND MAENADS

In one area women played a decisive role even in Athens: religion. The patron deity of the city was the goddess Athena, served by priestesses. In the great Panathenaea

Right: A vase from Apulia of 340BC showing Penelope, Odysseus' faithful wife, spinning wool.

every July, four nobly born maidens, the *arrephoroi*, led the procession. Other goddesses also had their own priestesses, especially Artemis, whose sanctuary at Brauron had female acolytes.

Some festivals were for women only. Men were excluded from the *Thesmophoria*, a major three-day festival throughout Greece. Celebrated in the autumn to honour Demeter, goddess of agriculture, the rites culminated in the sacrifice of a pig.

Another, far more thrilling, god offered women intoxicating release from their daily grind: Dionysus, god of wine and drama. His ecstatic rites took place in March outside the city, when women, drunk on wine and the god, went raving mad – the literal meaning of 'Maenad' – as they roamed the countryside. Men avoided these rites for their lives' sake.

Below: Preparations for a marriage, giving a relatively rare glimpse into domestic life. From a red figure vase of c.470BC.

FAMILY AND MARRIAGE

Above: A woman spinning with a distaff, spindle and whorl, typical activities expected of a housewife. From a lekythos (white background vase) of c.490BC.

Below: A wedding procession with the bride and groom in the chariot and Eros, god of desire, hovering overhead. From a red figure pyxis of the 5th century BC.

Women never legally came of age in classical Athens or in most other Greek cities. This meant that they always remained wards of their *kyrios* (master/lord), who might be their father, their uncle, brother or, of course, their husband. Woman could never control or own any property, nor could they choose their husband.

A girl, who would have spent her life inside her home, was betrothed, often as young as 5, and married around the age of 14 or 15 to a man, selected by her family, usually twice her age.

The overriding concern in Greece was the continuation of the family line, not a girl's happiness. Women's prime role in life was seen as producing children, as men's was fighting for the polis.

Xenophon, the historian and general, wrote: "My bride would have known nothing of how I lived, for until she entered my house she had had a very restricted life, trained from childhood … to ask no unnecessary questions." A wife then saw her husband only in private, his social, political and intellectual life being barred to her – at least in theory. In practice, relations between the sexes were often happier, Greek fathers being as fond of their children as any others. But Socrates was not that unusual in dismissing his family to debate with his friends before his death.

MARRIAGE AND WEDDINGS

In Athens wedding festivities lasted three days. At the betrothal (*egge*, pledge) the groom formally accepted his bride, who was given away by her kyrios with the words: "I give you this woman for the begetting of legitimate children."

The wedding itself was often set for the day of the full moon. Celebrations started on the day before, when sacrifices were made to varied gods, including Artemis, goddess of virginity, Hera, goddess of marriage and Aphrodite, the love-goddess. The bride then took a sad farewell of her childhood toys, offering them to the gods, while the women of her family fetched water in a torchlight procession from the Fountain of Callirhoe for her *loutron nymphikon*, ritual bath. She was then carefully dressed, with a special bridal veil. (This was, however, almost the only time Greek women wore veils.) The groom meanwhile had a similar bath. Olive and laurel branches adorned both houses as the groom, garlanded and anointed with myrrh, went with his relations and best man to the bride's house in the afternoon.

After sacrificing to the gods, they sat down to a banquet given by the bride's kyrios – one of the rare occasions women and men ate together in public, although they still sat separately. The traditional food included sesame seeds, symbolizing fertility, one of Persephone's attributes. Guests then gave the bride wedding presents and at night fall the kyrios formally presented the bride to the groom.

Bride and groom then went in a chariot amid a procession to her husband's house. An *amphithales*, a child with both parents still alive, escorted the bride. He represented prosperity and good luck for the couple and their expected children. The bride carried a sieve and a grill, symbolizing her coming domestic duties. On arrival, the crowd threw nuts and dried figs at the happy couple, who then retired to their bedchamber. Outside, the groom's friends sang marriage hymns lustily. The next day, the bride's parents or other relatives brought their gifts and the dowry to the couple in their new home. Then the door closed on a wife's life of domestic drudgery.

SPARTAN CUSTOMS

In Sparta, they organized things differently. The bride had her hair hacked off, she was dressed in a boy's short tunic, and her husband pretended to rape her. Such sexual violence was thought to help beget warriors. For the first years of marriage a husband could only slip away from his barracks at night to visit his wife secretly. Only later could couples properly set up house together.

Despite this, and perhaps because of the consequent fall in birth rate, a Spartan woman may have led a freer life than her Athenian counterpart, who bore an estimated nine children during her life.

INFANTICIDE

As the Greeks had no contraception and abortion was dangerous, the chief form of birth control was infanticide. Killing one's child was illegal in Athens, but a father could reject a child because it was an unwanted daughter or because it was sickly. (In Sparta the state decided which children should live.) The child was then exposed on a hill outside the city. Sometimes such babies were rescued by childless women and brought up as their own, but most of them died. The classical polis would have been surrounded by the tiny skeletons of such abandoned infants. It was a hard world.

Above: Callicrate and her daughters, one playing with a tortoise. From a relief at Smyrna of the Hellenistic era.

Left: Mother and child, a fine funerary relief from classical Athens. Women's quiet efforts were perhaps sometimes appreciated only after their deaths, although many couples were presumably devoted to each other.

CHILDHOOD AND EDUCATION

Above: A baby crawling, on a vase painting from c.400BC. Such family scenes were pictured in classical Athens.

Below: A terracotta figurine of a schoolboy, from c.300BC from the Lebanon, by then a Hellenized region.

Greek education aimed to produce soldiers for the citizen-armies, and for a select minority, orators for public life. For most Greeks education was limited to the three Rs. Music mattered, but physical education in the gymnasium was what counted for most. For a fortunate few, however, education higher than anything known before developed during the later 5th century BC.

FIRST STEPS

About a week after a baby's birth it was formally accepted in a ritual cleansing, the *amphidromia*, followed by a banquet. Richer mothers had wet-nurses and nannies to look after their infants. Children learnt fairy tales from Aesop's fables, as Socrates recalled in his death cell.

Elementary education was not compulsory, being private and fee-paying if inexpensive. From the age of six, most boys attended three types of school: one for gymnastics, under a *paidotribes* (physical trainer); one for music and poetry under a *kitharistes* (lyre player), for poetry was often accompanied by music; and one for the three Rs under a *grammatistes* (school teacher). Homer was the great authority whose poems every boy learnt by heart. There were no desks, boys sitting on stools using wood-backed wax writing tablets and a stylus of bone or metal. Papyrus, paper's precursor, was very expensive.

Many boys had a *paidagogos*, a slave tutor to teach them good manners and punish them if they misbehaved. Meanwhile, girls from wealthier families were taught at home to read, write and play the lyre. Most teachers were slaves or underpaid freedmen. The exception was the paidotribes, a stern-looking figure with cloak and stick, who supervised boys' exercises in the gymnasium or palaestra (wrestling-ground), who was well paid. In the Hellenistic cities scattered across Asia, gymnasia were far more than just gyms, being social and cultural beacons of Hellenism. Libraries now also became important for scholars.

THE FIRST UNIVERSITIES

On his return to Athens around 387BC after years of travel, Plato founded what became the first university. He chose an olive grove sacred to the hero Academus. It stood nearly a mile (1.6km) from Athens, outside the city that had executed Socrates but would tolerate his own muted yet more radical criticisms of it. The curriculum included mathematics, dialectic and political theory. Despite his belief in an ideal world, Plato intended to train philosopher-rulers for this world. But only one graduate, Dion of Syracuse, ever had real power, and his career proved disastrous. Plato headed the Academy for 40 years, his nephew Speusippus succeeding him. After a period dominated by the Sceptics, the Academy returned to Platonism in the 1st century BC. It later became a beacon of Neoplatonism, surviving until AD529, when it was closed by imperial decree. Aristotle, the Academy's most brilliant student, founded his own school, the Lyceum, in 334BC. Modelled on the Academy, with similar common meals and symposia, it was less exclusive and less anti-democratic. Systematic large-scale scientific research began in the Lyceum's large library and collections. After Aristotle's death, this encyclopaedic approach was neglected in favour of narrower philosophical studies. Rhodes, Pergamum and Alexandria later offered places of similar higher education.

Left: A master and pupil at an Athenian school, where the central curriculum included music. Teaching was an underpaid profession, some teachers even being slaves. From a red figure kylix of c.480BC by the Athenian artist Duris.

RHETORIC: AN AMBIVALENT GIFT

At the age of 12, the sons of wealthier men went to secondary schools offering courses in law, rhetoric or medicine. Then for two years, from the age of 18, ephebes did military training, although this appears to have become institutionalized only in the 4th century BC. For the politically ambitious, being able to speak well, to sway the Assembly or lawcourts, was vital. Rhetoric, the art of speech-making, was the glamorous new way to attain the gift of the gab.

The main teachers of rhetoric in the 5th century BC were Sophists (literally, wise men). Some were unscrupulous spin-doctors, but the best, including Protagoras and Gorgias, were profound thinkers. Isocrates (436–338BC), a notably prolific writer – or windbag – embodied the worst excesses of rhetoric.

The finest rhetorician was Demosthenes of Athens (384–322BC). Reputedly afflicted with a bad stammer when young, he cured himself, later delivering some of the most impassioned if ineffectual speeches in democratic history. Rhetoric became a revered subject –

Aristotle wrote a whole book on it – being widely taught under Roman rule, despite democracy's demise. A chair in rhetoric was even established in the new university of Constantinople, the Byzantine capital, in AD425.

THE SPARTAN EXCEPTION

In education the Spartans had their own special *agoge*, or upbringing. Boys, taken from their mothers at the age of seven, were for ten years brought up in singularly brutal boarding schools run by older boys. Institutionalized pederasty was the norm there. Dancing and singing were taught but were subordinate to overall physical toughening and testing.

This training included survival techniques such as having to steal their daily food and being savagely whipped if caught. With it went the regimentation that made Spartans both feared and mocked. From the age of 20 to 30, men lived in barracks undergoing yet further military training.

Below: Among the vital skills aspiring young citizens learnt in a democracy was rhetoric – oratory that could sway the Assembly or the courts. Demosthenes overcame a stammer to become one of Athens' greatest orators.

CLOTHING AND HAIRSTYLES

Above: Minoan women curled their hair and wore colourful dresses, typical of their cheerful culture, which was so different to later Greek severity.

The Greeks were never the slaves of fashion. Indeed at first glance their clothing seems to have remained unchanged over centuries. But styles did alter slowly, becoming simpler at the beginning of the Classical period and a bit more luxurious – for those who could afford it – in the Hellenistic Age. But the chief characteristic of Greek dress was its simplicity.

Minoan and Mycenaean styles differed radically from later fashions. Women in Crete wore long, elaborately flounced dresses, nipped in at the waist with little jackets that often left their breasts bare. Men went naked to the waist, with tightly belted kilts. Mycenaean women copied Minoan styles, but men usually wore breeches or shorts and tunics. Both sexes wore jewellery. The collapse of these palace-based civilizations after 1200BC meant the end of luxurious styles. Clothes became far simpler as classical Greek clothing emerged over the centuries.

THE MALE ESSENTIALS

Free men wore a loose-fitting tunic (*chiton*) made of wool or sometimes linen, fastened at both shoulders and tied at the waist. A young man's chiton reached to his knees, an older man's to his ankles. Over the chiton they often wrapped a cloak (*himation*), a large rectangular piece of cloth draped over the left shoulder with the back brought round under the right arm. Surplus material hanging down over the body could be gathered up in cold weather. The *chlamys*, a short cloak or cape, was worn for hunting or riding and by soldiers. Draped around the shoulders, it was fastened at the throat with a clasp,

Left: Women's hairstyles and clothes became far simpler at the beginning of the Classical Age (c.480BC). From then on, fashion changed only marginally over a long period.

Above: A koure (girl) showing her hair elaborately braided and wearing an ornate multi-coloured dress in the Archaic style. An Athenian statue of c.530BC.

for the Greeks did not use buttons, a much later invention. Nor did they wear underclothes of any sort. Men normally went bare-headed, but a wide felt or straw hat, the *petasos*, was worn at times by travellers and hunters, and a skull cap, the *pilos*, by labourers. The Macedonians were especially noted for wearing the petasos.

Labourers and slaves wore a single garment fastened over the left shoulder, the *exomis*, or in hot weather simply a loin cloth (*zoma*). Athletes, of course, competed and exercised naked.

Footwear was simple for both sexes and all classes, consisting of sandals of varying types, often no more than a sole with two or three straps. In winter, sturdier laced-up boots were sometimes worn but socks were unknown.

WOMEN'S CLOTHES

Female fashions were also simple and changed very slowly. In the Archaic period, women at times wore elaborate multi-coloured dresses, but by 500BC these had given way to the Doric style of dress, far closer to men's clothing. It consisted of a plain long woollen or linen chiton held by two pins at the shoulder and falling to their ankles. Some variety was introduced by sleeves being gathered at different points, creating pleats. The himation was draped over the tunic in much the same way as men's but could be wrapped around the whole head and body so that only the eyes were visible.

Women are often shown with bare feet on vases, but this was probably a convention or depicted them at home.

Silk from China became known after Alexander's conquests but remained very expensive, worn only by great queens such as Cleopatra. Cheaper but coarser was 'wild silk' from the island of Cos.

HAIR AND BEARDS

Down to the late 6th century BC, Greek men usually wore their hair long. A sign of the advent of Classicism, typified by the *Critios Boy* of *c.*480BC, was the adoption of shorter hair by men, although the Spartans were as always slow to change. This trend was not universal. Some gods and priests were still shown with long hair in the 5th century, as were some heroes. By the 4th century BC almost all men wore their hair short, but Alexander wore his romantically long.

Minoan men seem to have been clean-shaven, but Mycenaeans always wore beards. So did all adult Greek men right down to about 350BC. Then a fashion, started by the sculptors Praxiteles and Lysippus for showing men clean-shaven, was adopted enthusiastically by Alexander and his successors. From then on, men were clean-shaven, apart from philosophers and seers. This style was emulated by the Romans until Hadrian.

Women always had long hair, often pulled back in a ponytail or a bun and fastened by ribbons, or tied in elaborate patterns. Sometimes hair was artificially curled, judging by vase paintings. Head scarves of various types and colours were popular, allowing flashes of decoration.

Above: On the frieze of the Parthenon, carved under the direction of the master-sculptor Pheidias, the calm, timeless simplicity of Classical clothing is apparent for both men's and women's clothes.

Below: In the Archaic period (c.700–480BC) men's hair and even beards were often tightly curled, as this Athenian statue shows.

THE END AND REBIRTH OF ANCIENT GREECE

Above: Athen's Temple of Olympian Zeus, finally completed after 600 years under the emperor Hadrian in c.130AD, epitomizes the Graeco-Roman synthesis.

Below: Greek cultural prestige was so strong across the Roman Empire that even Leptis Magna in Libya, a city with no Greek connections, began importing pentelic marble from Attica for its finest buildings.

In 146BC the Roman general Lucius Mummius sacked Corinth, totally destroying the city and enslaving its inhabitants. This act of exemplary brutality – one of many at the time, as Rome stamped its power across the Mediterranean world – marked the end of independence in Greece proper. Over the next 120 years the whole Hellenistic world west of the Euphrates passed under Roman sway, at times being dragged into Rome's ruinous civil wars. Mummius had taken great care, however, to have Corinth's finest artworks packed and shipped to Rome, where they were displayed to appreciative observers. His actions symbolize the dual-faced nature of Roman rule. This preserved, indeed even revived, Greek cultural life while crushing the Greeks' final hopes of regaining their political liberty.

ROME, GREECE'S CAPTIVE

The Romans by c.120BC had the greatest admiration for Greek culture but almost no regard at all for contemporary Greeks, whom they saw as frivolous, unworthy heirs of the great age of Pericles. One building epitomizes Rome's philhellenism at the time: the temple of Hercules Victor in the heart of Rome. Built c.120BC as a perfect circle with slim marble columns, it is supremely Greek in form, owing very little to native Italian tradition. Equally Greek in form and spirit are the wall paintings of Pompeii, which were probably made by actual Greek artists copying Hellenistic masterworks. Horace, one of the greatest Latin poets, later wrote: "Greece made captive captured its conquerors and introduced the arts into backward Latium."

Greek culture transplanted remarkably well to Rome. It had shown it could thrive almost as much under monarchies as in democracies – from Pisistratus' enlightened tyranny in 6th-century BC Athens to the absolutism of Ptolemaic Egypt in the 3rd, when Alexandria's Museum/Library became the powerhouse of Hellenic culture. The Romans now showed a genius for absorbing, adapting and transmitting Greek culture across western Europe, albeit in vulgarized form. (The typical buildings of a Roman city were the amphitheatre, forum and public baths, not the theatre, library and gymnasium.)

PHILHELLENIC ROMANS

By the time of Cicero (106–43BC), almost every educated Roman spoke fluent Greek. Many, including Cicero, went to Greece to complete their education. (Few Greeks ever learnt much Latin, however.) Cicero, when he had a moment to spare from politics in the Republic's last years, translated and summarized Greek philosophy in books such as *De Finibus* (*Concerning Aims*) and *Republic*. In doing so he invented terms such as *moralis*, *qualitas*, *beatitudo* (moral, quality, happiness), still current today. Roman playwrights such as Plautus and Terence, poets such as Catullus, Virgil and Ovid and architects such as Vitruvius were all acutely aware of their debt to Greece.

Above: The well-preserved theatre of Sabratha in Roman Africa (Libya) reveals how Greek culture spread under the Pax Romana, *shaping life and art even in areas never previously Hellenized.*

Above: Roman statue of Cicero (106–43BC), who translated much Greek philosophy into Latin – a huge gain for a posterity in the medieval West after it had forgotten Greek.

Augustus, Rome's first emperor (reigned 30BC–AD14), was not as openly philhellenic as his defeated opponent Mark Antony, who had debated with philosophers in Athens and been hailed as Dionysus by Greeks in Alexandria. But, by establishing a lasting peace, Augustus allowed the Greek east to recover its wealth and, ultimately, its self-confidence. He ended being worshipped by Greeks as a saviour-god in gratitude.

The last of Augustus' dynasty, Nero (reigned AD54–68), went further, in effect trying to turn Rome into a Hellenistic kingdom. While Greeks might applaud acts of Neronian generosity such as granting Achaea (Greece proper) 'freedom' from taxes and starting the Corinth Canal, Romans, appalled by his extravagance, rebelled. Nero's reign ended in civil wars and was followed by a brief anti-Hellenic reaction.

THE ANTONINE SYNTHESIS

Under Hadrian (reigned AD117–38) and his Antonine successors, considered among Rome's finest emperors, the Greeks finally became Romans' social and political equals. Plutarch the biographer (AD46–125), whose grandfather as a boy had had to carry grain sacks across mountains to help feed Antony's troops, accepted imperial office as procurator of Achaea, although his heart remained in his native Chaeronea. More eloquently symbolic, the aristocratic Greek historian Arrian became a consul – the highest post in the empire after the emperor's – and then commanded a Roman army.

Hadrian himself became archon at Athens, ordering the completion of the vast Temple to Olympian Zeus begun 630 years earlier and being initiated into the Eleusinian Mysteries. He also had a very public affair with Antinous, a boy reputedly descended from Hellenized Bithynian kings, something which might be called truly Hellenic.

Right: The proudly imperial Prima Porta statue of Augustus, first Roman emperor, was based on Polyclitus' classical Diadomenus of 400 years earlier. The 'Classical Canon' was by then definitively established.

Above: The Neoplatonist philosopher-emperor Julian (reigned AD361–3), Rome's last non-Christian ruler, wanted to create an organized pagan religion to counter Christianity. But his reign ended in military disaster in Persia and he had no philhellenic successors.

Fifty years after Hadrian's reign, the philosopher-emperor Marcus Aurelius endowed four chairs of philosophy at Athens: the Platonist, Peripatetic (Aristotelian), Stoic and Epicurean. Marcus wrote his *Meditations* in Greek.

TWILIGHT OF THE GODS

A religion that satisfied people's varied needs as well as Graeco-Roman polytheism might have been expected to last indefinitely. Philosophical scepticism did not touch popular religion, which happily incorporated new gods such as Isis. Around AD250 the Olympic Games were still being held, sacrifices were still made to the Olympians and the Eleusinian Mysteries still promised initiates salvation in the afterworld. Urban decay did not harm a religion rooted in rural life.

Christianity could and did. After AD312 Christianity slowly became the officially favoured religion and then the only religion tolerated. Early Christians thought the pagan gods not charming myths but active malicious demons. Although at least 90 per cent of the population in AD312 was still pagan, Christians vehemently attacked the ancient cults, whose adherents lacked monotheists' fanaticism.

JULIAN, THE LAST PHILHELLENE

Rome's last non-Christian ruler, the philosopher-emperor Julian (reigned AD361–3), attempted to restore urban self-government, long decayed, and to create an organized pagan priesthood to counter Christianity. Although he refused actually to persecute Christians, he forbade them to teach Greek literature, the core of Graeco-Roman life. But Julian's reign ended in disaster in Persia and he had no philhellenic successors. In *c.*AD386 the fanatical Christian Theodosius I banned most pagan worship.

Even so, paganism was a long time dying. The cult of the healer-god Asclepius at Epidaurus thrived into the mid-5th century AD; a century later peasants in Asia Minor were still being converted en masse. In Athens the philosophy schools remained proudly Hellenic until closed in AD529. When the Byzantines reconquered the Peloponnese in *c.*AD830, they found peasants in remoter corners still worshipping Zeus.

HELLENISM REBORN

At the Councils of Ferrara and Florence in 1438, called to try to reunite the Catholic and Orthodox churches, the Greek philosopher Gemistus Plethon dazzled Westerners with his esoteric Neoplatonism. Bessarion, a more orthodox scholar, stayed on to rekindle knowledge of Greek in the West, where it had been forgotten. The fall of Constantinople in 1453 and the diaspora of Greek scholars fuelled Italian passion for things Greek. In 1462 the Academy was founded in Florence – its name deliberately recalling

Left: The Supreme Court in Washington DC shows the lasting influence of Graeco-Roman ideas. It was constructed in majestically Classical style in 1935.

Above: The rediscovery of truly Greek architecture in the later 18th century led to much simpler styles, such as that of the British Museum, London, built by Robert Smirke in 1823–46.

Plato's school – to study Greek literature and philosophy. It proved vastly influential, begetting similar bodies across Italy and inspiring artists such as Botticelli – whose *Birth of Venus* hides a Neoplatonist allegory – and Michelangelo. Michelangelo was moved by the spiritual anguish he discerned in the newly unearthed Laocoön group to create works on a gigantic scale, from his hopeful *David* to his overwhelming *Last Judgement* in the Sistine Chapel. When even Pope Leo X (reigned 1513–21) could celebrate the birthday of 'Saint Socrates', Hellenism was clearly resurrected and walking the streets of Italy.

By 1500 the passion for Greek culture had crossed the Alps. A chair in Divinity was founded at Cambridge University in England, Erasmus (1466–1536), the Dutch humanist and scholar, being among its first occupants. Erasmus had learnt Greek primarily to translate the New Testament. His new version revealed so many faults in the old Latin Bible that it helped trigger the Reformation. Protestantism and Platonism formed a fruitful synthesis at Cambridge. In the 17th century the scholars known as the 'Cambridge Platonists' found in Platonism a way of rebutting both fanatical Calvinism and Hobbesian reductionism.

REVIVALS AND REVOLUTIONS

The late 18th century saw a revolution in the arts as in politics. West Europeans returned from seeing at first hand the ruins of Greece (then under Turkish rule) with news of heroic, austere architecture and art. Superseding the impact of discoveries at Pompeii, this led to radically simpler fashions in art, architecture and even clothing. Jane Austen's heroines wore free-flowing 'Grecian' gowns.

This Greek revival led to a new appreciation of Hellenism, especially in Britain and Germany. The poet John Keats was overwhelmed on seeing the Elgin Marbles – carvings removed from the Parthenon by Lord Elgin, a deeply controversial act – as his poetry reveals. Almost the whole work of Shelley, his contemporary and a superb classicist, breathes Greek fire.

Some of Germany's finest poets, such as Goethe and Friedrich Hölderlin, were similarly moved. In the mid-19th century Richard Wagner, arguably the greatest opera composer ever, tried to recreate the totality of Greek drama in his huge *Ring* cycle, with results still resounding to this day.

In the 20th century Greek ideas also proved potently inspiring, in art, literature and philosophy. Martin Heidegger (1889–1976), among the century's most fundamental philosophers, grounded his radical thinking on Greek foundations, looking back partly to the Presocratics. Heidegger was the godfather of Existentialism, the century's most influential – or fashionable – philosophy. Ideas first aired by the Greeks seldom stay dead for long.

Below: In 1504 Michelangelo completed his heroic David, the first truly gigantic nude statue since antiquity. It incarnates Hellenic ideals both of male beauty and democracy – that of the Florentine republic, which Michelangelo ardently supported.

INDEX

ACKNOWLEDGEMENTS

This edition is published
by Hermes House
an imprint of
Anness Publishing Ltd
Hermes House
88–89 Blackfriars Road
London SE1 8HA

tel. 020 7401 2077
fax 020 7633 9499

www.hermeshouse.com;
www.annesspublishing.com

Anness Publishing has a new
picture agency outlet for images
for publishing, promotions or
advertising. Please visit our website
www.practicalpictures.com for
more information.

Publisher: Joanna Lorenz
Editor: Joy Wotton
Designer: Nigel Partridge
Illustrations and maps: Peter Bull
Art Studio, Vanessa Card and
Anthony Duke
Proofreading Manager: Lindsay Zamponi
Production Controller: Wendy Lawson

ETHICAL TRADING POLICY
Because of our ongoing ecological
investment programme, you, as
our customer, can have the pleasure
and reassurance of knowing that
a tree is being cultivated on your
behalf to naturally replace the
materials used to make the book
you are holding. For further
information about this scheme, go
to www.annesspublishing.com/trees

PUBLISHER'S NOTE
Although the advice and
information in this book are
believed to be accurate and true
at the time of going to press,
neither the authors nor the
publisher can accept any legal
responsibility or liability for
any errors or omissions that may
be made.

p. 1: *The Theseion, Athens.*
p. 2: *Porch of the Maidens,*
the Erechtheum, Athens.
p. 3: *Relief sculpture of horse racing.*
Above: Ruins of Olympia.

PICTURE ACKNOWLEDGEMENTS
The Art Archive: /Gianni Dagli Orti
2, 4.2, 7b, 8b, 9b, 21b, 22t, 24tl, 26t,
28t, 29t, 30b, 35tl, 36t, 44–5, 46t,
47t, 52b, 53bl and br, 66b, 67t,
128–9, 177t, 216t, 224t;
/Archaeological Museum Spina
Ferrara/Alfredo Dagli Orti 4.5,
106–7, 117t, 160b; /National
Archaeological Museum Athens/
Gianni Dagli Orti 5.5, 77t, 78r, 79tl,
80tl, 81tr, 82tl, 88tl, 94t, 98tl, 99t,
100m, 113, 148b, 208–9, 232b;
/Musée du Louvre Paris/Gianni
Dagli Orti 5.6, 102tr, 141bl, 142t,
168b, 169t and b, 170b, 176b, 179b,
214t, 215t, 218–19, 226b, 228b,
231t; /Galerie Berko Louvre des
Antiquaires/Gianni Dagli Orti
14–15; /Bibliothèque des Arts
Décoratifs Paris/Gianni Dagli Orti
19bl, 147b, 149b; /Archaeological
Museum Chora Greece/Gianni
Dagli Orti 23b; /Stephanie Colasanti
25b; /Archaeological Museum
Corinth/ Gianni Dagli Orti 30t;
/Alfredo Dagli Orti 46b; /Museo
Nazionale Reggio Calabria/Gianni
Dagli Orti 55bm, 103tr; /Agora
Museum Athens/ Gianni Dagli Orti
59b, 178b, 234b; /Olympia Museum
Greece/Gianni Dagli Orti 78l, 92tl;
/Archaeological Museum Cherchel
Algeria/Gianni Dagli Orti 88b,
136b; /Musée Archéologique
Naples/Alfredo Dagli Orti 90t,
127b, 139t, 143t, 148t, 172t, 217b;
/Museo Capitolino Rome/Alfredo
Dagli Orti 93br, 127t, 160t; /Museo
Nazionale Taranto/Gianni Dagli Orti
96tr, 138tl, 150t, 163tl; /Museo di
Villa Giulia Rome/Gianni Dagli Orti
112tl; /Eleusis Museum
Greece/Gianni Dagli Orti 112tr;
/Archaeological Museum
Florence/Gianni Dagli Orti 114tl,
240b; /Archaeological Museum
Ferrara/ Alfredo Dagli Orti 116b,
230b; /Musée d'archéologie
méditérranéenne, Marseilles/Gianni
Dagli Orti 117br; /Galleria degli
Uffizi Florence/ Alfredo Dagli Orti
123b, 140b; /Acropolis Museum
Athens/Gianni Dagli Orti 5.1,
130–1, 134t, 225b; /Museo
Nazionale Palazzo Altemps
Rome/Gianni Dagli Orti 133t, 243b;
/Antalya Museum Turkey/ Gianni
Dagli Orti 135b; /Harper Collins
Publishers 136t; /Galleria Borghese
Rome/Alfredo Dagli Orti 137, 145b,
146b; /British Museum/ Eileen
Tweedy 141br, 205b; /National
Gallery London/Eileen Tweedy
142b; /Musée Gustave Moreau
Paris/Marc Charmet 144t; /Antioch
Museum Turkey/Gianni Dagli Orti
144b; /Archaeological Museum
Aquileia/ Alfredo Dagli Orti 149t;
/Archaeological Museum
Paestum/Gianni Dagli Orti 153t;
/Neil Setchfield 156b; /House of the
Poet Menander Pompeii/Alfredo
Dagli Orti 163tr; /Archaeological
Museum Volos/Gianni Dagli Orti
173b; /Jean Vinchon Numismatist
Paris/ Gianni Dagli Orti 175t;
/Musée Archéologique
Naples/Gianni Dagli Orti 187b,
235t; /Museo Nazionale Romano
Rome/Alfredo Dagli Orti 192t;
/Archaeological Museum Ostia/
Gianni Dagli Orti196t; /Victoria
and Albert Museum London/Eileen
Tweedy 203br; /Archaeological
Museum Bari/Gianni Dagli Orti
227b; /Archaeological Museum
Delphi/Gianni Dagli Orti 229b;
/Archaeological Museum
Istanbul/Gianni Dagli Orti 233t;
/Archaeological Museum
Alexandria/Gianni Dagli Orti 233b;
/Archaeological Museum
Izmir/Gianni Dagli Orti 241t;
/Kerameikos Museum,
Athens/Gianni Dagli Orti 241b;
/National Museum Beirut/Gianni
Dagli Orti 242b; /Heraklion
Museum/Gianni Dagli Orti 244tl.
**The Ancient Art & Architecture
Collection:** 4.1, 6 l and r, 8t, 9t,
16–17, 18tl, 19t, 20t and b, 22b,
23t, 24tr, 26b, 27tl, tr and b, 28b,
31, 32tl and tr, 33t and b, 34t and b,
35b, 36b, 37b, 38t and b, 39t and b,
40t, 41t and b, 42 t and b, 43t, 48 t,
m and br, 49b, 51b, 55tl, 58t, 60t
and b, 61b, 62t and b, 64t, 65t, 66t,
67b, 68tl and tr, 69t, 70t, 71t, 72t
and b, 73t and b, 76b, 77b, 81bl,
82br, 84l, 85r, 86 t and b, 87l and r,
89t and b, 91b, 92b, 93t, 95, 96tl,
97l and r, 100t, 101t, 103b, 108t
and b, 109t and b, 110b, 111, 114b,
115t and b, 116t, 121t and bl, 124b,
126t and b, 132t, 133b, 138tr and b,
139b, 140t, 141t, 143b, 146t, 147t,
150b, 151b, 152t, 153b, 157t, 158t
and b, 159t and b, 161b, 162b, 164tl
and b, 165b, 168t, 171t, 178tr, 182b,
183t, 184b, 185b, 189b, 190t, 193t,
194t and b, 195t, 196b, 198b, 204t
and b, 205tl, 206b, 207t, 211b, 212t
and b, 213l and r, 214b, 216b, 217t,
220t and b, 221t, 222t and b, 223b,
225tl, 226tl, 227t, 229t, 231b,
234tr, 236t, 237t, 238b, 239t, 240t,
247tr and b; /C.M. Dixon 4.4, 48bl,
74–5, 210b, 224br, 236b; /Prisma 5.4,
79b, 105t, 180–1; /R. Ashworth 53t;
/G. Tortali 63b; /Ronald Sheridan
91t, 163b, 176t, 188t, 197t, 202t,
215b, 242t; /A. Pronin 102b.
The Bridgeman Art Library: 122t;
/© Birmingham Museums and Art
Gallery 58b; / Private Collection
/© Whitford & Hughes, London 99b;
/Vatican Museums and Galleries,
Vatican City 101br, 191b; /Museo
Archeologico Nazionale, Naples 104b,
203bl; /British Museum, London 112b,
234tl; /Tretyakov Gallery, Moscow
145b; /Louvre, Paris 162t, 170t;
/Private Collection/The Stapleton
Collection 177b, 200b; /© Ashmolean
Museum, University of Oxford 179t,
235b; /Musee de la Chartreuse,
Douai, France/Giraudon 188b;
/Biblioteca Estense, Modena 202b;
/British Library, London / © British
Library Board. All Rights Reserved
203t; /National Archaeological
Museum, Athens/ Lauros/Giraudon
228t; /Palazzo Ducale, Mantua 230t;
© Bradford Art Galleries and
Museums, West Yorkshire 237b.
Corbis: /© Wolfgang Kaehler 4.3,
56–7; © Araldo de Luca 90b.
Alan Hakim: 246b and 247tl.
Photo12.com: 35tr; /Oronoz 4.6,
5.2, 70b, 76t, 84tr, 85bl, 96bl, 98b,
104t, 110tr, 118–19, 120t and b,
124t, 125t and b, 151tl, 152br,
154–5, 157b, 161t, 164tr, 172b,
174t, 184t, 189t, 193b, 195b, 197b,
221b, 226tr, 244tr and b, 245t and
b; /Ann Ronan Picture Library 5.3,
121br, 122b, 134tl, 166–7, 186b,
190b, 200t, 206tl, 243t; /ARJ 19br,
65b, 83tr and bl, 105b, 132b, 152bl,
171b, 173t, 174b, 186t, 187t, 191t,
192b, 198tr, 199b, 210t, 211tl,
224bl, 232t, 239b, 248t; /JTB Photo
37t, 123t, 183b, 185t, 201b, 249t;
/Albert Arnaud 47b, 69b; /Société
Française de Photographie 71b;
/Oasis 156t; /Bertelsmann Lexikon
Verlag 182t, 201t, 206tr.
Werner Forman Archive: 52t;
/British Museum, London 94b.

ACKNOWLEDGEMENTS

This edition is published
by Hermes House
an imprint of
Anness Publishing Ltd
Hermes House
88–89 Blackfriars Road
London SE1 8HA

tel. 020 7401 2077
fax 020 7633 9499

www.hermeshouse.com;
www.annesspublishing.com

Anness Publishing has a new
picture agency outlet for images
for publishing, promotions or
advertising. Please visit our website
www.practicalpictures.com for
more information.

Publisher: Joanna Lorenz
Editor: Joy Wotton
Designer: Nigel Partridge
Illustrations and maps: Peter Bull
Art Studio, Vanessa Card and
Anthony Duke
Proofreading Manager: Lindsay Zamponi
Production Controller: Wendy Lawson

ETHICAL TRADING POLICY
Because of our ongoing ecological
investment programme, you, as
our customer, can have the pleasure
and reassurance of knowing that
a tree is being cultivated on your
behalf to naturally replace the
materials used to make the book
you are holding. For further
information about this scheme, go
to www.annesspublishing.com/trees

PUBLISHER'S NOTE
Although the advice and
information in this book are
believed to be accurate and true
at the time of going to press,
neither the authors nor the
publisher can accept any legal
responsibility or liability for
any errors or omissions that may
be made.

p. 1: The Theseion, Athens.
p. 2: Porch of the Maidens,
the Erechtheum, Athens.
p. 3: Relief sculpture of horse racing.
Above: Ruins of Olympia.

PICTURE ACKNOWLEDGEMENTS
The Art Archive: /Gianni Dagli Orti
2, 4.2, 7b, 8b, 9b, 21b, 22t, 24tl, 26t,
28t, 29t, 30b, 35tl, 36t, 44–5, 46t,
47t, 52b, 53bl and br, 66b, 67t,
128–9, 177t, 216t, 224t;
/Archaeological Museum Spina
Ferrara/Alfredo Dagli Orti 4.5,
106–7, 117t, 160b; /National
Archaeological Museum Athens/
Gianni Dagli Orti 5.5, 77t, 78r, 79tl,
80tl, 81tr, 82tl, 88tl, 94t, 98tl, 99t,
100m, 113, 148b, 208–9, 232b;
/Musée du Louvre Paris/Gianni
Dagli Orti 5.6, 102tr, 141bl, 142t,
168b, 169t and b, 170b, 176b, 179b,
214t, 215t, 218–19, 226b, 228b,
231t; /Galerie Berko Louvre des
Antiquaires/Gianni Dagli Orti
14–15; /Bibliothèque des Arts
Décoratifs Paris/Gianni Dagli Orti
19bl, 147b, 149b; /Archaeological
Museum Chora Greece/Gianni
Dagli Orti 23b; /Stephanie Colasanti
25b; /Archaeological Museum
Corinth/ Gianni Dagli Orti 30t;
/Alfredo Dagli Orti 46b; /Museo
Nazionale Reggio Calabria/Gianni
Dagli Orti 55bm, 103tr; /Agora
Museum Athens/ Gianni Dagli Orti
59b, 178b, 234b; /Olympia Museum
Greece/Gianni Dagli Orti 78l, 92tl;
/Archaeological Museum Cherchel
Algeria/Gianni Dagli Orti 88b,
136b; /Musée Archéologique
Naples/Alfredo Dagli Orti 90t,
127b, 139t, 143t, 148t, 172t, 217b;
/Museo Capitolino Rome/Alfredo
Dagli Orti 93br, 127t, 160t; /Museo
Nazionale Taranto/Gianni Dagli Orti
96tr, 138tl, 150t, 163tl; /Museo di
Villa Giulia Rome/Gianni Dagli Orti
112tl; /Eleusis Museum
Greece/Gianni Dagli Orti 112tr;
/Archaeological Museum
Florence/Gianni Dagli Orti 114tl,
240b; /Archaeological Museum
Ferrara/ Alfredo Dagli Orti 116b,
230b; /Musée d'archéologie
méditérranéenne, Marseilles/Gianni
Dagli Orti 117br; /Galleria degli
Uffizi Florence/ Alfredo Dagli Orti
123b, 140b; /Acropolis Museum
Athens/Gianni Dagli Orti 5.1,
130–1, 134t, 225b; /Museo
Nazionale Palazzo Altemps
Rome/Gianni Dagli Orti 133t, 243b;
/Antalya Museum Turkey/ Gianni
Dagli Orti 135b; /Harper Collins
Publishers 136t; /Galleria Borghese
Rome/Alfredo Dagli Orti 137, 145b,
146b; /British Museum/ Eileen
Tweedy 141br, 205b; /National
Gallery London/Eileen Tweedy
142b; /Musée Gustave Moreau
Paris/Marc Charmet 144t; /Antioch
Museum Turkey/Gianni Dagli Orti
144b; /Archaeological Museum
Aquileia/ Alfredo Dagli Orti 149t;
/Archaeological Museum
Paestum/Gianni Dagli Orti 153t;
/Neil Setchfield 156b; /House of the

Poet Menander Pompeii/Alfredo
Dagli Orti 163tr; /Archaeological
Museum Volos/Gianni Dagli Orti
173b; /Jean Vinchon Numismatist
Paris/ Gianni Dagli Orti 175t;
/Musée Archéologique
Naples/Gianni Dagli Orti 187b,
235t; /Museo Nazionale Romano
Rome/Alfredo Dagli Orti 192t;
/Archaeological Museum Ostia/
Gianni Dagli Orti196t; /Victoria
and Albert Museum London/Eileen
Tweedy 203br; /Archaeological
Museum Bari/Gianni Dagli Orti
227b; /Archaeological Museum
Delphi/Gianni Dagli Orti 229b;
/Archaeological Museum
Istanbul/Gianni Dagli Orti 233t;
/Archaeological Museum
Alexandria/Gianni Dagli Orti 233b;
/Archaeological Museum
Izmir/Gianni Dagli Orti 241t;
/Kerameikos Museum,
Athens/Gianni Dagli Orti 241b;
/National Museum Beirut/Gianni
Dagli Orti 242b; /Heraklion
Museum/Gianni Dagli Orti 244tl.
**The Ancient Art & Architecture
Collection:** 4.1, 6 l and r, 8t, 9t,
16–17, 18tl, 19t, 20t and b, 22b,
23t, 24tr, 26b, 27tl, tr and b, 28b,
31, 32tl and tr, 33t and b, 34t and b,
35b, 36b, 37t, 38t and b, 39t and b,
40t, 41t and b, 42 t and b, 43t, 48 t,
m and br, 49b, 51b, 55tl, 58t, 60t
and b, 61b, 62t and b, 64t, 65t, 66t,
67b, 68tl and tr, 69t, 70t, 71t, 72t
and b, 73t and b, 76b, 77b, 81bl,
82br, 84l, 85r, 86 t and b, 87l and r,
89t and b, 91b, 92b, 93t, 95, 96tl,
97l and r, 100t, 101t, 103b, 108t
and b, 109t and b, 110b, 111, 114b,
115t and b, 116t, 121t and bl, 124b,
126t and b, 132t, 133b, 138tr and b,
139b, 140t, 141t, 143b, 146t, 147t,
150b, 151b, 152t, 153b, 157t, 158t
and b, 159t and b, 161b, 162b, 164tl
and b, 165b, 168t, 171t, 178tr, 182b,
183t, 184b, 185t, 189b, 190t, 193t,
194t and b, 195t, 196b, 198b, 204t
and b, 205tl, 206b, 207t, 211b, 212t
and b, 213l and r, 214b, 216b, 217t,
220t and b, 221t, 222t and b, 223b,
225tl, 226tl, 227t, 229t, 231b,

234tr, 236t, 237t, 238b, 239t, 240t,
247tr and b; /C.M. Dixon 4.4, 48bl,
74–5, 210b, 224br, 236b; /Prisma 5.4,
79b, 105t, 180–1; /R. Ashworth 53t;
/G. Tortali 63b; /Ronald Sheridan
91t, 163b, 176t, 188t, 197t, 202t,
215b, 242t; /A. Pronin 102b.
The Bridgeman Art Library: 122t;
/© Birmingham Museums and Art
Gallery 58b; / Private Collection
/© Whitford & Hughes, London 99b;
/Vatican Museums and Galleries,
Vatican City 101br, 191b; /Museo
Archeologico Nazionale, Naples 104b,
203bl; /British Museum, London 112b,
234tl; /Tretyakov Gallery, Moscow
145b; /Louvre, Paris 162t, 170t;
/Private Collection/The Stapleton
Collection 177b, 200b; /© Ashmolean
Museum, University of Oxford 179t,
235b; /Musee de la Chartreuse,
Douai, France/Giraudon 188b;
/Biblioteca Estense, Modena 202b;
/British Library, London / © British
Library Board. All Rights Reserved
203t; /National Archaeological
Museum, Athens/ Lauros/Giraudon
228t; /Palazzo Ducale, Mantua 230t;
© Bradford Art Galleries and
Museums, West Yorkshire 237b.
Corbis: /© Wolfgang Kaehler 4.3,
56–7; © Araldo de Luca 90b.
Alan Hakim: 246b and 247tl.
Photo12.com: 35tr; /Oronoz 4.6,
5.2, 70b, 76t, 84tr, 85bl, 96bl, 98b,
104t, 110tr, 118–19, 120t and b,
124t, 125t and b, 151tl, 152br,
154–5, 157b, 161t, 164tr, 172b,
174t, 184t, 189t, 193b, 195b, 197b,
221b, 226tr, 244tr and b, 245t and
b; /Ann Ronan Picture Library 5.3,
121br, 122b, 134tl, 166–7, 186b,
190b, 200t, 206tl, 243t; /ARJ 19br,
65b, 83tr and bl, 105b, 132b, 152bl,
171b, 173t, 174b, 186t, 187t, 191t,
192b, 198tr, 199b, 210t, 211tl,
224bl, 232t, 239b, 248t; /JTB Photo
37t, 123t, 183b, 185t, 201b, 249t;
/Albert Arnaud 47b, 69b; /Société
Française de Photographie 71b;
/Oasis 156t; /Bertelsmann Lexikon
Verlag 182t, 201t, 206tr.
Werner Forman Archive: 52t;
/British Museum, London 94b.